Real Regulatory Reform, 1970–2000

Real Regulatory Reform, 1970–2000
The Need for Regular Order Today

Daniel V. Flanagan Jr.

HAMILTON BOOKS

HAMILTON BOOKS

Bloomsbury Publishing Inc, 1359 Broadway, New York, NY 10018, USA.
Bloomsbury Publishing Plc, 50 Bedford Square, London, WC1B 3DP, UK.
Bloomsbury Publishing Ireland, 29 Earlsfort Terrace, Dublin 2, D02 AY28, Ireland.

BLOOMSBURY and the Diana logo are trademarks of Bloomsbury Publishing Plc.

First published in the United States of America 2026.

Copyright © Bloomsbury Publishing, 2026.

Cover image © Mikhail Makarov/iStock

All rights reserved. No part of this publication may be: (i) reproduced or transmitted in any form, electronic or mechanical, including photocopying, recording or by means of any information storage or retrieval system without prior permission in writing from the publishers; or (ii) used or reproduced in any way for the training, development or operation of artificial intelligence (AI) technologies, including generative AI technologies. The rights holders expressly reserve this publication from the text and data mining exception as per Article 4(3) of the Digital Single Market Directive (EU) 2019/790.

Bloomsbury Publishing Inc does not have any control over, or responsibility for, any third-party websites referred to or in this book. All internet addresses given in this book were correct at the time of going to press. The author and publisher regret any inconvenience caused if addresses have changed or sites have ceased to exist, but can accept no responsibility for any such changes.

Library of Congress Cataloging-in-Publication Data Available

ISBN: HB: 978-0-76189-207-6
PB: 978-0-76187-481-2
ePDF: 978-0-76188-039-4
eBook: 978-0-76187-915-2

Typeset by Deanta Global Publishing Services, Chennai, India.

For product safety related questions contact productsafety www.Bloomsbury.com.

To find out more about our authors and books visit www.bloomsbury.com and sign up for our newsletters.

Contents

Acknowledgments	vi
Preface	vii
Introduction	1

Part One: Major Reforms

1	Railroad Deregulation, 1980	19
2	The Breakup of ATT, 1982	43
3	Tax Legislation in 1986, 1993, and 2017	71
4	Energy/Electricity Deregulation, 1992	93
5	Infrastructure Investment Commission Report and the Public Private Partnership Concept, 1993	125
6	Health Care Reform in 1993 (Clinton) and 2010 (Obama)	149

Part Two: Follow-On Efforts

7	NAFTA 1993, Mexican Energy Reform 2014, and Retreat 2022	179
8	Transportation Infrastructure Finance and Innovation Act (TIFIA), 1998	203
9	Thoroughbred Racing Reform Effort, 2007 and 2022/3	223

Part Three: Governmental Reforms

10	Technology Challenges within US Government Procurement	241
11	Government Information Technology (IT) Reform	259
12	The Need for Regular Order, Congress, and the Executive Branch	281

Conclusion	287
Afterword	301
Selected Bibliography	309
Index	311
About the Author	316

Acknowledgments

It is my hope that this book will bring you the satisfaction in reading it as I had in participating not only in the many actions described in the various chapters, but—in these confusing times—making the case for Regular Order as essential for quality congressional legislation.

There were many colleagues, teammates if you will, who were intimately involved.

There were the elected officials, the regulators, the staffers, the economists, the diplomats, and the constituencies for each of these reforms were achieved mainly through regular order, wherein legislation was reported from the House or Senate Committees before it was taken up on the floor of either the House or Senate.

Many friendships were formed, and I am forever grateful. We all had a great time and hit some real public policy home runs!

Writing a book is one thing; editing for publication is another, and Caitlin Flanagan deserves my gratitude for taking time from her early legal career to put it all together. She has been my invaluable editor. And, in that context, may I thank all my family members, particularly my wonderful wife, Fonny, who was always there!

Thank you all!
Dan

Preface

For quality legislation, important regulatory issues benefit from bipartisan legislation via regular order in the relevant congressional committees and in the executive branch budget process; otherwise, partisan agency rulemaking under the Administrative Procedure Act (regulatory ping pong) takes over, thus underscoring the lackluster performance of Congress over the last twenty-some years. The Administrative Procedure Act (APA) was enacted June 11, 1946, and is the federal statute that governs the way in which administrative agencies of the federal government of the United States may propose and establish regulations, and it grants US federal courts oversight over all agency actions.

In the earlier 1970-2000 time window, it was my privilege to observe at least a hundred committee hearings, markups, and bills reported from committee on a bipartisan basis. Rarely unanimous, the committee process was polite, informative, and very positive. The members were articulate, quite knowledgeable, and deferential to their colleagues and, in particular, to their Committee Chairman (majority) and Ranking Member (minority). Committee Chairmen were seen as powerful and worthy of respect. The Speaker of the House was, in effect, the conductor of the orchestra.

It was this decorum that permeated the entire Congress and sent that leadership message to the American public. The historical fact is that Congress was able to craft significant, bipartisan regulatory legislation, importantly often with timely executive branch proposals, going back to the 70s and up close to the millennium year 2000 based on the legislative discipline of regular order wherein only committee-reported bills could be considered on the House/Senate floor.

I was there and can attest to the many virtues of congressional and executive branch regular order. The initial eleven chapters of this book illustrate the number of major economic regulatory reform laws that I was closely linked to and that were passed by Congress within the regular order tradition of the 1970-2000 era, which is described in detail in a separate Chapter 12 for emphasis. It was a unique experience, compelling the need to write this book.

That same decorum applied to the Executive Branch as the White House, during that pre-millennium period, ensured timely State of the Union addresses and concurrent budget submissions and often specific legislative recommendations in keeping with the tradition of the executive branch proposing and the legislative branch disposing. And again, the American public was comforted by this display of good governance.

Rarely, since the millennium year, does a White House now prepare and send a regulatory proposal to Congress for its consideration, and the traditional State of the Union Address and budget submission are no longer delivered on time early in the year, leaving the congressional budget process in disarray.

As good as the US economic news seems to be these days, retail inflation notwithstanding, polls increasingly note that Americans are worried about their future and their concern about political instability, which is caused, in my view, by the lack of quality organizational leadership both in the Congressional Branch and in the White House Executive Branch.

For example, only twenty-eight percent of adults said they are satisfied with the way democracy is working in the United States according to a December 2023 Gallup poll. In an AP poll from November 30 to December 4, 2023, sixty-seven percent said the outcome of the 2024 election would be extremely or very important for the future of democracy in the country. My guess is that the actual results underscored this unease.

These sentiments have shown up in many surveys. In an August 2023 Morning Consult/Bipartisan Policy Center poll, eighty-two percent of participating voters said they were worried. And, in a January 2024 YouGov/CBS News poll, half of participating voters said having a functioning democracy was a bigger immediate concern than having a strong economy.

In the September 2023 Navigator poll, Democrats were especially worried that events similar to the January 6 US Capitol invasion could happen again, with eighty-seven (percent) saying they were somewhat or very concerned.

My response to this national concern is the lack of organizational leadership in Congress due primarily to the dismissal of Regular Order beginning under Speaker Newt Gingrich as we approached the Millennium year, and at the White House as they virtually ignore the Congressional Budget and Impoundment Control Act of 1974. They often delay the traditional January State of the Union presidential address to Congress and the delivery of the proposed fiscal year budget, which follows in early February over that same post-Millennium time period.

Regular Order is simply the congressional process wherein all legislative proposals (bills) must be reported from their related committee to be considered on the floor of the House or Senate. Additionally, the committee process itself encourages legislative expertise, bipartisan behavior, and cohesive, on-time policy results.

The Congressional Budget and Impoundment Control Act of 1974 established a new congressional budget process and timetable, established a Committee on the Budget in each House, established a Congressional Budget Office, and established a procedure providing congressional control over the impoundment of funds by the executive branch.

Today a Continuing Resolution (CR) has become a common, yet temporary solution any time that Congress and the President do not reach agreement on the spending levels and enact regular appropriations by the start of the federal fiscal year beginning on October First. There have been forty-seven CRs between FY 2010 and 2022. These ranged from 1 to 176 days (just under six months). On three occasions—in FYs 2014, 2018, and 2019—no CR was approved, resulting in a government shutdown.

The federal government was under a CR for FY 2023 that expired on December 16 and extended into early 2024. On February 29, 2024, Congress passed another short-term CR to avert a partial government shutdown that weekend, sending the legislation to the Senate one day before Friday's funding deadline from an earlier CR. The legislation cleared the House chamber in a 320–99 vote, extending two separate government department groupings' funding deadlines to March 8 and March 22 for the current fiscal year that began the prior year on October 1, 2023.

With the State of the Union slated for the following week, having the government partially shut down was a double embarrassment. Another CR was passed to continue government funding until after the November 2024 presidential election. With newly reelected Donald Trump and his ostensible advisor at the time, Elon Musk, opposing the bipartisan House spending legislation proposal and this existing CR about to expire just before Christmas, the chance for a government shutdown appeared likely, and House Speaker Mike Johnson was not very popular.

In the House, the Speaker's office has become the de facto legislative ombudsman, often ignoring regular order and sending bills directly to the floor, bypassing the relevant committee and, at best giving instructions to that committee. The floor voting process has, as a result, become a circus, with most members, never having experienced regular order, finding the chaos dispiriting or an opportunity for political mischief.

Beginning with Speaker Gingrich and continuing through his post-millennium successors to date, regular order has virtually disappeared. In its place, what I refer to as regulatory ping-pong has become a regulatory agency highway under the aegis of the Administrative Procedure Act of 1946, which requires administrative agencies to publish the rule or regulation in the Federal Register and hold public hearings if anyone objects to it.

And the Supreme Court bolstered the administrative agency role with the Chevron deference, named for *Chevron USA Inc. v. Natural Resources Defense Council Inc.*, a landmark 1984 Supreme Court case, which held that courts should defer to regulatory agencies when they interpret unclear laws passed by Congress, unless the agencies' interpretations are unreasonable.

Indeed, in 2023, the Supreme Court docketed Chevron deference for review, and a hearing was held. Justice Brett Kavanaugh countered during that hearing according to press reports, that the administrative leeway provided by Chevron had the opposite effect when he said that the reality of how this works is that Chevron itself ushers in shocks to the system every four or eight years when a new administration comes in.

And he is indirectly referring to what I have called regulatory ping pong, wherein the Biden administration actively seeks to overturn Trump administration rulemakings that, in fact, were used to overturn Obama administration rulemakings, and on and on it goes because the issues cannot be addressed in Congress without the regular order process.

In the House, the Speaker's office was now in charge, and Committee Chairman, historically important and well recognized, was now little known. As I have said, the Speaker was originally the conductor of the committee orchestra, and it worked well. The legislative train ran on time, the members were fulfilled, and the public was comfortable.

But, on June 28, 2024, the Supreme Court essentially ended the forty-year federal agency dominance of the Chevron doctrine, deferring once again to the role of the courts. Or preferably, calling once again for clear congressional bills passed under regular order after committee hearings and *markups* of the legislation, hopefully with written input from the Executive Branch as was the tradition prior to the millennium year 2000.

The press accurately followed up the next day, after the Supreme Court ruling, with various headlines about the pendulum now returning to Congress to properly legislate. Let's face it, there are about 180 executive branch and independent agencies, with nearly 2 million workers. They process, according to their reports and think tank analysis, thousands of new regulations in final form each year, and the law firms love it.

But the size of House committee staffs—where technical expertise resides and where legislative, oversight, and investigative work takes place—has shrunk by close to forty percent since the late 1970s, according to the Congressional Research Service, while Senate committee staffs have grown slightly overall. And the Congressional Offices of Legislative Counsel reported large staff attrition rates as members, frustrated by the lack of committee process, were introducing a record number of individual bills that they would write that would go nowhere.

So, the burden returned to the Congress to do a better job of legislating or the courts would return to umpire the confusion. And this necessitates a clear return to congressional regular order!

The derailment of regular order began when the new House Speaker Newt Gingrich unveiled the GOP Contract for America, which essentially eliminated the House discipline of Regular Order, wherein bills had to be considered and reported from the relevant committee before being voted on in the full House.

And I remember when White House executive legislative proposals, in writing, traditionally followed the on-time January evening State of the Union. In recent years, presidents on both sides take the easy way out and state they will work with Congress rather than that they will send recommended legislative proposals to Congress for their consideration. This lack of leadership is harmful and leads to public concern regarding their government's political instability.

The White House's Office of Information and Regulatory Affairs generally leads an administration's regulatory-reform agenda. I give credit to President Obama's 2011 and 2012 executive orders directing agencies to think more creatively in "identifying and reducing regulatory burdens" and improving their regulations by doing "retrospective" analyses of old regulations.

But the damage, particularly in the House of Representatives, had been done and by February 2024 close to two dozen Republicans were making it clear they were leaving their broken caucus and retiring from Congress. The surprise announcement that month of the departure of Rep. Cathy McMorris Rodgers (R-Wash.), a GOP leadership member, added to the evidence. Just days earlier came the retirement announcement from House Homeland Security Chair Mark Green (R-Tenn.), who later relented. Many Democratic members were also announcing their retirements. With the lack of regular order, the 2024 legislative process in the House of Representatives was on the verge of virtual collapse. When the House voted on supplemental bills on April 20, 2024, providing funding for Israel and Ukraine, just seven lawmakers missed those votes.

After that, absences skyrocketed, jumping into the twenties, thirties, and sometimes higher. According to an analysis by Derek P. Willis, a journalism professor at the University of Maryland, the missed votes tally on the final passage of bills jumped to 19.4 percent on average after the Israel and Ukraine votes in April, compared with 11.1

percent in the previous sixteen months of the 118th Congress. In the same analysis on amendment votes, the number of absences grew even more—to 25.8 percent between April 29 and June 30, 2024, compared with an average of just 12.2 percent previously.

And the House GOP leadership gave up and began a six-week summer recess on Friday, July 26, 2024, a longer-than-traditional break even for an election year. Unable to pass appropriations bills, members didn't have anything to do. So, they went home to campaign. The Senate, conversely, was working and sending legislation to the House; but it looked like another continuing resolution for government funding until after the 2024 election in November.

In fact, in December 2024, Congress would pass another continuing resolution for government funding into March 2025 as the Biden presidency would now shift once again to the Trump presidency on January 20, 2025.

Maybe this book, by illustrating the quality regulatory reform initiatives that were passed during that twenty-some-year period, will help turn the tide around. Importantly, traditional State of the Union addresses in early January, followed by timely executive branch budget proposals and legislative recommendations to Congress, will return to synchronize with the congressional budget process, which begins in February, and there will be presidential signing ceremonies once again.

There is a traditional regular order calendar of budget committee consideration in February and March, followed by the authorizing committees (policy) in April, May, and June to be finalized in the appropriations committees in July through September (staff work during the traditional August break), with their House and Senate conferees completing the final forthcoming fiscal year funding legislation by October first.

And authorizing committees will pass related policy legislation during this same time under regular order, which will then be taken up on the House and Senate floors, go to House and Senate conference, and then final votes in each chamber for final passage before being sent to presidential signature.

In this political climate dominant since the year 2000, I am not sure that the successful regulatory reform measures, of which I was honored to be a part in the 1975–95, period would be possible today unless our federally elected officers can return to the regular order that I have described.

Introduction

In my Washington, DC, career that spanned the 1975–2015-time frame, I had the good fortune to play a major role in the deregulation/regulatory reform of several of our major economic sectors. It seemed to be a rather unique experience. In fact, I was not aware of any other single individual who had walked down such similar public policy paths.

So, it seemed it was time to write that story and suggest other related reforms. The book journey began some twenty years ago following my USC faculty time. It ultimately evolved into two books that made better sense: *Real Regulatory Reform, and the Need for Regular Order*, along with *My Washington DC Story and, By the Way, We Blew the Millennium*.

"Real Regulatory Reform" is focused on successful policy accomplishments from bi-partisan laws being passed by Congress that, for the most part, began their legislative journey in committee (Regular Order) before going to the floor of either the House or Senate in the 1970–2000 period. Often, they received written proposals from the White House with detailed language.

But the book adds a much-needed spotlight on the instability of our current post-millennium regulatory process over the last twenty-some years due to the lack of congressional regular order and the resultant inability to pass needed regulatory legislation, hence adding the Need for Regular Order to the title.

As a result, while I am not a lawyer, my sense is that since the millennium year 2000, an unfortunate regulatory ping pong has evolved within administrative agencies, often with a partisan perspective on pre-millennium passed laws or Supreme Court decisions that lack the stability of good public policy and efficient funding cycles.

In the earlier decades, beginning in my case in the '70s, it seemed much better from a public policy perspective for the Executive Branch agencies and the White House to prepare the regulatory reform case and forward it to the Congress for their consideration under regular order.

The historical fact is that Congress was able to craft significant, bi-partisan regulatory legislation, often with Executive Branch proposals, going back to the '70s and up close to the millennium year 2000 based on the legislative discipline of regular order wherein only committee-reported bills could be considered on the House/Senate floor. That was the regulatory policy world that I knew, and it seemed conducive to updating and reform as the circumstances merited.

But, beginning with Speaker Gingrich and continuing through his successors to date in 2024, congressional regular order has virtually disappeared, along with the presidential State of the Union address traditionally in January, followed closely by the budget submission to Congress by the first week in February.

For example, in 2024, President Biden spoke to the nation in late March supposedly on the state of the union; but it really was the state of his re-election campaign, followed a week later by a quiet release of their FY 2025 budget proposal, totally out of synchronization timewise with the congressional budget committees' traditional February-March hearings.

In its place, continuing resolutions and partisan floor voting, including reconciliation, have been disastrous; and what I refer to as regulatory ping pong had become the regulatory highway under the aegis of the Administrative Procedures Act, until the 2024 Supreme Court removal of the Chevron Doctrine.

And a quality April 2023 US Chamber Risk of Policy Actions study that I read and agreed with attributed the increase in government risks to the repeated shifts in party control of the government; an increasingly partisan approach to policymaking; and a growing willingness by both parties to pursue aggressive policy changes through regulation, rather than Congress.

I would also note that the Brookings Center on Regulation and Markets and their Reg-Tracker, in April 2023, had some seventy-nine listed items, the majority being Biden administration rulemakings destined to overcome various Trump administration rulemakings that, in turn were designed to overcome various Obama rulemakings.

And, to repeat for emphasis, with the lack of congressional regular order, and thus the inability to pass real regulatory reforms, this rulemaking ping pong has become the new name of the game. The Brookings Re-Tracker and the Chamber Report illustrate this two decades long trend clearly. It is an added thesis of Real Regulatory Reform, which chronicles my eleven individual reforms and the need (the nexus) for regular order to encourage congressional bi-partisan, legislative expertise.

With the end of the difficult 2020 pandemic year and the start of 2021 with a new President, I had to reflect on a rainy Saturday afternoon, January 6, 2024, when an email arrived from former Speaker Nancy Pelosi noting that three years earlier, on January 6, 2021, she was presiding with then-Vice President Mike Pence over the House of Representatives Joint Session of Congress to certify the 2020 election and the peaceful transfer of power to President Joe Biden and Vice President Kamala Harris.

Suddenly, she noted, in a violent and shocking turn of events, demonstrators entered the Capitol building and our democracy would never be the same. Nancy, along with her husband Paul, was actually close friends with San Francisco friends. I had been on the same parochial grammar school basketball team with Paul (who was in the eighth grade while I was in the seventh) and had been working with Nancy on Democratic Party events beginning in the '70s and continuing into the millennium year 2000 and beyond.

Nancy's message was prophetic, for at the same time, I had been reading the chapters from former Congresswoman Liz Cheney's book, Oath and Honor, where she describes in vivid detail that same time on the House floor as the third-ranking Republican House member with the rampaging, Trump-inspired mob attempting to break into the House chamber.

Now, in 2024, we have suffered for some twenty-five years of congressional and White House legislative disarray, which had prevented bi-partisan, committee reported legislation from reaching the House and Senate floor, similar to the 1970–95 legislative regulatory reform accomplishments described in this book.

This underscores the timing for "Real Regulatory Reform, and the Need for Regular Order." I not only define what deregulation really means with the specific examples in which I was personally engaged, but the Trump administration's efforts to get rid of red tape, his executive orders, and consequent agency rulemakings did their damage.

It was not an accident that newly elected President Biden released twenty-nine executive orders in his first days in office. He absolutely had to revoke more than thirty ninth inning executive orders issued by his predecessor, former President Trump. Imagine this Washington Post February 7, 2021, front page headline: "Biden Inherits a Battered Civil Service," and Trump's second impeachment trial was to begin two days later. A president gets 4,000 appointees, and more than 1,200 of them must be confirmed by the Senate, so the sooner the transition began, the better.

I do talk about what has become the new normal, that is, regulatory ping pong when a new administration comes into office and quickly begins to undo the rulemakings, under the Administrative Procedures Act, of the prior administration. Both parties do it, and while law firms benefit, the fact is there is a lack of bi-partisan committee consensus that would have been needed to pass the legislation to address the issue due principally to the lack of regular order.

The regulatory reform successes that I review in the book hinged on congressional regular order being the legislative discipline that had been the norm for decades until we approached the year 2000.

The Wall Street Journal ran a lengthy op-ed by Chris DeMuth on June 10, 2023, in which he made the case for restoring the role of the legislature. Chris was correct, but he did not mention the pivotal role of regular order, wherein bills can only be taken up on the House or Senate floors after being reported from their relevant committees.

The Speaker's office has controlled this process since the millennium year 2000, and while a record number of bills are introduced singularly, as drafted by the Office of Legislative Counsel (with a high turnover/burnout rate), few ever pass Congress.

Since that millennium, Congress has been unable to pass legislation of similar regulatory quality, stymied by partisan bills drafted in the Speaker's office that rarely passed unless under reconciliation—an abuse of the budget process that has generally has been ignored in the post-millennium era. The relentless regulatory ping pong often sponsored by competing armies of lawyers, is capped by endless continuing resolutions. So, to repeat for emphasis from my experience, what is imperative is that Congress returns to regular order so that there is a system for writing laws that, while perhaps not perfect, are based on a bi-partisan majority that federal agencies follow dutifully in a bi-partisan fashion.

For background, over the Thanksgiving holiday of 2019, I was to read Bill Ruckelshaus's obituary. I met him during his second tour at the Environmental Protection Agency (EPA) as he was righting the agency that Reagan (and Nixon) had wanted in the face of an earlier Reagan EPA appointee, Colorado conservative Anne Gorsuch Burford (the mother of Supreme Court Justice Neil M. Gorsuch), who had done much agency damage as the EPA Administrator.

While an obituary, it really told that bi-partisan regulatory story describing how, during his tenure, he created policies that forced cities to adopt anti-pollution laws, held automakers to strict emissions standards, and banned the harmful pesticide DDT. Interestingly to me, President Nixon had created the EPA by executive order and appointed Ruckelshaus as its first administrator as the federal government lacked an individual agency to enforce the laws. So, regulation had been spread across fifteen separate agencies in a very inefficient way.

In August 2018, I was at a Barnes and Noble bookstore in Annapolis, Maryland, where we lived, to purchase a copy of Senator John McCain's new book, "The Restless Wave." (I crossed paths with him many times—a great guy.) He was to pass away shortly thereafter. In Chapter Ten, Senator McCain focused on the need for congressional regular order, which was essential and had been missing from our congressional protocol since around 2000.

I urged the Naval Academy Stockdale Leadership Center, endowed by our Class of 1965, to include this topic in their 2025 McCain Public Affairs Conference. While I knew the Senator from my Navy Memorial days with Admiral Bud Zumwalt, I had never met his wife Cindy, who generously endowed the annual public affairs conference. So, my guess was she would be very appreciative if Regular Order were included in his honor within the 2025 conference agenda.

Real Regulatory Reform

As a good friend, Senator Daniel Patrick Moynihan would say, every man is entitled to his own opinion but not his own facts. And getting rid of red tape was a new regulatory fiction!

The book is very relevant to today's public policy discourse as each of its first nine chapters focuses on specific and major deregulation/regulatory reform measures that I had the good fortune to play either a major role in or was part of the team that did.

And in the last two chapters, it is also about the necessary procurement reforms within the federal government itself.

"Real Regulatory Reform and the Need for Regular Order" allows the reader to proceed from both a lesson learned perspective as well as outlining a responsible path forward in the face of all the political noise. To do that, we need to regain that economic transparency; but it is not gutting our environmental or consumer protection laws.

It is about restoring the regulatory process to ensure it is once again bi-partisan, efficient and effective, that is, real regulatory reform. And that means Congress returns to regular order in order to initiate committee oversight hearings and, as needed, corrective or clarifying legislation so that the need for rulemaking is restored to its proper bi-partisan roll as well. The 2024 Supreme Court Chevron decision removing the primacy of federal agency rulemakings versus the courts emphasizes the importance of Congress passing clear, well-thought-out laws.

The various industry revamping's that I was involved with were essentially completed before the millennium year 2000.

As one can imagine, there are significant political debates about the benefits of regulation, with issues such as cost benefit analysis and the like, particularly at the national government level.

In many instances, there is a rhetorical flourish about the topic, as President Trump boasted in his October 2018 CBS sixty Minutes interview that he had achieved the biggest regulations cut in history, which was a totally untrue statement. Again, his mantra about getting rid of red tape was simplistic political rhetoric.

My professional experience was focused primarily on the public policy of a number of major regulatory reform initiatives. Each chapter in this book demonstrates the common sinews inherent in regulation but illustrates how each sector had a different solution. In some instances, those markets evolved with new technology, leading to new regulation.

I personally have always favored good government, if you will. In a recent 2023 essay on the thinking of my good friend, the late senator Daniel Patrick Moynihan (D-N. Y.), political scientist Jeffrey Tyler Syck recalled the distinction Pat made between liberals as people who would like to see things improved and conservatives as people who would like to see things not worsened. Exactly; in-fact I would always suggest you are better off saying I will support it if versus I will oppose it unless.

"Real Regulatory Reform and the Need for Regular Order" is a triangle connecting public policy, business/economic policy, and insightful I was present history. This triangle reflects the intersection of the executive, legislative, and judicial branches of our federal government. These were laws passed by Congress, many with executive branch assistance, based on a bi-partisan legislative process representing consensus. They were not the short-term partisan rulemakings that have become, as I point out, the ping pong of the Administrative Procedures Act. And, to repeat for emphasis, thanks to the recent June 2024 Supreme Court ruling curtailing the long-standing Chevron Doctrine regarding the primacy of agency rulemakings, we will have to return to well-written congressional laws (regular order) and court opinions.

This complex regulatory infrastructure represents an essential national framework of regulatory policies, agencies, laws, and rulings that can effectively monitor our many industry sectors, ranging from medicine to safety to electricity, for both the public good and economic success. Issues such as consumer protection, competition, technology, monopoly, and many other public interest maxims must be evaluated and put forward in the interest of the common good.

In the midst of this continuing debate, federal agencies such as the Environmental Protection Agency, Securities and Exchange Commission, the Federal Communications Commission, the Federal Trade Commission, and many others are challenged by changing political and economic circumstances, global commerce, technology, consumer protection, and other national and international policies, laws, and customs.

Washington, DC, is home to most of the nation's regulatory agencies and the related law firms, trade associations, and various interest groups. They focus their attention on the respective agendas of these various Executive Branch agencies led by their presidential appointees, as commissioners, following their US Senate confirmations.

Congress provides oversight and funding through its annual budget hearings, with the Commission members in attendance and giving testimony. The only exception is the relatively new independent Consumer Protection Financing Bureau, whose budget is provided by the Federal Reserve System and has a singular Director.

There are other regulatory initiatives and laws, that deal with procurement, operations, environment, immigration, safety, and even tourism.

As one can imagine, there are significant political debates about the benefits of regulation, and issues such as cost benefit analysis often integrate into the process. In many instances, there is a rhetorical side to the topic; but again, it is fair to say that there is a role for reform where there is consensus as to the need.

Always the starting point, in my experience, was defining the problem, developing a bi-partisan public policy regulatory solution, and engineering a successful advocacy effort, including the development of coalitions sensitive to the public interest, consumer benefit, and economic integrity.

Longstanding laws, many going back to the Depression and even longer to the 1890s trust-busting days, had become actually harmful to the public interest. So began a significant chapter of major deregulation initiatives in the United States in the 1970s!

There have been few chronicles written of these historic US deregulation initiatives. It was a privilege, therefore, for me to have played a lead role in many of these public policy achievements that carved out a new trajectory for our nation's economy and its citizens. As such, this book is designed to tell much of that unique story in personal historical terms intertwined with some related political and economic nuances of those times.

I do hope history buffs will find some very surprising information, such as why the US railroad network runs north to south versus east to west. Industry veterans will find answers to how they were deregulated and even why. What are the lessons learned going forward?

And there is a public interest in how these deregulation measures have positively impacted people's lives as consumers, inventors, investors, customers, taxpayers, and public officials. Often, the phrase, public private partnership, is adopted for some purpose! Where did that phrase originate?

The deregulation or regulatory reform effort in the United States truly began in the 1970s and was influenced by research from two of the leading "think tanks" in Washington, DC, the Brookings Institution and the American Enterprise Institute. Both were active in holding forums and in publishing studies advocating deregulatory initiatives, and I attended those sessions.

There are books written on the singular topic of a specific regulatory reform law and its application. However, I am not aware of any individual who has had the same experiences that I was to have regarding so many of these deregulation/regulatory reforms and to be able to authoritatively write a book about those individual histories in their entirety.

There is an interconnection, in subtle ways, to many of them. For example, by creating the independent power producer sector in the 1992 Energy Policy Act, we established the much-needed project finance expertise that would become a key discipline for US infrastructure investment and the infrastructure investment asset class that emerged after the millennium year 2000 in the country.

Chapters 5 and 8 focus on the infrastructure topic, and there has been some progress, such as the TIFIA and WIFIA lending programs (credit enhancement) and the Build America Bureau at the Department of Transportation launched under President Barack Obama.

But the congressional infrastructure legislative discourse spanning 2016 to 2024, despite all the ballyhoo and the billions, has been very narrow and disappointing. No wonder we trail other Western countries in terms of the quality of our infrastructure. Fortunately, we now have several dozen major infrastructure funds and very interesting projects that, in essence, allow a competitive infrastructure marketplace.

Senator Daniel Patrick Moynihan was the Chairman of the Senate Environment and Public Works Committee and enlisted my assistance in 1990. His words to me were, "Dan, government cannot do it all; help me with infrastructure."

Cornell economist Alfred E. Kahn played a central role in the Carter administration's efforts to deregulate transportation, and it was my privilege to meet with him on several occasions. This book describes the personal role that I played in the categories below:

1. Railroad Deregulation, 1980
2. Telecom Reform, AT&T Breakup, 1982, Sprint, the Internet and Content
3. Tax Legislation in 1986, 1993, and 2017
4. Energy/Electricity Deregulation/Reform, 1992
5. Infrastructure Investment Commission Report and the Public-Private Partnership Concept, 1993
6. Health Care Reform—1993 (Clinton), 2010 (Obama)
7. NAFTA 1993, Mexican Energy Reform 2014, and Retreat 2022
8. Transportation Infrastructure Finance and Innovation Act (TIFIA) 1998
9. Thoroughbred Racing Reform, 2007 and 2022/23
10. Technology Challenges in Government Procurement, (Maglev) 1998
11. Federal Information Technology (IT) Reform, Navy-Marine Corps Intranet (2000)

These were major efforts with myriad interests engaged. And the results were, for the most part, substantial! All eleven are based on my own personal experience, and I think it is fair to say that lessons learned in the early chapters were very helpful in guiding actions in later chapters. In two instances (railroad 1980 and electricity generation 1992), I was with the president at the signing ceremony.

Just before Christmas in 2017, President Trump emphasized his administration's efforts to prune the federal government of what he contended was burdensome red tape by using oversized gold scissors to cut a piece of red ribbon strung between two huge stacks of paper symbolizing, in short order, that his administration would excise some 165,000 of the more than 185,000 pages in the Code of Federal Regulations.

Federal reform is indeed needed, and those, from my experience, would be principally in the Federal Acquisition Regulations section of the Code of Federal Regulations, which are noted in the last two chapters and the Conclusion.

Noteworthy in this regard, Goldman Sachs reported in early February 2018 that the Trump administration's deregulation push was having little or no effect on the economy.

Rather, the prime Trump administration targets appeared to be CFPB consumer protection issues and EPA rulemakings (Clean Air Act, etc.). Those rulemaking processes relate to a 1970 law called the National Environmental Policy Act, sponsored by Senator Scoop Jackson, a good friend and fair-minded senator. NEPA requires agencies across the federal government to document the environmental impacts of major actions they plan to take. The rulemaking process (under the Administrative Procedures Act) includes a chance for the public to comment on the government's plans, and the Chevron decision had not changed that process, just its primacy. Once a rule is in place, there is a similar process to amend a rule. Unfortunately, today, when there is a change in the political party leadership, prior rulemakings are often under attack, as justice Kavanaugh pointed out in the Court's Chevron discussion.

The reality is that any meaningful reform requires a bi-partisan consensus and congressional action as we did in the 1970–2000 period under regular order. In its place was the regulatory rulemaking process under the Administrative Procedures Act which, unfortunately, as I have said, had morphed political into regulatory ping pong.

Under President Trump, getting rid of red tape seemed to be the rhetorical banner, but there was much agency mischief in their rulemaking efforts. First, I researched the term red tape, and it seems during the sixteenth century, the Holy Roman Empire of Spanish King Charles V began to use red tapes manufactured in Holland to bind important documents of state. This helped to identify them from less important documents.

And during the American Civil War, veterans' records were bound in red tape that were perceived as bureaucratic resistance to public access to such documents. President Donald Trump suggested at the ribbon-cutting ceremony in December 2017 that the never-ending growth of red tape in America had come to a sudden, screeching, and beautiful halt. His political base, as it was called, bought into it, but they did not really know what he was talking about. I am not sure he did either!

And in a subsequent regulatory defeat for the Trump administration, all five members of the Federal Energy Regulatory Commission (four were Trump appointees) rejected a White House move that would have kept some struggling coal plants running under the guise of reliability of the grid. Nuclear was noted as well, but since then, it has been cleared as free of carbon emissions.

Yet, the PJM regional grid operator (Maryland to Illinois) reported at the same time, during the coldest winter period in US history, that they had almost 35,000 megawatts available to meet their needed load of approximately 24,000 megawatts.

Mr. Trump's former campaign manager Corey Lewandowski suggested that the FERC move was evidence of the so-called deep state of bureaucrats undermining the president's agenda. But, to repeat, four of the agency's commissioners were nominated by President Trump.

Mr. Trump's deregulation agenda to get rid of red tape was slowed by unusually high losses in the courts. Since the summer of 2017, the Trump administration had lost twenty of twenty-two court cases challenging its deregulatory actions, according to data compiled by the Institute for Policy Integrity at New York University School of Law.

Perhaps some personal history would be in order, and a historical vignette in that regard. Senator Henry "Scoop" Jackson was twice an unsuccessful candidate for the Democratic presidential nomination, in 1972 and 1976. I was a volunteer in both of those races. In the 1972 edition, the Sierra Club, headquartered in my hometown of San Francisco, was to open its new national headquarters in a renovated fire station downtown.

While Scoop was well known for his national defense views, his environmental accomplishments, including NEPA, were not. I had met Dr. Edgar Wayburn, President of the Sierra Club and a renowned conservationist, several times. So, I called him up and asked if we could schedule the ribbon-cutting for the new headquarters when Scoop Jackson was in town; and Scoop would do the honors! Dr. Wayburn was all for it; and I alerted the national campaign headquarters in Washington, DC.

Two days before the event was to take place, the national campaign manager for Jackson called me to say they would have to cancel the Sierra Club event as Scoop had been invited to have drinks with the AFL-CIO executive committee on that same day at the St. Francis Hotel. That is when I knew Scoop would never be president! But it was difficult to call Dr. Wayburn!

There have been NEPA abuses, needless delays, and obstructionism; well thought out reforms would be warranted. However, there needs to be dialogue among the parties, and while some will never compromise for self-serving reasons, lessons learned on my part are to identify the agreed public policy objectives and then design the policies that will allow those to follow.

We do need to reform our regulatory review processes as the country needs new infrastructure investment. There was a quality proposal sponsored by The Common Good (Philip Howard) that takes a surgical approach focused on streamlining. I am very supportive of these recommendations just as we struggle to meet our global climate objectives via an energy transition. A prime example is the difficulty in permitting new electric transmission lines for renewable energy, particularly wind power.

Needed infrastructure project permitting just takes too long in the United States, it seems! There must be a better way! Frankly, if we are to meet our global climate goals, streamlining is an absolute necessity, for example, electric transmission for renewable energy, which I have advocated for over twenty years. We now have zealots talking about the "grid" in their own intellectual grid. The United States needs expert leadership in structuring the global climate strategy, not elected officials.

Congress in-fact addressed this very issue of permitting delay by creating the Federal Permitting Improvement Steering Council (FPISC) in the FAST Act in December 2015. FPISC would presumably lead government-wide efforts to modernize the Federal permitting and review process for major infrastructure projects and work with OMB, the Council on Environmental Quality, other components of the Executive Office of the President, and Federal agency partners to implement and oversee adherence. However, state/local and self-appointed environmental guardians have been able to stymie federal and private sector permitting and streamlining efforts for years.

Another area of regulation is the two-fold federal preemption of unneeded state laws (Staggers Act etc.) and the reverse when a new state law such as the 2023 Texas

Regulatory Consistency Act broadly prohibits local municipalities from creating laws that do not align with state law.

And the fact is companies often like existing federal rules, national standards, etc. In some cases, rules give companies advantages over rivals. So, it seems not everyone minds some red tape. But aside from earning goodwill, having a positive say in a rulemaking may beat the alternative. As I often suggested, support a solution where you, or put another way, "you will support if; versus oppose it unless."

If I can summarize my personal deregulation/reform efforts, they opened the economics of important industries and reformed antiquated governmental regulatory processes to encourage new technology, competition, and consumer/public benefit.

As noted, in the early 1970s, the deregulation discussion had begun. While working in New York at the time for the Martin Segal Company, I had attended Washington, DC, congressional meetings in Washington, DC, that ultimately led to the Employee Retirement Income Security Act of 1974 (ERISA), a federal law that set minimum standards for most voluntarily established pension and health plans in private industry to provide protection for individuals in these plans. It was very interesting to me.

But it was not until 1977, running Southern Pacific's Washington office, that I played a very significant role in a specific deregulation legislative effort, that is, The Staggers Act (1980), deregulating the railroad industry as Southern Pacific was one of the major US railroads at the time. This was the first of a dozen such deregulation initiatives that I was personally engaged in and described in succeeding chapters.

For the most part, these book chapters deal with economic deregulation scenarios where regulation was antiquated, essentially outdated, and unneeded. Markets had changed, new technology was available, and competition (consumer benefit) would be replacing monopolies from another era.

In the second chapter on SPRINT (Southern Pacific also), the breakup of AT&T (1982), telecommunications, and the internet, the point is added that now we are challenged with new monopolies such as Google, Facebook, and the like; and agencies like the Federal Trade Commission, the Federal Communications Commission, and the Antitrust division at the Justice Department continue to play important roles forty years later, as do their European Union counterparts today.

In Chapter 4, in deregulating the electricity sector (1992), a new wholesale trading market was created, catching regulators like the Federal Energy Regulatory Commission off guard as the enormous Enron bankruptcy occurred.

The point is made in Chapters 10 and 11 that there are significant opportunities for government to enjoy similar economic results by adopting new procurement reforms that inspire risk transfer, new technology, competition, and the like. Maglev technology, in Chapter 10, had tremendous potential (1998), and the Navy Marine Corps Intranet IT Procurement (2000) was a home run in that Millennium year.

The benchmark, from my experience, should be whether the reform opens up economic opportunities, stimulates new technology and competition, makes government more efficient, and provide a public benefit. Cloud IT technology is a good example.

Reforming the Federal Acquisition Regulation (FAR) would be a major achievement for government performance. Vendors might not like it conceptually, but here is a classic opportunity for them to participate in the design of a procurement process that results in a successful outcome for all the parties, particularly the public sector, that is, the government and its shareholders, namely the taxpayers.

The first comprehensive proposal to deregulate a major industry in the United States, transportation, originated in the Nixon administration. The proposal addressed both rail and truck transportation, but not airlines. Subsequently, the Ford presidency secured passage of the Railroad Revitalization and Regulatory Reform Act of 1976, which addressed the numerous railroad bankruptcies, Conrail, and Amtrak. I was to work with these same practitioners the following year on railroad deregulation itself.

To my surprise, I was to discover that fifty years ago, at a time of growing concern about rising industrial noise, President Richard Nixon signed the Noise Control Act of 1972, designed to give Americans the right to a reasonably quiet environment.

It created the federal Office of Noise Abatement and Control (ONAC) with a mandate to coordinate research on noise control, set federal auditory emission standards for products, and provide grants and technical assistance to state and local governments to reduce noise pollution. While the office didn't have the authority to regulate noise from most transportation infrastructure, it spearheaded a public education effort that built awareness of transport noise, eventually prompting airports, airlines, and freight companies to take the issue seriously. The Reagan administration defunded and largely dismantled the federal noise control programs as part of its anti-regulation push in 1982.

President Jimmy Carter devoted substantial effort to transportation deregulation and worked with Congressional leaders to pass the Airline Deregulation Act (October 24, 1978), Staggers Rail Act (signed October 14, 1980), and the Motor Carrier Act of 1980 (signed July 1, 1980). While not directly involved in the airline initiative, I was very engaged in the other two efforts, arriving in Washington, DC, in 1977 for this purpose and attended many White House-related meetings.

I remember well reaching consensus with industry sectors, labor, and the Congress that the Interstate Commerce Commission (ICC) was a bureaucratic backwater, and deregulation measures were needed to replace those antiquated regulatory systems put in place between the 1880s and the 1930s primarily to regulate railroads.

And we were very successful with the ICC being dissolved on January 1, 1996, having been formed on February 4, 1887. The agency was over 100 years old, and transportation economics were totally changed. It simply wasn't needed.

The dominant common theme was to lessen barriers to entry in markets and promote new technology and more independent, competitive pricing among service providers, substituting competitive market forces for detailed regulatory control of entry, exit, and price making in transport markets. It was the end of rate bureaus!

Under President Ronald Reagan, interstate buses were addressed in 1982 in the Bus Regulatory Reform Act of 1982. Freight forwarders (freight aggregators) received more freedoms in the Surface Freight Forwarder Deregulation Act of 1986. This was when I was advising my good friend, Lynn Fritz, who later sold his logistics technology company to United Parcel Service for about $500 million.

As many states continued to regulate the operations of motor carriers within their own state, the intrastate aspect of the trucking and bus industries was eliminated in the Federal Aviation Administration Authorization Act of 1994, which provided that "a State, political subdivision of a State, or political authority of two or more States may not enact or enforce a law, regulation, or other provision having the force and effect of law related to a price, route, or service of any motor carrier."

We included a similar provision in the Staggers Act in 1980 deregulating railroads that preempted unnecessary state regulation but bolstered national efficiency.

As a recent example, beginning in 2018, states looking to establish their own net neutrality policies in opposition to the new Trump Administration Federal Communications Commission (FCC) approach that favored the carriers over the content providers. However, virtually every industry sector prefers one national standard, not fifty different state requirements.

The Ocean Shipping Act of 1984 and the Ocean Shipping Reform Act of 1998 left in place the conference system in international ocean liner shipping, which included cartel mechanisms. However, independent rate-making by conference participants and contract rates, where permitted, opened up competitive activity in ocean shipping. I would brief shippers on these new laws at conferences.

Deregulation of the electricity sector in the United States began in 1992. I was very proud of my role in the passage of the Energy Policy Act of 1992 (Title VII Electricity), which eliminated obstacles for wholesale electricity competition. It essentially launched the independent power producer (IPP) industry responsible for the construction of most power generation facilities since 1992, including natural gas, solar, and wind power. The largest hearing rooms in the Senate were packed, attesting to the significance of Title VII Electricity and its PUHCA Reform provisions.

Earlier, the natural gas industry was deregulated, and its regional production and transportation monopolies opened up to new investors, pipelines, and the like. We no longer witnessed shortages, and I advised our utility clients accordingly in their distribution role.

Representing Mexico for the 1992–93 NAFTA negotiations, the stage was set for the successful energy reforms in that country ten years later; albeit President Obrador attempted to reverse that progress back ten years after that.

Deregulation was put into effect in the communications industry by the Justice Department and Congressional pressure, leading to the 1982 court order relating to the AT&T divestiture. The Telecommunications Act of 1996 was the first major overhaul of telecommunications law in many years, allowing anyone to enter any communications business, ameliorating the concentration of media ownership. My 1977—1982 role with SPRINT is reviewed in the second chapter.

The 1998 passage of the Transportation Infrastructure Finance and Innovation Act (TIFIA) stemmed directly from our 1993 Infrastructure Investment Commission report, of which I served as Chairman, and was critical to opening the transportation sector to new federal lending (not grants) and the companion investment of private capital, eventually including pension funds with infrastructure asset class allocations.

The Financial Services Modernization Act of 1999 repealed part of the Glass–Steagall Act of 1933, removing barriers in the market among banking companies, securities companies, and insurance companies that prohibited any one institution from acting as an investment bank, a commercial bank, and an insurance company under one corporate roof (Volcker Rule). It was a privilege to advise Wells Fargo during the late 1990s when their president, as well as chairman and CEO, was Paul Hazen. My Washington, DC, advice had been low-profile, good policy.

And amidst the sorry chapter of government Information Technology (IT) procurement failures, the 2000 success of the record-breaking Navy Marine Corps Intranet procurement, which I helped design, suggested a critical path for private sector risk taking and technology advancement while meeting federal government needs and requirements.

We attempted to revise the fiscal health of the US thoroughbred racing industry in 2007 with a state/federal regulatory reform/deregulation strategy; but unfortunately, it was not to be. The Sport of Kings was in desperate need of a king! In 2022, federal drug medication legislation was passed with the thoroughbred industry in support. However, it could have been much more.

Being with President Carter when he signed the railroad deregulation measure (The Staggers Act) in 1980 in the White House, and with President Bush when he signed the 1992 Energy Policy Act in Louisiana were singular honors. I still have my Carter autographed pen from that White House ceremony and the so-called blue copies of both measures framed and hanging on my office walls.

Texas Senator Phil Gramm served as a US representative from Texas as a Democrat (1979–83) and a Republican (1983–85) and as a US senator (1985–2002). He was to write an October 1 Wall Street Journal Op-Ed commending President Carter entitled "Jimmy Carter, Champion of Deregulation," by Phil Gramm which happened to be former President Carter's 100th birthday.

Coincidentally, that same day, I watched the C-SPAN documentary featuring President Carter's January 1980 State of the Union Address to Congress, in which he made proposals that he would shortly be sending to Congress in keeping with the much-needed tradition of regular order. Thus, this book's title and themes of this book, "Real Regulatory Reform and the Need for Regular Order."

My goal here is to tell a unique story in personal historical terms for a variety of reasons. First of all, there is the history of what happened and why. Secondly, each deregulation scenario had similar benchmarks even though the industries themselves were very different. And lastly, there are lessons learned that can be applicable to later-day deregulation efforts both in the private and public sectors.

A prime lesson learned is the bi-partisan consensus that comes from congressional regular order, needed to pass these very important laws that stand the test of time, in contrast to the political partisan rulemakings that have followed.

Much of this book is written based on my own personal experience, reports that I preserved, and research into my boxes of files saved over the years. There is also new material that was available in various trade publications and journals that I have read over the years and made notes on. Actually, I started on a longer memoir some fifteen years ago and have been reviewing my files as well as reading topical books, generating new information.

There are times when I think policymakers would save quite a bit of time if they could all learn from past successes. That certainly applies in this post-millennium technology era, as the reader will note the oversized lobbying wars relating to the regulatory policies of agencies such as the FCC and FTC. It is as if they have no knowledge of the regulatory reform accomplishments that began in the late 1970s under congressional Regular Order, wherein the committee process produced quality, bi-partisan legislation voted on by a majority for House and Senate floor consideration. Beginning around 2000, that process was essentially replaced by partisan leadership tactics that are doing damage to our country. That was a catalyst for writing this book.

As I look back, leading up to the Millennium year and beyond, we failed to take that Millennium opportunity here in the United States to reflect on where we have been, so to speak, and where we are going as a nation. We fell to the vicissitudes of a narrow security argument called Y2K.

Much of the old regulation stemmed from the 1900–1930 era and was simply outdated. For Republican members of Congress, I would emphasize the phrase, let the market work, and for Democrats, it was simply, let competition work, for the very same recommendation.

In writing this book with its emphasis on real regulatory reform, I would suggest that government IT procurement failure at all levels—federal, state, and local- is the sector most in need of procurement reform, as illustrated by the initial unveiling of President Obama's Affordable Care Act in 2010 and the subsequent failure of the IT sign-up process.

In 2015, the Code of Federal Regulations totaled 178,277 pages in 237 volumes. The Federal Acquisition Regulation (FAR) is a major part of this Code, primarily as the procurement arbiter; the last two chapters address federal procurement reform.

Ironically, just as our US deregulation era began in the 1970s, the FAR was issued under the auspices of the Office of Federal Procurement Policy Act of 1974.

In July 2024, the GOP convention again nominated Donald Trump, at seventy-eight years of age, for president to run against the incumbent President Joe Biden at age eighty-one. Donald Trump had survived an assassin's bullet earlier at a prior weekend rally, and Joe Biden was to contract the Covid virus just as the GOP convention ended. Biden, at age eighty-one, was to cancel his campaign events and isolate at his Rehoboth Beach home.

It was a strange time, and finally, the Biden family acquiesced, and Vice President Kamala Harris became the Democratic nominee, with being presidential as my campaign strategy for her. Open up the Biden White House to the public with televised cabinet meetings, task force sessions, and the like with the Vice President being asked by President Biden to preside. It did not happen, as Biden seemed resentful.

But on the post-election morning of November 6, 2024, the GOP hit the trifecta with Donald Trump returning to the White House and both the Senate and House under narrow GOP majorities. The fatal Democratic Party error was Biden running for a second term, without primaries, and a void of interest. Democratic turnout was much lower than in 2020, and Kamala Harris was unable to turn the abysmal Biden polling data around; every key state for the electoral college was won by Trump. It seemed there would be trouble ahead.

Trump's regulatory mantra during his 2016–2020 term had been a vocal call to get rid of red tape, while Biden from 2021 to 2024, generally left it to a team of unknown agency appointees, accompanied by an unfortunate, poorly drafted 2021 White House eighty-two-page omnibus regulatory package that, at best, brought confusion. The Need for Regular Order in Congress, as well as Executive Branch State of the Union/Budget discipline, was acute.

I do hope the reader finds Real Regulatory Reform, and the Need for Regular Order to be a helpful guidepost for their view of this important aspect of national economic policy and leads to smart regulation. Its many observations are based on my long professional career engaged in congressional/legislative activity, testifying, chairing a commission, attendance at two presidential signing ceremonies, and the passage of significant regulatory reform legislation. At eighty-three years of age, my message in this book is based on many years of experience and now concern.

I have added a Chapter 12 devoted to the mechanics of regular order as that important topic blossomed in my mind as the federal public policy process by 2020 was falling apart. There was a nexus to achieving real regulatory reform, but it was increasingly obvious that it would require retrieving the virtues of regular order.

Part One

Major Reforms

1

Railroad Deregulation, 1980

The Interstate Commerce Act of 1887 was the federal law that was designed to regulate the railroad industry, particularly its monopolistic practices. The Act required that railroad rates be reasonable and just but did not empower the government to fix specific rates. The Act created the Interstate Commerce Commission (ICC), which was charged with monitoring railroads to ensure that they complied with the new regulations. With the passage of the Act in 1887, the railroad industry became the first industry subject to federal regulation by a regulatory body.

By way of history, prior to the 1980 Staggers Act, Interstate Commerce Commission (ICC) regulation, along with state rate bureaus, had prevented railroads from any flexibility in customer pricing needed to meet both industry and intermodal competition. Regulation also prohibited carriers from restructuring their systems, including abandoning unneeded and little-used lines, a necessity for controlling costs. Trucking deregulation had preceded rail deregulation by six months in 1980, with similar provisions having been regulated by the ICC.

Added to these problems was the railroad industry's inability to cover inflation due to the regulatory time lag in rate adjustments. Consequently, nine carriers had gone bankrupt in the years following the Second World War; the industry had a low return on investment, was unable to raise capital, and faced a steady decline in market share to trucking competition. President Dwight Eisenhower signed the Federal-Aid Highway Act of 1956, which created a 41,000-mile National System of Interstate and Defense Highways and that changed the transportation marketplace.

As a result of the 1980 Staggers Act, after some forty years of its deregulation, the railroad industry's financial health has improved significantly, service to rail customers has improved dramatically, overall rates have decreased, and rail safety has also improved. The 2020—2021 pandemic put tremendous pressure on the global supply chain, including railroads. Railroad deregulation was a big deal, completing the triad with trucking and airline deregulation, which had also occurred in that same period. It was a personal accomplishment that was the first of several major deregulation/regulatory reform engagements well before the millennium year 2000. And President Carter, who passed away at the age of 100 on December 29, 2024, deserves much credit not only for railroad deregulation but for transportation deregulation in general.

In 1977, being active in San Francisco civic affairs, as well as national and state political campaigns, that city's Southern Pacific Corp. offered me the opportunity to take over their Washington, DC, office for governmental affairs. I had done my due diligence, talked with corporate governmental affairs execs, and learned these opportunities were highly sought after. I accepted their offer, and this chapter features my primary assignment: railroad deregulation.

In moving our family to Washington, DC, in early 1977, and while a relative newcomer to the governmental affairs community there, I was no stranger to the bipartisan political themes of the day and had excellent working relationships with the Carter White House and the Democratic-controlled ninety-fifth Congress. Within months, I was a veteran!

Southern Pacific (SP) was a great learning ground as the company was in several businesses, each with significant challenges. For starters, the company operated one of the nation's major railroads and was struggling with its strategic positioning, particularly in obtaining a direct rail line from Los Angeles to Chicago via its pending purchase of the Rock Island line.

Attending Interstate Commerce Commission (ICC) hearings in those days to monitor issues such as that railroad purchase was like being in an old-fashioned time capsule lost in the meaningless economic minutiae served up by the competing law firms to the commissioners.

The railroad industry was struggling with several bankruptcies earlier in the 1970s, and the conversion of the Penn Central into Conrail and the creation of Amtrak were only temporary band-aids. It was clear that a new, modern regulatory framework was needed to quickly replace the funereal atmosphere dominant at the Interstate Commerce Commission (ICC), which, incidentally, was terminated fifteen years after the passage of the 1980 Staggers Act.

The Interstate Commerce Commission (ICC), headquartered on Constitution Avenue (now the EPA's headquarters), was an old US regulatory agency created by the Interstate Commerce Act of 1887. The agency's original purpose was to regulate monopolistic railroads to ensure fair rates, eliminate rate discrimination, and regulate other aspects of common carriers, including interstate bus lines and telephone companies.

Congress expanded the ICC's authority, under President Teddy Roosevelt's leadership, to regulate other modes of commerce beginning in 1906 and to strengthen its railroad regulatory powers. This was a reaction to the monopoly control that J. P. Morgan had over the nation's railroads, which in turn controlled the anthracite coal lands of northeastern Pennsylvania that fed the iron and steel industries of the time.

The ICC was abolished in 1995, under President Clinton, as the Staggers Act was working, the market was opened, and competition was available. The remaining ICC functions were transferred to the new Surface Transportation Board. Good riddance to an unneeded agency, accomplished in a bipartisan, consensus "regular order" manner through the Congressional Committee process. It was real regulatory reform, good government for the national good!

Here is that personal history: Our railroad deregulation legislative effort came to a two-year head in Congress, between 1978 and 1980; and there was a political battle as the industry was split, as so often happens, I was to learn:

1. Major proponents included the Southern Pacific, Conrail, Chessie, Santa Fe, and the Union Pacific.
2. Opponents included Southern Company, Norfolk Western, Burlington Northern, Missouri Pacific, Kansas City Southern, and others. (Illinois Central Gulf and Seaboard Coast Lines seemed to be in the middle.)

Ironically, our first break came in the Senate when President Carter asked for Transportation Secretary Brock Adams' resignation in July 1979. On behalf of the proponents of deregulation, I immediately contacted Brock, and he accepted our invitation to serve as Counsel to our new coalition TRAIN, which I had created (Transportation by Rail for our Agriculture and Industrial Needs), composed of those railroads listed first above.

Brock testified shortly thereafter before the Senate Commerce Committee, with his statement on quickly printed TRAIN stationery with the five member railroads listed below Brock's name. I ensured that the committee staff had copies to distribute to the attending Senators and placed copies at the press table in the hearing room as well.

This action effectively broke the Senate filibuster letter signed by twenty-one Southern senators organized primarily by Southern Company's revered Washington lobbyist, former Kentucky Governor Ned Breathitt, who was a good friend of mine and a formidable opponent.

Democratic Senator Howard Cannon from Nevada chaired the Senate Commerce Committee and was ably assisted by his top aides, Ed Hall and Aubrey Sarvis, whom I talked to on a regular basis to review Senate strategy. It was one of their phone calls that prompted me to contact Brock Adams.

Earlier in 1978, House subcommittee Chairman Fred Rooney—a Democrat and rail deregulation supporter—convened a railroad deregulation summit at the Hershey Resort in his Pennsylvania District. The proponent railroads were in attendance along with the rail unions and others.

We had lost the first House floor vote, which was then simply entitled a "railroad deregulation" measure, and the rail brotherhoods (unions) had been, at best, neutral in the fight. We needed to rally the troops and bring them into the tent.

While Congressman Fred Rooney was the leader with his able staff, his GOP ranking member was Congressman Ed Madigan from Illinois. They were a great bipartisan team. Fred Rooney was to lose his seat in the 1978 election and was replaced as subcommittee chairman by Congressman Jim Florio from New Jersey, who picked up the baton and ran with it to the finish line.

Some history, in 1819, the committee was named the Committee on Commerce. The name changed again in 1891, becoming the Committee on Interstate and Foreign Commerce. The committee assumed its present Energy and Commerce name in 1981 to emphasize its lead role in the nation's energy policy.

Today, the committee has responsibility for matters including telecommunications, consumer protection, food and drug safety, public health and research, environmental quality, energy policy, and interstate and foreign commerce, among others. Railroads were transferred to the House Transportation and Infrastructure Committee years later.

In June of 2022, I was to read the obituary for J. Paul Molloy, who was a GOP House committee staff lawyer on Capitol Hill and had a key role in not only drafting the legislation that created Amtrak and other related federal programs but, most importantly, the 1981 Staggers Act deregulating the railroad industry. Our TRAIN coalition worked very closely with Paul throughout the committee hearings and markup and then the House floor action. I did not know it at the time, but this committee/floor sequence was to earn the name "regular order."

As it turned out when I first met Paul in 1977, he had been an alcoholic whose earlier drinking would eventually cost him his job, his family, and his home. A true Irish leprechaun, in 1975, he had been drinking heavily and thankfully entered a rehabilitation program. He moved to a county-run halfway house in Silver Spring, MD, to recover but soon learned that the facility was about to close.

Instead of being left to their own fates, Mr. Molloy and other residents decided to take over the house themselves, and importantly (as Paul would tell me) pay the rent and utilities, cook the meals, and keep watch over one another's path to recovery.

They called their experiment in group living and joint sobriety Oxford House. It was the first step in a nationwide movement, now almost fifty years old, that has been credited with helping thousands of people overcome addiction and lead productive lives. The key, Paul told me, was paying the rent (not buying) with all residents responsible for their share.

Through Alcoholics Anonymous and the intervention of congressional friends, Paul quit drinking and began to reclaim his life. When he landed a House Energy and Commerce staff job on Capitol Hill, he was warned, one drink, and you're fired.

Perhaps the most important part of his recovery, however, was Oxford House, the group home in Silver Spring where he lived for more than two years. Within two years of its founding, other Oxford House locations were sprouting up in the Washington area. The houses often encountered opposition from residents concerned that they would be living near a group of men (and sometimes women) with criminal records and addiction problems.

When an Oxford House location opened near Chevy Chase Circle in Washington in 1977, Paul, as the CEO, told me that he only asked for patient tolerance from the neighbors. When some communities tried to keep Oxford House from renting in their neighborhoods, Mr. Molloy and his lawyers went to court. Oxford House won a US Supreme Court victory in 1995 against the city of Edmonds, WA, on grounds that the city's efforts to block the group home violated provisions of the Fair Housing Act.

According to the new CEO Kathleen Gibson, Oxford House had more than 20,000 residents at more than 3,300 homes across forty-four states and several foreign countries. Hundreds of thousands of people have been through the program.

I was glad to read that, in 1988, after thirteen years apart, Paul and his former wife remarried and rejoined their five children. I can honestly say that there were several heroes in the passage of the Staggers Act, and Paul was one of them.

As noted earlier, the House Interstate and Foreign Commerce Committee—where railroads were held political hostage (all other transportation modes had long since been in the House Public Works and Transportation Committee)—was chaired by the venerable Chairman Harley Staggers, Democrat from West Virginia.

This was now 1979, and the House committee staffers, on a bipartisan basis, came up with the idea of naming the legislation after Chairman Staggers. He graciously accepted, the brotherhood unions came on board, and we went on—this time—to win on the House and Senate floors, the latter much to my credit, if I do say so to myself.

I will never forget joining my railroad colleagues standing on the Capitol steps, on the House side, just by the entrance to advise members I knew who were rushing to vote and had any questions.

The Staggers Rail Act of 1980 deregulated the American railroad industry to a significant extent, and it replaced the regulatory structure that had existed since the Interstate Commerce Act of 1887. Trucking deregulation (Motor Carrier Act) passed earlier that same year in 1980, with similar provisions that had also been regulated by the Interstate Commerce Commission.

The Staggers Act's purpose was to reform the economic regulation of railroads and was introduced in the Senate as the Harley O. Staggers Rail Act of 1980 (S. 1946) by Howard Cannon (D-NV) on October 29, 1979, and passed the Senate on April 1, 1980. It then passed the House on September 9, 1980. It was reported by the joint conference committee on September 29, 1980, agreed to by the Senate on September 30, 1980 (66-2) and by the House on September 30, 1980. Believe me when I say our coalition was engaged in each and every step noted here.

It was then signed into law by President Jimmy Carter on October 14, 1980, as Pub. L. 96-448. I was very busy during those two weeks working with the Association of American Railroads to coordinate the industry CEO participation in that ceremony, as I was in effect, the liaison for the industry with the Carter White House.

It was a very important legislation as many railroads had been driven out of business by competition from the interstate highways and airlines. The rise of the automobile led to the end of passenger train service on most railroads, and trucking businesses had become major competitors by the 1950s, with the Eisenhower National Highway System put in place.

The Staggers Act followed the Railroad Revitalization and Regulatory Reform Act of 1976 (often called the "4R Act"), which reduced federal regulation of railroads and authorized implementation details for Conrail, the new northeastern railroad system.

The 4R reforms included the allowance of a greater range for railroad pricing without close regulatory restraint, greater independence from collective rate-making procedures in rail pricing and service offers, contract rates, and, to a lesser extent, greater freedom for entry into and exit from rail markets.

Although the 4R Act established the guidelines, the ICC, at first, did not give much attention to its legislative mandates, as I can attest having attended some of those hearings in the 1977–9 period. It was clear Congress needed to pass more explicit instructions, and thus the major regulatory changes of the Staggers Act were as follows:

1. A rail carrier could establish any rate for a rail service unless the ICC were to determine that there was no effective competition for rail services. This was known as the zone of freedom, and within that zone, new services such as piggyback were deployed.
2. Rail shippers and rail carriers would be allowed to establish contracts subject to no effective ICC review unless the Commission determined that the contract service would interfere with the rail carrier's ability to provide common carrier service.
3. The scope of authority to control rates to prevent "discrimination" among shippers was substantially curtailed.
4. Across-the-board industry-wide rate increases were phased out.
5. The dismantling of the collective rate-making machinery among railroads begun in 1976 was reaffirmed, with railroads not allowed to agree to rates they could perform on their own systems and were not allowed to participate in the determination of the rates on traffic in which they did not effectively participate.

The Act also had provisions allowing the Commission to require access by one railroad to another railroad's facilities if one railroad had effective bottleneck control of traffic. The provisions dealt with reciprocal switching (handling of railroad cars between long-haul, rail carriers and local customers) and trackage rights.

It was very successful as, according to 1990 studies by the Department of Transportation, railroad industry costs and prices were halved over a ten-year period, the railroads reversed their historic loss of traffic (as measured by ton-miles) to the trucking industry, and railroad industry profits began to recover after decades of low profits and widespread railroad insolvencies.

In 2007, I was glad to read that the Government Accountability Office reported that the railroad industry was increasingly healthy and rail rates had generally declined since 1985. It also added that there is consensus that the freight rail industry benefited from the Staggers Rail Act.

The Association of American Railroads, the principal railroad industry trade association, stated at that time that the Staggers Act had led to a fifty-one percent reduction in average shipping rates, and $480 billion has been reinvested by the industry into its rail systems.

On October 14, 1980, I had led all the railroad representatives standing with President Carter in the White House when he signed the Staggers Act—with Chairman Staggers by his side. Later, we celebrated at a Georgetown landmark home that had a train set going around the ceiling in the reception room—it was perfect. The events planning firm, Washington Whirl Around, put it together. Chairman Staggers attended and retired at the end of the following year.

With the passage of the Staggers Rail Act of 1980 and its implementation by new leadership at the Interstate Commerce Commission, many regulatory restraints on the railroad industry were removed, providing the industry with increased flexibility to adjust its rates and tailor services to meet shipper needs (e.g., piggyback and double stack service) and its own revenue requirements.

As I said, we called it the zone of freedom wherein railroads were permitted to charge rates within the regulatory zone and not have to file tariffs in advance. I was very pleased! Boxcars slowly disappeared and eventually cabooses as well.

Later in the 2020 debates regarding Facebook and Google's monopoly practices, privacy, etc., I was to suggest this zone of freedom model to the FCC as a possible telecommunication's regulatory strategy.

The new law was a sea change event, and having been titled for the House Interstate and Foreign Commerce Committee Chairman, Harley Staggers (D-WV), it had passed the Congress. Although it is traditional for laws to be known by the names of their sponsors, this was believed to be the first case in which the sponsor's name was officially incorporated into the text of a federal statute.

Later, in 1994, the House GOP leadership finally reorganized this committee system by establishing the Energy and Commerce Committee and the Transportation and Infrastructure Committee; railroads were assigned to the latter, finally joining trucking, aviation, waterways, and pipelines.

The Senate, unfortunately, has not followed suit, and the Senate Commerce, Science, and Transportation regulates all transportation modes. Funding authorization for transportation and water occurs in the Environment and Public Works Committee for the most part, alongside the Finance and Appropriations Committees.

Slowly but surely, railroad industry profits began to recover after decades of low profits and widespread railroad insolvencies. A Government Accountability Office report in 2007 to Congress stated that the railroad industry was increasingly healthy and rail rates had generally declined since 1985.

Transcontinental Railroad

I very much enjoyed reading Steve Ambrose's yeoman work, Nothing Like It in the World, published in the millennium year 2000. His book tells the story, as he put it of the transcontinental railroad built from 1863 to 1869. It is the history of Abraham Lincoln's leadership in this project and of the veterans of the Civil War doing rail construction work from Council Bluffs Iowa and from Sacramento, California and ending with the Union Pacific meeting the Central Pacific at Utah's Promontory Summit on May 10, 1869. This was not actually a transcontinental railroad with its Iowa to California geography; but it was a momentous feat!

In May of 2019, the Union Pacific staged a reenactment of Promontory Summit with two of its antique locomotives facing each other. But there is another personal and truly transcontinental railroad story.

During 1978, Southern Pacific/SP (West Coast) had purchased close to ten percent of Seaboard Coast Line/SCL (East Coast) stock, suggesting the makings of the first east-west transcontinental railroad. The railroads met in several midwestern/southern city terminals, and their merger would have offered transcontinental rail coverage from coast to coast.

The negotiations—which took place in my Washington, DC, office (without my presence)—essentially floundered due to typical CEO disagreements as to who would be the CEO. It was either Prime Osborn from the SCL or Ben Biaggini from the SP; this was noted in the national financial press.

Another reason, though, was the failure to get ICC Chairman Dan O'Neal's permission to purchase more SCL stock, greater than the ten percent allowed at the time.

Dan O'Neal was a friend and neighbor in McLean, Virginia neighbor; and when I visited him in his ICC office with the Southern Pacific company's request letter in hand, he laughed, as he had no intention of helping those Republicans. Dan was from the Pacific Northwest and came to Washington, DC, as a staffer to Senator Magnuson.

I had anticipated Dan's response and had advised Southern Pacific to just keep buying, but the lawyers demurred. In September of 2020, the Federal Trade Commission (FTC) voted 3–2 along party lines to advance a proposed rule that would exempt those investments from reporting requirements as long as the investor doesn't already own a stake in the company, and the new purchase would put it over a ten percent holding, and the investor doesn't own more than one percent of the shares of a company that competes with the issuer.

North South versus East West US Rail Network

Later that year at the rail industry Hershey (Pennsylvania) Summit in Congressman Fred Rooney's district, Chessie CEO Hays Watkins and his Washington Representative, John Snow, latter CSX CEO and Secretary of the Treasury, approached Southern Pacific CEO Ben Biaggini and me and proposed to us that if the East-West SP-SCL merger was not working out, would the SP support the Chessie and tender their SCL shares in favor of a Chessie-SCL North-South merger?

We magnanimously answered in the affirmative, being close political allies, and the CSX was formed in the months to come with its headquarters in Richmond, Virginia.

Specifically, the Chessie System and the Seaboard System merged on November 1, 1980, under the holding company name CSX Corporation—CSX standing for "Chessie, Seaboard, and many times more." The combined road at that time had over 27,000 miles of track, importantly now on a North-South axis within the eastern half of the United States, not the earlier East-West transcontinental axis with the Southern Pacific and the SCL.

President Jimmy Carter had signed the Staggers Rail Act into law two weeks earlier on October 14, 1980. In the months to come, a domino succession of North-South mergers occurred, including Norfolk Southern, BN/Frisco, Union Pacific/Missouri Pacific, and others.

Kansas City Southern, already a north-south railroad, was to scale up some ten years later when NAFTA was signed in 1992. Coincidentally, I was a consultant for NAFTA to the Mexican government on how the bilateral infrastructure networks could be improved for both sides, including Kansas City Southern's ability to invest in rail assets in Mexico.

Railroad Industry

Years later, in 2010, there was interest in a type of infrastructure type concession investment (pension funds) in the old Conrail properties, now part of Norfolk Southern.

Our investment group, including a large Australian insurance company, made a sale-leaseback presentation in 2011 to the Norfolk Southern chief financial officers at their Norfolk headquarters; but it was too early. We were prepared to invest billions in the upgrade of those facilities to be paid back over many years, which was the infrastructure fund investment model.

A few years later, we attended a Washington Nationals baseball game with Admiral and Paul Reason (my Naval Academy roommate) and his wife, Diane. Paul was retired and a Norfolk Southern Board member. We noted the signs for the Norfolk Southern Club that ringed around from third base to first base and were very popular and apparently effective!

Norfolk Southern kept a railroad dining car at Union Station for entertaining senators, which was even more effective. I had attended luncheons there, and it was very hospitable.

Later in 2016, the Canadian Pacific Railroad, led by the talented Hunter Harrison, pursued a merger with the reluctant Norfolk Southern and then the CSX. The four major railroad CEOs in the United States had all been publicly quoted as saying to the effect that they were doing fine, and they did not need this Canadian railroad to rock the boat.

I would think someone at the Justice Department would have been alarmed at this antitrust behavior. (In the 2021 Biden administration, they were). Nonetheless, the odds were long that it would happen; even though it would have been the first transcontinental railroad if it did!

But the Canadian Pacific finally gave up in May of 2016, and Hunter Harrison disembarked on his own. Through Wall Street leverage, he surprisingly became the CEO of CSX in early 2017 with an outsized compensation scheme as if he was going to work some miracle. It made me wonder!

At the time, all transportation modes were looking for ways to optimize their operations. Rail transportation was no exception, and Class I railroads across the United States and Canada were implementing strategies to meet this demand.

Precision Scheduled Railroading (PSR) was one such strategy created by Hunter Harrison. The goal of PSR was to transport the same or an incremental amount of freight with fewer rail cars and locomotives, using a more simplified, direct line of transport across their network.

It is a railroad strategy that uses departure schedules and point-to-point delivery methods to achieve low operating ratios and consolidate railroad networks. Previously, shippers, as the customers had service that fit their operations. Now it is the other way around; shippers have to meet the railroad's new PSR schedule being implemented at most Class I railroads across North America, including Canadian National Railway (CN), Canadian Pacific Railway Limited (CP), CSX Corporation, Norfolk Southern Corporation (NS), Union Pacific Corporation (UP), and Kansas City Southern (KCS). The only major Class I rail line that hasn't completely adopted this strategy is the BNSF Railway, but the company has implemented certain aspects of a PSR strategy.

And in mid-2017, the shippers wondered at the rail chaos that ensued. Precision Railroading had arrived, and it was to become the modus operandi for the railroad industry. In the 2020–2021 pandemic, precision railroading was cited as one of the many causes of the global supply chain meltdown. And the dormant Surface Transportation Board now had its long-awaited agenda.

Forty years of Staggers Act success were now in jeopardy! In a way, the rail industry and its Washington trade association deserved this blowback. They had a good thing going but wanted to reach another level.

Amazingly, the 1980 Staggers Act was one of three major deregulation laws passed by Congress in a two-year period, the cumulative result of efforts to reform transportation regulation begun in 1971, during the Richard Nixon administration. The other two laws were the Airline Deregulation Act of 1978 and the Motor Carrier Act of 1980, signed on July 1 of that year, with the Staggers (Rail Deregulation) Act to follow some four months later.

Southern Pacific also had a major trucking line, Pacific Motor Transport (PMT), that required my attention but not anywhere near the concentrated focus on rail deregulation. However, the issues were similar; that is, unnecessary Interstate Commerce Commission and state rate bureau regulation.

Trucking deregulation was meant to allow in-house corporate trucking subsidiaries as well as independent truckers. In the new logistics era of online shopping, freight volumes were soaring, and large scale national and regional trucking companies were ordering thousands of new trucks for their fleets. In 2018 alone, estimates indicate that almost 50,000 ordered, a doubling from the previous year.

As this trend evolved, railroads had trouble with their urban expansion plans. For example, the closest BNSF terminal to the mega ports of Los Angeles and Long Beach was roughly 25 miles away. Its new terminal, which I was to work on when I joined the USC faculty in late 1999, would be 4 miles away from the ports.

Meanwhile, Union Pacific had been locked in what it called "environmental review purgatory" at the ports for nearly a decade as it tried to double capacity to handle 1.5 million containers annually.

The 2015 Panama Canal expansion was bringing bigger ships and more business for those US East Coast ports that were ready for them depth-wise. The Port of Baltimore was one of only a handful of East Coast ports with deep enough harbors to unload post-Panamax ships carrying around 14,000 containers. (In 2023, a severe drought greatly impacted the water supply for the Panama Canal, and ships were restricted as to containers.)

But Baltimore did not have enough rail capacity to handle the cargo volume those ships can bring, despite decades of effort. They are probably the only major port from Florida to Maine that doesn't have double-stack capability, the ability to stack one container on top of another on rail, due to very old tunnels that are the only entry/exit points. Finally, in 2022, work commenced to allow double stack capacity.

CSX Corp. had tried to build a $90 million rail terminal near the Port of Baltimore, a process that ended in 2014 after residents balked at expected noise and traffic. Now, in 2022, the railroad and port were planning a $450 million project to lower the floor of an existing tunnel to accommodate stacked rail, the railroad said. With my infrastructure investment hat on, they finally got it right, and project finance came to the rescue.

But in 2024, the Francis Scott Key Bridge was struck and destroyed by an out-of-control, fully loaded container ship. It would be years before it was rebuilt, with every politician, from the president to the mayor, claiming bragging rights for supplying the political finance.

The positive effects that the Staggers Act had on the industry have been substantial. In the thirty-year period before 1980, railroad freight market share measured in revenue ton-miles declined by thirty-three percent, from 56.1 to 37.5 percent. Market share in the post-Staggers era became stable and then increased to 41.7 percent. Other measures show similar improvement. Return on investment now averaged around seven percent, up from a two percent average in the '70s, according to the Association of American Railroads, the rail industry trade association I had worked with during this period.

And with the industry's improved financial condition, railroads were investing an average of over $6 billion a year in roadway, structures, and equipment. Between 1980 and 2002, the railroads had expended $364 billion in capital improvements and maintenance of track and equipment. Prior to 1980, the rail plant was not in good condition.

I listened to a railroad panelist in mid-2018 explain that his railroad, Norfolk Southern alone would implement a capital program of $1.845 billion in 2018, approximately $100 million above what it spent in 2017, with the main focus on core infrastructure. Asked about public-private partnerships, the response indicated they had done a number of PPP projects where it made sense for both the company and the public agency, and that was in keeping with my 1993 Infrastructure Investment Commission recommendations.

The Staggers Rail Act's major thrust was to limit the authority of the Interstate Commerce Commission, shortly being replaced by the smaller Surface Transportation Board, to regulate rates only for traffic where competition was not effective in protecting shippers. The Surface Transportation Board (STB) estimated in the mid-1990s that only sixteen percent of traffic was still regulated.

Rates are not regulated when competition keeps them at levels below the statutory threshold where the ratio of the revenue to the regulatory variable cost of the move is less than 1.8—the zone of freedom, when a class of traffic has been specifically exempted, or when traffic moves under contract. For example, all traffic moving in trailers or containers on flatcars was exempted in the early 1980s.

The Staggers Act also legalized railroad-shipper long-term contracts. These contracts represent privately negotiated agreements between railroads and shippers over rates, service levels, equipment, and volume of traffic. According to the Surface Transportation Board, at least fifty-five percent of all traffic moves under contract, enabling railroads to improve asset utilization through better planning of their freight cars. These service contracts were to influence my thinking years later in government procurement and electricity deregulation.

It was very satisfying to see how the industry leadership was reinvigorated, taking the initiative regarding new services, pricing, and product. Since Staggers, shippers (customers) have seen a significant decline in rates. Freight rates adjusted for inflation have declined by one to two percent a year. I was a witness to this transformation and was proud of the results.

The industry has also has showed remarkable safety improvements since the Staggers Act, with train accident rates declining by sixty-eight percent, although there were warnings about several oil train derailments in 2014–2015 during the oil fracking boom. I was worried that these oil train derailments during the oil shale fracking phenomenon would bring back regulation, and while generating new revenue was worth the regulatory risk.

A Union Pacific oil train, for example, derailed in the Columbia River Gorge near Mosier, Oregon, on Friday, June 3, 2015, catching fire and sending a plume of black smoke into the sky. Union Pacific spokesman Aaron Hunt said eleven cars of the ninety-six-car freight train, which was heading from Eastport, Idaho, to Tacoma, Washington, derailed around 70 miles east of Portland. Authorities evacuated residents living within a quarter mile of the site and shut parts of Interstate eighty-four.

Ironically, of the 719 people killed in US rail accidents in 2016, only two were paying Amtrak passengers; the rest resulted from a variety of grade crossing accidents and other pedestrian or auto/truck collisions.

But in late 2017 and early 2018, there were, unfortunately, four separate Amtrak related accidents, one of which was carrying the GOP congressional delegation to their annual retreat at the gracious, long-time Greenbrier Resort, a railroad-built hotel in West Virginia. Generally speaking, people are not familiar with the history of Amtrak, which took over passenger rail years earlier in a compromise allowing Amtrak passenger trains to utilize private sector rail lines.

Before 1970, the railroads had to run passenger service. I will never forget riding the Southern Pacific to Chicago and transferring to the Penn Central to Washington, DC, when our family moved there for our father's new government assignment representing workforce needs during the Korean War.

But as passenger service declined, various proposals were brought forward to rescue it. The federal government passed the High-Speed Ground Transportation Act of 1965 to fund pilot programs in the Northeast Corridor, but this did nothing to address passenger deficits. In late 1969, multiple proposals emerged in the United States Congress, including equipment subsidies, route subsidies, and, lastly, a "quasi-public corporation" to take over the operation of intercity passenger trains.

On June 21, 1970, the Penn Central, the largest railroad in the Northeast United States and teetering on bankruptcy, filed to discontinue its passenger trains. Months later, in October 1970, Congress passed, and President Richard Nixon signed into law, the Rail Passenger Service Act. There were several key provisions relating to the new National Rail Passenger Corp. (NRPC), to be known as Amtrak:

1. Any railroad operating intercity passenger service could contract with the NRPC, thereby joining the national system.
2. Participating railroads bought into the NRPC using a formula based on their recent intercity passenger losses. The purchase price could be satisfied either by cash or rolling stock; in exchange, the railroads received NRPC common stock.
3. Any participating railroad was freed of the obligation to operate intercity passenger service after May 1, 1971, except for those services chosen by the Department of Transportation (DOT) as part of a "basic system" of service and paid for by NRPC using its federal funds.
4. Railroads that chose not to join the NRPC system were required to continue operating their existing passenger service until 1975 and thereafter had to pursue the customary ICC approval process for any discontinuance or alteration to the service.

Of the twenty-six railroads still offering intercity passenger service in 1970, only six declined to join Amtrak, which has taken on a life of its own, achieving profits in urban areas like the Northeast while losing millions on long-distance trains spraining the county.

While Amtrak owns its Northeast Corridor, everywhere else they must contact the related Class One rail carrier, and that has always caused some tension. President Biden has been known as "Amtrak Joe" from his years of commuting daily from his Wilmington, Delaware home to Washington's Union Station, just two blocks from his US Senate office.

And hundreds of millions of dollars were now available to Amtrak from the pandemic avalanche of federal funding. Unfortunately, the argument continues by passenger rail zealots to focus on expansion while others said to modernize the existing network. Regardless, there was little encouragement or expertise for Non-Amtrak passenger rail, including the doomed California High-Speed Rail debacle.

The rail industry had resumed an oil shipping schedule, but in the 2020s, as fracking had slowed and some pipelines were being built, there was misplaced environmental opposition. There is nothing worse than seeing dozens of rail cars carrying refined oil falling into a river, as happened from time to time, including in 2023 into the Yellowstone River in Montana.

A pipeline is a far better option, and many have been successfully built and operated for many years. However, it was increasingly difficult to build a pipeline in this country with the global climate issue at the forefront. The failure to understand and provide leadership for this energy transition was becoming a major economic problem, stymieing any progress on all fronts and causing gas at the pump to exceed $5 as the Russians invaded Ukraine in 2022.

I was to read that in the spring of 2016, Fred Smith, founder of FedEx Corp., at his fiftieth-anniversary reunion of the Yale University class of 1966, saluted the

Carter administration and their academic research and the example of ultra-low fare intrastate airlines compared with high-cost national carriers. As a result, many Republican and Democratic lawmakers alike pushed for federal economic deregulation of transportation. He was correct; that is what happened. I similarly say to Republicans, let the market work, and for Democrats, let consumers benefit, as Mr. Smith also pointed out.

I was very pleased that, in the ten years following the 1980 Staggers Act deregulating railroads, the perennially loss-making rail industry was able to halve the rates charged to customers while restoring financial stability. Surface-transport deregulation also spawned an entirely new industry of flexible truckload common carriers to meet the needs of emerging "big box" distribution and retailing models such as Wal-Mart and Target. Our advocacy predictions were confirmed.

As railroads charged their customers by the distance and timing deliveries were made, much of their intermodal infrastructure could engage in sale leasebacks, have new facilities built by third parties (build to suit and lease) as in Joliet, Illinois, or have ports load/unload containers on special spurs. Truckers were also paid by the mile, and this raised their hours-of-service issues.

By the beginning of the twenty-first century, overall logistics costs were reduced from sixteen percent of GDP during the 70s to fewer than nine percent years later. For example, spending in the United States logistics and transportation industry totaled $1.48 trillion in 2015 and was eight percent of annual gross domestic product (GDP).

In 2018, logistics costs started to rise amidst a booming economy and huge increases in global trade and e-commerce. There was a shortage of truckers, a tough job to begin with, so pay increases were needed to stimulate driver recruitment. Trucking freight rates in 2018 had skyrocketed. It appeared that millennials do not want to be truck drivers!

I was very proud of what we accomplished in 1980 and, doubly so, as I had been in Washington, DC, for only four years. It was a tremendous victory and, for me, a personal achievement.

Fast forward, now the Environmental Protection Agency (EPA) occupies the old Interstate Commerce Commission's cavernous hallways in this Federal Triangle building! It was odd walking down those halls in 2015 to a meeting with my thoughts focused on the new WIFIA law (Water Infrastructure Finance and Innovation Act), a successor to our very successful TIFIA legislation described elsewhere in this book.

Those austere, wooden-paneled conference rooms, once the scene of bureaucratic regulatory hearings, are now alive with new topics such as water resources financing.

In the 1992 electric/energy deregulation effort, twelve years later, I would extol PUHCA Reform's creation of the independent power industry, saying to the GOP members, "let the market work," and to the Democrats, "let competition work."

Before I came on board in 1977, the Southern Pacific (SP) had made the decision to diversify. The result was a decision to make only a minimal investment in improving its railroad due to the inept regulatory environment, and to use profits derived from the operation of the railroad to move into other sectors of the economy such as real estate, telecommunications, fiber-optic cable lines, and oil exploration and development.

Ironically, the Southern Pacific owned the Black Mesa Coal Slurry line in Northern Arizona—the only one in the nation as the other railroads fought any expansion of this pipeline technology for Powder River coal in the late 1970s. It was a battle!

In 2019, the dramatic decline in US coal production due to the hundreds of coal-fired power plants that had been shuttered could cost US freight railroads billions, according to Moody's Investment Service. My 1992 Energy Policy Act efforts to launch the independent power industry had much to do with this transition from coal to natural gas, wind, and solar.

Due to climate change concerns and resultant state and federal regulatory policies, coal demand from utilities was estimated to drop by more than 50 percent by 2030. As a result, US railroads could see an estimated $5 billion in lost revenue, which constituted about 5.5 percent of 2018 industry revenue, Moody's said in a September 4, 2019 report.

US coal consumption was declining because relatively clean natural gas prices were effectively competing against coal as a generating fuel, and Federal mandates for clean air emissions in the global climate context had also resulted in utilities seeking other fuel sources for power generation.

As a result, Appalachian coal production has already fallen in the eastern United States, affecting railroads such as CSX and Norfolk Southern; and this was solid Trump "coal" country.

Surprisingly, railroads that delivered coal from the Powder River Basin (PRB) in the western United States were likely to be more exposed to weakening coal demand, including BNSF and the Union Pacific. While its coal had a lower heat content than other coal types, utilities were mandated to install scrubbers to reduce emissions of sulfur oxides. That advantage was no longer the case.

Coal slurry was opposed by the railroads, and they were victorious in that battle with the pipeline promoters. But now, almost forty years later, the Powder River Basin is experiencing economic challenges. Electric utilities respond to their state regulators regarding fuel choices! Southern Pacific had been in the middle of this battle; it was very interesting to look back on this experience.

I also spent much time representing Southern Pacific as the largest land owner in California and played a strategic role in the Congress eventually passing the Reclamation Reform Act in 1982, boosting allowable irrigated land to 960 acres and eliminating the provision that landowners remain near their lands.

I often think of this when driving the direct Los Angeles to San Francisco federal highway five and see, for the most part, water-nourished agriculture. But there are some dry spots with dead rows of almond orchards and signs blaming Congress for a water shortage! Climate change was identified as the culprit amidst the 2020–2 droughts.

Southern Pacific also owned forest lands, so RARE II was another chapter. A second roadless inventory, RARE II, was initiated in 1977, which culminated in a recommendation of wilderness designation for 15,000,000 acres of national forest land and further study for another 10,800,000 acres.

I attended many meetings on the topic, as my general theme was to learn as much as I could about every issue available. I was hooked on public policy!

People are generally surprised that Southern Pacific also launched SPRINT, which I will talk about in the next chapter.

In early 1981, still serving as the Washington representative for Southern Pacific (SP), President Ronald Reagan was now in the White House succeeding Jimmy Carter. SP Chairman and CEO, Ben Biaggini, was also the Chairman of the California Business Roundtable and a leading Republican who knew President Ronald Reagan well.

In fact, just weeks after the Reagan inaugural, the two of us had visited newly installed Secretary of Defense Cap Weinberger (a fellow San Franciscan) at his Pentagon office to review a western rail network chart and make the case for using mobile rail infrastructure to house anti-missile platforms. It was something else!

That same week, walking down K Street in sight of the White House off 16th Street after several meetings, Ben Biaggini indicated to me his concern for President Reagan. This was early 1981; and in 2011 I was to read that Ronald Reagan's son suggested in a new book that his father suffered from the beginning stages of Alzheimer's disease while he was still in the White House.

I had to hand it to Mike Deaver, the President and Mrs. Reagan's closest confidant and public relations/media counselor, to carry on the great communicator strategy despite this obstacle. Perhaps there is a lesson here for every president since that time. In simple terms, it was quality versus quantity in public speaking! Stay focused on the big picture! A good friend of ours, Mamie McDonough, was Mike's special assistant.

Today, in 2024, we have an even older president, Joe Biden, whose handlers seem convinced that they need to have him on point every day on every issue to reassure American voters that he is on top of his game. A rail example was the Norfolk Southern 2023 derailment in East Palestine, Ohio, which caused political havoc with President Biden visiting the site early in the 2024 election year.

This was done to the detriment of his cabinet team's effectiveness, and the low polling numbers seem to bolster the case for a needed Mike Deaver type. Again, it is about quality, not quantity! That propensity had much to do with President Biden giving up on his campaign for a second term in July of 2024, which led to his vice president, Kamala Harris, replacing him on the Democratic ticket. And all of a sudden, we discover that she had chaired a number of White House task forces unbeknownst to the American public during those four White House years.

In the early 1980s, the Atchison, Topeka and Santa Fe Railway (SF) in Chicago and Southern Pacific Transportation Company (SP) in San Francisco attempted a merger. It began with the merger of holding companies Santa Fe Industries and Southern Pacific Company on December 23, 1983, to form the Santa Fe Southern Pacific Corporation (SFSP), which held the SP shares in a voting trust pending ICC approval. The new company was headquartered in Chicago.

The holding company controlled all the rail and non-rail assets of the former Santa Fe Industries and Southern Pacific Company, and it was intended that the two railroads would be merged. They were confident enough that this would be approved that they began repainting locomotives into a new unified paint scheme.

But the SF/SP merger was opposed by the Justice Department in 1985 and denied in a four–one vote by the still-in-existence Interstate Commerce Commission (ICC) on July 24, 1986, when it ruled that such a merger included too many duplicate routes and was therefore monopolistic. The Commission denied SFSP's appeal (again in a four–one vote) on June 30, 1987.

It was what was called a parallel merger, as many of the Southern Pacific and Santa Fe tracks were next to each other figuratively (particularly in California), versus a longitudinal merger such as the earlier proposal with Seaboard Coast Line, which might have eventually been approved by the Interstate Commerce Commission despite the earlier setback.

After the Interstate Commerce Commission denied the merger, SFSP in Chicago sold the SP to Rio Grande Industries (having been purchased by billionaire Phil Anschutz) on October 13, 1988. Rio Grande Industries was rechristened the Southern Pacific Corporation on April 25, 1989. In 1996, Union Pacific finally captured the Southern Pacific by purchase, ending some 130 years of history.

During the SF/SP honeymoon, many top SP executives had moved to Chicago (including good friends Rob Krebs and Bill Denton) assuming management roles. When the ICC aborted that merger, the Santa Fe eventually merged with the BN in 1996 to create the BNSF now owned by Berkshire Hathaway (Warren Buffett) in the largest infrastructure investment in US history.

Rob Krebs, a San Francisco SP executive and Stanford/Harvard MBA grad, became the CEO of BNSF from April 1997 to 2000 and Chairman from April 1997 to April 2002. We were similar in age and worked well together.

In 1984, being in San Francisco for the Democratic Convention and having supervised Southern Pacific's Washington office in recent years, I was asked to meet with then Mayor Dianne Feinstein at City Hall regarding Mission Bay, a huge tract of land made up of old SP rail yards in the sunny Mission District where my mother's family had lived up the hill looking out at the Bay.

The meeting began with her criticism of the SP management at One Market Plaza and how frustrated she was with their refusal to negotiate on the Mission Bay site. I explained that they were not in charge anymore as Santa Fe had merged with the SP the prior year in 1983 and moved the management to their Chicago headquarters. Amazingly, she was not aware of this and asked me for my assistance and to make some introductions.

Upon my return to Washington, I contacted my colleague and friend Bill Denton at Santa Fe, expressed the mayor's concerns, and he flew to Washington, DC, to meet with me.

Within a month, the Santa Fe management sent out a new team led by Jim O'Gara, and a memorandum of understanding was agreed to shortly thereafter in 1985. Ultimately, the SP/Santa Fe merger was disapproved, as I noted; but nonetheless, the Mission Bay project had begun its development journey.

Mission Bay was officially created in 1998 by the San Francisco Board of Supervisors as a redevelopment project. Much of the land was a rail yard of the Southern Pacific Railroad Company, but it had been transferred to its subsidiary Catellus Development Corporation, which latter was spun off as part of the aborted merger of Southern Pacific and the Santa Fe Railway.

Catellus subsequently sold or sub-contracted several parcels to other developers under the leadership of Jim O'Gara and later Nelson Rising, who I knew well from the John Tunney for Senate campaign. Catellus eventually merged into Prologis, which was the largest logistics/industrial/warehousing company in the country. Nelson was a great fellow—UCLA football, Democratic campaigns, smart businessman—and it was unfortunate to read of his death in the spring of 2023.

Mission Bay was a unique transaction revolving around San Francisco's derelict rail yards located in optimal urban settings. Today, it is prime real estate hosting a major University of California, San Francisco (UCSF) medical complex as well as numerous high-tech companies. Even the San Francisco Giants moved their baseball park to the area, as did the Warriors.

Interestingly, I had helped UCSF earlier look at acquiring Treasure Island when it was closed by the Navy in the 1993 Base Realignment and Closure Commission (BRAC), which recommended closing thirty-three major United States military bases, including many in the San Francisco Bay Area.

We launched the first Washington, DC-based "National Infrastructure Week" in 2012 and suggested it be an annual event, which it became, with the "Seventh Annual" having taken place in May 2019, featuring record events and turnout just before the pandemic. During National Infrastructure Week 2014, the BNSF CEO Matt Rose participated in a panel discussion at the Bloomberg event, which was terrific. Matt and I had talked about innovative finance/TIFIA when he was still working under Rob Krebs at the BNSF. Matt went on to praise the Staggers Act as the most important event in American railroad history; and I guess it was!

Another panel at Infrastructure Week 2014 had FedEx and UPS executives praising the Staggers Act and noted how many of their trucks go by rail/piggyback, as it is faster, more economical, and cleaner for the environment.

Trucking and railroad deregulation had a huge impact on the logistics of our nation; however, there are challenges. For example, trucking tonnage—the weight of freight carried—was up by more than thirty percent in the United States since 2009, but the industry's labor force had grown only by about ten percent. The American Trucking Association estimated there were 48,000 open jobs, a 2018 figure that was expected to more than triple over the next decade.

The 2020 event was postponed amidst the coronavirus pandemic, and in 2021 it was a virtual event under the new logo of United for Infrastructure. National Infrastructure Week had morphed into some press sarcasm for having accomplished relatively little. The fact was it was very successful everywhere in the private sector; but in the United States, historically, infrastructure was owned by Congress, and instead of the project finance discipline, it was political finance.

I will talk more about infrastructure (project) finance in chapters five and eight in this book.

When I arrived in Washington in 1977 to run Southern Pacific's Washington office, nine rail carriers were bankrupt, the industry had a low return on investment and was unable to raise capital, and faced a steady decline in market share. The effects that the Staggers Act had on the industry were remarkable. Our TRAIN coalition team had done well!

In February 2014, I watched Norfolk Southern CEO Wick Moorman extol the virtues of the Staggers Act at the US Chamber of Commerce Transportation Summit;

and I noted to myself that his predecessor companies, the Southern Company and the Norfolk and Western, were bitterly opposed to what became the Staggers Act back in the late 1970s.

It is funny, I was a leader of the supportive companies that had to defeat the Southern Company (Ned Breathitt) led filibuster; and we did so with the launch of my TRAIN coalition with Brock Adams as our Counsel. But once the Staggers Act passed back in 1980, the new Norfolk Southern went all out under the new law. I often wondered why they had been in opposition earlier!

So, you had CEOs like Matt Rose and Wick Moorman singing the praises of the Staggers Act with little knowledge of its intrinsic history. And yet, Ed Hamburger, the President of the Association of American Railroads at the time, ignored the notion that, after thirty-five years since passage, a panel of veterans should be assembled to explain how we did it! Ed told me it was a great idea! And it still is!

Ed appeared on the news in July 2015 to respond to the latest in an increasing number of railroad derailments throughout the country. With the huge increase in fracking, oil shipments by rail at the time had dramatically increased, as noted earlier, and many of the older cars had blown up in these accidents.

I watched as Ed stated that there are thousands of rail car shipments every day and that the industry safety record was 99.95 percent. That was not the point, as people in small towns were being driven from their homes every few months and often injured or killed. East Palestine, Ohio, in 2023 as I noted, was the final nail in that public policy coffin.

During this 2015-to-2020 time span, there were also huge new deposits of clean natural gas needing pipelines to get to their new markets like New England from the Marcellus Shelf region of Pennsylvania. What surprised me was the opposition to building new pipelines as a far safer transportation mode alternative. There had never been such opposition before! A sign of the times!

The list of stalled new pipelines at the time included three major oil systems in the Midwest and six natural gas transmission lines across the Eastern United States, mainly in New York and Virginia. These nine projects totaled roughly $27 billion of US infrastructure investment.

Pipelines are the safest and most environmentally friendly means of transporting oil and gas around the country, especially compared with alternatives such as rail or trucking. The 2.8-million-mile system of oil, product, and gas pipelines currently blanketing the lower forty-eight states has a safe delivery rate of greater than 99.999 percent (Transportation Department).

But the new environmental, not-in-my-backyard, movement was throttling worthwhile projects for adding renewable energy transmission or gas pipeline transmission infrastructure that would benefit consumers and the global climate energy transition effort of the 2020s.

While in 2016, all the railroads were laying off thousands of employees as shale oil shipping had slowed due to the dramatic drop in oil prices; in 2018, they were signing up new employees with bonuses due to the thriving US economy at full employment and recovering from the "Great Recession" of December 2007 to June 2009.

Interestingly, in the new ecommerce economy, the supply chain sector, including railroads, boomed. The Association of American Railroads pointed out that both trains and the people working in the rail yards are more productive. CSX's operating ratio, a measure of the amount of operating revenues consumed by operating expenses, went from more than sixty-seven percent in the second quarter of 2017 to fifty-nine percent in the second quarter last year, then fell further to fifty-seven percent in the second quarter this year. The intermodal business matters greatly. It made up eighteen percent of revenue among top-tier, or "Class I," railroads the prior year.

The point I would make is that none of this new business model would have been possible in the pre-Stagger's days. You would have had to go to the Interstate Commerce Commission, and there would have been interminable bureaucratic delays. Now the market and competition can work!

But the industry had its problems. In 2018, coal made up nearly a third of the total tonnage of Class I railroads as originated carloads of coal had dropped by almost half in the decade leading up to the end of 2018 amidst pricing pressures from natural gas (our 1992 Energy Policy Act is reviewed in Chapter 4) and related environmental concerns, regardless of what the Trump administration attempted to do in easing clean air regulations.

And the truckers were already hurting! Some 640 carriers went out of business in the first half of 2019, up from 175 for the same period in 2018, according to transportation industry data.

In 2020, as the coronavirus took its economic toll, people had forgotten that we were already heading downward in 2019 with the Trump tariff strategy. The Institute for Supply Management's (ISM) manufacturing index fell below fifty percent in August 2019, which indicated a contraction in the manufacturing sector.

And global trade was down as the Trump tariffs escalated. The Trump trade war with China had also impacted agricultural exports, which move in large numbers over the nation's railways.

The agriculture sector was dramatically impacted, and the Trump Agriculture Department responded with two subsidy programs of $16 billion and $19 billion to ease the burden in these red states that had voted for Trump.

Ever since I was involved in passing the Staggers Act in 1980, I have found rail freight numbers to be a good, early barometer of the economy, both up and down or the reverse. We saw this in the 2019 Trump tariff situation. And when the next recession arrived in the spring of 2020 with the coronavirus, railroads were once again the first stocks to go down.

The railroad freight picture from the early weeks of 2020, just before the coronavirus, illustrated the 2019–20 downward economic trend from the Trump tariffs. The Association of American Railroads (AAR) reported US rail traffic for the week ended February 15, 2020, was 479,137 carloads and intermodal units, down 8.6 percent compared with the same week in 2019.

Coincidentally, I wrote a note to Ian Jeffries, President of the American Association of Railroads, commemorating the fortieth anniversary (October 14, 1980) of the passage of the Staggers Act right in the middle of the 2020 pandemic. He had written an op-ed entitled When Democrats Were Deregulators, and I remarked on my Southern

Pacific Washington office roll at the time and was very proud of that 1980 event at the White House, as I was the "Democrat" who made all of the arrangements for the signing ceremony.

The country had frozen its 2020 economy as the coronavirus pandemic arrived and enveloped the United States. Still, in early August of 2020, the Washington, DC-based Surface Transportation Board (STB), the successor to the ill-fated Interstate Commerce Commission for resolving railroad rate and service disputes and reviewing proposed railroad mergers, said it had issued a final rule regarding market dominance.

I was to read that the STB objective of this rule was to establish a streamlined approach for pleading market dominance in rate reasonableness proceedings.

I mentioned earlier the Zone of Freedom, wherein railroads could charge rates and services on an unregulated market basis as long as they did not cross over similar standards. It had worked well, and I was beginning to wonder about the STB, as later in 2020, three railroads wanted the regulatory agency to consider financial health in the broad context of the S&P 500 rather than based on individual company balance sheets. In other words, what's the problem? The railroads were doing well, providing good service. Let's not return to the bankruptcy days of the early 1970s.

Norfolk Southern, CN, and Union Pacific filed a joint petition to the Surface Transportation Board (STB) asking that the revenue adequacy calculation used by regulators be seen as a floor instead of a ceiling, as the independent agency had proposed. To me, it was becoming obvious that the shipper organizations were up to their old tricks, essentially lobbying the STB.

The Staggers Act of 1980 changed the rules to let rail carriers establish rates for service unless the commission found there was no competition for rail. Carriers and shippers could also now enter into contracts without commission review. In other words, let the market work and let the consumer benefit.

The next STB steps ranged from no action to announcing a Notice of Proposed Rulemaking for public comment. No action was the right answer. I was now convinced! This was a lobbying exercise by major shippers and reminded me of the old Interstate Commerce Commission days.

And to my surprise, newly inaugurated President Biden signed a wide-ranging executive order on Friday, July 9, 2021, taking aim at certain companies that supposedly dominated their market, including railroads, suggesting STB action.

The executive order—which contained seventy-two initiatives—was like a shotgun striking in its scope and ambition, challenging the business practices of America's technology, health care, agriculture, transportation, and manufacturing firms. But it reached these conclusions after only a few months in office. It seemed strained and rather political.

This now made fifty-two Biden presidential executive orders as of July 9, 2021, after taking office, which surprisingly surpassed his predecessors at this juncture in their presidencies: Trump with thirty-nine, Obama with twenty-two, and Bush with twenty-three. They needed to slow down and be credible!

On Thursday, November 4, 2021, Biden's Deputy Secretary of Transportation Polly Trottenberg sent me a Global Supply Chain question regarding the packed Southern California ports and the open Port of Oakland, wondering why is Oakland underutilized and what are the economics?

I sent her a note the next morning telling her that historically, the fastest route was from LA to Chicago with no mountains, while Oakland to Chicago had both the Sierra Nevada and the Rockies.

Also, California-bound freight could be Oakland while Chicago/Texas etc. can be LA/LB. The latter two have access to a huge inland warehousing infrastructure. Oakland does not have that scale; but there is plenty of open land just miles away by rail in the Central Valley.

I noted that a good friend was on the Board of Walmart years back when the ILWU went on strike in LA/LB. He told me they would just move much of their shipping to Savannah, and they did.

Lastly, the trucking and port logistics sectors need attention. LA/LB might be the biggest port structure in the United States, but it is only #8 in the world. (China has at least five of the others.) And the container revolution beginning in the '60s is a big part of the story. Growing up on a San Francisco hill, I watched it happen by the Golden Gate.

I noted separately that the United States had fallen to fourth place with a total of $96 billion in shipping assets; however, some $56 billion of this is comprised of cruise ships, which comes as no surprise as the largest cruise companies Carnival and Royal Caribbean are both based in the United States.

In the 2021–2 supply chain crisis amidst the pandemic, shipping charges tripled, and there was little oversight. US lawmakers and regulators were taking a hard look at these charges, and new measures in Congress and actions by the US maritime regulator, the Federal Maritime Commission, were focused on a container shipping sector dominated by foreign-based carriers that made profits last year estimated by London-based Drewry Shipping Consultants Ltd. at about $150 billion. However, the 50 percent of US ship inventory in cruise ships did not help.

And the Biden administration, in July of 2021, jumped in and asked the chair of the independent Surface Transportation Board to consider a rule to allow shippers to seek competitive bids for moving freight.

On Monday, February 14, 2022, the STB finalized the comment period and scheduled a public hearing on the proposal for March 15. The Biden administration proposal would force railroads to share cargo with competitors in an effort to supposedly make shipping more cost-effective. What they miss is the tremendous profits and charges noted earlier that the essentially unregulated non-US ocean shipping industry has reaped during this pandemic period.

But the political backlash was mounting in April of 2022 as House Transportation and Infrastructure Chairman Peter DeFazio indicated at his committee hearing that Wall Street pressure to cut costs and maximize profits for shareholders had put the freight-rail industry in a deteriorating state.

In the same hearing, Brotherhood of Locomotive Engineers and Trainmen (BLET) National President Dennis Pierce, from a rail labor perspective, noted that precision-scheduled railroading and similar business strategies at railroads have led to furloughs, very long trains, clogged ports, and a workforce forced to work beyond the point of safe operations.

On April 22, 2022, the Surface Transportation Board voted unanimously to propose an update of its emergency service rules, which enable the STB to compel railroads to respond when shippers say they aren't receiving sufficient and timely service. Among other measures, those rules enable the board to order railroads to share tracks with competitors to get freight loads moving.

Much of this regulatory backlash, in my view, was caused by this new precision-scheduled railroading strategy. Since the passage of the Staggers Act in 1980, US railroads had been very creative in their marketing strategies, particularly intermodal, and the shippers appreciated the advances and were comfortable with the railroad's approach to providing a service anchored around a pickup schedule integrated with the shipper's output.

But the new precision-scheduled railroading strategy changed that to my paraphrase: here's our new schedule, and you the shipper had better be ready or you will miss that train. Frankly, the rail industry's attitude was reverting to its old inward tendencies, and the regulators were on the march, unfortunately. The pendulum, I feared, was swinging in the wrong direction after forty years of success.

While I was also working on trucking and maritime deregulation issues years ago, the maritime sector was reporting extraordinary profits during the 2020–2 pandemic global supply chain. It made me wonder, and sure enough, in late May of 2022, Federal Maritime Commission (FMC) Chairman Daniel Maffei (a former staffer for Senator Moynihan, whom I knew well) admitted he may have been too optimistic about the ocean carriers' ability to self-regulate, particularly as it related to late fees associated with container demurrage and detention.

While he did not want to see vessel alliances eliminated, he did want his FMC to review an alliance if there was an issue of concern to the agency.

A few weeks later, President Biden signed the Ocean Shipping Reform Act into law in the presence of US Senator Maria Cantwell, Chair of the Senate Commerce Committee, and other officials.

The bipartisan Ocean Shipping Reform Act of 2022 would allow the Federal Maritime Commission (FMC) to deploy tools required for the better monitoring of international ocean carriers, creating a level playing field for domestic exporters and importers, as Dan Maffei pointed out.

With oversight and enforcement tools, the new law would help the FMC remove unfair charges, prevent the irrational denial of American exports, and restrict other unfair practices that negatively impact the country's businesses and consumers. With regard to the overcharging of certain fees, the new law will allow the burden of proof to be shifted from the complainant to the international ocean vessels.

The Ocean Shipping Reform Act would also help bar retaliation by international shipping companies against importers and exporters and create the FMC Office of Consumer Affairs and Dispute Resolution Services for the improvement of complaint and investigation processes for American firms.

Most importantly, it was a bipartisan effort developed in the regular order process in committee, representing consensus and avoiding the regulatory ping pong of regulations only. This was a law that would have lasting benefits.

On December 2, 2022, President Joe Biden signed legislation sent by Congress to bring to a close any threat of a rail strike by enshrining into statute a contract between labor unions and the freight rail industry. In mid-September, the Biden administration brokered a deal to avert the threat of an earlier work stoppage, including a significant pay increase.

On the same day as the presidential rail signing, three of the big four US Class I railroads told federal regulators that their service is at or near pre-pandemic levels, thanks to improved train crew staffing levels in their new performance-based rail service strategy, which I believed had much to do with the sick leave issue.

But it seemed the Surface Transportation Board (STB) was starting to resemble its antiquated predecessor, the Interstate Commerce Commission. Perhaps the industry deserved some scrutiny. Surely, they did not want to jeopardize that economic freedom. The Staggers Act had worked, but precision-scheduled railroading (PSR) had not. The STB cited statistics in 2024 compiled by the Federal Reserve of St. Louis showing a steady decline in carload traffic over the past twenty years, including a 28 percent drop in the past decade. At the same time, since 2004, the rate of annual price increases for rail shipping nearly doubled to 3.8 percent, a railcar technology company stated in comments filed with the STB.

Earlier in the 1980s, when my wife's cousins moved to a very large family-oriented home on the beach in Mantoloking, New Jersey, we often visited during the summers and almost all holidays.

I helped their Congressman Jim Howard convert the Conrail (Jersey Central) Commuter lines to the status of State DoT contractors eligible for UMTA grants. Jim's congressional district was the New Jersey Shore area. As Chairman of the House Public Works and Transportation Committee, he was totally frustrated by his inability to impact railroads as they were still in the Energy and Commerce Committee's jurisdiction.

I told him to create a state transit agency as a conduit for mass transit funding, and then contract out to Conrail. That is what he did, and the money flowed to improve service. In some ways, the idea came to me from my San Francisco days, and the issue of double-decking the Golden Gate Bridge was being debated. The bridge overseer at the time was the Golden Gate Bridge and Highway District, so the district changed its name in 1969 to the Golden Gate Bridge, Highway and Transportation District, and launched new bus and ferry services as an alternative, now being eligible for federal mass transit funding.

2

The Breakup of AT&T, 1982

The Role of Sprint, MCI and What Was to Come

Under congressional pressure, prompted by new long-distance fiber entrants such as MCI and Sprint, the breakup of the AT&T Bell System was mandated on January 8, 1982, by an agreed consent decree (Judge Harold Greene, US District Court for the District of Columbia) which required the AT&T Corporation, as had been initially proposed by AT&T, to relinquish control of the Regional Bell Operating Companies (RBOCs) that had provided local telephone service in the United States and Canada up until that point.

The RBOCs were also called the ILECs (incumbent local exchange carriers). In contrast, CAPs (Competitive Access Providers) and CLECs (competitive local exchange carriers) were companies that competed against the RBOCs in the local service areas. IXCs (interexchange carriers) were long-distance service providers such as AT&T, MCI, and Sprint. Long distance was the real battle, as Sprint and MCI fought both in the courts and at the FCC for equal access as their long-distance fiber infrastructure was cheaper than monopoly AT&T's age-old copper lines.

At the time, the cable industry was growing, the three TV networks were dominant, and the computer was landing on office desks. But market forces, new technology, and regulatory policies had been unleashed, leading to Apple, Google, Oracle, Microsoft, and many others.

And AT&T never entered the computer business even though it was allowed under the original consent decree. Alphabet, parent of Google, hit a milestone on January 16, 2020, as a stock rally took it above a $1 trillion valuation for the first time, solidifying the dominance of technology and internet stocks as the biggest titans of Wall Street.

Some 150 years earlier, in the bestseller biography, *Grant*, author Ron Chernow noted the critical role that the telegraph played in 1864 in allowing the Union generals to communicate with each other. Sherman and Grant communicated every day and coordinated their winning strategies. The Union side strung 15,389 miles of wire during the Civil War, operated by 1,500 linemen and operators. And they won the Civil War!

Competition has pushed down the pre-tax cost of cell phone service by 26 percent since 2008, but subscribers haven't enjoyed the benefit because wireless taxes have risen about 50 percent over the same period, the Tax Foundation says. In the year 2020, the main reason for the increase was a jump in the federal Universal Service Fund tax rate, from 9.1 percent to 9.8 percent.

I read that the first coin-operated public telephone appeared on the outside of a Harford, Connecticut, building downtown in 1889. By 1999, more than 2 million public payphones were still available across the United States, according to the Federal Communications Commission; they later reported in 2016 that less than 100,000 remained. In 2021, the Pew Research Center reported that 97 percent of US adults now had cell phone service.

As I had been in charge of Southern Pacific's Washington office, and Sprint was part of the company's business portfolio back in that 1977–81-stime frame, I was very involved in the earlier efforts that led to the 1982 AT&T breakup consent decree and will describe that exciting time.

First off, for perspective, the Google experience in the last two decades is a good analogy. The United States regulatory apparatus for telecommunications today in the 2020s has begun peeling the monopoly onion that began as content of all varieties was now the coin of the advertising realm, with new technologies such a search, ads, and content streaming bursting onto the scene with new emphasis on sports content in particular.

The US lawsuits against Google compounded the legal issues the company faced worldwide while broadening the scope of the government's allegations. Google was now in battle mode. It hired high-powered lawyers, including a former litigator from the Justice Department's antitrust division, to build a defense as it tried to protect its position in the search, mobile software, online video, and ad-tech businesses that helped make it a $1.2 trillion company.

In 2023, Google completed its largest layoffs in company history, signaling it felt pressure to cut costs. But unlike our SPRINT team's coalition that managed to break up AT&T, I had my doubts that there would be a breakup of Google. So we begin that AT&T story:

Under congressional pressure, the breakup of the AT&T Bell System was mandated on January 8, 1982, in an agreed consent decree (Judge Harold Greene, US District Court for the District of Columbia) which required the AT&T Corporation, as had been initially proposed by AT&T, to relinquish control of the Regional Bell Operating Companies (RBOCs) that had provided local telephone service in the United States and Canada up until that point.

Under the decree, AT&T would continue to be a provider of long-distance service, competing against MCI, Sprint, et al, while the now independent Regional Bell Operating Companies (RBOCs) would provide local service, capture the burgeoning wireless sector, and no longer be directly supplied with equipment from AT&T subsidiary Western Electric. Now customers would be able to shop for new technology!

Eventually, the government loosened RBOC telecommunications restrictions, and the Telecommunications Reform Act of 1996 changed the telecommunications landscape yet again. RBOCs were allowed to merge, and those mergers or acquisitions took place in the following years, winding up with Verizon and AT&T.

It is hard to comprehend the immense changes brought on by the computer and the internet in these millennium times. If AT&T had not been broken up, none of this technological phenomenon would have happened. And, believe it or not, the Defense Department had supported AT&T under the banner of "national security" against the Justice Department.

This was to be a very important Millennium moment as it unleashed American technology and Silicon Valley. In that vein, on October 9, 2023, amidst another continuing resolution (lack of congressional regular order), the ouster of the House Speaker, and two major foreign conflicts, that day's Wall Street Journal chose to recognize the fortieth anniversary of the AT&T breakup, which is the prime topic of this chapter.

In representing Southern Pacific Corporation and just finishing railroad deregulation (the Staggers Act) as described in the preceding chapter, it was another exciting yet personal regulatory reform moment.

People don't commonly know it, but Southern Pacific Communications Company (SPC) – later to be called Sprint – was originally a unit of the Southern Pacific Corporation, the railroad holding company headquartered in San Francisco. SPC was headquartered on Adrian Court in Burlingame, California, where it also maintained a technology laboratory.

Competition in the long-distance market was the issue that inspired Sprint and its MCI ally to support the Justice Department and advocate in the courts and Congress for long-distance telephone competition.

AT&T had a national telephone monopoly, including the telephone in your home, and their long-distance service was slow, expensive, and archaic based on antiquated copper lines. In 2024, the Justice Department antitrust suit against Apple brought back the memory of how AT&T owned everything; now Apple wanted to sell you everything.

While effective competition in long lines was the near-term goal for Sprint and MCI, public policy favoring new technology and competition in all aspects of the telephone market went even further, ultimately resulting ultimately in the breakup of the entire AT&T colossus. I was very excited!

Sprint was building out a low-cost fiber network for long-distance that would provide better service at competitive prices for consumers.

Southern Pacific had maintained an extensive microwave communications system along its rights-of-way that the railroad used for internal communications. After the 1978 Execunet II decision, Southern Pacific expanded its internal communications network by laying fiber optic cables along the same rights-of-way.

Earlier in 1972, Southern Pacific Communications had begun selling surplus system capacity to corporations for use as private lines, circumventing AT&T's then-monopoly on public telephony. Prior attempts to offer long-distance voice services had not been approved by the Federal Communications Commission (FCC), although a fax service (called Speed FAX) was permitted. SPC was only permitted to provide private lines, not switched services.

Competitor, but political ally, MCI Communications won its court battle giving MCI the right to begin offering Execunet services; that is, AT&T had to allow its long-distance rivals to complete the local call. Long distance was the real battle, as Sprint and MCI fought both in the courts and at the FCC for equal access as their long-distance fiber infrastructure was cheaper than monopoly AT&T's age-old copper lines.

Southern Pacific Communications, represented by Attorneys Bob Ross and John Kenny from our 1801 K Street, SP Washington, DC, offices, took the Federal Communications Commission to court to obtain the right to offer switched services and succeeded in the Execunet II decision.

At that point, Southern Pacific Communications decided they needed a new name to differentiate the switched voice service from Speed FAX and ran an internal contest to select a name. The winning entry was Sprint, an acronym for Southern Pacific Railroad Internal Network Telecommunications. I truly enjoyed being a part of the Sprint team; it was exciting.

The first fax machine I ever saw was Japanese-made and brought to our Washington office around 1979 by Gus Grant, the president of Sprint. Gus, along with our Washington office attorneys, John Kenny and Bob Ross, ran circles around AT&T's lawyers. They were a great team!

In April 2022, I once again attended the Annapolis Book Fair at the Key School campus by the South River. Besides some excellent panel discussions with various authors, there was also a "book market" with donated books for sale at $2 each. I always picked up several non-fiction items!

On this trip, there was a book, still wrapped in cellophane, entitled 1968—88: The History of MCI, *The Early Years by Philip Cantelon*, written in 1993 and sponsored by MCI. I included it in my purchase, and after unwrapping the cellophane, I went through the pages and pictures; it brought back memories of an important time in national communications policy.

Representing Sprint, I was in the Rayburn House Office Building hearing room in Congress in the late 1970s when AT&T Chairman John deButs (a native Virginian) said "no" to competition. I was in the same committee hearing room a year later when new AT&T Chairman Charlie Brown said "maybe" and later proposed spinning off the regional bells, which then led to the January 8, 1982, consent decree.

Interestingly, Mr. deButs resided on a family farm in Upperville, Virginia. This is beautiful country where we later had a modest but very pleasant weekend home. Mr. deButs died of a heart attack in Winchester, Virginia, on December 18, 1986, only four years after the consent decree which he had opposed.

In the case of this initial chapter of US telecommunications reform, there was no legislation passed; rather, a court decision was rendered. But I will give credit to Congressman, and later Senator, Tim Wirth from Colorado for being the front-line member of Congress who drove this issue. Tim was a Stanford PhD graduate and a good friend!

AT&T's history, going back to 1885, was a highly profitable company and a government-supported monopoly. However, the communications giant lost its government backing in 1980 when charges were filed against it under the Sherman Antitrust Act.

This was the second time that AT&T found itself in an antitrust suit. In 1949, AT&T was excused from antitrust laws because it was believed that a single company providing nationwide service was a vital part of national security and any deregulation might interrupt service.

It was Judge Harold Greene who presided over the momentous United States v. AT&T case in the US District Court for the District of Columbia, which resulted in the 1982 consent decree between AT&T and the Federal Trade Commission represented by the Justice Department.

This divestiture had a long history beginning with the filing in 1974 by the United States Department of Justice in the first Bush administration of an antitrust lawsuit against AT&T, noting that AT&T was, at the time, the sole provider and owner of telephone service throughout most of the United States.

Prior to the breakup, the broadcast networks relied on AT&T Long Lines' infrastructure of terrestrial microwave relay, coaxial cable, and, for radio, broadcast-quality leased line networks to deliver their programming to local stations.

However, by the mid-1970s, the then-new technology of satellite distribution offered by other companies started to give the Bell System competition in the broadcast distribution field, with the satellites providing higher video and audio quality, as well as much lower transmission costs. These long-distance carriers like Sprint and MCI were giving AT&T competition in that long-distance sector where their new fiber wires were far more efficient than the old AT&T copper.

And long distance was the real battle, as Sprint and MCI fought both in the courts and at the FCC for equal access to the local service networks, as their long-distance fiber infrastructure was cheaper than monopoly AT&T's age-old copper lines.

Some more background: In 1982, the Federal Trade Commission (FTC) moved to spin off local telephone services provided by the Bell operating companies from AT&T. In that case, the Justice Department brought charges against AT&T, accusing it of violating the Sherman Antitrust Act by improperly using its monopoly profits.

AT&T then adopted this breakup strategy as it sensed it would lose in the courts. So, it proposed that it retain control of Western Electric, Yellow Pages, the Bell trademark, Bell Labs, and AT&T Long Distance.

And internally agreed to turn over cellular to the RBOCs, which was hard to believe in retrospect. A lawyer friend later told me he had been in the room when the question came up at the AT&T headquarters on lower Broadway in New York City; and the casual decision was to just give it to the RBOCs, which gave me a mental picture of the AT&T management mediocrity.

It was an exciting time; our three-man Sprint team was there participating in the hearings, fundraisers, panel discussions, and the like. John and Bob were fully engrossed in the legal network at the time, including the agencies, while I focused on Congress and the political landscape.

The RBOCs, AT&T argued, would achieve the Government's goal of creating competition in supplying telephone equipment and supplies to the operating companies. These Baby Bells were some of the most successful spinoffs in history, as AT&T had already installed the infrastructure and their businesses were established and producing cash flow from day one.

The 1982 breakup of the Bell System resulted initially in the creation of seven independent companies that were formed from the original twenty-two AT&T controlled members of the system. At the time of the breakup, these companies were:

1. NYNEX, acquired by Bell Atlantic in 1996, is now part of Verizon Communications.
2. Pacific Telesis, acquired by SBC in 1997, is now part of AT&T Inc.
3. Ameritech, acquired by SBC in 1999, is now part of AT&T Inc.
4. Bell Atlantic merged with GTE in 2000 to form Verizon Communications.
5. Southwestern Bell Corporation, rebranded as SBC Communications in 1995, acquired AT&T Corporation in 2005 and renamed itself AT&T.
6. BellSouth, acquired by AT&T Inc. in 2006.
7. US West, acquired by Qwest in 2000, which in turn was acquired by CenturyLink in 2011.

As well as these two: Cincinnati Bell, covering the Cincinnati metropolitan area; Southern New England Telephone (SNET), acquired by SBC in 1998, is now part of Frontier Communications.

The AT&T breakup led to a surge of competition in the long-distance telecommunications market by companies such as Sprint and MCI with their lower cost fiber infrastructure. AT&T struggled in this competition, and AT&T Computer Systems failed.

After spinning off Western Electric, which became Lucent, then Alcatel-Lucent, and now Nokia, it was left with only its core business with roots as AT&T Long Lines and its successor AT&T Communications. It was at this point that AT&T was purchased by one of its own spin-offs, SBC Communications, the company that had also purchased two other RBOCs and a former AT&T associated operating company (Ameritech, Pacific Telesis, and SNET), and which later purchased another RBOC (BellSouth).

Local residential service rates, which were formerly subsidized by long-distance revenues, initially began to rise faster than the rate of inflation. Long-distance rates, meanwhile, fell both due to the end of this subsidy and increased competition. But it brought the country together. I personally remembered how it had been a big deal and costly to make an East Coast to West Coast telephone call, and now it was routine and an economic plus.

And as for technology, AT&T had owned the entire US land line phone network; and they were in a regulated rate base. As a result, there was no incentive to develop new technology for the customer, even though Bell Labs in New Jersey was one of the top research organizations in the world. So, they depreciated those phones and slowly surrendered to the wireless iPhones.

The cellular/RBOCs decision ultimately led to the multiplicity of cellular broadband carriers that were known as Verizon, AT&T Wireless, Sprint (SoftBank), and T-Mobile (Deutsch Telecom). The latter two merged in 2020 and it was now known as T-Mobile. The Sprint name was gone, much to my disappointment.

In 1993, the "new" AT&T moved into the mobile phone business by acquiring McCaw Cellular, for $12.6 billion. But in 2001, the AT&T Wireless Services became an independent business.

MCI was purchased by WorldCom in 1998 and became MCI WorldCom, with the name afterwards being shortened to WorldCom in 2000. WorldCom's financial scandals and bankruptcy led that company to change its name in 2003 back to MCI Inc.; and that name disappeared in January 2006 after the company was bought by Verizon.

In 1980, SPRINT decided to move its California headquarters in Burlingame to the Washington, DC, metro region, noting this was the home of telecom public policy. Southern Pacific Land Company CEO Greg Linde asked for my recommendation regarding the locality.

As I often traveled in and out of Dulles Airport from San Francisco on United, my strong recommendation was that the region in Northern Virginia would be an excellent location as there was little development there at the time; but I sensed that this was about to change. And I was right as AOL and a host of tech companies and then numerous data centers converged on this Northern Virginia area. But the Southern Pacific Land Company back in San Francisco was more conventional and purchased an established location in Bethesda, Maryland.

It was all for naught as, in 1982, SPC/Sprint and GTE entered merger negotiations, and in 1983, they merged under the name "GTE Sprint." I had known the GTE governmental affairs staff well. In 1989, United Telecom purchased a controlling interest, and in 1991, it completed its acquisition of US Sprint, and Kansas City was its new home.

In 1992, United Telecommunications adopted the nationally recognized identity of its long-distance unit, changing its name to Sprint due in large part to the increased brand recognition because of the successful Candice Bergen "Dime Lady" advertisement campaign.

Sprint and MCI were the catalysts for competition; but this is primarily a history of the break-up of AT&T, which was critically important to moving the United States forward to the era of computers, the internet, and Silicon Valley with its legion of successful high-tech telecommunications companies.

It is hard to believe today, but as I said earlier, prior to the 1982 breakup, AT&T owned your phones! They owned everything, and Bell Labs products were only brought online as AT&T so deemed. Again, it is a mystery that they did not succeed in the computer business, as the 1982 consent decree had allowed. It seems when they spun off the RBOCs, they also spun off their customers!

Interestingly, pollsters now in this cell phone era are having a hard time with the accuracy of their polls as they have based their interview strategy on the availability of landlines. Now they cannot locate the right demographics, particularly the millennials, who use their mobile cellular phones wherever they happen to be. This was an issue in the polling results of the 2016 presidential election and earlier for several reasons:

1. A landline-only sample conducted for the 2014 elections would miss about three-fifths of the American public, almost three times as many as it would have missed in 2008.

2. Since cellphones generally have separate exchanges from landlines, statisticians have solved the problem of finding them. The problem, though, is that the 1991 Telephone Consumer Protection Act had been interpreted by the Federal Communications Commission to prohibit the calling of cellphones through automatic dialers, in which calls are passed to live interviewers only after a person picks up the phone, now conventionally known as robocalls.

In 1993, the "new" AT&T moved into the mobile phone business by acquiring McCaw Cellular, for $12.6 billion. But in 2001, the AT&T Wireless Services became an independent business.

MCI was not listed anymore as they had been purchased by WorldCom in 1998 and became MCI WorldCom, with the name afterwards being shortened to WorldCom in 2000. WorldCom's financial scandals and bankruptcy led that company to change its name in 2003 back to MCI Inc.; and that name disappeared in January 2006 after the company was bought by Verizon.

In July of 2023, AT&T RBOC alumni had left behind a sprawling network of cables covered in toxic lead that stretched across the United States, under the water, in the soil, and on poles overhead. This was not long distance but rather local/regional. One region was Lake Tahoe where, in 2024, it was disclosed that there were miles of copper cable at the bottom of that pristine lake.

Here is some of my earlier Sprint history when we worked closely with MCI in advocating for the AT&T breakup. Bill McGowan, an investor from New York with experience in raising venture capital, met with the board of Microwave Communications Inc. (MCI) in 1968. His critical investment provided him with a stake in the company and a seat on the board, eventually becoming MCI Chairman and CEO. Bill was the guiding spirit of MCI (headquartered in New York), and Sprint and MCI were closely aligned in terms of public policy goals. We became good friends, and Bill went on to win a big antitrust settlement ($1.8 billion) from AT&T.

I recommended to Southern Pacific that they hire my tennis partner and former FCC Chairman Dick Wiley to pursue a similar strategy, which his firm, then Kirkland and Ellis, was willing to do on a contingency basis. But Southern Pacific stubbornly demurred and stayed with their railroad firm, Steptoe and Johnson, and did not get a dime. Dick's successor firm (Wiley, Rein, and Fielding) went on to major successes.

I remember visiting with Dick and exploring the lottery approach for acquiring cellular spectrum, the prime artery for wireless traffic. This was the precursor to the auctions of the late 1980s. Fast forward, and FCC cellular auctions in 2015 generated some $45 billion in proceeds, with a smaller amount received in early 2016.

With my 1993 Infrastructure Investment Commission hat on, I had been arguing for some portion of those proceeds to also be directed to a national infrastructure investment strategy, marrying the old economy with the new economy by funding a National Infrastructure Corporation (Bank) as called for in our Infrastructure Investment Commission report. But members of Congress seem to think they are the infrastructure experts in their districts. This topic is dealt with in more detail later in this book.

But those auctions continued and were now being suggested for building out rural (and urban scholastic) broadband, particularly after the 2020 pandemic and the need for long-distance learning as schools shut down. 5G was to make its debut at the same time.

The Sprint long-distance service was first marketed in six metropolitan areas: New York, Boston, Philadelphia, Los Angeles, San Diego, and Anaheim. The switches were in Los Angeles and New York. A customer was required to have a private line connection to one of these switches to use the service and paid an access fee per private line. Access was also available by dialing an access number to connect to the Sprint switch. Customers were then billed at 2.6 cents per tenth of a minute increment.

I remember vividly how cell towers multiplied around commercial centers throughout the United States to allow major companies to connect directly to the Sprint long-distance network, and this first episode of "cherry picking" stayed with me throughout my public policy career.

I was very proud to have been a part of the deregulation of telecommunications in this country.

Having just completed my active role in the 1980 Staggers Act, it was a sign of the times.

In 2019, I was to enjoy reading former FCC Chairman Tom Wheeler's new book, From Gutenberg to Google, published by the Brookings Institution Press, just before the pandemic and its disappointing closure.

Tom had been a good friend during the 1982 AT&T breakup drama, serving then as the President of the National Cable and Television Association. Michael Powell, son of the General and a former FCC Chairman, was now the president of the NCTA, with their website logo: We are NCTA—The Internet & Television Association.

I very much enjoyed Tom's book and would have added just a few thoughts:

1. He was right to salute Bill McGowan, founder of MCI, as I have also done in Real Regulatory Reform. But our Sprint team should have been mentioned as well.
2. My point about Ron Chernow's biography of Grant emphasizes the role of the Union forces under General Grant, focusing on logistics and the building out of an enormous telegraph infrastructure that the Confederacy could not come close to matching. This superiority had much to do with Lincoln and Grant ultimately winning the Civil War.
3. The role of Robert Kahn and Vinton Cerf as Fathers of the Internet is right on point. While I was at USC from 2000 to 2004 (National Center for Innovations in Public Finance), I had occasion to visit Dr. Kahn at his Corporation for National Research Initiatives (CNRI) offices, based in Reston, Virginia. The topic was, of course, infrastructure investment, particularly our 2000 Navy Marine Corps IT Procurement, which is Chapter 11 in Real Regulatory Reform.
4. The US Naval Academy had delisted celestial navigation as a mandatory course in the 90s due to GPS technology; but as a result of cyber warfare, it had reinstituted that celestial curriculum twenty years later in 2014. It was a back-to-the future moment!

Reading book reviews recently, I came across these two together coincidentally that are certainly related to Tom's references to railroad networks and Edison's speaking telegraph, both in 1877:

1. Rail networks review of The Europeans (Orlando Figes) by Dan Hofstadter. Chief among these was the rapid construction of railways, such that in France alone, for example, well more than 8,000 miles of track were laid down between 1850 and 1870.
2. Edison's speaking telegraph from Edison (Edmund Morris essay) By mid-June, Edison had been able to construct a combination telephone transmitter-receiver that tested "far plainer and better."

In a similar way, decades later, Robert Kahn and Vinton Cerf were the Fathers of the Internet, launched as a Pentagon project during the Cold War. It has played a central role in our twenty-first century economy, and during the 2020 coronavirus, even more so.

The internet and Zoom technology became essential to our lives. For example, on Easter Sunday of 2020, our family (Washington, DC, San Francisco, and San Diego, etc.) united via a virtual conference meeting platform named Zoom, which had taken off as the go-to option to solve the stay-at-home requirement of combating the Covid pandemic.

At that same time, Comcast, the nation's largest source of residential Internet with its cable legacy, serving more than 26 million homes, reported peak traffic was up by nearly one-third that March, with some areas reaching as high as sixty percent above normal. Demand for online voice, video, and connections—all staples of remote work—had surged during the pandemic, and peak usage hours shifted from evenings, for entertainment, to daytime work hours.

Vinton Cerf, along with fellow computer scientist Robert E. Kahn, would have been pleased. They were the driving force in developing the key Internet protocols in the 1970s for the Pentagon's Defense Advanced Research Projects Agency, which provided early research funding. They were headquartered in Northern Virginia, where we had moved in 1977.

Cerf, who lived and worked in Northern Virginia, was featured during this 2020 virus outbreak in the Washington Post and talked about his gang of self-described Netheads who led an insurgency against the dominant forces in telecommunications at the time, dubbed the bell heads for their loyalty to the Bell Telephone Company and its legacy technologies.

This was fascinating to me and brought back memories of our Sprint effort in the late 1970s and early 1980s, and in 2002 while at USC visiting Robert Kahn at his office in Reston, Virginia.

Bell, which had dominated US telephone service until it was broken up (by us) in the 1980s, and similar monopolies in other countries wanted to connect computers through a system much like their lucrative telephone systems, with fixed networks of connections run by central entities that could make all of the major technological decisions, control access, and charge whatever the market—or government regulators—would allow. I remember it well!

The vision of the Netheads was totally different, relying on technological insights and a lot of faith in collaboration. The result was a network of networks—with no central control. That was the idea! There were technical protocols, arrived at through a process for developing expert consensus, that offered anyone access to the digital world from any properly configured device.

And the lack of a central authority was the key to why the Internet works today as well as it does, especially at times of unforeseen demands like the coronavirus pandemic in the early 2020s, a social benefit that has been a regulatory challenge ever since, offsetting the concerns of privacy, and the so-called Section 230 provision giving the internet carriers liability coverage.

Cerf's comments about the telephone company titans of the day made me laugh. They (the Bellheads) were treating the Netheads as misguided children who, someday, might understand how telecommunications technology really worked. I guess we were the Netheads!

But we all celebrated when the telephone companies gradually abandoned old-fashioned circuit-switching for what was called Voice over IP or VoIP. It was essentially transmitting voice calls over the Internet—using the same technical protocols that Cerf and others had developed decades earlier. I remembered that happening from our Sprint activity, but had never interacted with these Netheads at the time.

On February 15, 1985, .us was created as the Internet's first domain; its original administrator was Jon Postel of the Information Sciences Institute (ISI) at the University of Southern California (USC). He administered .us under a subcontract that the ISI and USC had from SRI International (which held the .us and the gTLD contract with the United States Department of Defense).

On October 1, 1998, the National Science Foundation transferred oversight of the .us domain to the National Telecommunications and Information Administration (NTIA) of the United States Department of Commerce.

John Postel died that same month, leaving his domain administration responsibilities with ISI. In December 2000, these responsibilities were transferred to Network Solutions, which had recently been acquired by Verisign. I had joined the USC faculty just months earlier and had read about John Postel and their USC ISI offices in the Marina Del Rey area of Los Angeles.

Earlier, in 1997, while still a part of Lockheed Martin, Neustar won the contract to administer the North American Numbering Plan (NANP). It created a massive database in need of a neutral steward to give telephone companies equal access to everybody's digits. To ensure that neutrality, in 1999 they were divested by Lockheed Martin and renamed Neustar. The internet was growing by leaps and bounds. The Neustar contract was renewed by the National Telecommunications and Information Administration (NTIA) periodically.

Interestingly, Lockheed Martin was a client of my firm at that same time but on the topics of maglev technology for high-speed transportation.

During these years, the Corporation for National Research Initiatives (CNRI), founded by Robert Kahn in 1986, was headquartered in Reston, Virginia, by Dulles Airport. It was a not-for-profit organization formed to undertake research around the strategic development of network-based information technologies, and providing leadership and funding for information infrastructure research and development.

This was all amazing to me, and interested as I was in our nation's infrastructure, including digital, I contacted Robert Kahn while I was at USC and, as noted, visited him at his CNRI offices around 2002. He was a very nice person, very focused on the public benefit aspect.

I briefed him on my infrastructure initiatives at USC and indicated my surprise that USC had essentially ignored all the work that John Postel and he had been doing in creating the infrastructure of the internet. He concurred, saying, in effect, that they seemed to ignore what we were doing.

This early history of the internet underscores how, between the late 1970s and 1990s, this country would totally revolutionize key components of its economic infrastructure; and I was fortunate to have been directly involved early on with the deregulation of railroads, trucking, and telecommunications. But the trendlines were there, and the waves began to land on the beach as the ensuing chapters will address, including natural gas and electricity generation.

This experience was to help me later in working with infrastructure funds to identify investment opportunities in these important sectors.

But backing up a bit, I should mention my Naval Academy classmate and friend, Roger Staubach, as he was retained by MCI in the early 1980s. Roger's prime role off the gridiron was always in commercial real estate. When MCI began their rollout in the 1980s after the consent decree, they quickly needed office space in multiple cities throughout the United States.

Dan Akerson, also a Naval Academy graduate whom I knew, was at MCI in those days; and he wanted to move a large system software group to Dallas. He was determined to have Roger find a large parcel of land, have the zoning and other issues straightened out, and have the move completed—fast. It had to happen within a year instead of the usual two.

Out of that exercise began the first national tenant services real estate business in the country; the Staubach Company was on its way. Knowing both Roger and Dan, I suspected that both having gone to the Naval Academy only made Roger work harder, as Dan had high expectations, as demonstrated by his later role as chairman of General Motors. Roger went all out to meet his demands, and I could appreciate that loyalty.

The Staubach Company had an exclusive to represent MCI, at no cost, to establish MCI offices throughout the country, and they were paid by the building owners in keeping with the typical commercial leasing commission tradition. It was a real turning point for the real estate industry, launching the tenant representation business, and Roger was uniquely qualified to take it to that next level.

Dan Akerson retired in 2014 as Chairman of General Motors, and we had become good friends earlier when he joined the Board of the Navy Memorial Foundation.

A decade earlier, Admiral Tom Lynch was retiring as Superintendent at the Naval Academy, and all of us went out on the aircraft carrier, USS George Washington, for two days courtesy of Dan's private business jet from his Wall Street firm, Forstmann Little, at the time.

In the early 2000s, Dan had been the CEO of XO Communications, an internet services provider founded by telecom billionaire Craig McCaw. I had launched a startup called Bright Net, later Local Crossing when Global Crossing invested. It was a consortium of utilities that would make their unregulated conduit available for last-mile connections of fiber (that we would install and manage or light the fiber) to downtown office buildings versus digging up streets.

I was asking Dan's XO to invest in us and was giving him a status report in his McLean, Virginia office. Dan was well known as a hard driver and said they would invest if we gave them an exclusive on each building we connected. I told him this was probably impossible from a regulatory perspective, but I should have said, okay, let's give it a try!

Dan did very well and is the largest donor now to Naval Academy athletics with the new Akerson Tower at the Navy football stadium in Annapolis. Retiring from General Motors at the time was a surprise. However, Dan's wife, Karin, was ill fighting cancer, and I was saddened to read in our Naval Academy alumni magazine that she passed away in early 2018.

Merger proposals—seeking content and/or scale—were a major issue for the FCC throughout this period. Some state attorneys general continued to oppose the SPRINT—T-Mobile merger, and that was an unfortunate delay as SPRINT lost some 91,000 of its top subscribers to its larger rivals in the third quarter of 2019. It made sense for T-Mobile and SPRINT to merge.

The T-Mobile legions coming to Washington, DC, always stayed at the new Trump Hotel, possibly thinking that it was a good lobbying strategy now that Donald Trump was president, until the Washington Post ran a front-page story! Another reason I thought to rename the combined company as simply SPRINT (again, keeping that SP railroad heritage alive).

But at the end of the day, on April 1, 2020, the $32 billion merger was finally approved by the judge; and unfortunately, the surviving entity would be known as T-Mobile, not as SPRINT! Then T-Mobile CEO Mike Sievert's compensation totaled $54.9 million, most of which came in the form of stock grants.

Other executives with long tenures at T-Mobile also gained payouts in the double-digit millions. Neville Ray, the company's president of technology, received a 2020-package of $33.2 million.

T-Mobile jumped over rival AT&T Inc. in 2022 to become the country's second largest wireless network operator in terms of subscribers. Sprint also provided its merger partner with a valuable cache of wireless spectrum licenses that would support the bandwidth for T-Mobile's 5G network. I had my doubts not only about the tawdry T-Mobile corporate behavior but also the huge compensation awards for what?

It was a shame that the SPRINT spirit, ingenuity, talent, and huge fiber network had been overcome by its swashbuckling corporate partner.

Resultant US Telecommunications Technology Sector Expansion

To date in this chapter, we have talked primarily about the breakup of the AT&T communications monopoly and the various technology companies that were spawned. Now, positioning for this new marketplace, I had to pay close attention as some corporate strategists thought that content was the key. So that is where we now steer this conversation, albeit content turned out to be a bucking bronco!

Some history here is in order, and all well reported in the public business press, which I read avidly. In 2007, Apple's iPhone had only just gone on the market. The new AT&T (anchored by Southwest Bell), unlike its old predecessor, made a smart, conservative decision to make wireless the cornerstone of the company's growth, using the iPhone to gain wireless market share. In fact, by 2023, the AT&T/Verizon landline business was roughly 25 percent of its original US footprint, with the South being the only region with a real landline presence.

AT&T CEO John Stankey announced a proposed mega-merger with Time Warner, seeking content to shore up their economics as they lost customers through cord-cutting to the internet despite their 2015 purchase of DirecTV. In 2015, well into Netflix's rise, AT&T, having already spent $49 billion on DirecTV, launched an ambitious campaign to buy Time Warner for $85 billion, with entertainment content as the goal.

As to corporate performance, AT&T's shares had produced a total return of 80 percent since Randall Stephenson's (Stankey's predecessor and fellow careerist) arrival as CEO in 2007. Cable-and-entertainment rival Comcast's stock had more than tripled its value while wireless rival Verizon's shareholders had gained 150 percent during that same time span. (Both AT&T and Verizon had a regulated rate base history while Comcast, as a cable company, had enjoyed a franchise approach that is relevant to the net neutrality issue.)

The Time Warner purchase, on top of the DirecTV purchase, resulted in a heavy debt load complicating Stephenson's commitment to maintaining the healthy dividend. And hedge funds sensed an opportunity. The entertainment content strategy was looking questionable. It was not long after its 2019 consummation when institutional investors criticized AT&T for this foray into entertainment content.

Fast forward, on Friday, April 8, 2022, AT&T Inc. completed the planned separation of its relatively new film-and-TV empire into a new publicly traded company called Warner Bros. Discovery.

AT&T Chief Executive John Stankey noted at the time that inflation could prompt the company to raise prices for some core services while it continued to cut costs and reduce debt after getting out of the media content business. Inflation had raised the cost of everything from labor to router parts. But the rate that US cellphone carriers charged for wireless service had barely budged.

AT&T faced challenges that included a high debt load and said it planned to use most or all of the $39 billion of cash from its media transition strategy to help pay down this debt. In March 2022, it outlined a plan to halve AT&T's network of copper telephone lines by 2025.

There had been a brief pipes and content strategy, but AT&T determined to give that combination up and focus on the pipes. A few months later, AT&T ordered 60,000 managers to report to one of just nine offices nationwide—drastically consolidating its footprint and leaving 9,000 workers with the choice to relocate or resign.

The US telecom giant, with 350 offices across fifty states, was calling in workers who had been remote since the onset of the pandemic to report to a handful of outposts to save money and inspire collaboration, according to Bloomberg.

Stankey announced the on-location assignments would take effect in July 2023 in Dallas and Atlanta, and would be implemented everywhere else by September 2023. He told Bloomberg that the 60,000 managers would be required to report to one of the nine designated offices at least three days per week based on their specific duties.

Of AT&T's 300-plus hubs, two core central offices in Dallas and Atlanta, plus locations in Los Angeles, San Ramon, Calif., Seattle, St. Louis; Washington; and Middletown and Bedminster, N. J., would make up the nine.

About 9,000 AT&T managers would be forced to relocate or resign under the telecom giant's new return-to-office mandates, which would assign workers to a hub no matter where they currently lived, according to AT&T press releases to the media. There were no hubs, apparently, in Pebble Beach.

On October 1, 2019, Stankey had become the COO of AT&T while continuing to serve as the CEO of Warner Media. Content was the strategy then (perhaps with his LA background), and billions were invested only to be divested a few years later.

AT&T also indicated publicly that it would upend the $70 billion traditional television advertising market, using its reams of data—on everything from its DirecTV subscribers to where its customers take their phones—to help advertisers target consumers with ads across their TVs and digital devices. Aha, so this was the strategy, joining up in the Google, Facebook club!

And sure enough, the Federal Trade Commission was scrutinizing how AT&T and other internet service providers used consumer data for advertising. The agency ordered AT&T's advertising subsidiary and other companies to provide information on their privacy practices for user data last month. AT&T said at the time that it would respond appropriately.

And in 2024, it was announced in the press that DirecTV would pay Dish's owner, EchoStar, just $1 for Dish in exchange for assuming its billions of dollars in debt. Private equity firm TPG, meanwhile, would acquire AT&T's remaining 70 percent stake in DirecTV. I was not impressed with AT&T, but had met the TPG CEO years earlier in San Francisco and was impressed with them.

I have followed Comcast for a long time, as well as Steve Burke, who served as the executive vice president of Comcast and chief executive officer of NBCUniversal. Steve grew up in the content business under his father's tutelage. Dan Burke was a former president of Capital Cities Communications, which acquired the ABC network.

Steve had earlier graduated from Colgate University in 1980, and in 1982, he finished his Harvard Business School MBA, just after the AT&T breakup.

Ultimately, Comcast purchased NBC, which reminded me of their 2001 attempt with Walt Disney in Los Angeles. David Seltzer was a good friend and had coincidentally hitched a ride on the Comcast corporate jet with Steve to join me at USC for a joint lecture. David's brother-in-law was Brian Roberts, the CEO of Comcast.

Steve Burke was the architect of this transaction for Comcast and the purchaser of the Mantoloking, New Jersey beach house where we visited our family cousins for many years. He paid $3.5 million for it in 1999, and after it was demolished by Hurricane Sandy, sold the two beach lots for $7 million, doubling his money and enjoying the beach.

For their content strategy, Comcast was locked in battle with Disney for Murdoch's entertainment empire, 21st Century Fox, which in 2017 agreed to sell its film and television studios, its pay-tv operations including its stake in Sky, and a clutch of other assets to Disney.

Comcast Corp. in mid-2018 said it was dropping out of the hunt for 21st Century Fox's entertainment assets, handing a major victory to Walt Disney Co. Chief Executive Bob Iger, who had championed the $71-billion purchase.

Comcast would have had to offer more than $80 billion to stay competitive with Disney's sweetened $71 billion bid. It had separately offered $34 billion for Sky, the European pay-tv service. Brian Roberts, as CEO of Comcast, had seen the light, probably lit by Steve Burke. Content was not king; it was an asset that needed smart management, and Steve Burke provided just that.

And at CBS, back in May 2000, upon the first merger of CBS and Viacom, my old Democratic Party friend Marty Franks was named Executive Vice President of CBS Television and Senior Vice President of Viacom.

Marty worked on the staffs of President Jimmy Carter, Senator Patrick J. Leahy, and Congressman Tony Coelho. I knew Marty at the White House, and when he served at the Democratic National Committee, we were building its new headquarters on Capitol Hill.

He retired in September 2013.

Les Moonves was Marty's very highly paid CBS CEO and said that Marty had been the glue that kept it all together—a fine compliment! Unfortunately, Moonves also said publicly to the press in 2016 that this election may not be good for America, but it's damn good for CBS. Donald's place in this election is a good thing. Go Donald Go!

While AT&T no longer owned everything as they did back in the 70s, there was now interest in new consumer technology. AT&T owned/controlled Bell Labs but never exploited that, much to my surprise, and eventually sold it to Alcatel—Lucent.

Alcatel-Lucent then announced the opening of a new Bell Labs Research Center in Israel and also runs the original Bell Labs in Murray Hill, New Jersey.

For Bell Labs, the Murray Hill folks seemed to have lost the technology chase to Silicon Valley. While I cannot identify one recent consumer product from Bell Labs, Silicon Valley is keeping its assembly line moving forward as technological inventions break out every month with San Francisco-based announcements. And today, in Silicon Valley, the so-called new AT&T was looking more and more like the old AT&T that we had effectively broken up.

Reading an article on this topic, I remembered how Intel's CEO Paul Otellini, a fellow St. Ignatius High School grad from San Francisco, was always gracious. Unfortunately, Paul passed away years ago at the young age of sixty-six at his Sonoma home. He lived on Green Street in the city not far from our family boyhood home.

We both were at a dinner party in San Francisco, and Paul asked what I was working on. I mentioned Bright Net, using my electric utility background to launch a last-mile fiber build-out, having utilities as unregulated partners and using their conduit into the building basement. Paul thought it was a very good idea and something that Intel Capital might invest in. He set up an introduction, and several meetings ensued. It was always the same question: Who would be the CEO? I responded, "Commit to investing, and I will interview CEO candidates and give you the answer."

Paul was truly a great leader; I always enjoyed chatting with him. At a San Francisco reception a few years back, I mentioned to Paul that my niece (international antitrust lawyer for Intel) really appreciated the Intel offices in the Presidio, so she did not have to commute to their Santa Clara headquarters every day. He quickly responded that he had that office set up because he was tired of the commute as well.

Net Neutrality

Net Neutrality was now the Maginot Line for the current battle for supremacy of the open access theory originally born to allow new technology, including content, to flow uninterrupted to the consumer. Several years ago, a prominent investor asked me what the key was to this topic.

I explained that historically you had different infrastructure build-out regulatory practices, that is, public utility rate base and cable monopoly concessions. In the former, customers paid for the regulated utility build-out in rate base and public access was implicit. In the latter, shareholder equity paid for the cable build-outs, and they could charge market rates.

Comcast's fiber build-out was paid for via shareholder equity, so they "own it" and can charge an access fee to their customers.

In my Senior Fellow role at the Progressive Policy Institute, I made the same argument amidst the noise of the FCC Net Neutrality rulemaking. I explained my theory to my good friend David Seltzer and suggested he pass it along to his brother-in-law Brian Roberts, CEO of Comcast.

For background, in early 2015, after several visits from White House National Economic Council Director Jeff Zients, and Council of Economic Advisors Chairman Jason Furman, they convinced FCC Chairman Tom Wheeler to move forward and announced a "net neutrality" proposal that shocked me and many observers as running counter to the Congressional hearings and testimony in late 2014!

Tom Wheeler, my old friend from the SPRINT days, as President of the National Cable Trade Association, testified in March 2015 before the House Oversight and Government Reform Committee. He had a difficult time responding to then Chairman Jason Chaffetz's (carrier fee preference) line of net neutrality questioning on these visits and the new FCC policy supporting free content versus fee carriage.

Before the 2024 Supreme Court decision rescinding the Chevron Doctrine, a Democratic majority on the FCC reclassified broadband providers as common carriers under Title II of the 1934 Communications Act. This allowed the commission regulate broadband rates and impose non-discrimination obligations. But months later, the three-judge Sixth Circuit panel explained the law doesn't allow the FCC regulate broadband providers as common carriers—and the US Supreme Court concurred. Under Chevron, judges routinely deferred to administrative agencies, but Chevron was no longer applicable.

And on a related topic, Rupert Murdoch suggested it was time for Facebook to make content providers pay to be in the Facebook pavilion to separate legitimate from fake news; and I agreed with him. This pay-for-content issue became international, as Canada, for content became an international issue as Canada for example passed such a requirement in 2023.

In 2015, CalSTRS Infrastructure asked me about telecom as an infrastructure investment strategy, and I stated that the "net neutrality" debate was going to confuse investment strategy.

And then the new AT&T auctioned off their landlines to Frontier (stranded assets) for 9 billion dollars to help defray their wireless auction bids. Frontier was to find out a few years later that the landline sector was slowly disappearing. I was glad not to have recommended that idea.

Importantly, new digital/technology positions were established at the Obama White House and were all taken by Microsoft and Google alumni, which was good public policy in terms of federal internet grid procurement.

And as a result of the Obama health care rollout IT debacle in 2014, the White House at that time also named former Salesforce executive DJ Patil as its first chief data scientist and VMware's Tony Scott as chief information officer. Also, 18F at the GSA along with the US Digital Service were established as in-house federal IT consulting platforms which I will talk about more in later chapters. So, lesson learned: The way policy works in Washington, DC. If you are inside the White House, that beats being on the outside, even with seventy-six lobbying firms on retainer.

Remember the opportunities old AT&T had under the consent decree years ago and how they failed to follow up on the computer opportunity. Well, in 1998, I was in a Washington, DC, office and asked the receptionist a question. She responded, in her British accent, "Let me Google that!" That was the first time I had ever been exposed to that company and its name.

At the time, I was intrigued and thought of going to see them at their campus down the San Francisco Peninsula on my next trip to San Francisco. But they retained a UC Berkeley professor to study their public policy exposure and strategy. He would not answer my calls, and the rest is history.

The more I thought about it, the more I became convinced that their coin of the realm was information, much of it was government information, and immediately saw the ramifications in Washington, DC.

It was last year that I discovered the true currency was information on their users; and Google gathered that as the user searched for information from the libraries and newspapers that Google had brought into their ecosystem.

In the aftermath of the Edward Snowden spying episode, Google and the others switched from being supporters of post-9/11 government security measures to being opposed. They knew more about us than the government ever will!

I had breakfast with George Soros many years prior in 1982. California Senator Alan Cranston had been running for president, and I was chairman of his Political Action Committee, and George Soros was considering a contribution. I was to visit him in his New York office a few times.

He sounded the alarm at the 2018 Davos World Economic Forum by applauding the European Union's heightened enforcement aimed at web giants, Facebook and Google, and calling for greater US regulation. The internet and its ecosystem had enjoyed a virtual free ride, including sales tax exemption, since its inception; but it was now a mature, successful sector.

On March 21, 2024, Europe's new Digital Markets Act went into effect, requiring Apple, Google, and other operators of digital platforms to allow third-party app stores and alternative payment options on those platforms. It was a major change for Apple, which had practiced a closed approach since launching its first iPhone in 2007. Earlier in January, Apple announced a series of changes to its App Store for the European market to comply, but not in the United States.

Apple's App Store is a far more lucrative business, now generating more than $26 billion in annual revenue compared with about $13 billion for Google's Play Store, according to press estimates, and accounted for nearly one-third of Apple's service revenue for its most recent fiscal year. It was expected that over time, Europe's regulatory approach would become global policy.

As noted earlier, in July 2019, the $26 billion T-Mobile-Sprint merger cleared its last major regulatory hurdle. The Justice Department approved the combination with some provisos, including the sale of Sprint's Boost Mobile prepaid carrier to Dish Network, and the FCC approval followed three months later.

Considering our success in breaking up the AT&T monopoly in 1982, it was fascinating to watch as the United States in 2018 was in the midst of an intensifying debate over monopoly power and privacy, with Democrats calling for much tougher antitrust enforcement and Republicans joining them in accusing big tech companies of abusing their market dominance. Much of this was politically motivated smarting over the new campaign-related ads and messaging on these platforms.

And it turned out that our US cellphone customer usage plans were more expensive in the United States than in Europe due to this concentration and lack of competition. Just the same, the Justice Department approval was the last major federal step for the merging of the nation's No. 3 and No. 4 wireless carriers into T-Mobile and the No. 2 position behind Verizon.

AT&T, Verizon Communications Inc., and T-Mobile US Inc. collectively controlled more than 90 percent of mobile phone connections in the United States; however, there was competition unlike the old AT&T monopoly.

Still, a permanent price change at one of the big three carriers sometimes prompts rivals to follow suit, like gas stations across from each other at intersections.

US Telecom Public Policy Influence

In 2014, Google had been the first political/public policy mover, spending a league leading $16.8 million on lobbying. They continued to set records in subsequent years! They were trying to keep the regulators at bay. It was just a matter of time, I thought, but it was still the same in 2024.

Some historical background would be in order. In 1996, the US Congress passed the telecommunications law, and besides the RBOC merger approval provision, included another provision to protect free speech online. More than twenty-five years later, that provision, known as Section 230, is seen as crucial to the business models of companies including Facebook Inc. and Alphabet Inc.'s Google. Section 230 was part of the Communications Decency Act that was originally marketed by its bipartisan sponsors as a "Good Samaritan" law for the internet. It has two key provisions: (1) shields internet companies from liability for most of the material their users post and (2) gives the companies legal immunity concerning "any action voluntarily taken in good faith" to remove materials.

A report from Harvard's Shorenstein Center on Media, Politics and Public Policy and New America suggested that the business models attached to digital advertising platforms like Facebook Inc. and Alphabet Inc.'s Google continued to undermine user privacy and incentivize disinformation campaigns despite recent reform efforts by tech companies to prevent abuse.

We need to completely reorganize the way that industry works, Dipayan Ghosh told me. He previously worked on privacy and policy issues at Facebook and was now a fellow at the Shorenstein Center. I had worked for Walter Shorenstein years earlier in San Francisco and was with him when he launched this Center in honor of his deceased daughter, Joan, who had been a CBS news producer. It was good to see this regulatory reform product emanate from there.

I had lunch with Dipayan in Washington, DC, and we agreed to work on a regulatory paper together. I sent him an outline for a zone of freedom concept to start the process. In the zone of freedom that I had worked on in the railroad scenario, railroads were free to innovate with services and rates if the rates were within the zone. If not, a regulatory response was required.

In late September 2023, under the Biden administration, the FCC finally had a Democratic chairman confirmed for a 3–2 majority, and headlines appeared regarding the return to the returning to the Democratic supported net neutrality policy and a threat to the expansion of 5G. We would see!

With the unbundling of cable viewing packages, it seemed timely in this chapter to review the content topic in a more holistic way, as billions of dollars were being spent on mergers and buyouts. To be honest, I had been dubious about the debt being taken on, particularly by AT&T, which had no experience in the Hollywood sector. Within a few years, they reached that same conclusion.

It appeared the content providers, be it Netflix, Disney, Viacom, Time Warner et al., were erstwhile competitors but seemed intent on mergers to achieve market dominance. This is the fundamental tightrope that the Federal Communications

Commission walks. The internet was new, and public policy favored its growth. But now there seemed to be a very even matchup, with Comcast in the lead at around 20 percent; change was quickly coming, and merge they did.

In August 2019, ViacomCBS remarried and was now around #4 or #5. Sure, the content providers have the visible glamour. Disney, as mentioned, offered to pay $52.4 billion in December 2017 for a good portion of 21st Century Fox from Rupert Murdoch, seeking to bulk up their content. They didn't seem concerned about the Trump FCC actions on net neutrality.

But the Viacom-CBS kicker was that the new CEO of the combined company, Bob Bakish from Viacom, would get a 55 percent raise in total compensation to $31 million annually, while his CBS rival would be awarded a one-time $70 million for staying on as number two! It was not a pretty picture! Then Comcast offered $65 billion for 21st Century Fox, setting up a bidding contest with Disney. It was a crazy time!

Sport as Content

The Justice Department determined that Disney, which is the majority owner of ESPN, would have too much market power in sports TV if it were allowed to acquire the large-scale Fox Sports networks, so it ordered Disney to sell them off as a condition of the deal with 21st Century Fox.

And shortly thereafter in early May 2019, conservative TV-station giant Sinclair Broadcast Group Inc. struck a deal valued at more than $10 billion to acquire the twenty-one regional sports networks from Disney. Sinclair, headquartered outside Baltimore, is the nation's biggest owner of local television stations, and this presumably would make them a force in cable sports programming. We would see!

While content had the glamour, and the carriers got to send billings every month to their customers for their services, the unbundling phenomenon exploded, particularly with ESPN owned by Disney and the lower ratings for National Football League and World Series games. In fact, all the networks had declined among the coveted eighteen to forty-nine age group that advertisers favored. NBC was down 8 percent, while Fox, CBS, and NBC were down by double digits. Sports were key!

Now sports content entered the picture as regional sports networks suffered from cable-TV cord-cutting and audience erosion along with the rest of the traditional television business. Younger viewers often got their sports fix online, and ratings for most sports leagues had declined over the years while compensation for the superstars escalated significantly. Maybe the owners needed more tax depreciation! Salaries for players (and coaches) were going out of sight, and that was the depreciation asset.

This was hard to believe for some sports fans, but under a 2004 law, owners of sports teams may deduct the cost of purchasing a team over fifteen years from their taxable income.

Also, under IRS rules, player contracts can be depreciated as assets—the annual decline in a player's value can be figured as a cost to the owner. This is because players, unlike franchises or broadcasting rights, but like machines, wear out. So, the more you pay them, the better from a tax avoidance perspective, and wealthy individuals have paid enormous sums in recent years to buy a team. The Washington Commanders, for example, were purchased for some $6 billion in late 2023 from the previous owner who had paid less than $900 million back in 1998.

In July 2023, this headline appeared in the Wall Street Journal: College Sports Powers Stall Bid to Pay Players in California. Finally, there was some pushback! Sports as Content may have reached a pinnacle of overexposure when you have ESPN struggling to meet this changing market in recent years. And this content was the financial mother lode for all of these mega-companies. Yet the debt they were taking on seemed challenging, and this was to change dramatically later that year.

But for a historical perspective, here is a personal story about football's foundation!

Bert Bell was the National Football League (NFL) commissioner from 1945 until his death in 1959. During the Great Depression, he was an assistant coach for the Temple Owls and a co-founder and co-owner of the Philadelphia Eagles, who finally won their first Super Bowl in 2018. Following WWII, as commissioner, he implemented a proactive anti-gambling policy, negotiated a merger with the All-America Football Conference, and—on his own—crafted the entire league schedule before each season with an emphasis on enhancing the impact of late-season games with the best matchups!

My wife, Fonny, was a classmate of Bert's daughter Jane at the Convent of the Sacred Heart out on the Main Line in the Philadelphia suburbs. Fonny was a boarder and would visit with Jane and other friends at the Bell home; she told me she would see Mr. Bell working out this schedule on the dining room table. That was how sports content began in the 1950s!

One of the more interesting content issues is the role of sports and television. At first, there was the cable network bundling of sports channels and the ESPN phenomenon; and now the unbundling of such cable packages to focus in on a few favorite viewing packages.

Sports were now tied with movies (before the pandemic) as the two super-weights of viewing, and the resultant monetary impact on the leagues whether college or professional, was mercurial.

Even former President Obama had an opinion as probably the most sports-minded US president, calling for colleges to take greater responsibility in providing for student-athletes and challenging the NCAA to address compensation for student-athletes in addition to scholarships.

In early 2018, former Secretary of State Condoleezza Rice, serving as the chair of a sports-related commission, made similar comments, particularly on the one-and-done practice.

And I was impressed when President Barack Obama reaffirmed his concerns with sports earlier in 2018 at an MIT Sloan Sports Analytics Conference in Boston. He was calling for change to college basketball's order under the current NCAA-administered system so that the NCAA was not serving as a farm system for the NBA, with unpaid players under enormous financial pressure.

But I personally would add the suggestion that the NCAA could support its member schools establishing investment trusts for their student-athletes, and the revenues in the trust would be available to the individuals after they graduate.

But it was off to the races five years later; words like collective, Name, Image, Likeness (NIL), gambling, and the portal etc. became the new vocabulary. All of this was based on TV revenue for this content, which had an unknown shelf life!

In talking about diversity, President Obama went on to say at this 2018 conference that Bill Russell was a really good hire, as those teams that did not hire Bill Russell were walloped for a long time. I enjoyed this Bill Russell comment, as I had watched his great national champion University of San Francisco (USF) Dons team practice in our St. Ignatius High School gym across the street every day after classes, as they did not have a gym of their own in those days.

Our high school basketball team had to wait and watch them play. It was great! Once they finished, we took the court. USF was right across the street, and ten years later, they were to build their own gymnasium for thousands of fans.

But by 2020, the athletic conferences across the country were paying top dollar to their commissioners because they arranged the new long term TV contracts. The Big Ten Commissioner Jim Delany jumped from $558,000 per year (not bad) in 2004 to $3.1 million in 2014, while the ACC Commissioner went from $571,000 to more than $2 million.

Many of the major programs were spending $4–5 million a year on head football coaches' salaries. Maybe the base is $500,000, but when the alumni booster clubs finish, they have the coaches up there with the CEOs. Georgia's head coach saw his salary go to $10 million a year for ten years after winning their first national championship in decades. And 80 percent of alumni contributions had been tax deductible plus they received prime season tickets, although the new 2017 tax law changed that.

This growth in compensation has been fueled primarily by new generous long term contracts with television, particularly ESPN, in short order. However, it cannot last with fan viewing fatigue becoming a reality and ratings declining, including pro football in its recent season.

Will the whole system implode at some point? Clearly, the sports viewing audience by age and income is in decline regarding viewership. For example, the television ratings for NASCAR's Daytona 500 drew a 5.1 overnight rating on Fox for 2018, down 22 percent from the overnight rating scored by the 2017 edition, down 16 percent from 2016, and down 30 percent from 2015. The numbers for all sports were also down. And then this headline:

On the collegiate side, Stanford University had won the Learfield Athletic Directors Cup award for twenty-three straight years with wins in NCAA tennis, track, baseball, and swimming championships every year. It is not content; it is not content, it is accomplishment. During the pandemic, they announced some pruning, including rowing and men's volleyball, which surprised me as they had around twenty-five Olympic medalists as students. In the 2024 Paris Olympics, it was reported that Stanford students had won thirty-nine medals after reinstating those same varsity sports.

My sister, Sarah, was a Stanford alum and longtime outside counsel for Stanford, reporting to the General Counsel and Executive VP, Debbie Zumwalt. I was happy for them both. My younger brother had been a two-year starter on their football team.

Sport has an important role in our society for both men and women, but it is crucial for character development. Content was an added benefit for the networks; however, the statistics are a concern.

The Aspen Institute reported in 2019 that team sports participation in the United States was down from 45 percent of children in 2010 to 38 percent in 2019.

Then you look at how the money is spent! The United States Olympic Committee (USOC) has some 500 employees compared to just 558 athletes sent to the 2020 Summer Games. With revenues of $336 million, it gave just $28 million to athletes in direct cash and assistance.

There are 129 six-figure salaried USOC executives. The USOC's most recent tax filings illustrate that $45 million went to USOC administrative staff wages and salaries. Another $21 million went to travel, which included the cost of getting the US Olympic and Paralympic teams to Rio, as well as first and business class for executives.

I will never forget when I was on the USC faculty, and Senator and Mrs. Moynihan came out to give the President's lecture in 2001. We were seated in the beautiful library with University President Steve Semple and many other tables of prominent guests. It was in the middle of the NCAA basketball championships, and I heard President Semple say to the senator that everyone was excited here on campus as our USC Trojan basketball team had made it to the Sweet Sixteen. Then Senator Moynihan asked President Semple, "Steve, what is the Sweet Sixteen?" and we all laughed.

During the summer of 2020—with schools and sports closed because of the coronavirus pandemic—there was an important question. Colleges and their athletic departments were struggling with how to reopen their campuses, academics being the top priority, but also their athletic programs.

College athletics exist in the most fragile ecosystem. The entire enterprise depends on football. If college football can't be played, it affects not only the wallets of the players but also the opportunity for gymnasts and lacrosse players, wrestlers, and runners.

For example, Ohio State annually hosts seven games at Ohio Stadium—capacity 104,944—because they need the revenue from seven home games at Ohio Stadium. Playing without fans would cost the Buckeyes between $5 million and $7 million per game in lost ticket revenue. If seven games go away, there goes somewhere between $35 million and $49 million—potentially nearly a quarter of the $210 million in expenses the department needed to keep thirty-six sports afloat last year.

And that doesn't include the revenue football brings in through television broadcasts, so there must be football. But if college football punts an entire season, the infrastructure that supports so many of the 170,000 Division I athletes would all but collapse. In early July, the Big Ten Conference announced they would drop non-conference opponents from their schedule. Somehow, they survived and by 2023 had a banner year.

College sports are often referred to as the front porch of a given university. Most big-time athletic departments operate as separate corporations.

The Ohio State Buckeyes paid their assistant coaches a total of $7.245 million in 2019, according to data compiled by USA Today. Head coach Ryan Day was due $5.4 million in 2020. Five members of Day's staff make at least $900,000 each.

Clemson Coach Dabo Swinney made more than $9.3 million in 2019, according to USA Today, just one of ten coaches who made more than $6 million. Thirty-one head coaches made at least $4 million, and thirty-one schools pay their staffs of ten assistants at least $4 million. So maybe there would be some cutbacks to keep these programs from losing money. Even Navy's coach was now making $2 million.

Major sport-related compensation was out of hand, and it was damaging the goodwill of college sports and, hence, the value of its content.

In the good news department, we learned in late 2017 that there were university sports programs that are highly academic in their priorities:

Top ten Graduation Success Rates (All Sports/FBS Schools Only):

1. Notre Dame—98 percent.
2. Duke, Northwestern, Stanford—97 percent.
5. Vanderbilt—96 percent.
6. Boston College—95 percent.
7. UCF, Wake Forest—94 percent.
9. South Carolina: 93 percent.
10. Bowling Green, Rice, Tulane—92 percent.
13. Naval Academy, Clemson, Miami (Ohio), Miami (Fla.), Michigan, Missouri, Syracuse—91 percent.

I was very pleased to see Notre Dame at the top with Stanford just a notch down, and surprised that the Naval Academy, my alma mater, was not higher.

Overall, the NCAA graduation rate for the 2018 student athlete increased by a point to 88 percent, the highest rate ever. There were some specific subgroup differences worth noting:

When my younger brother, Fergus, (who recently passed away) was playing football at Stanford in 1966 and 1967, starting at tackle, #75, he was always was free to have summer jobs and worked in construction. This helped him finance his education in addition to his athletic scholarship. Today, the student athlete cannot do that.

In 2023, UCLA and USC shocked the college sports landscape by announcing their move to the Big Ten. The Times reported that Pac-12 university presidents and chancellors were conflicted over how to move forward, spurning potential media rights deals with ESPN and Apple. I was astonished. After Oregon and Washington joined the Big Ten, Arizona, Arizona State, and Utah left for the Big 12. The defections were a major blow to the Pac-12 Conference.

It was sad, but sports as content was showing some problems. It was all about the TV contracts, which were more expensive in the Big Ten and even the Big Twelve than for the West Coast brand. I wondered what about the Big Game between Cal and Stanford annually and even the Rose Bowl. Then, leaders from Stanford, Cal, and SMU leaders announced they had accepted invitations to join the ACC and will compete in all sports. It was odd to watch a Cal or Stanford game on an ACC-branded court. You had to think the jet travel costs would be ruinous. Sports as content was now more like Sports as cancer. And college stars were making millions in so-called Name, Image and

Likeness (NIL) payments from advertisers spurred on by so-called booster clubs called collectives to lure prospects from another university to go through the portal.

The word collective reminded me of the Soviet Union destroying its agriculture through its version of collectives. This university version could destroy its crop, otherwise known as academics, as the Knight Foundation predicted.

The NCAA is composed of more than 1,100 schools, serving hundreds of thousands of athletes, and its CEO said athlete representatives from all three NCAA divisions had stated they do not want to be employees of their schools. He said that without congressional action, Division II and III schools might abandon their athletic programs.

And on June 21, 2021, the Supreme Court ruled against the NCAA in the Alston Decision, in a unanimous 9–0 vote. The decision opened up further ways for student athletes to be compensated. Justice Neil Gorsuch, who delivered the court's opinion, explained that the NCAA was violating antitrust law.

Much of this revenue was essentially brokered by ESPN (Entertainment and Sports Programming Network), which was launched back in 1979 along with many other cable channels as we approached the 1982 breakup of AT&T.

Today in the 2020s, it is a complicated content world in cable land. Whether it is "net neutrality," sports exhaustion, or competition, much investment has been made to support a large downstream ecosystem of highly paid coaches, players, and the like.

But once that freshman season is over, forget the books! The John S. and James L. Knight Foundation is headquartered in Miami, and one of its projects is the Knight Commission on Intercollegiate Athletics. Fr. Hesburgh, a long-time president of Notre Dame, was a co-founder along with William Friday, a long-time UNC president.

I agreed with the point Bill Friday made in 1993 that trying to superimpose an entertainment industry on top of an academic structure would not work. It never has worked. What you are seeing now is the consequence of not controlling that very enterprise.

Gambling

In 1992, President George H. W. Bush signed the Professional and Amateur Sports Protection Act. Known as the Bradley Act after its principal author, Sen. Bill Bradley (D-New Jersey), a basketball Hall of Famer deeply concerned about the integrity of competitive sports, the bill forbade states to "sponsor, operate, advertise, promote, license, or authorize by law . . . betting, gambling, or wagering" on sports competitions.

In 2018, however, the Supreme Court overturned the Bradley Act in the name of states' rights. Congress can regulate sports gambling directly, Justice Samuel A. Alito Jr. wrote for the majority, but if it elects not to do so, each state is free to act on its own.

Since then, legal sports gambling has spread to thirty-eight states and D.C. The US sports betting market is expected to grow from $119 billion in 2023 to more than $150 billion in 2025. Sports gambling ads, prohibited by the Bradley Act, were now everywhere.

Well, it turns out that National Basketball Association Commissioner Adam Silver saw great potential for the NBA in a legal sports betting economy when I read his public statements that it's a fabulous hedge against volatility with future TV contracts, but it must be handled with care, which was an understatement as betting scandals were breaking out often.

Sports betting—once only inside Las Vegas casinos—has invaded US sports since its legalization in the United States. Studies have shown that young adults are at a higher risk for sports-gambling-related problems, and studies have also suggested that 75 percent to 80 percent of college students report having gambled in general within the previous year, according to a report in the Journal of Gambling Issues.

But we're just beginning to get our heads around the effects of gambling on sports, which has been legalized in thirty-eight states over the past six years. This summer, for instance, researchers at the University of California at Los Angeles' Anderson School of Management published a paper that examined consumer credit data and analyzed what sports betting did to the financial health of the states where it was legal.

The findings were staggering: a 28 percent jump in bankruptcies and an 8 percent increase in debt sent to collection, as well as growth in late auto loan payments and weakened credit scores. The fact that we can find anything in the aggregate suggests that the impact for individuals is quite large, said UCLA professor Brett Hollenbeck.

Broadband Availability

One of the most challenging 2020 pandemic events was the massive shift to remote learning for all students. However, it was clear that both urban and rural school districts did not have adequate broadband infrastructure for low-income, disadvantaged students. In response, on December 7, the US Federal Communications Commission (FCC) awarded $9.2 billion to provide high-speed broadband internet service to 5.22 million unserved rural homes and businesses.

My infrastructure investment coalition, emanating from my 1993 Infrastructure Investment Commission report, strongly suggested that they would invest in public private partnerships that could address rural broadband with federal funding partners. The FCC said in its "Rural Digital Opportunity Fund" auction that Charter Communications Inc. won $1.22 billion to provide service to 1.06 million locations, while Elon Musk's SpaceX won $885 million to serve 642,000 locations.

The Rural Electric Cooperative Consortium won $1.1 billion to serve 618,000 locations, and LTD Broadband LLC won $1.32 billion to serve 528,000 locations. An FCC report said 18.3 million people in the United States lacked access to broadband, but Democrats say that this underestimates the problem, while Republicans noted the report found the number without access had fallen by thirty percent since 2016. Broadband access is now like mail-in voting.

One of the endearing traditions of the World Series was to view the red, white, and blue bunting gracefully displayed along the first-tier stands, particularly in the home plate area (television viewers). For some reason, that multi-decade tradition has been abandoned.

It was a busy December 2020 for the telecommunications sector as the US government and forty-eight state attorneys general filed landmark antitrust lawsuits against Facebook on December 9, seeking to break up the social networking giant over charges it engaged in illegal activity.

At the end of the day, having been a participant in the 1982 breakup of AT&T, it seemed we had inadvertently unleashed technology with tremendous advances to our quality of life. But in this new content streaming arms race, just where were we going? Well, internet search was also in the courts and on August 5, 2024, in a Washington, DC, federal district court, Judge Amit P. Mehta found that Google illegally abused its market power to suppress competition in internet search, saying that Google is a monopolist, and it has acted as one to maintain its monopoly. In 1982, Judge Harold Greene, in that same US district court, ruled on the AT&T consent decree. Congress had been stymied in both instances; the remedy was the courts.

In 1989, my wife Fonny and I were attending a Pat Moynihan book signing party at the Smithsonian's Wilson Center. Tim Russert was there, and we had a nice chat. Tim had been Pat Moynihan's Chief of Staff and was now running Meet the Press and the NBC Washington office. His wife, Mori Orth, had been a roommate at Lone Mountain College (now within the University of San Francisco) with my wife, Fonny. I congratulated him on his recent assignments and asked what his goals might be in bringing an informed, educational approach to political journalism, and he told me that he was not interested in that; his goal was market share.

3

Tax Legislation in 1986, 1993, and 2017

The 1986 Tax Reform effort was strongly bipartisan and, very importantly, had momentum with a detailed tax-simplification proposal from President Reagan's Treasury Department, and was designed to be tax-revenue neutral.

The congressional legislation bill was also sponsored by Democrats Richard Gephardt of Missouri in the House of Representatives and Bill Bradley of New Jersey in the Senate.

My role in the successful 1986 bipartisan tax reform effort was to chair the Alliance for Philanthropy, representing a broad coalition of art museums, university endowments, and other well-known foundations. Memorial Sloan Kettering had retained my firm, but we organized the coalition as a more effective advocacy strategy. Our goal was to preserve the appreciated property charitable contribution tax deduction.

There had been abuses by marking up or exaggerating the market value of the donated property, artwork, etc.; but prominent Harvard economist Larry Lindsey, whom I latter helped to be confirmed to the Federal Reserve by the Senate, would make the congressional and administration rounds with me, arguing that philanthropy would take a precipitous drop in the United States without this treatment.

It was my privilege to have chaired the Alliance for Philanthropy when Congress passed the historic bipartisan Tax Reform Act of 1986 under the leadership of Senator Bill Bradley with added impetus from a detailed tax-simplification reform proposal from President Reagan's Treasury Department. Senator Daniel Patrick Moynihan was a senior member of the Senate Finance Committee, a supporter of tax reform, and he recruited me for the task.

Keep in mind that as Ronald Reagan became President in 1981, inflation was nearly 10 percent. The Federal Reserve, under Paul Volker, had pushed interest rates into double digits beginning in the last years of the Carter administration. The federal debt was about half what it is today, measured as a share of the economy. The 1981 Reagan tax cut was very large, with the top rate reduced from 70 percent to 50 percent. It turned out to be too large.

Some history here as the truth is most of the top Reagan administration officials didn't think their 1981 tax cut would pay for itself. They were counting on spending cuts (budget prioritization) that would follow to avoid blowing up the deficit (Speaker Ryan had the same idea in 2017). This was the beginning of so-called "supply-side economics" championed by OMB Director David Stockman and others. (Stockman coincidentally had been a boarder earlier in the Moynihan home on East Capitol Street a few blocks from the Capitol.)

Contrary to GOP rhetoric, the 1981 tax cut did not pay for itself and reduced federal revenues by about 9 percent in the first couple of years. As the deficits worsened, it became clear that the 1981 tax cut was too big. So, with Reagan's signature, Congress raised taxes in 1982, 1983, and 1984 before taking up the 1986 tax reform legislation. It seemed to me that the GOP needed to stop reciting this myth about tax cuts growing the economy citing the unique success of the President Kennedy tax cuts years earlier; but it was the lead in their songbook for years to come.

I remember the political atmosphere in 1986 well, and the tax reform legislation was designed to be tax-revenue neutral, as Reagan stated that he would veto any bill that was not revenue neutral. The detailed proposal's goal was to simplify the income tax code, broaden the tax base, and eliminate many tax shelters. Revenue neutrality was achieved by offsetting tax cuts for individuals by eliminating $60 billion annually in tax loopholes and shifting $24 billion of the tax burden from individuals to corporations by eliminating the investment tax credit, slowing depreciation of assets, and enacting a stiff alternative minimum tax on corporations.

I fondly recall complaining to Senator Daniel Patrick Moynihan, as a senior member of the Senate Finance Committee and later its chairman, that he should do something about the proliferating automobile advertisements noting the tax advantages of buying an expensive luxury limo vehicle like a BMW or Mercedes-Benz.

The German government expressed alarm, but Pat liked the idea and added an amendment in 1984 on the Senate floor, adding limitations on tax benefits, including depreciation and investment tax credits. He sent me a note after the provision was enacted into law, and that is in a large frame in my office.

Moving on to 1993, I review extensively our 1992 Infrastructure Investment Commission hearings in Chapter 5 and our report that was issued in 1993. One key finding was that the United States was the only country that had a tax-exempt bond policy available to state and local governments. That same year, the Omnibus Budget Reconciliation Act of 1993 was enacted by Congress and signed into law by President Bill Clinton on August 10, 1993. The bill grew from a budget proposal made by Clinton in February 1993; he sought a mix of tax increases and spending reductions that would cut the deficit in half by 1997, and a budget surplus did occur the following year in 1998. Leon Panetta was Clinton's Chief of Staff and, as the former Chairman of the House Budget Committee, he really knew the numbers and the process.

At the same time, I remember well drafting an explanatory memo for Senator Moynihan in 1993 on the budget advantages of federal lending via infrastructure loans versus federal grants to discuss with then Treasury Secretary Bob Rubin. Rubin agreed, and that was the beginning of federal infrastructure project lending, but with investment grading required, which was to be very important.

Hard to believe, but every congressional Republican voted against the Omnibus Budget Reconciliation Act of 1993. However, it passed by narrow margins in both the House of Representatives and the Senate. In 1998, the effects of the bill helped the US federal government achieve its first budget surplus since the 1960s. It was a good model for the millennium period; unfortunately, regular order in Congress was starting to wither on the vine.

One policy phrase that is clearly overused is tax reform, and its camouflage is often penetrated. For example, years later, the so-called Tax Reform of 2017 was to pass; however, the bipartisan leadership was not in place as it was in 1986. The 2017 "Gang of Six," which included GOP congressional leadership, the Trump White House, including the Secretary of the Treasury and the Chairman of the National Economic Council, met behind closed doors and developed the principles that ultimately were drafted by the House Ways and Means Committee's GOP majority staff.

There was not one hearing before the bill was reported from Committee by a GOP partisan vote (I was there) to the House floor in December 2017. Our well-respected PIRC Coalition that I informally chaired, including the US Chamber of Commerce, had spent the preceding several years coordinating with the Obama administration and key House Ways and Means Committee staff to develop a broad, imaginative infrastructure financing component for a future tax bill. The key funding requirement, as recommended by then Secretary Jack Lew, was to reduce the corporate tax rate only down to 25 percent and dedicate the repatriation of overseas corporate taxes to this infrastructure financing component.

The final 2017 legislation was far removed from reform and was a very partisan and controversial tax cut. In fact, it was the largest cut in history, with most Americans having misgivings according to the polls, particularly with the added debt of $1.5 trillion to pay for the cuts, which favored the corporate sector and wealthy according to most analysts. Most disappointing was the one-time repatriation of overseas corporate cash proceeds targeted for tax cuts, as opposed to the original Obama/congressional plan to include an infrastructure investment. The US corporate minimum was reduced to 21 percent in the 2017 legislation, which differed from many corporations recommending 25 percent, allowing for an infrastructure investment bank provision.

In 2017, there was immense confusion as to GOP loyalty to tax reform and revenue neutrality. Somehow, the GOP adopted, once again, the mantra that the more you cut taxes, the more the economy will grow! Conversely, the 2017 tax cuts were so draconian that the plan to set aside repatriation dollars and a 21 percent corporate rate to fund a major infrastructure initiative that our infrastructure coalition, during the Obama administration, had worked on for several years was abandoned.

As to the supply side theory, right after the 2017 tax cuts, Speaker Paul Ryan announced that entitlement reform (Medicare and Social Security) would be next; but as often was the case, while reform was needed, Congress could not deal with the optics. It just did not look right to reduce government funding and then claim a shortfall due to the tax cuts and assert that entitlement cuts were needed.

If there had been a legitimate entitlement reform proposal passed beforehand in 2017, as controversial as that might have been, I felt it probably could have passed. But it could not be done right after the enormous 2017 tax cut.

But that is the GOP rhythm: Cut the revenue base and, with deficits, force entitlement reform on the poor and elderly. It is time for Social Security reform, but stop cutting taxes as a prelude.

Hard to believe, but on May 31, 2019, the White House announced that President Trump would award the Presidential Medal of Freedom on June 19 to economist Arthur Laffer, one of the pioneers of the idea that tax cuts can boost government revenue. I heard Senator Moynihan say, at a Reagan-era reception I attended, that the Laffer curve is Laughter.

Art Laffer was one of the founding theorists of supply-side economics, and in 2020, the 2017 tax cuts did not pay for themselves nor will they. Although the economy grew 2.9 percent in 2018, federal tax revenue fell 0.4 percent, according to the Treasury Department, despite Laffer's assurances, just as he assured Ronald Reagan in 1981, as noted in the press.

Art Laffer earned a bachelor's degree from Yale University in 1963 and a doctorate from Stanford in 1972, working with our good friend John Donaldson from Mclean, Virginia. John was from a prominent family in Nashville and convinced Art to move his office there.

Ironically, in mid-2014–15 (before the 2016 elections), there was considerable public policy discussion on tax reform by both congressional Republicans and Democrats. The Obama White House and Treasury had spoken in support of corporate tax reform (reducing the rate) only, coupled with repatriation to fund infrastructure. I attended a number of hearings and meetings to assess the political possibilities and was encouraged. However, the infrastructure investment community and their political supporters in Congress were very disappointed as, unfortunately, no detailed tax reform-repatriation infrastructure proposal was ever sent to Congress by the Obama Administration, in keeping with their modus operandi focused on talking points. There was excellent testimony by Treasury Secretary Jack Lew, but no bookmark so to speak! They would work with the Congress!

You would have thought that the 2000–2024 public policy chaos with unending continuing resolutions would be replaced with stability, statesman-like behavior, and results including reducing the federal deficit. The Fed had reduced its interest rates, but mortgage rates were stubbornly high due to their reliance on the US Treasury's ability to market their borrowings, with the historically large 2024 federal deficit clouding that market.

And we had watched Trump sign that 2017 tax cut law at the White House in a celebration with a large GOP congressional contingent; only a few months later, the Treasury announced that over $700 billion in new Treasury borrowing would be needed just to meet the 2018 budget shortfall resulting from the unfortunate 2017 tax cut legislation.

But back to 1986, in our Alliance for Philanthropy meetings, revenue neutrality was acknowledged as the congressional/administration dictum while decreasing individual tax rates, eliminating $30 billion annually in loopholes, and increasing corporate taxes. Still, the 1986 bill reduced overall tax revenues by $8.9 billion, so it was not revenue neutral, but President Reagan signed it anyway. A $8.9 billion deficit was not as dramatic as the 2017 deficit estimate of some $1.5 trillion over ten years for that GOP-passed tax package.

Conversely, the Tax Reform Act of 1986, passed in October importantly on a bipartisan vote, was a major simplification of the tax code, drastically reducing the number of deductions and the number of tax brackets. That had been Bill Bradley's goal!

In 1986, the top tax rate was lowered from 50 percent to 28 percent while the bottom rate was raised from 11 percent to 15 percent. This package ultimately consolidated tax brackets from fifteen levels of income to four levels of income. This would be the only time in the history of the US income tax (which dates to the passage of the Revenue Act of 1862) that the top rate was reduced and the bottom rate increased at the same time.

There were some humorous times! As a boat owner on the Chesapeake Bay, I was aware that the boating industry was going to lose one of its tax breaks. As a member of Boats USA, now owned by Warren Buffett's Berkshire Hathaway, I called their Washington, DC, government affairs office to alert them. It turns out they were all in Australia for the 1986–87 America's Cup competition, and they lost that tax benefit for boat manufacturing.

Getting to the final passage wasn't easy! But there was a leadership team in place in the Senate with Bill Bradley, Pat Moynihan, and Bob Packwood, and in the House with Dan Rostenkowski; and at the White House itself with President Reagan. In 2017, that bipartisan leadership issue was totally missing. Committee chairmen had loss their power as the "regular order" tradition of sending only committee-passed bills to the floor had been their privilege; but now it was in the Speaker's office.

Since our 1986 advocacy focused on the appreciated property charitable deduction, an explanation is in order. This provision had allowed taxpayers to deduct donations, including property such as paintings at their appraised value, to nonprofit organizations. A donation could be made from pre-tax income, effectively reducing the "cost" to the donor. It was first enacted in 1917, four years after the modern income tax.

Taxpayers who made a charitable donation could deduct the donation from their income but could not reduce their income by more than half. Not all donations to tax-exempt organizations qualified for the deduction. Traditional 501(c)(3) non-profits and churches (even if they were not registered as a non-profit) qualified, but donations to many other types of tax-exempt organizations, such as political committees, labor unions, and chambers of commerce, were not deductible.

In 2011, there was nearly $300 billion given to 1.1 million charities, but only $175 billion was deducted as a charitable contribution. The rest was either donated by non-itemizers (who cannot claim the deduction) or simply not reported. Interestingly, in 2019, it was reported that donations were down 4 percent for those giving less than $1,000, while up 2.6 percent for major donors as a result of the new 2017 tax cut standard deduction.

Our Alliance for Philanthropy issue was labeled the Appreciated Property— Charitable Deduction and encouraged major donations, allowing a donor to deduct the appraised value of the gift. Senator Moynihan was a major supporter as this was important in New York, and that is how I became involved. The Senator and I had strategic discussions throughout the process, and he agreed with my Alliance coalition strategy, as did our client, Memorial Sloan Kettering Hospital in New York.

We had our work to do as there was some controversy over appraisals being too high; but on balance, universities, museums, and other such institutions were very pleased to receive these gifts. Real estate was not that welcomed as it required significant administration, and liquidity could be a challenge, albeit a Delaware Trust approach could solve that problem.

Our Alliance meetings were usually held at the American Association of Universities conference room, and representatives from America's universities, museums, hospitals, and various charitable organizations would attend. The Alliance for Philanthropy stationery I designed and had printed was very effective, with the roster of members printed down the left side border. For advocacy, I will never forget the President of MIT coming to my office to volunteer to make calls to his Senators.

During this 1985–6 period, Harvard's Larry Lindsey and I were on our congressional rounds making the economic case for the provision. The abuse from market evaluations of donated art was a challenge, and we urged stronger appraisal requirements.

While our Alliance did a very good job, we did lose at the end. Senate Finance Committee Chairman Bob Packwood (plus his Staff Director Bill Diffendorfer) went behind closed doors with House Ways and Means Chairman Rostenkowski, the Big Two as they were called, and made the final decisions in those days. And we were a victim of that process!

Packwood and Rostenkowski could do this as their members, on both sides of the aisle, trusted them to be responsible in making the final policy decisions. Also, many of us knew Bill Diffendorfer and had great respect for him.

In later years, the Appreciated Property—Charitable Deduction was restored, although impacted by the 2017 provision allowing an overall charitable deduction, thus eliminating the incentive to actually make the contributions. However, that applied to the smaller donor.

Later in the 2020s, it was relatively common for wealthy homeowners to leave art or real estate to charities, foundations, or universities in the event of their death, or to donate a portion of the proceeds of a major sale as a result of the restored Appreciated Property—Charitable Deduction.

It was unusual to see high-net-worth individuals directly transfer title to a major single-family property as a donation while they were still alive. But the tax strategy was now well recognized in the 2020s thanks to major property donations by very wealthy individuals. Donating a home rather than donating the proceeds of the sale of a home comes with sizable tax benefits. If the homeowner has held title to the property for more than a year before the donation, they can deduct the fair market value of the property from their taxable income following the transfer of the property.

While the tax deduction for the charitable donation of a home is limited to 30 percent of a taxpayer's adjusted gross income, the unused deduction can be carried forward for an additional five years. A home donation can also be made within a year of purchasing the home, but in that case, the deduction would be limited to the lesser of the fair market value or the original purchase price.

The fair market value is typically determined by a third-party appraiser, who attributes a value to the house based on factors such as comparable sales in the local market. The IRS requires that such an appraisal be conducted no more than sixty days before the donation and could challenge the amount if the charity ultimately sells the property for a significantly lower sum. Appraisals were a major debating point during our advocacy in 1986 for the appreciated property charitable deduction.

Wealthy individuals often choose to make such a donation in a year when they are expecting a particularly large tax bill. The merits of the appreciated property charitable deduction had been our 1986 Alliance; it had been our driver. Museums, universities, and others were our members, and it was a comforting advocacy. However, to witness these multi-million-dollar tax-driven transactions with the donation of huge mansions was not what we had in mind.

Historical Views

The 1986 tax overhaul was originally deemed impossible to achieve when Sen. Bill Bradley, D-N. J., first proposed it in 1982, and it nearly died multiple times before it finally passed, 292–136 in the House and 74–23 in the Senate in 1986. The project succeeded because President Ronald Reagan was behind it, and the leaders of Congress, dubious though some of them were, thought they had to produce something.

In 1993, newly elected president Bill Clinton had inherited major budget deficits left over from the Reagan and Bush administrations; for example, fiscal year 1992 had seen a $290 billion deficit. In order to cut the deficit, Leon Panetta, President Clinton's Chief of Staff, and Treasury Secretary Bob Rubin—both of whom I knew—urged Clinton to pursue both tax increases and spending cuts.

They felt that by balancing the budget, Clinton would encourage Federal Reserve Chairman Alan Greenspan to lower interest rates and be politically beneficial since it would potentially help Democrats shed their supposed "tax and spend" label perpetuated by the Republicans.

Sure enough, the 1993 deficit reduction plan produced smaller budget deficits each year. In 1998, the federal government experienced the first budget surplus since 1969. For some reason, the Omnibus Budget Reconciliation Act of 1993 became a leading target of Republican criticism of the Clinton administration. Republicans argued that Clinton's tax hikes on high-income earners violated earlier promises he had made to not raise taxes and reduce the deficit. The rest is history!

The 2017 House GOP plan was unveiled on November 2 and passed through the reconciliation process. I reported to our infrastructure coalition later that day that there were several infrastructure/repatriation hearings in the Senate in the last Congress; we were assuming earlier this year that might be the route they would take. However, Gary Cohn was on C-SPAN today discussing the tax bill and said not a word on infrastructure. They were holding it hostage.

The House GOP Ways and Means Committee Chairman Kevin Brady, the Secretary of the Treasury Steve Mnuchin, and the Chairman of the National Economic Council Gary Cohn were all new to this legislative challenge. Their attitude regarding the expected deficit from their tax cut proposal was very surprising considering the supposed conservative GOP base, mostly now from the red states and of modest means.

But the GOP messaging was a constant "middle-class tax cut, middle-class tax cut" mantra; and even though the expert tax analyst pointed out that only 10 percent of the tax cuts would go to the middle class, the red states bought into the Trump theme.

And Rep. John Delaney (D-Md.), with whom we were working with closely, was right on target when he wanted the effort to overhaul the tax code to be bipartisan and argued that putting infrastructure into tax legislation was the best route. He added that the GOP would be making a huge mistake by leaving infrastructure out of their plan, because that's something we all agree on and it's a way to start having a real bipartisan negotiation.

And if they do jam through tax reform without any new funding for infrastructure, there won't be any infrastructure bill because there won't be any money left to pay for one. He was right on target as I had attended those partisan GOP Ways and Means Committee hearings. Delaney was smart and did a really good job for infrastructure, but he was not on the Ways and Means Committee and was to resign then to run unsuccessfully for president two years later in 2020.

In the tax cut proposal, there was a one-time tax on US companies repatriated foreign profits; a 12 percent rate on cash and a 5 percent rate on illiquid investments, with an eight-year repatriation payout. However, the GOP failed to link any of the proceeds to infrastructure.

While tax reform/repatriation was the infrastructure funding solution, the effort quickly morphed into the largest tax cut in US history, with the repatriation windfall essentially grabbed for the corporate rate reduction from 35 percent to 21 percent, coupled with many other corporate and wealthy benefits in the GOP bill. It clearly lacked the fairness label. As noted, there was not one hearing! We had been advocating for 21 percent, and with the modest contribution of corporate tax receipts, it seemed logical and worthwhile.

As a result, our infrastructure investment coalition was very disappointed with the 2017 tax bill and finally gave up in 2021 after the bipartisan infrastructure proposal ignored any national infrastructure bank lending proposal and focused on grants only in a very political way and shortly was adopted as the "Biden Build Back Better" manifesto.

A real mystery to me was the red state insistence on eliminating the deduction for state and local income and sales taxes (plus capping the deduction for state and local property taxes to $10,000). They knew that many blue state Republicans in the Northeast and California, the donor states, would vote "no," forcing a very tight partisan vote on the House floor. It's as if Kevin Brady, Chairman of the House Ways and Means Committee from Texas, wanted to ignite another North-South Civil War.

This trend toward an all-south GOP does not bode well for the country. The GOP did it again in their infrastructure proposal with 75 percent of the funding targeted either for rural or state/local incentive grants with a clear red state governor's bias; and then again opposing a "national" project to participate in the funding of a new train tunnel under the Hudson River from New Jersey to New York City. A $6 billion grant from the Federal Transit Administration, under President Biden, solved that problem in June 2023.

All through the Trump days, there were many grants announced, invariably to rural red states; under Biden, the numerous grants were going to blue states, and our infrastructure coalition, having made such good progress in the area of federal credit enhancement (loans), was very discouraged by this.

Maybe the Tax Reform Act that I worked on back in 1986 was not quite revenue neutral. But this 2017 version makes you wonder as there has been some very positive legislative activity in earlier years.

In 2013, House Ways and Means Chairman Dave Camp and Senate Finance Committee Chairman Max Baucus had planned to produce a tax overhaul that would put regular families on a level playing field with those who can pay high-priced tax advisers. But Max, a good friend, was not the needed leader and moved to China in 2014 to be our ambassador there. Friends who worked for Max in the Senate tell me he would call once a week from Beijing wanting to know what was going on in Washington, DC.

In mid-February 2015, in the new 114th Congress, Senate Finance Chairman Orrin Hatch and Ranking Democrat Ron Wyden held a "setting the table" Senate Finance hearing with testimony given by former Senators Bob Packwood, who chaired that same committee in 1986, and his colleague former Senator Bill Bradley.

The topic was essentially a review of the "lessons learned" from the 1986 tax reform experience. I had been in this hearing room several times for related hearings, but was to watch this one on the committee's website via YouTube.

I read in the press coverage that Bradley described a conversation with President Reagan wherein he told the President that he was in the 90th percentile bracket when making movies; and as a professional basketball player, he himself was a depreciable asset.

And in the previous chapter, we talked about sports as content and that sports teams are considered businesses for tax purposes. So, players' salaries are what are depreciable by the owner of the team! Today, these extraordinary salaries to sports stars are a write-off for the team owner.

I have always admired Bill Bradley since the day I saw him playing for Princeton against Navy at the Naval Academy in 1964–1965, his US Senate career, and his interest in running for president after retiring from the Senate in 1996.

In fact, we exchanged letters at the time urging him to run for president in 2000. His response was vintage Bill Bradley and fits with his February 2015 lessons learned testimony before the Senate Finance Committee, where he pointed out that the income tax system is unfair, inefficient, and overly complex. He added that by cutting tax rates and eliminating most of the nearly $1 trillion in individual and corporate tax loopholes, we allow people to keep more of each additional dollar they earn, and we deal a blow to the special interests and quoted Justice Oliver Wendell Holmes, who said that taxes are the price we pay for civilization.

On a flight back from California to Washington, DC, in 1996, a huge snowstorm redirected our plane to Newark Airport. Publisher Steve Forbes was designing a presidential run for the White House at the time, and was similarly snowed in at the same Newark terminal, unable to fly out to California. We were seated next to each other in the terminal waiting area, and I asked him where he was going in California.

He told me he was going to Stanford, and I responded that he must be going to meet with Stanford flat tax specialists Bob Hall and Alvin Rabuska. He was impressed, and I explained that I had been through this flat tax episode back in 1986 with Pat Moynihan and had met Alvin Rabuska and Bob Hall. He grunted, as I recall.

Then a small plane flight to Charlottesville, Virginia was announced. I got on it, spent the night with my son Clay and his young family as he was getting his master's degree at the University of Virginia, rented a car, and drove home to the Washington, DC, area.

In 2015, I attended several hearings in the Senate Finance Committee and House Ways and Means Committee on the related topics of corporate tax reform, repatriation, and the resultant funding of a major infrastructure investment program, including some form of a national infrastructure fund/bank/authority, a long-time goal of mine. I wanted to assess the chances! "Repatriation" would require companies to bring back earnings to the United States at a 14 percent tax rate, generating an estimated $238 billion in revenue for the government that could be used to pay for infrastructure improvements.

Then in September 2016, the European Union hit Apple with a $14.6 billion tax bill based on special tax arrangements that Ireland provided to Apple. Both the United States and Ireland opposed this action: US Secretary Lew stated that any Apple tax revenue belongs to the United States Treasury; and Ireland said they would appeal as they wanted to maintain their tax advantages for jobs in Ireland.

Just days after the European Union announcement, Apple CEO Tim Cook said he expected to transfer billions of dollars in profit to the United States in 2017. I was impressed, and seeing the magnitude involved, I was optimistic about a major infrastructure funding opportunity, as had been Treasury Secretary Jack Lew's suggestion. I was encouraged to read Cook's news interview in 2016 where he stated that Apple had set aside several billion dollars for US payment as soon as we repatriate it, and right now he forecasted that repatriation would occur the next year, that is, 2017.

US companies are supposed to pay federal taxes on their global profits, but the tax on money made overseas is only due when it's brought back (repatriated) to the US

Cook said that year that he wanted to repatriate Apple's foreign profits but that he couldn't because it would cost them 40 percent, referring to the combined US federal and state tax rate Apple would likely owe. Estimates are that Apple was holding $181 billion offshore, and that the company's effective tax rate was 25.9 percent between 2008 and 2014.

I agreed with Apple CEO Tim Cook that, with a worldwide income tax rate at 26.1 percent being a reasonable level, US repatriation proceeds could be dedicated to infrastructure investment in the United States.

It is amazing that since Apple launched the iPhone in June 2007, the smartphone revolution was unleashed, and it had changed the way people work and socialize while reshaping industries from music to hotels. It has put its unique stamp on the Millennium and the millennials themselves.

Ten years later, the iPhone was one of the best-selling products in history, with about 1.3 billion sold, generating more than $800 billion in new revenue. Apple's willingness to repatriate at a reasonable rate and see some of those proceeds flow back to their nation's infrastructure would be a millennial win-win. I was optimistic.

As noted earlier, the Obama administration's 2016 "principles" proposal was geared toward (1) corporate tax reform (25%) exclusively with the added proviso of (2) repatriating overseas profits at a 14 percent rate to fund infrastructure, including the highway trust fund and a national infrastructure bank.

Apple's repatriation alone would generate over $45 billion at the 14 percent rate, and our infrastructure coalition panel of experts has devised a holistic infrastructure plan that would require $75 billion over ten years in budget allocations, stimulating an overall investment effect of $615 billion.

Secretary Lew's daughter was an assistant secretary at the Transportation Department, and we had several meetings leading to a strong Treasury-Transportation infrastructure relationship. From my experience, this was a strategic breakthrough leading to the establishment of the Build America Bureau at Transportation and an infrastructure task force at Treasury led by a close ally, Elaine Buckberg who is now the Chief Economist for General Motors.

Interestingly, in a nod to regular order, in 1986 Congress completed action on the Tax Reform Act of 1986 with the following votes: On 09/27/1986, the Senate agreed to the conference report by a bipartisan Yea-Nay Vote of 74–23; and earlier on 09/25/1986, the House had agreed to the conference report by a bipartisan Yea-Nay Vote of 292 to 136, 2017.

It was noteworthy that there was a House-Senate Conference, in keeping with the regular order tradition. It was my honor to witness those votes in the galleries of both congressional chambers!

Conversely, in 2017, the House of Representatives, on a strictly GOP partisan vote, passed the Tax Cuts and Jobs Act of 2017 in mid-November, and the Senate GOP, on my November 30 birthday, followed with a similar GOP partisan version. Still, further action was needed as there were differences.

Just before Christmas, the House voted 227 to 203 to pass the House-Senate conference compromise bill, with twelve Republicans voting against it and no Democrats voting for it. Eleven of the twelve Republicans were from California, New Jersey, and New York, states that would be impacted by the provision limiting the deduction for state and local taxes to just $10,000. The Senate followed and voted fifty-one to forty-eight, with only Republican votes in support and all Democrats opposed. This was done under reconciliation, a budget act maneuver with a majority vote requirement.

Earlier that fall, the House Ways and Means Committee had reported The Tax Cuts and Jobs Act of 2017 by a partisan vote of GOP majority vote 24–16 after several days of markups and straight partisan votes on amendments. The Senate Finance Committee voted 14–12, again with only GOP votes in support. I was to watch both of those sessions. There were no hearings, as I noted earlier, including nothing on infrastructure.

Individuals would see tax cuts including a top rate of 37 percent, down from 39.6 percent. The size of inheritances shielded from estate taxation would double to $22 million for married couples; and owners of pass-through businesses, whose profits are taxed through the individual code, would be able to deduct 20 percent of their business income.

But it was as if the Civil War South attacking the North was being reinvented with the elimination of the state and local tax deduction. It is true that the more liberal and well-educated the state, the more the surplus they pay to the Treasury. This epitomizes the Blue State versus Red State rivalry, and the GOP tax policy suggestion to eliminate the State and Local Tax Deduction underscores this political rivalry, as Blue States historically pay Uncle Sam far more than they receive; and with Red States, it is the reverse according to the Rockefeller Institute for Government Policy.

I was alarmed by the deficit expansion and the inability to fund infrastructure legislation. The one-time repatriation windfall, to be targeted for infrastructure investment, was lost in the shuffle, forgotten by the GOP in what became a significant tax cut as opposed to tax reform.

Contrary to GOP assertions that they were simplifying the tax code in 2017, the bill was very complicated at 1,097 pages in length. Originally referring to this legislation as Tax Reform, the consensus was indeed a major tax cut for the rich.

In fact, even the Wall Street Journal had a December 19 article with the headline, "Middle Class Gets 10% of Cut," underscoring that 90 percent of the benefits were going to either corporations or the wealthy in the United States. Polls confirmed that most Americans understood that was the case, much to the GOP's chagrin. They voted in 2018 to bring back the Democrats to control the House.

While this 2017 legislation was a tax policy bill, the GOP also eliminated the individual health insurance mandate beginning in 2019 to begin their attempted sabotage of the Obamacare program despite record 2017 sign-ups.

And it was particularly troubling, in this era of wealth imbalance, that the GOP doubled the estate tax threshold, so now the first $11 million that people pass on to their heirs in property, stocks, and other assets won't be taxed ($22 million for married couples). And this was to protect the family farms!

And Republicans had decided it would be all right to go into debt up to $1.5 trillion to fund the tax cut. In the end, they nearly hit that mark. The official estimate—released that Friday evening alongside the bill—came in at $1.46 trillion. The next generation would inherit not only this debt but the added trillions from the pandemic expenditures.

And later you would read IRS-reported taxation data that really put this major 2017 tax cut legislation in perspective:

1. The IRS audited 1 in about 160 individual tax returns in 2017, the lowest since 2002 and the sixth consecutive year that audits have declined, as budget cuts had reduced the number of staff at the federal agency.
2. The Internal Revenue Service lost nearly a third of its enforcement employees since a 2010 peak, when it audited one in ninety individual returns—audited 0.62 percent of individual returns in the 2017 fiscal year.
3. In 2017, the IRS audited 4.37 percent of returns with income of $1 million and higher, less than half the 9.55 percent audit rate for such returns in 2015.
4. The number of taxpayers reporting income above $1 million rose nearly 25 percent between 2015 and 2017.

5. In 2017, IRS funding was $11.2 billion, down nearly 8 percent from its high in 2010, although the number of individual returns grew nearly 5 percent over the same period.
6. From a revenue standpoint, filers earning over $1 million in calendar year 2015 accounted for 28 percent of total income taxes, up from 25 percent in 2013. For 2015, filers earning between $200,000 and $500,000 paid nearly 21 percent of the total. Filers earning between $100,000 and $200,000 paid 22 percent.
7. Revenue from individual income taxes is the single largest source of federal receipts and has been growing as a percentage of the total. In fiscal 2017, it accounted for nearly 48 percent of federal revenue, up from 45 percent a decade earlier.
8. The revenue from corporate taxes accounted for 9 percent of total revenue in 2017, down from 12 percent a decade ago, the committee's data show.
9. There are approximately 1.7 million non-profits (1.3 million are charities) and 112,000 private foundations in the United States, all enjoying tax policy privileges and experiencing a very low IRS audit rate due to personnel shortages.
10. The IRS indicated that the drop in audits of high earners reflected the continuing decline in IRS compliance personnel from some 23,000 in 2010 to roughly 15,000 in 2017, including highly skilled staff.

Shortly after the 2017 tax bill's passage, Speaker Ryan indicated that the next GOP goal was entitlement reform, which meant a structural revamp of Social Security, Medicare, and Medicaid, along with reducing the food stamp program.

The Progressive Policy Institute at the time announced that Moynihan was right: The GOP tax giveaway would lead to safety net cuts. My good friend, Senator Daniel Patrick Moynihan, had been correct. There should have been a bipartisan discussion in 2017 as was done back in 1986. The Senator from New York, working with his GOP colleague, Senator Robert Dole, said doing something big had to be bipartisan! Indeed, the results would have been far better!

I had sat through several of the House Ways and Means Committee hearings, and it was very discouraging how the well-prepared infrastructure topic was dismissed.

I was surprised to read, after the bill's passage, that President Trump's priority all along was to fix a broken system, according to Treasury Secretary Steven Mnuchin. Indeed, the IRS had been under relentless attack by the GOP, and still was not broken.

Every responsible analysis stated how the wealthiest Americans would be the major beneficiaries for years to come, not the "middle class." The polls supported that conclusion. The political stage had been set for the November 2018 midterm elections. The GOP had used partisan budget reconciliation to pass it, so the house Democrats would return the favor when they reclaimed the majority. Meanwhile, the federal deficit mushroomed!

There could have been some corporate tax reform, particularly rate reduction, coupled with infrastructure investment via some portion of the repatriation proceeds. The individual income tax cuts were unnecessary and uncalled for and would encourage the wealthy to pursue all sorts of "tax avoidance schemes."

Plus, the debt taken on for these tax cuts will have long-term negative impacts. Already in early February, a little over a month since the tax bill was signed into law, the Treasury Department announced that the federal government was on track to borrow nearly $1 trillion in the 2018 fiscal year, that is, the first Trump administration budget year. That was almost double what the government borrowed in fiscal 2017. I was worried as were many other Americans.

Interestingly, in the millennium year 2000, many were pleased that the budget was balanced in that last year of the Clinton presidency. Here is where we were in 2016. The federal government ran a budget deficit of $588 billion in fiscal year 2016, the Congressional Budget Office estimates—$149 billion greater than the shortfall recorded in fiscal year 2015. The 2016 deficit equaled an estimated 3.2 percent of gross domestic product (GDP), up from 2.5 percent of GDP in 2015.

Congressional Republicans, in 2016, said once again that tax-cut-induced deficits aren't the same as those brought on by increased spending, in part because they believe the former can generate growth in ways that recoup lost revenues over time. The term now is dynamic scoring, but it was really so-called supply-side economics with the discredited Laffer curve. However, it never works out that way. Art Laffer had drawn the curve on a restaurant napkin during a lunch with Dick Cheney.

The last two times Republicans reclaimed the White House from Democrats—in 1981 and 2001—they pushed for large tax cuts. Deficits nonetheless rose during their administrations. And sure enough, the FY 2017 Federal Budget Deficit exploded to $666 billion, reminding me of the famous Top of the Sixes restaurant, atop a 41-story building at 666 Fifth Avenue that Jared Kushner bought before entering the White House.

With the 2017 GOP partisan tax cut leaving over 1.5 billion dollars in deficit by design, I felt the GOP had lost its way. Just the long-term interest payments on the US debt were consistently projected to be over a trillion a year in and of themselves. The abuse of the Budget Reconciliation Resolution Act by the GOP was a disgrace, and the Democrats would use the same maneuver in 2021.

Mr. Trump's deficits would be the largest relative to the economy of any president in more than fifty years save for Barack Obama during the devastating "great recession." The United States was actually a low-tax country in 2017 to start with, but the new tax law would reduce federal revenue in fiscal 2019 to 16.3 percent of GDP, a figure normally seen only around recessions; and then the 2020–1 pandemic would inspire a US spending tsunami with deficits multiplying dramatically. The Biden administration deficits would follow a similar trajectory.

Leon Panetta, who I knew well, in his autobiography, Worthy Fights, talks about the budget balancing strategy he initiated as Bill Clinton's Chief of Staff. Leon had been Chairman of the House Budget Committee and was really a very good numbers man from that experience. He doesn't mention the millennium in his book, but that is when the balanced budget happened! It is a shame, as we squandered the millennium opportunity on the spurious Y2K alarm.

GOP Senator Jeff Flake, whom I admired for his heroic opposition to Trump's behavior, stated before a March National Press Club lunch (that I watched) that he supported a needed corporate tax reform to a lower, more competitive international percentage. However, he was alarmed by all the other inclusions that hemorrhaged the deficit by over a trillion dollars.

The 2017 Tax Cuts and Jobs Act was a substantial blow to the integrity of the income tax and increased the complexity of the code under the guise of reform. It was very unfortunate—the GOP should have done nothing, and we would be better off. The previous GOP attacks on the Internal Revenue Service went into temporary hibernation in the face of this mammoth regulatory challenge ahead. But sure enough, that GOP anti-IRS venom was to reemerge just a few years later.

In early 2018, after the 2017 tax cut passage, some corporations were awarding $1,000 bonuses to employees as a gesture; but some said it was a public relations ploy. After all, the Bank of America gave CEO Brian Moynihan a 15 percent total compensation raise to $23 million that year. Furthermore, his income tax bracket declined from 39.6 percent to 37 percent in the future.

Coincidentally, the new SEC (Dodd-Frank) executive compensation/employee median ratio reporting requirements began in early 2018, and the ratios were typically in the 200 to 300 to one times range, much higher than in other developed countries. Corporations were to keep their ratios under wraps and the Biden administration seemed oblivious to what had been a hard-earned fairness policy issue. Instead, the work equity was thrown out there as camouflage for the reality.

Going forward on a positive note, the 2017 Tax Cuts and Jobs Act changed the taxation of executive compensation by eliminating the exemption (some say loophole) for performance-based pay from the corporate deduction limit of $1 million per year in compensation paid to chief executive officers.

The tax legislation also expanded the scope of covered individuals to include CFOs, along with the CEO and three highest-paid employees, beginning in 2018. There was a transition rule applied to remuneration provided under a written binding contract that was in effect on November 2, 2017. That was how Mr. Bryan Moynihan got his 2017 raise at the Bank of America.

The bulk of this corporate bonanza, though, according to a Morgan Stanley survey of 556 companies, indicated: 43 percent would either do share buybacks or increase dividends, 19 percent would pursue mergers, only 17 percent would allocate funds for capital spending and 13 percent would direct funds toward higher wages.

In February, Cisco announced they would repatriate $67 billion and use $44 billion for share buybacks and dividends, confirming the survey. Share buybacks, as it turned out, allowed corporations to report higher earnings, which are directly related to executive compensation. It also allowed companies that were not performing that well to boost their earnings as camouflage.

Numerous companies had declared bankruptcy in recent years after the leveraged buyouts of the last two decades, including Toys R Us in early 2018, as their new private equity owners loaded them with debt coupled with large dividend payments to enrich themselves. The Toys R Us CEO at the time, in 2005, John Eyler, received a payment of $65.3 million for his cooperation at the completion of the deal. It is an interesting and immoral comparison!

And now, in reality, we have the ultimate Wall Street leveraged buyout (LBO) with over $1.5 trillion in debt leveraging a buyout of our national government for the benefit of the 1 percent ownership cadre of wealth in the United States who enjoyed substantial and unneeded tax cuts in the new law. Many of whom had said publicly they did not need or want a tax cut, including Bob Crandall, the retired CEO of American Airlines.

What a difference 2017 was from the successful bipartisan tax reform effort in 1986. It had been a privilege to be engaged directly in that process. In 2017, our PIRC coalition advocated project financing tools such as infrastructure tax credits, incentive/performance grants, private activity bonds, federal project loans, and federal public private partnerships. We had bipartisan meetings with the Senate Finance and House Ways and Means Committees, but the House GOP was disinterested, and they were in the majority. Tax cuts were the mantra!

I had been optimistic about the corporate rate tax reform repatriation proceeds funding a dramatic infrastructure strategy, as there were billions of corporate dollars overseas. However, the House GOP assigned all of those repatriation dollars to corporate rate relief, bringing that rate all the way down to 21 percent.

But the tax cut/deficit spending story was just beginning; in a July 2023 decision, US District Judge Tom Barber, who was appointed by President Donald Trump, ruled that, astonishingly, a Maryland couple was required to pay federal income tax on stolen money from their IRA savings. A similar story emerged at the same time when a former White House scientist was scammed out of $655,000 IRA savings. Judge Barber cited the Tax Cuts and Jobs Act that Trump signed in 2017, which temporarily repealed deductions for losses from storms, fires, earthquakes—and theft. Known as personal casualty loss deductions, they were suspended through 2025.

Our infrastructure coalition had been meeting for over two years. How infrastructure legislation would be funded in 2018 or 2019 was an open question that reemerged once again in 2021. And the solution, as noted was deficit spending!

The Trump White House infrastructure plan, after it was finally released in February 2018, would have spent $200 billion in federal dollars over ten years with incentives that the Administration predicted would leverage over $1 trillion in total spending. We liked the concept! But the White House could not explain how it would work nor pay for the plan. Our PIRC Coalition had worked with the White House's DJ Gribben, and we had sent him our material and briefed him. I always felt his proposal would be critical, and somehow it went off on a rural/state/local tangent. The GOP Five Cabinet members' testimony on the plan in the Senate on March 14 was like a "Kabuki Dance."

The committee members were totally confused, as were the cabinet secretaries. They could not define "rural." And before long, it was "dead in the water," as is so often said; and the next Congress would draft a new infrastructure plan.

In that context, a Senate Democratic infrastructure plan was released that would spend $1 trillion in real federal dollars over that same ten-year period, increase funding for existing programs, and fund new programs such as our PIRC Coalition proposals.

In 2018, the Senate Democrats proposed to pay for their infrastructure plan by repealing some of the GOP tax cuts. Later, the House Democrats made a similar proposal.

But the 2018 mid-term elections would come first, and the House and its Ways and Means Committee reverted to Democratic control. They argued that because business was clamoring for infrastructure, it would make sense to raise the corporate tax rate to 25 percent from the 21 percent enshrined in the 2017 law, pulling back on some of its other provisions to fund an infrastructure proposal that would have included some of our PIRC Coalition's innovative finance proposals for project finance.

We had excellent meetings with the House Ways and Means Committee Democratic staff in early 2019 and were optimistic.

The 26 percent level was the rate that I noted Apple's CEO Tim Cook had suggested in earlier testimony in the Obama administration when Treasury Secretary Jack Lew was presenting an infrastructure/tax reform strategy with emphasis on the repatriation of corporate dollars overseas and a reduction of the corporate rate.

But reopening the 2017 tax reform act for infrastructure was a non-starter, declared Senate Majority Leader Mitch McConnell.

Then a week after National Infrastructure Week, President Trump sabotaged the effort he had nurtured with the congressional Democratic leadership (the 2-trillion-dollar plan) as he had no way of coming up with any funding for all of his bravado.

There was also, behind the scenes, a high-level acknowledgment by President Trump, in a White House meeting, that tariffs and trade would have to wait until after this 2017 tax cut was enacted. Trump had assembled his trade team along with the economic team to launch the trade strategy in early 2017, but Secretary Mnuchin pointed out that the GOP control of the House, Senate, and White House was a lifetime opportunity for a major GOP tax bill.

And Mnuchin also noted, according to Bob Woodward in his book, FEAR, that many GOP members were free traders and putting trade and tariffs on the table before the tax bill passed would jeopardize the tax legislation's passage. Trump finally agreed but said they would move to steel tariffs right after the tax bill passed!

The US Treasury projected that they would borrow a total of $1.3 trillion in 2019, more than double the amount borrowed in 2018 and the largest annual borrowing figure since 2010. In only 2009/2010, during the Great Recession, did the government borrow more money? The US Treasury also confirmed that the gross US national debt topped $22 trillion for the first time in history on February 11, 2019.

Earlier in April 2019, the Social Security Trustees released their annual report, continuing to show that the Social Security program must address its funding imbalances to prevent across-the-board benefit cuts or abrupt changes in tax or benefit levels. I read their following reports:

1. Social Security will be insolvent in only sixteen years. At that point, all beneficiaries will face a 20 percent across-the-board benefit cut, which will grow to 25 percent over time.
2. Social Security faces large and rising imbalances. The Social Security program will run cash deficits of nearly $1.8 trillion over the next decade.
3. Social Security's shortfall has grown dramatically since 2010, from 1.92 percent of payroll to 2.78 percent in this year's report.
4. Lawmakers must start making changes immediately. The sooner changes are made, the less severe they will need to be.

Our nation needs Social Security reform more than ever. Personal savings have been difficult to accumulate because middle-class wages have remained stagnant for three decades. More than half of all workers have no retirement plans at work, and millions more have no retirement savings.

Yes, on the facts, it was pretty glum in 2019; some combination of a payroll tax increase and benefit reform was urgently needed. Senators Moynihan and Dole were very proud of their work in 1986. Liz Moynihan was always talking to me about how they did it! It seemed time for a similar effort.

With the Democratic House victory in 2018, future Ways and Means Committee hearings would be interesting as there never was a hearing by the GOP in 2017 before the passage of their mammoth tax cut legislation. Hard to believe but true!

But there was quite a bit of reaction across the country in 2018 and 2019 to the 2017 tax bill:

1. My tax consultant, in sending out my 2018 income tax forms, noted that the so-called 2017 tax reform bill was actually 300 pages longer than the preceding law had been, and they would therefore have to raise their preparation fee!
2. And in February, the IRS reported that the average tax refund check was down 8 percent this year compared to last, and the number of people receiving a refund had dropped by almost a quarter.
3. And unfortunately, charitable giving in the United States rose only 1.6 percent in 2018 despite a good economy. Charities had warned that could happen; but the GOP promoters of the standard deduction change said economic growth would more than make up for the deduction's loss.

And on February 26, the Federal Reserve Chairman, Jerome Powell, testified before Congress that they now expect the US economy to only grow 2.3 percent in 2019 versus 3 percent in the prior year. Moody's Investors Service reported that companies were using the 2017 corporate tax overhaul to benefit shareholders through buybacks at the expense of paying off debt. In the second half of 2018, share repurchases accounted for 60 percent of cash outflow versus about one-third in the first half of the year.

And sure enough, the federal government would run a trillion-dollar deficit for the year. President Trump suggested to his staff that the US should buy Greenland.

Finally, there was a House Ways and Means Committee infrastructure hearing entitled "Paving the Way for Funding and Financing Infrastructure Investments" on January 29, 2020; however, it was very disappointing with a weak witness list and parochial member questions that revealed the need for more education and expertise.

But now the majority Democratic staff was in charge and included many of our PIRC Coalition infrastructure finance recommendations in the proposed legislation that Ways and Means Chairman Neal had outlined in their House report, such as:

1. Direct Subsidy Bonds—Provides taxable bonds, such as Build America Bonds, that state and local governments can use to finance projects while the bondholder receives a direct subsidy, rather than tax-free interest like municipal bonds.

2. Qualified Private Activity Bonds—Expands the national volume cap for qualified infrastructure facilities to allow for greater investment in surface transportation public private partnerships.
3. Advanced Refunding—This restores state and local governments' ability to invest in infrastructure projects with favorable financing terms by allowing them to use one bond's proceeds to replace existing bonds.
4. Tax Credit Bonds—Provides a taxable bond that state and local governments can use to finance surface transportation projects while the bondholder receives a tax credit, rather than tax-free interest like municipal bonds.
5. Tax Credits—Expands existing infrastructure tax credits and creates new credits to improve all sectors of infrastructure investment, including community development projects.
6. Energy Storage Incentives —providing incentives for renewable energy projects and new technologies to modernize the electric grid and improve resiliency.

Our coalition analysis suggested that some $75 billion invested in these infrastructure financing tools over ten years could generate approximately $400 billion in program volume and $615 billion in net investment effect, plus generate some 8 million jobs over that ten-year period using CEA standards. This leverage could also include federal sector public-private partnership provisions and performance incentive grants.

And then the coronavirus exploded in our midst. The $2 trillion coronavirus relief package Congress approved in late March 2020 included hundreds of billions of dollars to increase unemployment insurance benefits, send $1,200 checks to tens of millions of American families, and provide relief to small businesses. It also included more than $500 billion in GOP tax cuts in the must-pass legislation.

And as nonprofit groups struggled during the pandemic, bipartisan efforts for charitable donations were gaining momentum in Congress, allowing taxpayers deduct charitable donations, even if they don't itemize their deductions.

Some religious congregations reported donation declines of more than 30 percent. The YMCA's national office was reducing its staff from 300 to 170.

In 2000, 66 percent of Americans donated to charities; by 2016, that proportion had dropped to 53 percent, according to the Indiana University Lilly Family School of Philanthropy's Philanthropy Panel Study. The 2017 tax law dealt another blow to charitable giving.

By nearly doubling the standard deduction in 2017, the law reduced the number of people who have enough deductions to make itemizing worthwhile to about one-tenth of households, down from about one-quarter.

With former Vice President Biden leading Trump in the polls in late October, a week before the November 3 election, Democrats were backing away from vows to reverse President Trump's 2017 tax cuts if they took control of the Senate and White House. Instead, the priority was the pandemic and spending to create jobs and raise wages, investments in green technology and infrastructure, and a national plan to contain the coronavirus pandemic.

Some of those stimulus and relief bills would include tax incentives for clean energy infrastructure and strengthening the nation's supply chain and domestic manufacturing base. Tax relief in the form of child tax credits and earned income tax credits for lower- and middle-income families is also on the table.

Biden's plan also called for raising the corporate tax rate from 21 percent to 28 percent and increasing taxes on foreign profits. When asked during an interview at the time with CNN whether he would wait to raise taxes until unemployment goes down, he stated he would make corporate tax changes on day one.

Biden's tax policy was to be merged into the Biden infrastructure (Global Climate) strategy as he approached his first State of the Union address on April 28, 2021. But nothing came of it, albeit a minimum 15 percent global corporate rate policy was adopted by the OECD countries that year. That was probably the latest State of the Union address date-wise in modern US history, practically eliminating any Congressional follow-up. And the needed 15 percent overseas rate vote was ignored.

Finally, the Infrastructure Investment and Jobs Act (IIJA), also known as the Bipartisan Infrastructure Law (BIL), was signed into law by President Biden on November 15, 2021. The law authorized $1.2 trillion for transportation and infrastructure spending, with $550 billion of that figure going toward "new" investments and programs over multiple number of years. Our PIRC Coalition surrendered as this was a 100 percent political grant program that originated in the Senate on a bipartisan basis and was later adopted as the Biden Build Back Better grant program under the White House Infrastructure Czar Moon Landrieu.

The following year, 2022, the State of the Union was on March 1 again, over a month late, and this time there were no excuses relating to the 2021 outgoing Trump administration OMB budget mischief. However, I had yet to read a Biden Administration/Congressional Democratic tax proposal, generally speaking, in 2021–2, one that might include estate tax reform as an issue of logic and fairness.

What always confused me was the GOP's stubbornness on the corporate tax rate, now with a minimum, but according to the Joint Committee on Taxation, for FY 2022, corporate taxes amounted to only 8.7 percent of total federal revenue while individual returns amounted to 53.8 percent and social insurance was 30.3 percent.

From 2010 through 2019, according to a study by the Government Accountability Office, the number of audits of taxpayers earning more than $500,000 dropped by three-quarters, from 53,000 to 14,000. Over this period, the number of key IRS enforcement personnel also dropped 40 percent, according to agency data.

But now, with the 2022 legislation, there was significant funding to recruit and restore the Internal Revenue Service, adding $79 billion to the Internal Revenue Service over the next decade.

Looking back, in 2017, the tax system might have seemed unfair to some, with certain corporations and individuals escaping payment of any tax at all. More than $400 billion a year less in taxes being paid than is estimated to be owed, and with some industries paid a far lower tax rate than others.

Until the Trump administration, I had not known that cabinet members enjoyed unusual tax exclusion from required sales of their personal holdings for Senate confirmation, with the requirement that they invest the proceeds tax-free in Treasury securities. While capital gains and income are taxed on that second portfolio, it pays to be in the cabinet as your earlier capital gains portfolio was not taxed at all.

Surprisingly, corporate tax revenues make up only between 9 percent and 11 percent of government tax revenues; however, they were the center of the 2017 tax cut rhetoric. I was in attendance at those hearings, hoping for an infrastructure investment bank opportunity based on a corporate tax rate of 25 percent, but the GOP members settled on 21 percent, and that was the end of that infrastructure proposal from Obama Treasury Secretary Lew.

To me and many other tax policy observers, once again this is a GOP bromide that has proven over and over to be false, and is actually a supply-side/shrink the government strategy that has not worked! And sure enough, after the 2017 tax cut, Stephen Moore of the Heritage Foundation, who advised the Trump campaign, stated publicly that they were not backing away from the supply-side agenda.

As I said, we gave up in 2021 after the bipartisan infrastructure proposal ignored any national infrastructure bank proposal and focused on pork barrel in a very political way and shortly was adopted as the Biden "Build Back Better" manifesto with former New Orleans Mayor Moon Landrieu as the infrastructure czar.

Landrieu resigned from the White House in late 2023 to join the Biden re-election campaign as he knew where all the infrastructure grants had been placed and could call in those chits. Plus, he was close to President Biden, who favored political advice to balance out his staff policy recommendations.

4

Energy/Electricity Deregulation, 1992

In September 2016, just before the elections, I listened attentively to then Secretary of Energy Ernest Moniz at a Washington, DC, global climate event at the Mayflower Hotel that had political competitors, billionaire Tom Steyer of Next Gen Climate and Sean McGarvey of the AFL-CIO Building and Construction Trades Department, on the same program. Quite a feat!

The Secretary outlined in detail the many changes happening in the US energy/electricity sector. It was a long list focused on the need for large-scale infrastructure investment in the grid in every category, including the distribution sector. Coincidentally, I had listened to the Secretary testify before the Senate Energy and Natural Resources Committee two years prior; when—in answering a Senator's question—he agreed that the electric utility vertically integrated business model was broken.

All of this began with the passage of PUHCA Reform Title VII (Electricity) in the 1992 Energy Policy Act, which created the independent power industry and was a proud personal moment, having led the key supporting coalition of utilities. Being present with President Bush when he signed the 1992 Energy Policy Act was very satisfying. This would be a major consumer benefit!

For example, during the five years from 2011 to 2016, roughly 350 coal-fired generating units shut down across the United States, ranging from small units at factories to huge power plants, according to data from the Energy Information Administration (EIA). A clean natural gas plants replaced them along with renewable energy sources such as wind and solar, almost all developed by independent power producers responding, for the most part, to electric utility RFPs and, in some renewable cases, corporate power purchase agreements.

And according to the EIA, that trend has continued since then. The US was expected to source more of its electricity from wind and solar than coal in 2021–2 as more renewable energy projects came online and utilities shuttered more coal plants under pressure from state regulators.

While President Trump withdrew the United States from the Paris Climate Change Accord in early 2017 and Russia invaded Ukraine in early 2022, the die was already cast as to our nation's energy transition. Repair work was quickly addressed in 2021 as the Biden administration took charge, but the Global Climate Energy Transition effort seemed lacking in direction with elected officials in key post such as Secretary of Energy.

With the 2024 presidential campaign underway and Vice President Harris leading in the polls against former President Trump, it was clear that our next Secretary of Energy needed to be someone with technical knowledge, like former Secretary of Energy Ernest Moniz. Here is that 1992 Energy/Electricity Deregulation story, first its history!

In late 1976, my Vietnam boss, Admiral Bud Zumwalt, asked me to fly back from my home base of San Francisco to Washington, DC, after the elections and meet with Jim Schlesinger at the John Hopkins Washington, DC, campus on Massachusetts Avenue on a snowy Saturday morning. Jim Schlesinger had been nominated to be the first Secretary of Energy by President Carter, and it was his task to design the structure of the new Department of Energy, which was signed into law in August 1977. I was to suggest a congressional/public relations strategy for that endeavor!

The Department headquarters was to be the new Forrestal Building on Independence Avenue, which the Defense Department conveniently surrendered. The Department of Energy itself was activated on October 1, 1977.

Also in 1977, super lawyer, friend, and Democratic Party Chairman Bob Strauss entered the Cabinet of President Carter, serving as Special Trade Representative. Over the next two and a half years, he successfully concluded the Tokyo Round of Multilateral Trade Negotiations and directed its passage through Congress, which culminated in the Trade Act of 1979.

And coincidentally, during that summer of 1977, I was to move our family to Washington, DC, to oversee the Southern Pacific office there, with its transportation (rail and trucking), telecommunications (Sprint), and natural resources activities.

My advice to Jim Schlesinger regarding the structure and contents of a national energy plan, which included much of the policy for the new Department of Energy, was to take the time necessary to build a consensus as Bob Strauss was doing on trade and get it right! He asked me to go over and meet with the energy planning staff, which included future TVA Chairman David Freeman. I did so, but the reception was polite yet non-committal.

Sure enough, President Carter—on the advice of his political staff—instructed that the new energy plan being drafted by that same transition team, including David Freeman, be sent to Congress by that April. It was correct to send up a written legislative proposal but to develop that consensus first. So, my strategy was ignored at that time. Looking back, most energy experts would agree that the needed time should have been taken as the Department has had its intrinsic challenges over the years, particularly in meeting the global climate challenge years after its birth.

They were fortunate to be given the new Forrestal Building on Independence Avenue as their home (originally planned as an annex of the Pentagon) to assist their long-range energy policy coordination with the Congress in the midst of the energy crisis at the time.

Still, I was pleased to note that there is now the James R. Schlesinger Medal for Energy Security honoring an individual's distinguished contributions to advancing our understanding of the threats, opportunities, and energy policy choices impacting the domestic and international energy security interests of the United States through analysis, policy, or practice.

The first Medal was given to Daniel Yergin on October 1, 2014, which was the thirty-seventh anniversary of the Energy Department's formal opening in 1977. The second was given to Dr. Phil Sharp, President of Resources for the Future and former US Congressman from Indiana, on January 20, 2016. The third Medal was awarded on January 13, 2017, to Charles Curtis, the first FERC chairman and former Acting Secretary of Energy under the Clinton administration. I had known and worked with all three, particularly Phil Sharp and Charlie Curtis.

And, some forty years later, on January 5, 2018, the House Energy and Commerce Committee announced its first step in a push to reorganize the Department of Energy (DOE). Rep. Fred Upton (R-Mich.), who chaired the panel's subcommittee on energy, announced a hearing on DOE Modernization, saying it would feature current DOE officials and outside science and policy experts. Watching on C-SPAN, Upton noted that the nation's energy landscape had changed dramatically since the Department of Energy was created in the 1970s amid energy scarcity and global market turmoil. It was time for the department to meet twenty-first-century challenges ranging from its continuing nuclear security responsibilities to what he called the geopolitical benefits of energy abundance. But global climate also needed to be on the list.

But my energy/electrical deregulation story begins much earlier in 1987 when a good dozen US electric utilities retained my firm, established six years earlier, to assist them in charting a new public policy course for their industry. We sponsored an analytical process for determining what structural changes would bring the maximum economic value to the nation's vertically integrated electric utility sector and its customers. The industry was in trouble with cost overruns on nuclear plants, and the requirement to purchase power at avoidable cost (PURPA) was creating confusion in utility boardrooms. The old utility-owned generation/transmission/distribution business model was not working!

My firm had Virginia Power/Dominion Resources as an existing client, and their Chairman and CEO was Bill Berry, the intellectual leader of the argument for opening up the wholesale generation market to what became the independent power industry. It was a pleasure to work with Bill. He was very flexible, and when he needed to testify on Capitol Hill, he was there.

Unfortunately, meetings on this industry structure topic had turned into filibusters by some utilities at the Edison Electric Institute trade association. I finally stood up and announced that those companies that wanted to move forward in a constructive manner should meet at a pre-arranged corporate location in Washington, DC.

Well, the response was overwhelming as a good number of the largest utilities in the country, including PG&E, Public Service Electric and Gas, Con Edison, Entergy (where the weekly meetings took place), and a dozen others, all showed up. That was the beginning of the Utility Working Group, which became a formidable presence in Washington, DC, energy policy.

I had learned earlier from my varied deregulation experiences that you were better off supporting policies for change by being part of the process and supporting a proposal if it squared with your group's concerns. In short, "you would support if; versus oppose unless!"

You had to appreciate that the traditional US system of regulating energy production and delivery dated back to the New Deal era, when Congress brought an end to the reign of large interstate holding companies that controlled more than seventy-five percent of the country's electric generating capacity.

The Public Utility Holding Company Act of 1935 (PUHCA) forced the holding companies to break up and gave utilities a government-sanctioned monopoly, a franchise, over a limited territory. In exchange, utilities agreed to provide reliable electric service to all customers at a state-regulated rate. The law resulted in the formation of nearly 300 power systems and 800 rural cooperatives. Importantly, to own a power generation plant, you had to be a utility or get an SEC waiver.

Top economists, including MIT's Paul Joskow and Dick Schmalansee, were retained by our coalition to assist our analytical process. The so-called Utility Working Group that we organized and coordinated over a five-year period eventually included Virginia Power, Duke Power, Baltimore Gas & Electric, Consumers Power, Entergy, Public Service Electric and Gas, Pacific Gas & Electric, San Diego Gas and Electric, Pacific Power and Light, Consolidated Edison, Commonwealth Edison, and New England Electric.

After first exploring the potential benefits of a "retail access" approach, being pushed then by ENRON, the group set this aside in favor of opening up the wholesale generation market—where seventy-five percent of utility capital investment occurred—to leverage more fully the benefits of competition and new technology in generation.

This entailed an amendment to the 1935 Public Utility Holding Company Act (PUHCA), which we called PUHCA Reform; and while natural gas power generation was foremost on our minds, renewable energy was not far behind. Essentially, PUHCA Reform created the independent power producer (IPP) industry, albeit the phrase in the new law was "exempt wholesale generator." I still have my 1992 "tombstone" with a miniature summary of the Act contained therein! The US IPP industry was to be a global leader in new power generation and, incidentally, the precursor of today's formidable project finance industry.

Retail access (or "direct access") did eventually evolve at the state level, allowing a retail consumer to purchase generation directly from a generation provider (e.g., green power). This usually applied to both large industrial consumers as well as smaller retail customers, including households. This varied state by state as to what was allowed; but, as the case may be, utilities were required to support this state retail access policy and are compensated for their transmission/distribution services. However, state Renewable Portfolio Standards (RPS) were the driver for renewable energy.

The Federal Energy Regulatory Commission (FERC) oversaw the wholesale power market, particularly transmission rates; however, permitting for new transmission emerged as a significant challenge, especially for building out new transmission for renewable energy, such as new wind power from the Midwest to the coastal states.

The environmental community at large, particularly regarding the future need for the energy transition to meet the global climate change challenge, was opposed to virtually all new infrastructure activity, particularly transmission for wind power from rural, wind-prone states. There are numerous environmental groups by region, both local and national, and their agendas often collide. However, today they agree on the need to invest in the "grid"; yet the not in my backyard (NIMBY) crowd remains a challenge. Permitting reform has been included in legislation but has been ineffective.

Today, in the 2020s, there has been much talk about "distributed generation," which deals with rooftop solar and utility remuneration, net metering, etc. This has led to controversy and some questions regarding the viability of the electric distribution utility as wholesale generation and even transmission become increasingly independent and no longer part of the so-called "rate base," the all-important state public utility-approved revenue stream received from customer billings.

California's 2018 ruling that all new housing would have solar energy roofs would only intensify this issue. But years later, there was state PUC retreat as the financial integrity of the distribution utility was being undermined by paying customers high fees for their surplus solar electricity.

But back to 1989, and after three years of hard work reaching agreement on the structuring of PUHCA Reform, in 1990 we were focused on the fact that Secretary of Energy Jim Watkins (retired four-star Admiral, former Chief of Naval Operations, Old Town Alexandria neighbor, and son of a former utility CEO) was to unveil the new Bush administration's national energy strategy (NES). Our Utility Working Group was now holding regular meetings of its member Washington representatives, and I would chair those gatherings and set the agenda.

The successful inclusion in the NES of our provisions modifying the Public Utility Holding Company Act (PUHCA Reform) providing for competition in wholesale generation would prove to be this pivotal accomplishment leading to congressional momentum. It became clear to me over the years that major initiatives fared best in Congress if the White House submitted a well-thought-out plan at the beginning of a Congress, as was the case here. As a result, the independent power producer industry was about to launch; but there was work to be done, particularly at the White House and the Department of Energy.

Dick Schmalansee, then Chairman of the White House Council of Economic Advisors and now retired Dean at MIT's business school, would call me periodically seeking our assistance to ensure inclusion of "PUHCA Reform" in that pending National Energy Strategy soon to be unveiled and forwarded in writing to Congress. I would assemble our utility CEO team, and we would go over to the White House, offsetting the visits from our opponents. And it worked; the provision stayed in the National Energy Strategy sent to Congress.

Much credit goes to the first Bush White House as issues like PUHCA Reform are complicated, and it really helped that they sent a detailed proposal to Congress for its consideration via the committee process of "regular order" and the administration's proposal being introduced "by request."

During our congressional advocacy effort, I remember promoting the virtues of this legislation by telling Republican members of Congress that this proposal would let the market work, and for the Democrats, the message was that this would let competition work. It's all in the eyes of the beholder!

I recall visiting with senior Congressman Joe Barton from Houston and telling him that it was time for Texas to get out of its ERCOT in-state regulatory ghetto. It was to be a prophetic message!

Years later, the Electric Reliability Council of Texas (ERCOT), the grid operator for roughly ninety percent of Texas's electric load, set another record in 2020 for peak electricity demand in the summer season: 75.2 gigawatts. This occurred even as overall US summer electricity demand was expected to fall to the lowest level since 2009, according to projections published by the Energy Information Administration. In the summer of 2024, the combination of heat domes and Hurricane Beryl left the Houston area without power for thousands of its CenterPoint customers.

Earlier, in February 2021, an unanticipated deep freeze paralyzed Texas, and ERCOT came minutes away from collapse as the state energy infrastructure had not been winterized. There were companies marketing electricity they did not own beforehand, essentially speculating at high risk.

I was to write to Speaker Nancy Pelosi's energy/environmental staff director in 2021, including this Electricity Chapter, to make it clear that the 1992 Energy Policy Act Title VII (PUHCA) was a real consumer success story, creating the independent power industry leading to natural gas, wind and solar technology with public utility commission approved for power purchase agreements as state renewable portfolio standards kicked in. The customer no longer took risks as their distribution utility paid for energy delivered. I pointed out that before, it was essentially coal and nuclear, plus hydro with the customer taking all the construction risk, and there was plenty.

At the time, ENRON had been trying to convince Congress to deregulate the retail electricity market, and we convinced Congress not to; rather, we opened up the wholesale market. However, ENRON and other forces convinced states like Texas and California to open up retail years later and essentially experiment. It was state deregulation that prompted the California 2000–2001 disaster (the Power Exchange).

PUHCA Reform was a big deal, but it was about opening federal energy policy. The largest hearing room in the Senate is in the Hart Senate Office Building. The Senate Energy hearings were held in that room, and it was packed, and I was there! I would have to say that the Senate Energy Chairman, Senator J. Bennet Johnson from Louisiana, was the top congressional leader on this effort. I remember sitting in his office with other members of our team, and the Senator pointed out that with the passage of PUHCA Reform, we were going to sell a lot of natural gas in this country, and he was right!

I would tell members of Congress that utilities had ignored conservation because most of the generation was in their inventory; and the goal was to maximize its sale. But now their behavior would change as they would buy just enough electricity to meet the needs of their customers. And sure enough, electricity conservation became a major accomplishment twenty years later.

When Congress finally completed and enacted the Energy Policy Act of 1992, the Electricity Title VII of the electricity bill was based on our coalition working with both the White House and the Department of Energy and the FERC, and of course with congressional staff. We concentrated on evaluating the best way to: (1) advance a restructured wholesale (federal-regulated) electricity power market; (2) allowing independent power producers to compete to supply electricity to utilities; and (3) also have transmission access to the utility grid.

It should be noted that Nuclear Licensing Reform was another title in this 1992 legislation, and I remember vividly telling nuclear executives that we would be seeing nuclear IPPs in the future. They did not believe me, but eventually there were many, all existing facilities, and with the global climate challenge, now they were in the "Clean Energy Club," and governors/and state PUCs were asking them to keep active versus the earlier pre-global climate shutdown chorus.

Interestingly, at the same time we were finishing up the passage of this energy legislation in 1992, I was chairing the US Infrastructure Investment Commission, and our recommendations, after many hearings, focused on the need for credit enhancement to support private investment, the need for the disciplines of project finance, and a national infrastructure corporation to provide this credit enhancement and project finance expertise to state and regional infrastructure projects.

Ironically, in one of the great paradoxes, the IPP industry launched the project finance industry in the United States.

In 1992, I was invited by Secretary of Energy Admiral James Watkins to witness President George H. W. Bush sign the 1992 Energy Policy Act, which included the PUHCA Reform as Title VII (Electricity). The October ceremony was to be in Louisiana, so Bill Berry, CEO of Dominion Resources (Virginia Power), charted a private jet, and we invited the EEI President Tom Kuhn and ANEC President Ed Davis as well. It was a great day!

In 1996, the Federal Energy Regulatory Commission (FERC) issued what would become one of its most famous orders. Order 888 required utilities to open their transmission lines to competitors per the 1992 legislation. But utilities fought this for years, particularly for new transmission, a forerunner of challenges to come for renewable energy in the years to come.

On average, retail electricity prices in the United States changed little from 6.57 cents per kWh in 1990 to 6.81 cents per kWh ten years later in 2000, reflecting the impact of the competitive independent power sector now building nearly all the new power plants (natural gas initially).

In 2005, there was a jump to 8.14 cents per kWh in tandem with the passage of the Energy Policy Act of 2005, which launched the rebuilding of the transmission grid after the Northeast power blackout. Ten years later, in 2015 prices plateaued at 10.28 cents per kw/hr).

The 2005 Energy Policy Act allowed FERC to provide incentives to independent transmission companies (Transcos) in their rates of return. Utilities, as a compromise, were allowed to own independent Transcos. Transcos, by definition could not own generation or distribution in the traditional generation, transmission, distribution scheme.

It was August 8, 2005, when President George W. Bush signed the 2005 Energy Policy Act, the sequel to the 1992 Act, not only repealing PUHCA entirely but also enacting new national electric reliability and transmission investment incentive provisions (Title XII) at the FERC.

I was a frequent participant in various electric policy roundtables leading to the passage of these provisions, which launched the independent transmission (Transco) business with companies such as Clean Line, run initially by family friend Michael

Skelly, Energy Capital Partners, and LS Power to name a few, not counting the various utility-sponsored joint Transco ventures.

But Michael Skelly, after launching a half dozen major renewable energy-based transmission projects, finally gave up due to state politics and NIMBY opposition, and sold his projects in 2018. It was disappointing.

Unfortunately, the Department of Energy had performed miserably in assisting Transco permitting issues under Presidents Clinton, Bush, and Obama, so we would see what Trump Secretary of Energy Rick Perry could do. His track record as Texas Governor was exemplary in the buildout, under ERCOT, of a large-scale transmission network for wind power.

Mike Gent was a good friend and ERCOT Board member and supported this buildout. Mike and I coordinated during my years at USC (2000–2004) after he had retired as CEO from the New Jersey-based North American Electric Reliability Corporation (NERC), which was the guardian of our nation's electric grid and headquartered in Princeton. We both were living in San Diego.

In early January 2017, the East Coast of the United States was hit by one of the coldest storms in history. Yet the region's electric grid known as the PJM stretching from Maryland to Illinois weathered the storm. For example, the New York regional grid had 38,777 megawatts of power generation capacity—more than enough to handle the anticipated peak demand of 24,340 megawatts on that Friday, January 5.

But Secretary Perry was surrounded by the Trump White House chaos, and his experience in Texas could not to be duplicated at the federal level. President Trump could not understand that coal-fired plants were being shut down despite his presidential orations.

In summary, my firm represented those investor-owned utilities that wanted to open the wholesale power markets to competition, new technology, and project finance expertise. They wanted to open the "G" in the traditional GTD utility structure; and the "G" made up roughly seventy-five percent of a utility's cost structure.

Invariably, each state had three to six or so major electric utilities, and they had both urban and rural customers. Samuel Insull had already "consolidated" the electric utility industry, and his monopoly led to the passage of the 1935 Public Utility Holding Company Act to facilitate regulation of electric utilities by either limiting their operations to a single state and thus subjecting them to effective state regulation or forcing divestitures so that each became a single integrated system serving a limited geographic area.

Another purpose of PUHCA was to ensure that utility companies engaged in regulated businesses did not engage in unregulated businesses. The compromise there was to allow utility holding companies to own separate generation assets. In 2023, after some thirty years of this, utility holding companies sold off those unregulated assets—primarily renewable—to independent power producers in what was becoming a very competitive market. Additionally, investment in the utility grid had become the priority in meeting the energy transition need.

When Congress finally completed and enacted the Energy Policy Act of 1992, the Electricity Title VII of the electricity bill had been heavily influenced by our coalition, which concentrated on evaluating the best way to advance a restructured electricity market. There were two pivotal "PUHCA Reform" provisions:

1. Henceforth, an exempt wholesale generator, or EWG class was established with the added proviso that to be a US-owned power generator, you did not have to be a regulated utility. This action launched the independent power industry.
2. The Federal Energy Regulatory Commission (FERC) was instructed to ensure transmission access for this new power generation to the electrical grid.

I was very pleased and proud! Our newly launched independent power industry initially focused on natural gas-fired, combined cycle plants and then utility-scale renewable energy power plants. Virtually all power plants built in the United States since the 1992 passage of PUHCA Reform have been independent power plants, including natural gas and renewables.

Importantly and to repeat, these plants and their utility issued power purchase agreements were not in the utility's rate base, the economic engine traditionally for utilities. And, as already noted, generation made up roughly seventy-five percent of a utility's cost structure, and distribution (connections and local transmission—state regulated) was now their principal line of business.

Since the 1992 passage of PUHCA Reform, the independent energy industry has grown dramatically. By 2002, ten years following the passage, independent producers operated roughly one-third of the nation's power plants; and in 2014, virtually all power plants in the United States were operated by independent producers.

Electric utilities, as noted, are now distribution utilities; before 1992 they owned the generation (nuclear cost overruns and coal) as well, and so, conservation was not on their agenda. The more kilowatts they could sell, the better. Today, they buy only the amount of electricity they need. As a result, conservation has been enhanced and consumption has been greatly reduced. Consequently, utility power purchase agreements (PPAs) are no longer plentiful as the transition from coal to natural gas and renewables has run its course.

And electricity prices for the customer because of this competition, new technology, and project finance expertise have been relatively stable. It is a great story!

Independent power producers built their market share by developing power plants for less than the utilities could. Utilities actually never built anything as they outsourced all design and construction while retaining ownership. As a result, their customers took all the risk for the outside contractors' mistakes (nuclear!). When state utility commissions opened development to authentic competition, IPPs bid intensively against one another and against the local utility. The result was consistent: the IPPs came in far below the utilities for the same increment of capacity.

The IPPs put all types of fuel to use, including renewable energy sources, especially favoring the cleanest and most efficient form of thermal electric conversion: combined cycle combustion turbines (CCCTs) fired with natural gas. Much of this trend was state-inspired, particularly as over thirty states adopted renewable portfolio standards (RPS) that started at maybe ten percent in the early 2000s but are now twenty percent;

in California the goal is fifty percent, and the utilities issue their power request procurements to the IPP industry accordingly in most states, but not all.

When Congress opened the wholesale power market to competition in 1992 with the National Energy Policy Act (Title VII, Electricity, PUHCA Reform), it allowed independent power producers (Exempt Wholesale Generators) to compete in the FERC regulated wholesale power market for the sale of electricity to utilities.

As noted earlier, there were no instructions to state regulatory powers over their retail distribution powers. The states should have stayed with their status quo. However, they were worried that their existing utility-owned generation inventory would become stranded assets in the competition with the lower-cost IPP plants to come.

So instead, many went astray! New Hampshire launched a pilot program allowing retail direct access competition, as did Arizona, California, Massachusetts, Pennsylvania, and Rhode Island. Enron, headquartered in Houston, Texas, was to be the champion of this new electricity trading market; and unregulated utility subsidiaries opened trading floors in Houston as well.

We (our coalition) had gone to Senate Banking Chairman Senator Phil Gramm from Texas in 1992 to alert him to this new energy trading market that was essentially unregulated as neither the FERC nor the CFTC had direct jurisdiction over this emerging market. By coincidence, the Senator's wife was on the Enron Board! In summary, they did not take any action in the Banking Committee at that time. Ten years later, we had the ENRON debacle as a result.

In 2018, it was like being back in the Enron days, and the FERC needed a wakeup call when I read that two Ex-JPMorgan traders had lost millions on bets in the power market that year. Their strategy depended on certain parts of America's largest electric grid being congested, driving up power prices. But there was no congestion, so their betting portfolio, valued at more than $150 million, cratered. Their firm, Green Hat, based in Houston, had bought transmission rights hedges in a market administered by PJM Interconnection LLC, which oversees the wholesale electric grid from Chicago to Washington.

This energy trading sector, as I noted to Phil Gramm, never had the oversight platform established that was needed back in the '90s. And a huge multi-billion-dollar natural gas trade fiasco occurred during the 2021 Texas ERCOT freeze that February, when the Lone Star State's energy freedom strategy (actually a version of Russian roulette) collapsed.

Phil Gramm's July 15, 2021, op-ed in the Opinion section of the *Wall Street Journal* appeared just after the Biden White House had announced its omnibus (and excessive) regulatory reform executive order with seventy-two different agency action items. I was surprised to read that former Texas conservative Senator Gramm, with whom I had meetings with, was indicating that the deregulation of the 1970s—which he supported—allowed the US economy to expand.

For once, I agreed with Phil. Funny, but in 2024, energy traders were back at it, making huge energy bets and being highly compensated. Memories are short at these trading desks!

The word freedom is big in Texas, but Congressman Barton should have remembered my energy ghetto phrase back in 1992, as he was later the House Energy and Commerce Committee chairman, and should have transitioned ERCOT into a neighboring regional transmission coordinator.

As I pointed out, in the aftermath of the 1992 Act, several states and their utilities panicked on the topic of stranded assets. California was by far the worst, but New York, Texas, and others made mistakes.

I can remember flying to California with my client Harkins Cunningham law firm team to meet with PG&E in San Francisco to help them with their strategy development. We suggested they not be forced to buy short-term on the state-planned exchange in Pasadena; rather, they should have long term contracts.

But they made their 1996 deal with the legislature on stranded assets and got stuck with that power exchange (same-day trading) that was the trade-off that nearly bankrupted both major utilities amidst the Enron market manipulations.

These actions at the state level, as I said, were primarily a reaction to utility concerns regarding these so-called stranded assets; that is, their traditional rate-based plants would no longer be economically viable in the face of a barrage of new combined cycle gas turbine plants.

Compromises were made regarding stranded asset relief in rates, direct access by consumers, and this new power exchange (mandatory utility day-to-day purchasing of electricity supply, no long-term contracts) in California that hemorrhaged in the years immediately following the 1996 passage of the "Golden State" electricity deregulation measure.

PG&E actually entered into bankruptcy in 2001 and in 2004 emerged with the judge overseeing Pacific Gas & Electric Co.'s bankruptcy approving the fees of lawyers and consultants working on the three-year case. The tally: Approximately $450 million, making it one of the most expensive bankruptcies in state history.

Several San Francisco Bay Area law firms (not experts in energy) earned millions working for PG&E or other interested parties on the 2001 bankruptcy. In early 2019, PG&E once again declared bankruptcy due to the calamitous forest fires of 2017 and 2018, and once again these law firms benefited. "When will they ever learn," as the famous 1960s song by Peter, Paul and Mary went.

As I said, we had exhorted the California utilities to make sure they could buy long-term power purchase contracts; but that was lost in the din. The new Power Exchange was approved nonetheless as a pilot and built in Pasadena. In one of the remedial actions taken a few years later, the Exchange was shuttered, and utilities could sign long-term contracts; but not before the carnage began, led by ENRON.

Inexperience and failure of state regulators to fully anticipate the ramifications of the state's new spot market system for power purchases resulted in the opportunity for electricity trading floors like ENRON to game the system and hold back on releasing generation until supply tightened and they could increase prices. By the time state regulators recognized the significance of the power exchange problem, the utilities and states were nearly bankrupted by having to pay inflated prices for generation.

The California electricity crisis of the millennium years 2000 and 2001 was a situation in which the state faced a shortage of electricity supply caused by market manipulations, illegal shutdowns of pipelines by the Texas energy consortium Enron, and capped retail electricity prices. The state suffered, and the economic fallout greatly harmed Governor Gray Davis's standing; as a result, he was recalled.

A false demand supply gap was created by energy companies, mainly Enron, to create an artificial shortage. I remember when energy traders took power plants offline for maintenance during days of peak demand to increase the price. Traders were able to sell power at premium prices, sometimes up to a factor of twenty times its normal value.

The crisis cost the California economy between US $40 and $45 billion. And it was all for naught! They should have done this years ago and, nothing; but in their experimental naiveté, the progressive regulators brought the state to its knees. There were many experts in California who knew little about the 1992 Energy Policy Act, and they didn't listen to those who did!

I was at USC then beginning in late 1999, and we organized two well-attended conferences in 2000 on the situation, one on campus at the USC Town Hall and the other at San Francisco's City Hall. And remember, this was during the year 2000 Y2K fiasco and the Gore/Bush presidential election/Florida recount/Supreme Court decision. It was a terrible start to the Millennium indeed.

In 2001, Southern California Edison CEO John Bryson offered to sell its wholesale transmission system to the State of California to stave off bankruptcy in the disastrous marketplace. I had helped Trans Elect get launched and remember going to Sacramento to tell state legislators that we were prepared to buy the Edison transmission system rather than the state having to make that purchase.

It was a real eye opener and an early infrastructure asset class investment opportunity. Legislators were amazed that the private sector was so interested! John Bryson, who never understood PUHCA Reform, after I had explained it to him in 1992, withdrew his transmission offer. John made a huge salary for many years and was typical of the new utility holding company CEOs who seemed motivated solely to make more money in this new environment.

Despite this disaster, many states decided to move forward on their own to implement a competitive retail access electricity market. This resulted in a patchwork of states with deregulated retail open access/direct access markets operating next to states that did not. Eventually, twenty-five out of fifty states had some measure of open access/direct access.

Ironically, Enron was to declare bankruptcy in 2001 amidst the chaos it had initiated. And some history: in medieval Italy, when a merchant did not pay his debts, the bench at which he conducted business was smashed to force him to stop trading. The word bankrupt derives from banco-rotto, meaning broken bench. It seemed to fit!

So, Enron, along with California, was at best a broken bench! Under Italy's bankruptcy laws until 2006, debtors lost their right to vote and had their mail read by liquidators. Not a bad idea! In early 2019, I was to read and view the photo of former ENRON CEO Jeff Skilling being released from prison after serving twelve years for market manipulation.

Since 1992, US electric utility companies in this industry have changed their business model; numerous mergers have occurred, and utility holding companies have both regulated and unregulated subsidiaries, such as independent transmission companies.

Combined, the US electric industry is the largest industry in the world. However, the largest electric utility in the world is the State Grid Corporation of China. It is state-owned and transmits and distributes power in China and in overseas markets, with annual revenues of almost $330 billion per year.

As noted, retail distribution in the United States remains regulated by state commissions, while wholesale generation and transmission are overseen by the Federal Energy Regulatory Commission (FERC). In the states that have had partial deregulation, many incumbent utility subsidiaries (unregulated) own and operate nonregulated generating companies. In fact, some utility holding companies get more than half of their profits from the nonregulated side of their business.

Virtually every US power plant built since 1992 (primarily clean natural gas), including renewable energy, has been constructed by an IPP, and major transmission projects have been carried out by independent Transco's since 2005. Most of these plants are not in the utility rate base, nor are the power purchase agreements that the utilities sign.

Utilities, unregulated subsidiaries, did invest in IPPs early on, but the competition was becoming an economic threat, and they were to sell off their plants to the IIP firms in the 2020s.

The distribution utility has become the economic "rate base" orphan, and there is an opportunity for large-scale infrastructure transactions. Additionally, the typical distribution utility has significant infrastructure upgrade requirements.

Some of these distribution utilities desire more generation to be owned in their rate base now and are working with their state commissions to have both power purchase agreements (risk transfer) and new (design-build) owned generation assets in the rate base. In traditionally regulated states, particularly in the South, utilities still commission the construction of generating units by outside construction firms; they recover their costs as the facilities are under construction, and recover their investment, and earn a return on it after the plant has attained commercial operation.

Unfortunately, the two major nuclear plants that the Southern and Scana utilities commissioned with Westinghouse (now in bankruptcy and owned by Toshiba and being bought in 2018 by Brookfield Partners in Canada) were originally in the customer rate base category; but recently the utilities have agreed that their shareholders would also be liable as well for the huge cost/budget overruns.

The public, generally speaking, does not understand the utility regulation outlined here:

1. Interstate sales of electricity on the wholesale power market and by public utilities (e.g., investor-owned utilities, power marketers, independent power producers, and non-exempt electric cooperatives) are subject to regulation by the Federal Energy Regulatory Commission (FERC).
2. Power marketing became a huge industry for a while, with many utilities setting up unregulated trading floors in Houston competing with Enron. As I said earlier, FERC was not ready nor empowered to adequately supervise this new market, and there were many abuses.
3. FERC also regulates interstate transmission service provided by transmission owning public utilities. In addition to regulating transactions in interstate commerce, FERC licenses hydroelectric facilities on navigable waterways.

4. Licensing the construction and operation of nuclear power plants, safety, and nuclear waste disposal management is under the jurisdiction of the Nuclear Regulatory Commission and
5. Retail sales and unbundled distribution services provided by investor-owned utilities are subject to State regulation. In some states, municipal utilities and electric cooperative rates are also subject to State regulation.

That is why the independent power industry has been such a positive addition, bringing risk transfer, new technology, conservation, new investment, and project finance discipline to the electric energy marketplace. The consumer has benefited in many ways. I was very proud of our 1992 accomplishment.

Many of my utility clients had natural gas distribution utility subsidiaries, and so, I was actively engaged in advising them on the gas-related policy actions that were taken just as the Department of Energy was being established in 1978.

In November 1978, at the peak of the natural gas supply shortages, Congress enacted legislation known as the Natural Gas Policy Act (NGPA), as part of broader legislation known as the National Energy Act (NEA). The price controls that had been put in place to protect consumers from potential monopoly pricing were now hurting consumers in the form of natural gas shortages, particularly in the northern tier states during frigid weather.

The federal government sought through the NGPA to revise the federal regulation of the sale of natural gas. Essentially, this act had three main goals: creating a single national natural gas market, balancing supply and demand, and allowing market forces to establish the wellhead price of natural gas.

Later in 1985, FERC issued Order No. 436, which altered how interstate pipelines were regulated. This order established a voluntary framework under which interstate pipelines could act solely as transporters of natural gas, rather than as natural gas merchants.

Three years later, Congress passed the Natural Gas Wellhead Decontrol Act (NGWDA) in 1989, which completed deregulation of wellhead prices.

In 1992, FERC Order No. 636 completed the final steps toward unbundling the natural gas supply industry by making pipeline unbundling a requirement. The order stated that pipelines must separate their transportation and sales services so that all pipeline customers have a choice in selecting their gas sales, transportation, quantity, and storage services from any provider.

Of course, that was the same year as the passage of the Energy Policy Act that embraced natural gas generation with its combined cycle turbines (we called them "cookie cutters") that could be easily assembled into large-scale 900-megawatt power plants.

The industry took off! General Electric made a fortune supplying turbines to the new independent power industry, per my advice to their Vice Chairman.

Being recognized widely for my 1992 PUHCA electric energy reform accomplishment, in 1995 I was contacted by Mr. Millard Carr, Director of Energy Procurement in the Office of the Assistant Secretary of Defense for Economic Security.

As it turned out, Millard coordinated all three services in their efforts to enable the Department of Defense to enjoy the full benefit of this dynamic, competitive wholesale power market. I attended several meetings of this group.

As noted in other chapters, after my own firm The Flanagan Consulting Group was launched in 1981, electric and gas utilities retained us for our experience in the emerging field of regulatory reform, and Millard sought similar input. Later, we formed a coalition to support the needed reforms.

We recommended that a new Government Service Enterprise (GSE) be established called the Forrestal Corp. to serve as the energy procurement/trading arm of the Pentagon for all three services. Legislation was introduced noting my observation that the then Department of Energy building had originally been constructed in 1970 for the Department of Defense (Corps of Engineers) and thus christened after its first secretary, James Forrestal. Because of our Forrestal Corp. coalition efforts, legislation establishing the Forrestal Corporation was introduced in the Congress.

About that time, I was asked to meet with Defense Department Deputy Under-Secretary. Paul Kaminski in March 1995 on this energy topic. At that spring meeting, he asked me to join the Department as the Principal Deputy Under Secretary of Defense for Industrial Affairs and Installations. I accepted and was asked to stand by until Mr. Kaminski returned from a spring vacation.

During that lull, there was a speed bump as Vice President Gore had his own candidate, John Goodman, whose wife, Sherri Goodman, was already serving as Deputy Under-Secretary for Environmental Security at the Pentagon. A proverbial Mexican standoff ensued as my supporters, particularly Senator John Warner and Navy Secretary John Dalton, were committed. However, I was concerned that we needed to have the Forrestal Corporation proposal in the upcoming DoD Authorization request for FY 1997.

So, I indicated in the interest of timing and much to my disappointment, that John Goodman should take the position; and my firm be retained by the Department of Defense to analyze their energy procurement profile and to suggest modernization steps to take advantage of our 1992 work in opening the wholesale energy power market.

The Defense Department was paying top dollar for energy supply at their domestic bases, and the Forrestal Corp. would allow them "to shop around" in this new electricity trading market. We designed the concept for budget authorization purposes, but the timing was off as the Defense authorization request had already been submitted. Timing is everything, and the appointment delay came at a cost. If the Forrestal Corporation had been established in FY 1997, it would have been very effective in meeting today's Defense renewable and alternative energy goals.

I worked closely with Millard Carr, who ran the energy desk for the Office of the Assistant Secretary of Defense for Economic Security. Millard had contacted me after the passage of PUHCA Reform, and I enjoyed reading an article he had written in 1996 about the opportunities for the Pentagon with this new competition in the electric power sector, making the following points:

1. The Department of Defense (DOD) has responded to the electric utility deregulation process by trying to achieve consensus on what the Department expects and wants.

2. Historically, the Defense agencies' relations with public utilities had often been adversarial.
3. The agencies' objective in rate negotiations had been equity: rates that reflected the true cost of service. Today's changing circumstances demand:

He wanted a new relationship with power suppliers that would provide the ability to take advantage of competition for supply and the economic benefits that result from it, as well as reducing utility costs, increasing energy use efficiency, and improving the power infrastructure.

Our Forrestal Corporation concept would have been perfect for that mission. Today, in the 2020s with the AI/Data Center power expansion need, it would be even more timely. The Navy, along with the other services, should dust off the Defense Forrestal concept and put together a proposal for a government-sponsored enterprise that will be able to recruit top-flight energy marketing and project finance expertise to accomplish their renewable energy goals.

The Navy did create a renewable energy office, and I met with them in 2016 (retired Admiral Dennis McGinn). I asked where they got their people to perform these project finance deals (thinking about the Forrestal concept). The Admiral explained that they outsourced it to Booz Allen Hamilton Inc., a US management consulting firm, sometimes referred to as a "government-services company," headquartered in McLean, Virginia.

Here is another story: Public Service Electric and Gas Company (PSEG) in New Jersey was one of our coalition companies, and Joe Kelliher represented them and attended our meetings. A few years later, in 1994, the GOP took the majority in the House (Newt Gingrich), and Congressman Tom Bliley of Richmond, Virginia, became chairman of the House Energy and Commerce Committee. Tom and I were good friends, and his chief of staff asked for my staff recommendations.

I enthusiastically recommended Joe Kelliher. Joe was hired, and the rest is history. Joe did some great work both in Congress and at the Department of Energy, including the 2005 Energy Policy Act (I helped him with transmission). After chairing the Federal Energy Regulatory Commission (FERC), he joined NextEra as their Federal Counsel; what a career!

And around 1993–4, engineering professors at the University of West Virginia contacted me about the new legislation and what it meant for their coal-based economy and curriculum. Twice I visited with them on their campus and gave lectures to their engineering school faculty.

I emphasized that the days of state utility commissions mandating coal-fired plants were over and that the independent power industry would become the dominant force in replacing coal with natural gas as it was cheaper, cleaner, and easier to build the plants themselves.

My advice was for that engineering school to be the academic home (project finance, gas, and clean coal technology) of the new independent power industry. They were polite, but this was West Virginia!

In a May 2019 CBS TV News feature story, Eric Ritchie, a former coal miner from West Virginia whose family had worked in coal for generations, successfully switched to a new career in wind energy. I was impressed with his comments; as I watched the show, he went on to say that West Virginia has everything it needs to be a competitor to some of the Midwest states that are going largely renewable. He had spent nine years looking through the windshield of a piece of underground mining equipment and traded it in for this, he said, scanning the 360-degree views of rolling West Virginia hills. I think he made a pretty good trade.

This is what I was telling the University of West Virginia engineering school faculty after we had passed Title VII Electricity in the 1992 Energy Policy Act; when they invited me out to their Morgantown campus on those two occasions to lecture on the future of the electric utility industry. But the state political establishment would have none of it. I was introduced to some of that leadership and got the cold shoulder—coal was king.

Still, the professors, as I said, should have focused on project finance and natural gas technology for power plants, as our coalition's 1992 legislation created the independent power industry.

It had been twenty-seven years since 1992 when Eric Ritchie figured it out, and he heard from a friend about a job opening at Invenergy LLC, a Chicago-based energy company. They had a wind farm job opening in central West Virginia. Ritchie was skeptical at first, noting in the TV interview that for much of coal country, alternative energy is almost a bad word, and many of his coal miner friends gave him a hard time—though he added it wasn't long before some of them were calling him up to ask for a job.

Well, it had only been about thirty years but finally, the professors at West Virginia University might have the political support to focus on teaching project finance and clean energy technology.

Coal mining jobs have declined by 88 percent since their heyday, and today only about 14,000 still work in West Virginia's mines. Automation and more efficient mining practices have been a factor behind the change. But since our 1992 PUHCA Reform (electricity wholesale market deregulation), most utilities—prodded by their state commissions—have issued power purchase procurements almost exclusively for competing clean energy sources, particularly natural gas initially and then renewable energy under state political/regulatory policy. This has led to near-record coal plant closures in recent years.

I wish the professors could have followed my 1993 advice as, from 2011 to 2016, roughly 350 coal-fired generating units shut down across the United States, ranging from small units at factories to huge power plants, according to the Energy Information Administration. And natural gas plants replaced them—some were retrofits from coal fired to gas fired—along with renewable energy, all developed by independent power producers.

Now in December 2020, I was to read that mayors from the Appalachia region want the Biden administration to embrace their proposals for billions of dollars of spending, with a heavy emphasis on clean energy projects, as a way to reinvent the region as coal declines.

Finally, to my surprise, on June 15, 2020, the US Supreme Court removed a legal barrier to the construction of an $8 billion pipeline that would deliver natural gas from

West Virginia to the East Coast, ruling that the project could run under a major hiking trail.

The court, in a 7–2 opinion, overturned a lower-court ruling that found the US Forest Service didn't have the authority to grant a special-use permit that allowed developers of the Atlantic Coast Pipeline to construct an underground segment beneath a section of the Appalachian National Scenic Trail in Virginia.

Environmentalists had argued that the pipeline's path could harm ecologically important national forests, with threats of soil erosion and damage to wildlife habitat.

Despite the court ruling, delays continued, and Dominion Energy, along with Duke, gave up and the former selling their entire natural gas subsidiary to Berkshire Hathaway. Building pipelines in the United States was becoming a challenge.

In the late 1990s, my Harkins Cunningham law firm team was asked to come up to Niagara Mohawk's office in upstate New York to advise them on their restructuring. The cab driver asked if we were there to buy the company. It was too soon!

But in 2015, I set out to bring this combination of distribution utilities and pension/infrastructure funds to fruition. With power generation now primarily an independent power enterprise and transmission heading in a similar direction, the distribution companies had an opportunity to become a technology platform leveraging their proximity to the customer.

It may be time to unite pension funds with infrastructure allocations to become new owners of distribution utility infrastructure assets and provide the utilities with the capital to reinvent themselves as technology leaders in the clean energy and energy conservation sectors. Warren Buffett did this years back, and it worked well (Mid-American). They have been major investors in all sectors of energy generation, and I was hopeful that this would continue with transmission at both the wholesale and retail levels.

FERC had asserted jurisdiction over independent transmission (Transco) siting, from the states, but unfortunately, the courts intervened, making it very difficult for Michael Skelly and his Clean Line Energy colleagues to obtain state transmission siting approval due to unfair and anti-consumer local opposition. Pipelines and transmission lines now faced that same "Not in My Back Yard" (NIMBY) opposition. Michael finally sold his company in frustration, I would think.

As to clean energy and global climate concerns, state and local renewable portfolio standards were driving the energy markets and utility decisions to go clean. Thirty states had adopted a mandatory renewable or clean energy standard for their electricity sectors. Fourteen of them had plans in place to transition to 100 percent renewable or zero-emissions energy.

Dozens of utility companies pledged to decarbonize their electricity in the coming decades, and 40 percent of American households are now served by utilities that have pledged to completely decarbonize by 2050. State legislatures and public utility commissions have been the primary drivers of this trend. The US Department of Energy continues to disappoint, whether on the new technology topic or strategic leadership, leaving consumers to wonder about the so-called energy transition. EV sales and charging stations seem lost at sea in 2024.

But the IPP industry performs, and while initially focused on combined cycle gas turbine plants, IPPs, as pointed out, are now the developers of most renewable wind and solar generation as well in the wholesale power market.

I am personally very proud that under the 1992 Energy Policy Act, the independent energy industry grew so dramatically. Reading through some of my 1992 correspondence for this book, I came across a memo to Federal Reserve Governor Larry Lindsay who, as noted in the preceding tax reform chapter, I had helped get nominated and confirmed.

In my note, I referenced then Treasury Secretary Nick Brady and noted the importance of the investment tax credit (ITC) and the production tax credit (PTC), even then, to support the development of renewable energy.

Another facet of the IPP movement has been the introduction of the disciplines of project finance to the US infrastructure marketplace. While infrastructure fund focus during the last ten years has been on the energy sector, more and more public-private partnerships are now being launched in a variety of infrastructure sectors, and project finance is the core discipline.

In 1992, we launched IPPs, and in late 1993, the phrase PPPs or public-private partnerships was introduced. Now, the PPP is ubiquitous and project finance has been key for both IPPs and PPPs.

In retrospect, our Infrastructure Investment Commission recommendations in 1993, regarding the need for project finance in the United States, have been greatly assisted by this new IPP industry stemming from the 1992 Energy Policy Act's PUHCA Reform provision, passed by Congress a year earlier. At the time, I was pleasantly surprised to see the connection and was pleased to envision what progress was to come.

Independent power producers built their market share by developing power plants for less than the utilities could with their construction partners. When state utility commissions opened development to authentic competition, IPPs bid intensively against one another and against the local utility. The result was consistent: the IPPs came in far below the utilities for the same increment of capacity.

Plus, they took design/construction risks and were not compensated until the new generation was providing service. The utilities were not the builders themselves; they would outsource that process but would keep the risk. (Actually, utilities never built power plants themselves; they outsourced).

The IPPs put all types of fuel to use, including renewable energy sources, especially favoring the cleanest and most efficient form of thermal electric conversion: combined cycle combustion turbines (CCCTs) fired with natural gas.

In a similar vein, IPPs were responsible for commercializing wind and solar energy and making it what it is today: the leading new source of power generation in the world. The environmental community owes this IPP sector a major "thank you."

The IPPs' unique role is to accept the development, permitting, financing, and operational risks of power generation. By taking these risks, IPPs—funded by private investment dollars—relieve utility ratepayers of assuming them. The result has been that the cost of the electric power itself has declined by 35 percent because of the 1992 Energy Policy Act, of which I am very proud today.

A number of large regulated electric utilities had established unregulated power generation subsidiaries competing in the wholesale power market beginning in early 1993. This was very successful for some thirty years, but competive pressure in the renewable energy market convinced some of these regulated utilities to sell off their unregulated subsidiaries in 2023.

Natural gas accounted for nearly 32 percent of US power generation in 2017, up from about 22 percent a decade earlier, according to federal data. Coal was now 30 percent, after falling from 49 percent over the same time span. Nuclear accounted for 20 percent in 2017, and wind and solar combined totaled 8 percent, rising from less than 1 percent a decade ago.

A core reason was the governors and state legislators passing laws regarding their renewable portfolio standards, starting out at maybe 10 percent but escalating every few years to 20–30 percent and even higher. It became a political competition; that is, we are the cleanest energy state, etc., in terms of global climate change.

In just some twenty years since the 1992 act, total installed wind capacity in the United States through the first quarter of 2014 was 61,327 MW. This translates into 15.5 million American homes-equivalent operating wind power capacities. Wind energy's percentage of new generating capacity installed from 2009 to 2013 was 31 percent, and there were 46,100 operating utility-scale wind turbines at the end of 2012.

Most of these wind farms, as well as the solar equivalents, were developed by independent power producers (IPPs) responding to utility requests for proposals urged on importantly by state renewable portfolio standards.

There were at least thirty-nine US states with operating utility-scale wind energy projects, and the wind industry average annual investment in new wind projects from 2009 to 2013 was $15 billion. There were some 50,000 wind-related jobs in the United States at the end of 2013, across fields such as development, siting, construction, transportation, manufacturing, operations, and services.

US renewable electricity had grown to 16.7 percent of total installed capacity and 13.8 percent of total power generation in 2015 in the United States, according to the National Renewable Energy Laboratory (NREL).

In the year 2015, renewable electricity accounted for 64 percent of the country's power capacity additions compared to 52 percent a year earlier. Total renewable power production went up by 2.4 percent, with solar electricity generation jumping 35.8 percent and wind production rising 5.1 percent.

Hydroelectric plants produced over 44 percent of total renewable electricity generation in 2015, and federal policy includes hydro as a renewable; however, California does not, as they want wind and solar to be developed, rather than hydro damming up the rivers.

Wind turbines generated a record 226 million megawatt-hours of electricity in 2016, the EIA data showed. This is about four times the amount of solar production and close to what hydropower generates in the United States.

Offshore wind, in US waters, has started, but it is of modest size and therefore expensive at almost 25 cents a kWh versus 10 cents in Europe. I was always told that the Pacific Coast would never have offshore wind power due to the depth of the water offshore. We shall see; but so far, that prediction has been holding, but there are designs floating around.

In mid-2018, the Energy Information Administration reported similar energy sector numbers for 2017 as the trends continued into the next decade; this energy transition was historic. By January 2020, the switch to renewable power was accelerating. Renewable power would be the fastest-growing source of electricity over the next three decades, accounting for 38 percent of generation by 2050, according to the US Energy Information Administration's Annual Energy Outlook released in January 2020. That was up from a forecast of 31 percent in the prior year's report, and it came as costs for solar and wind continued to decline.

Coal, meanwhile, would provide 13 percent of US power in 2050, down from 24 percent today, as power plants closed. Natural gas, currently the largest source of electricity at 37 percent, would be surpassed by renewables by 2045, according to the EIA. And it was the IPPs that were building this generation.

And infrastructure/pension funds were to invest billions in these new plants as infrastructure investments just as I had predicted back in the millennium year 2000 in a USC speech. I was very pleased to be retained in 2000 by General Atomics in San Diego to find a private sector outlet for their skilled staff of electrical engineers working on the Navy aircraft carrier maglev launches and recovery system discussed in a later chapter. I selected wind power, and we designed a very innovative medium voltage inverter for Clipper Wind in Santa Barbara (now owned by Platinum Equity Group in Los Angeles).

Clipper Wind had a contract with the Crown Estate in England, which I had not been familiar with at the time. However, in the summer of 2024, the Crown Estate (Royal family/Government Partnership) had become the owner of a vast offshore wind portfolio featured in press reports.

Energy efficiency has finally had a major impact on the growth of electricity consumption, confirming our arguments in 1992 that it would be good economic policy to separate ownership of generation from the distribution utility so that they would align directly with the customers' economic interests. No longer was the utility obliged to maximize sales from its inventory; now they just purchased (just-in-time delivery) exactly what they needed for its customers.

The utility now sells only the Kilowatt hours, the customer needs, not the Kilowatt hours the utility wanted to sell. I had fun explaining this to a young salesman for an energy efficiency company when he asked me to do a survey in a shopping center.

Also, the independent power industry introduced new technology ranging from natural gas combined cycle turbines to wind and solar farms, medium voltage inverters, direct current transmission, electric battery storage, etc.

The advent of the electric vehicle mesmerized the marketplace as we moved through 2020. There were many companies entering the EV charging market, and it reminded me of the railroad industry in the 1880s with their various gauges. But increasingly, it appeared the Tesla EV charging stations were becoming the standard. Elon Musk had another monopoly on his hands, yet he sold it off in 2024, laying off hundreds.

With all the talk in 2022 about investing in "the grid" for renewable energy, the US electrical distribution system was becoming less dependable. Large, sustained outages had occurred with increasing frequency in the United States over the past two decades, according to a Wall Street Journal review of federal data. In 2000, there were fewer than two dozen major disruptions. In 2020, the number surpassed 180, much of this due to major weather disturbances including forest fires.

Utility customers on average experienced just over eight hours of power interruptions in 2020, more than double the amount in 2013, when the government began tracking outage lengths. The data doesn't include 2021, but those numbers are certain to follow the trend after a freak freeze in Texas, a hurricane in New Orleans, wildfires in California, and a heat wave in the Pacific Northwest left millions in the dark for days.

The power system, that is the grid, was challenged just as millions of Americans were becoming more dependent on it—not just to light their homes but to work remotely, charge their cars, and cook their food—as more modern conveniences became electrified.

At the same time, the grid was undergoing the largest transformation in its history for good reasons, particularly the renaissance of independent power producers.

Several states have enacted mandates to eliminate carbon emissions from the grid in the coming decades, and the Biden administration has set a goal to do so by 2035.

The pace of change, hastened by market forces and long-term efforts to reduce carbon emissions, has raised concerns that power plants are being retired more quickly than they can be replaced, creating new strain on the grid at a time when other factors are converging to weaken it. A good example is the PG&E Diablo Canyon Power Plant's return to long-term service in California.

Much of the transmission system, which carries high-voltage electricity over long distances, was constructed just after the Second World War, with some lines built well before that. The distribution system, the network of smaller wires that takes electricity to homes and businesses, is also decades old and accounts for most of the outages.

Weather-related problems have driven much of the increase in large outages shown in federal data, topping 100 in 2020 for the first time since 2011. Scientists have tied some of the weather patterns, such as California's prolonged drought and wildfires, to climate change. These weather extremes are raising the costs of power network upgrades for utilities all over the country.

In the spring of 2022, US electric grid operators were warning that power-generating capacity was struggling to keep up with demand, which could lead to rolling blackouts during peak periods. For example, California's grid operator (Cal ISO) said that it anticipated a shortfall in supplies this summer, especially if extreme heat, wildfires, or delays in bringing new power sources online occurred. But with the heavy rains of 2023, they were back in business, for example, hydro.

Power grids were feeling the strain as the United States began this historic transition from conventional power plants fueled by coal, nuclear, and natural gas to cleaner forms of energy such as wind and solar power, which had their own challenges, including transmission infrastructure and supply chain/tariff issues.

Second thoughts were occurring as this energy transition was more complicated than the politicians had bargained for, be it wildfires in California or the Russian invasion of Ukraine, which set off a new global fuel supply remake.

Much of this naive cadence was driven by strident environmental interests, including Biden administration appointees ignoring the immense challenges in making such a historic transformation for what appeared to be near-term political points.

The grid depends on independent system operators (ISOs). An ISO is an organization formed at the direction or recommendation of the Federal Energy Regulatory Commission (FERC). In the areas where an ISO is established, it coordinates, controls, and monitors the operation of the electrical power system, usually within a single US state, but sometimes encompassing multiple states.

Like an RTO, the primary difference is that ISOs either do not meet the minimum requirements specified by FERC to hold the designation of RTO, or that the ISO has not petitioned FERC for the status. But the reality is they are interchangeable; they are the grid.

Electric utilities that are located within the United States and engage in interstate commerce fall under FERC authority. Not all utilities are members of ISOs. All utilities and ISOs, however, are responsible for meeting the compliance of a larger organization called the North American Electric Reliability Corporation (NERC), which overlays the entire FERC footprint and includes a Mexican utility and several Canadian utilities.

International reciprocity is commonplace, and rules or recommendations introduced by FERC are often are voluntarily accepted by NERC members outside of FERC's jurisdiction. Therefore, one Canadian province is a member of a US-based RTO, while two others function as an Electric System Operator (ESO), an organization essentially equal to a US-based ISO.

Within the United States, one ISO, and its participating utilities do not fall under FERC authority: The Electric Reliability Council of Texas (ERCOT). ERCOT does fall under the authority of NERC and operates a reliability function, separate from its market function, to comply with NERC requirements. It has had its problems during the 2022 winter freeze and the following summer power challenges as it does not connect to other utilities outside its state borders. Yes, in 1992, I told senior Texas congressman John Barton that his state was essentially going to be an electricity ghetto, and I was right unfortunately.

As of 2009, there were nine ISOs within North America: CAISO—California ISO, NYISO—New York ISO, Midcontinent Independent System Operator—Midcontinent ISO, ISO-NE—ISO New England, SPP—Southwest Power Pool, PJM—Pennsylvania New Jersey-Maryland Interconnection, AESO—Alberta Electric System Operator, and the Independent Electricity System Operator (IESO) Hydro One transmission grid for Ontario, Canada.

Today, seven of these grid operators, either independent system operators (ISOs) or RTOs, coordinate the power grid to ensure the reliable delivery of two-thirds of the electricity used in the United States to two-thirds of its population. Most are overseen by FERC. ISO/RTOs play an essential role in managing and enhancing all power flows, and they are the so-called grid.

In California, in 2019, 34 percent of energy consumed was renewable (primarily solar and wind), with natural gas and large hydro supplying most part supplying the difference. Starting in 2020, California became the first US state to require almost all new homes to draw some power from the sun, retreating somewhat in 2024.

Representing utilities led me to spend an enormous amount of time on the 1982 Nuclear Waste Policy Act and the 1992 Nuclear Licensing Reform measure included with PUHCA Reform in the 1992 Energy Policy Act. Both successful efforts were led by the American Nuclear Energy Council (ANEC), occupying two floors above a restaurant on the House of Representatives' side.

Under ANEC's leadership, first by Tom Kuhn (who went on to be the longtime president of the Edison Electric Institute), and later by Ed Davis, we were very effective interacting on a bipartisan basis with Senator J. Benet Johnston and Congressman John Dingell, chairmen of the Senate and House Energy committees respectively.

Later, Tom Kuhn assisted me in building of the US Navy Memorial complex as his Edison Electric Institute was to be our anchor tenant. Tom and I would often go over to Senator Bennett Johnston's house in McLean and play tennis. Bennett did a great job as Chairman of the Senate Energy and Natural Resources Committee, and we honored his leadership with a luncheon at the National Press Club where I presented a memento to him.

We used to explain to our nuclear clients in the 90s that they had a role to play in the clean air/global climate debate: that there would be nuclear IPPs. Many of them were US Navy nukes, and for the most part, they did not get it!

The one notable exception was Corbin A. McNeill, Jr., a fellow Annapolis/Naval Academy graduate who served as the President of Commonwealth Edison Company and later as a Co-Chief Executive Officer and Chairman of Exelon Corp. from October 10, 2000, to 2002. Corbin bought a number of nuclear plants at a discount for the unregulated side of their generation business.

In 1993, the nuclear operators were tired of the American Nuclear Energy Council (ANEC) and wanted their own trade association. They now have it in the Nuclear Energy Institute (NEI), widely acclaimed as the worst trade association in Washington, DC, yet with some highly paid executives. The NEI is actually run by the Institute of Nuclear Plant Operators (INPO) located in Atlanta, Georgia.

Senator Moynihan, who served on the Senate Environment and Public Works Committee that oversaw nuclear energy policy, told me that he was touring a New York state nuclear power plant in the late 1970s and was concerned by the general dress and lack of discipline/decorum of the plant employees. He returned to Washington, DC, and introduced legislation to create a government training academy for nuclear plant operators.

There was a great industry fear of this proposal, and a compromise reached to establish an industry-sponsored Institute, hence INPO. Every time we did a vote count, the nukes would record Senator Moynihan as an expected "no" when he was in fact a supporter. It annoyed me!

The one thing NEI was supposed to get done was the Yucca Mountain nuclear waste repository in Southern Nevada. In the 1980s, Senator Harry Reid was not opposed to the Yucca Mountain nuclear waste repository; yet his Senate colleague, Richard Bryan, was. The Nuclear Energy Institute, since its founding in the mid-1990s, managed to alienate many members of Congress, including Senator Harry Reid, who had become the Senate Majority Leader.

Nuclear power advocates yearned to be a "clean energy" source, but they have their back-end challenges in waste storage. Although with the 2016 retirement of Nevada's Senator Harry Reid, they hoped that this would allow the Yucca Mountain facility in Nevada to move forward. We would see, as nuclear power was deemed "clean energy" around 2020 amidst the challenges of global climate.

There are thirty-one countries operating nuclear power plants; only fourteen produce their own nuclear fuel, while the others purchase primarily from Russia, the United States, and Europe.

In early 1992, the French Nuclear attaché was impressed with our work and asked me to visit with Electricite de France CEO Remy Carle when I was going to be in Paris. I predicted to Mr. Carle that the US was soon to open the electricity wholesale power market and launch the independent power industry. Unfortunately, he did not believe me.

In a surprise, General Electric Co. Chief Executive Officer John Flannery abruptly stepped down on Monday, October 1, 2018, just over a year after taking the role, as the company warned it would fall short of its 2018 earnings guidance due to cash flow issues in its GE Power division and a write-down of $23 billion.

I will never forget attending a Business Roundtable reception around 1990–1 at the Willard Hotel in Washington, DC, when Larry Bossidy (then Vice Chairman of General Electric) sat down next to me in the bar area to order a drink. He asked what I was up to, and that led to a discussion of the recently announced White House Energy Strategy, including PUHCA Reform. In response to his question, I commented that, having won at the White House, I was confident we would be successful in Congress.

While they were timely regarding the natural gas/combined cycle IPP market in 1992, probably due to my alert, they later missed the renewable energy signals in the US electricity utility market a decade later.

Earlier in March 2018, in this new electric power grid market, General Electric (GE) announced a comprehensive energy storage platform that would deliver customized energy storage solutions for customers to address new challenges. They called it the Reservoir, which I liked.

The Reservoir, which already had a 20-megawatt, 80 megawatts-per-hour commitment, expanded GE's ten-year footprint in the energy storage space.

I was glad to read that Russell Stokes, president and CEO of GE Power, predicted that the energy landscape was undergoing an unprecedented paradigm shift, as the growth of renewables, decentralization of power, and digitization were creating both new challenges and opportunities in how power was generated, transmitted, and distributed. He pointed out that GE's Reservoir system would deliver the new type of energy system that customers were looking for to help manage electricity supply, and he was right, as energy storage investment was booming in 2024. It would be very interesting to watch how this Reservoir developed as General Electric commenced its historic downsizing strategy amidst the collapse of its power turbine business.

On April 18, 2024, the *Wall Street Journal* reported that GE was now a top stock market performer as it prepared to reorganize into three different companies, one being GE VERNOVA, which had been GE Power. The headline, "GE Power Spinoff to Be Supercharged," noted the growth in AI-related electricity demand

At the White House infrastructure Summit that I attended on September 9, 2014, Commerce Secretary Pritzker (Don Pritzker's daughter—Hyatt) noted the need for a review of disaster relief protocols to ensure that such rehabilitation efforts are undertaken efficiently to rebuild and optimize the damaged transmission infrastructure. I was to sit beside her at another Washington Conference and told her how I knew her father, the founder of the Hyatt Hotel chain. We had a nice chat!

The Stafford Act was written in the 1980s and is an antiquated public sector-oriented grant program. Yet it is our prime agent for dealing with disaster relief and a political pork barrel, as anyone who attended Congressional disaster relief hearings can attest.

Private sector utilities, in my opinion, should be eligible for large-scale "loans," as opposed to grants, under the Stafford Act to rebuild their systems importantly with the latest technology. Their state commissions can approve a long-term reimbursement schedule; however, the lesson learned from Sandy was that there was a need to quickly rebuild a new grid with new technology, which was very difficult, and the remedial work was done in the conventional way.

In late 2013, I had a social visit with Paul Hanrahan, a fellow Naval Academy graduate and CEO of American Capital's relatively new Energy and Infrastructure Fund (2013), located coincidentally in Annapolis, Maryland, where both of us lived. (Paul lived on the Eastern Shore).

Paul, after his naval service and Harvard Business School, began a career with AES Corp., a large international energy company in twenty-one countries across five continents with 30 GW of generating capacity, nine utility companies including 8 GW of generating capacity, $18 billion in annual revenues, and a global workforce of approximately 25,000 people. Virtually all this growth came from the passage of the 1992 PUHCA Reform statute.

Paul retired from AES as its President and CEO in 2012. While AES Corp. owned both Indianapolis Power and Light and Dayton Power and Light, the bulk of their power generation activities has been overseas since moving beyond their 1981 origin as a cogeneration developer here in the United States.

Paul's experience had been virtually all overseas (he told me it is easier from a regulatory perspective and more rewarding earnings-wise), with generation as the lead, but surrounding infrastructure, including transmission, distribution, ports, and another project-related infrastructure, included in their AES portfolio.

The exit strategy was to sell the up-and-running assets to the infrastructure fund sector, including the US, for the long-term, lower-return brownfield returns of 8–10 percent and pocket the change. Their secondary market potential might be of interest to US infrastructure funds in the years to come.

In November to December 2015, as the world watched Paris and the UN Conference on Global Climate Change, I sent a note to Heidi Crebo Rediker, who had worked for Senator John Kerry on his National Infrastructure Bank legislation and followed him to the State Department as Chief Economist, telling her that, as a visiting lecturer at Stanford, I spoke on the campus last month about my ideas for customer infrastructure where World Bank type lenders focus on subsidizing the distribution/social development sector. With customers (even subsidized), you can finance the more capital-intensive upstream transmission and generation sectors (and avoid corruption in the process).

It is an approach that could fit into this Climate Change aid strategy with upstream clean energy financed based on distribution grid buildout for customers (social/economic development). While I chaired the 1993 Infrastructure Investment Commission, I was leading the US utilities in opening the wholesale power market and creating the independent power business. It is this combination that led me to this conclusion.

I also sent a similar note to fellow San Franciscan Kate Brandt now that she was at Google as their lead officer on sustainability. It turns out Kate was in Paris at these talks and caught up with me and our Stanford team for lunch on campus upon her return. I later alerted her that when we visited Stanford, we discussed former Senator Tim Wirth (a Stanford PhD) and good friend who went on to run the United Nations Foundation for donor Ted Turner in 1998. I suggested to Tim that, as the UN has its Security Council focused on international security topics including military-type initiatives, it might consider adding environmental security to that agenda, establishing an Environmental Security Council. Maybe that is what finally happened in Paris in 2014.

Michael Skelly did not give up on transmission after his Clean Lines disappointment and was now the founder and CEO in 2021 of Grid United, an early-stage transmission development company that would integrate the Biden administration's funding commitment to the grid. He was serving as well on the new Secretary of Energy Advisory Board.

But his Clean Lines experience underscored the fact that we can't get the projects approved and built due to America's outdated and unpredictable permitting process. Fortunately, the 2023 Congressional debt ceiling agreement included the first significant reforms to America's permitting process in more than fifty years. These were the 2023 updates to the National Environmental Policy Act (NEPA) permitting process, and they were very practical and reasonable:

1. Sets a deadline of two years for an agency to complete the project's permitting process.
2. Allows project sponsors to petition a court if the agency misses the deadline.
3. Mandates that there to be a lead agency when more than one agency is involved in the permitting process to ensure a better-coordinated process.
4. Requires the development of a single environmental permitting document when more than one federal agency is involved in the permitting process to reduce preparation costs.
5. Instructs agencies to consider reasonable project alternatives that are technically and economically feasible, guided by the defined purpose of the project.
6. Allows project sponsors to prepare the environmental permitting document, with the agency having ultimate control, to help expedite drafting and offset the cost burden.

As for the lessons learned:

The role of the state public utility commissions has been key—over the last twenty-five years—in implementing renewable portfolio standards set by their governors and state legislatures. Organizations like NARUC can be very helpful. The PUCs control customer rate policy, and that is the hammer! FERC governs wholesale rates, but that is it!

Laws like the Clean Air Act are where the federal government's role begins. Hundreds of coal-fired plants have been shuttered by utilities under pressure from both the state and federal perspectives and because they were non-competitive with new natural gas-fired plants.

The Stafford Act is long overdue for modernization in dealing effectively with disaster planning and relief (resiliency and technology); plus "lending" (not just pork barrel grants) to allow all utilities to borrow quickly to rebuild the grid to the highest standards and allowing long-term rate increases to pay back these loans.

Battery storage is necessary to support the electric grid during high demand periods, and the technology has improved a great deal in recent years.

Up until 1977, it was the Senate Committee on Public Works, and that year Environment was added, validating the important nexus between infrastructure development and environmental standards. It is a truism that certain environmental organizations do not like to hear, but the nexus of infrastructure investment and environmental progress would certainly be a helpful ingredient in some of our infrastructure policy discussions. This infrastructure investment and environmental sustainability linkage is also good for the infrastructure fund community.

I had noticed and was pleased to read in early 2020 that US businesses, led by the tech industry, had now been aggressively buying electricity from wind and solar farms. In 2019, companies signed power purchase agreements (PPAs) for a record 9.3 gigawatts of renewable energy, according to the Renewable Energy Buyers Alliance, roughly half of average demand on the New York state power grid.

The largest purchaser, for the second straight year, was Facebook Inc. Amazon, Microsoft, and Google were all in the top seven. None of this could have happened without our 1992 Energy Policy Act Title VII Electricity title opening up the wholesale power market to competition and the new independent power industry.

And I was very pleased that these corporate commitments mattered to incoming employees such as Amanda Willis, a twenty-nine-year-old MBA student at the University of Michigan's Ross School of Business. For her, sustainability action tops salary and location as criteria for choosing an employer this spring. She said that her goal was to work somewhere that aligned with her values.

It was very satisfying for me to read this sentiment.

In a similar way, it was very nostalgic to view on television the weeklong funeral ceremonies to honor President George H. W. Bush, who had died on November 30 (my birthday) in 2018; and I wrote to family and friends that it was a wonderful program today honoring President George H. W. Bush from the US Capitol to the National Cathedral and on to Andrews Air Force Base and the Air Force One return flight to Texas. Along the route, bystanders honored the forty-first president and greeted the Bush family. Here is my Bush story in reflection:

When I came home from Vietnam and "retired" from the Navy in December 1969, I went to work in February for White Weld, located then in the Crown Zellerbach building downtown. My boss, George Pfau, was a great guy and had been George H. W. Bush's roommate at Yale.

In January 1989, when George H. W. Bush was to be inaugurated at the US Capitol, we then lived on Capitol Hill, just a long block from the Capitol grounds. I called George and told him we would host him and their friends for lunch afterwards. We all attended the inaugural ceremonies on a beautiful but cold day. Everyone walked over to our warm home, which we had decorated with festive bunting both inside and out in front, and everyone had a great time and a wonderful lunch.

A few years later, I was representing numerous utilities in the deregulation of electricity generation and had many meetings at the Bush White House.

When Congress passed the legislation in 1992, I was invited by the Bush White House to attend the signing ceremonies down in Louisiana as it was during his reelection campaign. We chartered a jet (clients paid for it), and I invited our allies to join the trip. One was a good friend Tom Kuhn, the president of the Edison Electric Institute. It was great to be there watching President George H. W. Bush sign the Energy Policy Act with our Title VII included, and it was fun to tell them all that Tom Kuhn had been his son, George W. Bush's, roommate at Yale!

Having invented the phrase "public private partnership" described in the next chapter on infrastructure reform, HR 359 illustrated the utility need and the government's unique security role and technical prowess. As a Naval Academy graduate (1965), I was impressed to view the new Hopper Hall Building on that campus (The Yard) that would be the first cyber security academic center in the country.

Since our passage in 1992 of the Energy Policy Act, and its Title VII on Electricity, the market for new technology in natural gas, wind and solar took off. State Renewable Portfolio Standards had been very influential; but it truly was the entrepreneurial role of the independent power producers financing their projects based on utility-issued power purchase agreements after a competitive bidding process by the utility with new infrastructure funds and now equity investors.

In all my years in the energy-related sectors, I personally was not aware of even one new technology that had its birth in the Department of Energy university research program—launched in 2009, as it has a political tilt in its award selection from my experience. But energy supply was now out in the marketplace, and public private partnerships were key.

As an example, more than a dozen US natural gas and electric utilities joined a $100 million effort to study and develop clean technologies over the next five years. The Low-Carbon Resources Initiative aimed to advance the development of energy sources such as hydrogen, synthetic fuels, biofuels, and other alternatives to fossil fuels, according to the Electric Power Research Institute and the Gas Technology Institute located in Silicon Valley near Stanford University.

Sempra Energy, Dominion Energy, Consolidated Edison, Duke Energy, and Southern are among those sponsoring the effort, according to the statement. I remember well how all of these companies, except for Southern, supported our 1992 PUHCA Reform effort. Now everyone is on board as the market encourages this research and new technologies such as battery storage to, in essence, combat global climate change. It is simple; this is what the customer wants!

The 2020 pandemic had been a true challenge, and recovery would require an "all hands-on deck" approach not this spurious special interest type of action defending a fading fossil fuel initiative.

The environmental "movement" is made up of hundreds of different organizations, many of which many are obstructionists. They have been slow to appreciate the role that infrastructure investment can play in achieving environmental goals. Issues such as streamlining the permitting process make for good consumer oriented public policy.

With the Biden 2020 election victory, we would restore our leadership role in the Paris Accords, assist with infrastructure project development and financing, support new technology and research, and understand the need for progress. Unfortunately, political grant money seemed to be crowding out private capital, and the global climate energy transition was going astray.

John Kerry would be the special envoy for global climate policy, and he had also been the chief supporter in the United States Senate for our National Infrastructure Bank idea, and I was with him—as the former Chairman of the congressionally mandated US Infrastructure Investment Commission—when he did so. He retired from that role in early 2024 as the public momentum for global climate action was in remission due to the inconsistencies of harsh environmental community demands and consumer budget reality. The energy transition had morphed into energy confusion.

In 2023, I was pleased to read that US utility companies were selling off their wind and solar farms to free up capital to make record investments in the power grid. It was a great business strategy, as utilities, while owning and operating unregulated power plants, faced a compromise thirty years ago when we passed PUHCA Reform; it never made sense to me.

The sales highlighted the stress on the country's aging power infrastructure and the need for new investment; but also, how rising competition among renewable-energy developers was pushing margins lower. Off-loading these generation assets was long overdue. But utility management had been dominated by the engineers for decades, and hence the compromise at the time.

Now the utility trade association, the Edison Electric Institute, predicted that utilities would invest roughly $159 billion in 2023 and $155 billion in 2024, more than any year since 2000, when the group began tracking spending. Obviously, upgrades would be needed to account for more electric vehicles and the prospect of more severe hurricanes, tornadoes, and flooding.

Suddenly, our nation's capital was filled with "experts on the grid." And my longtime friend Tom Kuhn, who had presided over this anchor trade association, retired as its president after almost thirty years of service in that role.

Utility spending is generally low risk yet rewarding because state public utility commission regulators allow the companies to earn set rates of return on investments primarily in their distribution and transmission infrastructure.

That isn't the case, since our 1992 US deregulation of electricity allowed spending on unregulated businesses, including portfolios of renewables and conventional power plants that operate in competitive power markets throughout the US; hence, the recent exit taking place by utilities.

For example, Duke recorded nearly $1.5 billion in impairment charges in mid-2023 as it wrote down the value of its renewable's portfolio, which it once pegged at $4 billion. If utilities were to retain their unregulated renewables portfolios, it would require them to spend increasing amounts of capital outside of their core utility business.

So, with both my electric and infrastructure hats on, the issues of global climate, sustainability, and resilience are solvable by combining market-oriented research, infrastructure investors, infrastructure projects, and public understanding. My Washington, DC, public policy firm specialized in regulatory reform (transportation, telecommunications, electric energy, and infrastructure), and we represented all of the utilities (Utility Working Group) that assisted the Department of Energy in drafting and supporting Title VII (Electricity) of the all-important 1991 Energy Policy Act.

And in February 2021, there were numerous articles on the passing of George Shultz at the age of 100 at his home by the Stanford campus. It brought back memories. Around 1993, after my utility coalition led the effort to pass the 1992 Energy Policy Act (Title VII Electricity) creating the independent power industry, I was at Bechtel's San Francisco headquarters giving their senior leadership a briefing. They had been a client for several years, and Cordell Hull was #2 in the company and a good friend. During my briefing, Cordell asked how Bechtel could have built and owned power plants overseas before this new law. I explained that you had to get an SEC waiver. After the briefing, he invited me to join him for a visit with George Shultz, who happened to be in an executive office down the hall just checking in (as a board member). He had just returned from a visit with his ophthalmologist, and his eyes had been dilated. He was very friendly, humorous, and even funny, as I recall. With all his accomplishments, I was very impressed.

5

Infrastructure Investment Commission Report and the Public Private Partnership Concept, 1993

Good things have been happening since our 1993 Infrastructure Investment Commission report, and here is that history. First off, Senator Daniel Patrick Moynihan asked me in 1990 to assist him in designing new approaches to funding US infrastructure, particularly private capital. He noted to me, "Dan, you have worked with other industries and their reform; help me with infrastructure; government cannot do it all."

We went to work, but with the lack of new infrastructure financing ideas from the traditional industry, I suggested to Senator Moynihan that he take an Infrastructure Investment Commission approach to be incorporated in the seminal 1991 transportation bill known as ISTEA, which was spearheaded by the Senator as Chairman of the Senate Environment and Public Works Committee and included many other innovations, including mass transit eligibility for highway trust fund assistance, plus transit/employer/commuter reimbursement of $240 per month commensurate with corporate parking privileges, along with new metropolitan planning organizations to prioritize urban transportation infrastructure projects.

I was appointed by the Speaker of the House Tom Foley to the Commission and elected its chairman by my fellow commissioners, and our hearings—seven in all—took place in 1992.

And our historic report, "Financing the Future," was issued a year later in 1993.

Our commission had a great support team including: David Seltzer from Philadelphia (Lehman Brothers alumni) who later authored TIFIA while a consultant to the US Department of Transportation, Bryan Grote (former OMB official) who was the Federal Credit Reform Act of 1990 guru, Doug Koelemay who authored our report and later served as the Director of Public-Private Partnerships for Virginia, the late Mort Downey who served as Under-Secretary of Transportation under President Clinton and always preceded me in providing congressional testimony on the innovative finance topic, and Jack Basso who served as the Assistant Secretary of Transportation for Budget and Programs during that same time period.

All of them were generous with their time, including the many congressional and administration meetings that moved these infrastructure investment policies forward.

After our seven Commission hearings in 1992, we published our report in February 1993, over thirty years ago. It was entitled "Financing the Future," and emphasized the importance of project finance, credit enhancement, federal lending, leverage, and project investment-grade credit ratings. It is fair to say that those principles have stimulated the growth of private capital investment in our nation's infrastructure, which had been our commission mandate by Congress.

Our prime recommendation for lending and credit enhancement, TIFIA, described more in Chapter 8, was passed by Congress in 1998 with the goal of leveraging federal dollars to attract private and non-federal capital into transportation infrastructure.

TIFIA is administered by the US Department of Transportation's (DOT) Office of Innovative Program Delivery in tandem with the Build America Bureau. The program provides loans, loan guarantees, and lines of credit to qualified public or private borrowers, including state governments, private firms, special authorities, local governments, transportation improvement districts, or a consortium of these entities, such as public-private partnerships.

I was very proud of this accomplishment and, in looking through my files, noticed the draft letter for Senator Moynihan to send to Treasury Secretary Bob Rubin, thanking him for meeting with the Senator and his colleagues and agreeing to this new lending program, provided there was a credit rating agency report in the project application, which was added to the legislation and was an important addition.

It was a first in federal credit lending! Build America Bonds (which revamped the municipal bond subsidy toward the project itself) followed, and President Obama and bipartisan members of Congress consistently called for a national infrastructure bank modeled after our project finance expertise recommendations and the need for what we called a National Infrastructure Corporation, which led, as a first step, to the 2014 establishment of the Build America Bureau at the US Department of Transportation.

When testifying on our innovative finance recommendations (new infrastructure), I remember a congressman asking me whether, under my new program, a new bridge can still be named after a congressman. I responded in the affirmative!

In a Senate hearing, I stated that we needed a domestic version of OPIC, and a Senator responded, "do you mean a DOPIC?" which generated much laughter from the audience. I could see it was going to take time to turn the infrastructure funding battleship around! This was in 1994! But we were pleased when the Transportation Innovative Financing Act (TIFIA) was enacted in 1998, administered by the DOT, and its water cousin, the Water Innovative Financing Act (WIFIA) in 2014, administered by the EPA.

And then in 2018, Congress passed legislation (The Build Act) creating the US International Development Finance Corporation (DFC). The DFC assumed the activities of the Overseas Private Investment Corporation (OPIC), USAID's Development Credit Authority, USAID's Enterprise Funds, and other programs. The Senate Foreign Relations Committee reported that: The DFC would have the authority to issue direct loans, including local currency loans; issue guarantees, including local currency guarantees; provide political risk insurance; fund first losses; participate in equity investments; provide technical assistance; make limited grants to unlock larger investments; and attract private sector talent.

The IDFC would prioritize support for projects in low and lower middle-income countries where it furthers US national security and economic interests and where the project can be shown to have a demonstrable development outcome.

This action validated the establishment of a similar institution for US infrastructure investment as I had testified before the Senate years ago as part of our Infrastructure Investment Commission recommendations. I specifically called for the establishment of the domestic equivalent of OPIC for our own domestic infrastructure needs to assist US infrastructure project development. So, if we can do it overseas, how about our own country with our recommended National Infrastructure (Investment) Corporation?

The Build America Bureau at the Department of Transportation, established under the Obama administration, was an important step forward but was restricted to transportation when infrastructure finance needs were quite evident in water, energy (renewable), telecom (rural broadband), and social (public buildings, educational facilities).

Yes, TIFIA for transportation (1998) and WIFIA for water (2014) were passed by Congress and have been very successful infrastructure lending programs, but there are still three others.

Shortly after our report was published in February 1993, I was asked—as the chairman of the Infrastructure Investment Commission—to speak at the Forbes Rebuild America conference at New York City's Plaza Hotel. The sponsors included the Privatization Council, the Pepper Hamilton law firm, Goldman Sachs, and Forbes magazine.

During my speech extolling the need for private capital investment in US infrastructure, I commented that the word "privatization" was an unfortunate misnomer, and we needed a new phrase. Privatization had the wrong image, particularly as it had enriched dozens of oligarchs in Russia when state assets were sold in that same period via stock offerings that were quickly bought up at below market prices by these individuals.

When the conference adjourned and noting my comments, I was asked by the sponsors to meet that afternoon to discuss possible options for a new, redefined phrase. A half dozen or so attendees/sponsors gathered in an adjacent Plaza Hotel meeting room, and we spent some two hours reviewing the topic.

It was at that meeting that a never-before-heard phrase, public private partnerships, was suggested and embraced. Soon thereafter, the Privatization Council was rechristened as the National Council for Public Private Partnerships and has its offices on K Street in downtown Washington, DC.

The rest is history, as that phrase, has become increasingly popular and serves a unique purpose in uniting both the public and private sectors in crafting new infrastructure investment strategies.

The Public-Private Partnership phrase has become ubiquitous. In 2020, during the terrible coronavirus pandemic, there was a desperate need for a new serum to combat the virus. The pharmaceutical research experts all called for a public-private partnership to bring both the drug research and public sectors together. There was the need for the serum but also a need for a binding long-term commitment to purchase the serums that would underwrite the cost.

Our commission was told in 1992 that we did not have a project finance discipline in the United States due principally to our unique reliance on municipal tax-exempt bonds, particularly general obligation bonds. That same year, 1992, as President George H. W. Bush signed the Energy Policy Act, it dawned on me that we were not only launching the independent power producer (IPP) industry but also the US project finance sector. Today, project finance expertise in the United States is best in class!

And when this expertise involves public-private partnerships (PPPs), they are time-sensitive, and the private sector has been critical of the delays that can often occur due to bureaucratic indifference and often in delays in permitting. I have seen it many times, and it is a disservice to the taxpayer and consumer.

Our Performance Infrastructure Review Committee (PIRC) coalition, launched in 2016, was focused on targeted/leveraged federal infrastructure investment, particularly as a credit enhancement tool to invite other capital (public and private) to participate in the project financing of major infrastructure developments throughout the country. We were aligned with the AFL-CIO and the US Chamber of Commerce, and they hosted a number of our meetings. Much of our work stemmed from the original 1993 Infrastructure Investment Commission report.

In 2016, both presidential candidates Donald Trump and Hillary Clinton were espousing infrastructure investment, which inspired us to form PIRC and provide recommendations to both campaigns. Later, the Biden White House would espouse infrastructure as well but focused on billions of grant dollars to state and local officials via the Infrastructure Investment and Jobs Act.

Our 1993 Infrastructure Investment Commission recommendations contained in our report, "Financing the Future," have been recognized by Public Works Financing and many other infrastructure professionals as essential tools in financing America's infrastructure. By this, we are referring not just to highways, but investment in energy, telecom, water, transportation, and social (educational facilities/hospitals/public buildings) infrastructure in either new construction or modernizing/upgrading existing facilities.

In my Public Works Financing letter that follows, there is this statement: to attract both public and private capital to financially feasible projects. There are numerous projects that can be developed with this investment strategy. However, we all know that there are projects, particularly in rural areas, that need grant funding; albeit even some of those can be financed, for example, locks and dams, which are an integral part of our national supply chain. The focus needs to be on the projects, not the politics!

Unfortunately, the noted 2021 bipartisan Infrastructure Investment and Jobs Act (IIJA), also known as the Bipartisan Infrastructure Bill, signed into law by President Joe Biden on November 15, 2021, went exclusively in the political direction, with the President appointing a White House Infrastructure Czar who then recruited state and regional infrastructure czars to fill the pipeline with their favored projects. From the signing ceremony onward, the White House identified it as the Biden infrastructure plan, even though the White House had never sent a proposal to Congress.

The act was initially the traditional Senate Environment and Public Works infrastructure package that included $715 billion for provisions related to federal-aid highways, transit, highway safety, motor carriers, research, hazardous materials, and rail programs of the Department of Transportation.

After Senate bipartisan congressional negotiations, it was amended and renamed the Infrastructure Investment and Jobs Act to include funding for broadband access, clean water, and electric grid renewal, as well as an Infrastructure Financing Authority in addition to transportation.

But the Biden infrastructure grants were going to be distributed wherever the local infrastructure czars designated. Our public-private partnership coalition gave up and disbanded! The inadvertent lobbying deletion of the Infrastructure Financing Authority provision was deeply disappointing.

Still, there was a real need for a state/regional/local debate and related policy options to open up the US infrastructure investment market beyond the private sector energy generation and telecom sectors.

State and regional agencies need to do far more in performance-based project development and value-added financing benefits. They need to develop expertise in the public-private partnership model as that is the critical path for the other three infrastructure sectors (water, transportation, and social) with their public histories.

I am convinced that every Governor should have a first-class project finance expert on their staff to facilitate and encourage local and regional infrastructure implementation within their state, and that a comparison of the best financing strategy should be required by the states to encourage project development and performance based life cycle funding. You do need expertise.

A good example of public-private partnerships going off the deep end is sports stadium funded by taxpayers via municipal bonds that greatly inflate the value of the franchise for the team owner exclusively. The 2020 coronavirus shut down all sports in the United States, and these municipal bond-financed stadiums (Glendale, Arizona had two) were now silent and financially vulnerable.

The unique role of tax-exempt bonds in the United States is a related issue. During our 1992 Infrastructure Investment Commission hearings, it was a surprise to discover we were the only country in the world where state and local governments could sell tax-exempt municipal bonds for infrastructure purposes. This skewed our national approach to project finance and delayed our new infrastructure investment public private partnership based concept by many years.

Wall Street public finance, in those days, was not project finance (in some ways it was political finance), but they called it public finance with the emphasis on selling municipal (debt) bonds. I had many discussions about this with reluctant Wall Street leaders back in the 1990s, but almost twenty years later they all had large infrastructure funds! And I attribute that to our painstaking efforts over those years with little reward at the time.

On March 17, 2021, I sent a note to the Speaker of the House, Nancy Pelosi's Chief of Staff, Robert Edmondson, telling him it took me over ten years to get the University of California to do an infrastructure public-private partnership (PPP model) for its new Merced campus; and now these university infrastructure PPP models were taking off—there were a half dozen and growing. For example, I mentioned Fresno State, which had just selected a Meridiam-led consortium and its partner NORESCO as the preferred bidder for a thirty-three-year public-private partnership (PPP) contract valued at about $170 million to modernize and maintain its energy utility system. I suggested there should be a PPP provision in the upcoming infrastructure legislation.

It is noteworthy, and I am pleased that pension/infrastructure funds are now quite active in the United States, and there is a critical role they can play while offering their future retirees stable, long-term revenue streams from projects that are so structured. Having spoken on this topic many times, it was very satisfying to finally see it happening.

Pension funds are now major investors in the deregulated energy generation market (telecom as well but not as much) and could be investors, as I mentioned, in the other infrastructure categories of water, transportation, and social if they are structured appropriately. The Goethals Bridge project is a good example.

In 2010, Nancy Pelosi and I were visiting in her speaker's office in the United States Capitol; and she asked what I was working on these days. I explained that my professional work now was primarily with infrastructure funds, and that completing my 1993 Infrastructure Investment Commission recommendations was the public policy goal to fully open US infrastructure to much-needed private capital investment.

I explained that our commission had first recommended federal infrastructure lending/credit enhancement (TIFIA 1998—Chapter 8) coupled with a National Infrastructure Corporation to recruit independent project finance expertise to administer such infrastructure lending/credit enhancement programs. I was pleased when she called for a National Infrastructure Investment Plan that same year.

Nancy mentioned Felix Rohatyn, and I pointed out that we had jointly testified in the '90s and differed significantly. His approach was basically to provide more liquidity for bond issuance, which was not what we needed.

In 1990, while spending weekends at our place outside Middleburg, we became good friends with Democratic doyenne and wealthy landowner, Maggie Bryant. She was sponsoring a new toll road to enhance the value of her land beyond Dulles Airport to Leesburg and asked for my help.

We went to see her project director, Ralph Stanley, at their Leesburg office. I asked Ralph how they were going to collect the toll, and he showed me a fast-track device that you put in your windshield. I asked Ralph where he got this, and he replied that Auto Strada in Italy was going to operate our Dulles Greenway.

Ralph allowed me to take the device, and I brought it to Senator Moynihan in his office and said, "Pat, this is the future." Pat was the chairman of the Senate Environment and Public Works Committee.

Being a deregulator, I saw how new technology evolves when industry sectors are opened, and this experience was helpful later in our Commission findings. Ralph was to serve on the Infrastructure Investment Commission as well with me and did a great job!

In 2011, I was honored to stand with Senators Kerry and Hutchinson in their US Senate press conference introducing their national infrastructure bank legislation—also recommended by our 1993 Commission. Kerry's legislative aide was an economist, Heidi Credo Redeker, and I was meeting with her to review our 1993 Infrastructure Investment Commission report.

When I handed her a copy of our report, she saw that Senator Kay Bailey Hutchison had been on the Commission with me (when she was the Texas Treasurer). Heidi borrowed the report and disappeared for fifteen minutes. Upon her return, I learned that Kay had agreed to be a co-sponsor, as we had recommended a national infrastructure corporation.

After the ceremony, Senator Hutchinson told her staff gathered in her office that I was the one who started all of this infrastructure investment and innovative public finance focus. It was a proud moment!

I have been a leading advocate for a national infrastructure corporation (bank) since our 1993 Infrastructure Investment Commission report recommended this measure, and President Obama also called for the creation of a National Infrastructure Bank in his FY 2010 budget proposal with funding of $5 billion annually for five years.

Surely, it could have been in the 2009 economic stimulus package. We drafted it then and sent it to the White House; but we were later told that Rahm Emanuel and Larry Summers took it out. However, it resurfaced a year later.

I worked with Senators Kerry and Hutchinson only to see them ambushed by GOP attacks in a losing, very partisan US Senate floor vote.

But the Congress was prepared once again to tackle the issue in 2014, with Senator Mark Warner taking the lead in the Senate, and the House launching a special public-private partnership panel. Both efforts were based on a bipartisan approach, and I was hopeful. He moved the National Infrastructure Bank effort forward with his BRIDGE Act and its Infrastructure Financing Authority with a dozen bipartisan Senate co-sponsors.

In the spring of 2014, I was in a roundtable with Mark Warner and his Senate colleague, Roy Blunt from Missouri at the Bi-Partisan Policy Center. I made the point that pension funds, with their large infrastructure allocations, would welcome a national infrastructure bank; and Senator Warner immediately interrupted, saying to me that an infrastructure bank was Obama talk and this was an infrastructure financing authority as he had described in the bill. That response spoke volumes! My number one priority had been our Commission's recommendation to create a National Infrastructure Corporation (Bank, Fund, or Authority... whatever it was called).

Mark and I first met in the mid-1990s, on my Cape Dory Open Fisherman motorboat that I docked in Old Town Alexandria a few blocks from our respective homes on South Lee St. Mark lived three blocks over and was contemplating a political debut after a successful business career in the wireless industry as an investor.

Our coalition partners, including labor and the US Chamber of Commerce, all had worked hard during the Obama administration, but the legislative clock was ticking.

By now, pension funds were major investors in the US infrastructure asset class, particularly in existing energy generation assets including wind and solar with long-term power purchase agreements. However, we still had several public policy goals that would further assist this progress. Initially, our infrastructure investment policy effort in 2017 had a promising start, picking up from the progress in the prior election year. We had a number of well-received recommendations, briefed senior members of Congress and their staffs, and had early signs of interest from Gary Cohn, who had been the president of Goldman Sachs and was to serve for the first Trump year as head of the National Economic Council before resigning over trade policy. He also oversaw the infrastructure strategy with DJ Gribbin reporting to him. But these were the policy speed bumps:

1. The early 2017 GOP congressional leadership decision to take up the "repeal Obamacare" issue first and not infrastructure (Trump White House preference).
2. The 2017 tax cut legislation later that year exhausted all infrastructure funding options.
3. The confusing February 2018 rollout of the Trump infrastructure proposal.
4. The early 2018 White House resignation of DJ Gribbin (the first and only Special Assistant for Infrastructure Policy).

Bottom line, the support for funding an innovative infrastructure proposal was virtually ignored in favor of the very large GOP 2017 tax cuts, even though the stage had been set in the prior Obama administration, which focused on a corporate tax repatriation strategy coupled with a 25 percent corporate tax rate.

Later, I was to read in the press about a leaked Trump White House summary which seemed to be their infrastructure consensus plan beginning in the New Year 2018. My notes indicated:

1. Investing $200 billion, with half of that directed toward incentivizing state and local governments to find new resources for public works.
2. Earmarking $50 billion in block grants for rural infrastructure, such as expanding broadband access; another $25 billion would go toward large, complex projects.
3. The last $25 billion would go toward projects with innovative forms of financing.

I sent a note to my Stanford colleagues at the Global Projects Center, Mike Bennon (a West Point grad, Corps of Engineers, Stanford MBA and ME), giving him an update and suggesting we advocate that every Governor should have a first-class project finance expert on their staff to coordinate infrastructure implementation.

In February 2018, the Trump administration finally sent to Congress their complicated state/local infrastructure proposal. The shifting of the project funding and development responsibility to the state/local sector (with federal incentives) was criticized by many public officials and members of Congress. In summary, their rural/state/local proposal was mishandled (too political) by the Trump administration, and the initial congressional hearings were indeed very confusing.

Our coalition proposals targeted $75 billion in lending and grants over ten years in five program categories to generate $615 billion of infrastructure investment. Our prime 2017 coalition goal had been to have our infrastructure policy options embedded in the Trump administration proposal that would be sent to Congress as soon as possible so that the educational process could begin. We were successful in that regard, but the proposal itself was held hostage, unfortunately, by the tax cut legislation and the inept administration testimony.

We included a provision calling for a Strengthened Platform for Federal Credit, referring to some form of a national infrastructure lending entity (a national infrastructure bank!) that would be either independent or within the Treasury Department. And, short of some federal financing platform, at a minimum there needed to be a federal office (at Treasury?) established to provide coordination with state/local offices and federal support for regional projects.

We were very encouraged when Treasury Secretary Mnuchin early on called for a National Infrastructure Bank as well in the Trump plan to provide the necessary lending platform with the expertise in both project finance and federal credit. But that did not happen!

As one of our key 1993 Commission recommendations for what we called a National Infrastructure Corporation (project finance expertise), I was hopeful that we would finally be successful. The Democrats had won back the House in 2018, and we had good meetings with the House Ways and Means Staff as well as the Senate Finance Committee.

But there were significant questions as Congress had quickly dismissed the 2018 Trump infrastructure proposal and indicated they would draft their own versions. Additionally, the funding issue had to be resolved.

Some Democrats noted that $150 billion of the $200 billion federal funding in the ten-year Trump administration proposal was targeted for rural and state/local incentive grant proposals and seemed to be focused politically on the red or rural states. The congressional hearings with Transportation Secretary Chao trying to explain the definition of rural were embarrassing.

We indicated that our PIRC coalition of experts was standing by to assist Republican and Democratic members, particularly on the four key committees (Senate Finance and Environment and Public Works; and House Ways and Means and Transportation and Infrastructure) plus their staffs. The usual House and Senate highway bills were announced in late 2019.

In essence, we were working hard to rejuvenate US infrastructure practices, primarily from the perspective of project finance, time value of money, and risk transfer disciplines in this country. There is now an infrastructure asset class and many infrastructure funds seeking investment opportunities. State, regional, and local project expertise and leadership are improving but are needed in many states.

My home state of California, for example, was a top prospect as its track record on major projects has been more than disappointing! The lack of infrastructure/project finance discipline in California (notwithstanding the erstwhile efforts of our Global Projects Center at Stanford University where I served on its Board of Advisors) is a major concern; this is the nation-state after all. The hemorrhaging of costs for the SF/Oakland Bridge replacement project or the failure of the high-speed rail project are not attractive stories of competence:

Roughly ten years ago, my younger brother called me about the California High-Speed Rail Authority. He is a very successful real estate investor, and his group owns various properties, including a large-scale office building in Sacramento at the time when the Authority was a tenant. He asked me about how the Authority was doing, and I gave him an update and responded that I wasn't aware that he was a supporter of the high-speed rail project. He clarified everything by saying that he just wanted to make sure they could make the lease payments.

Some of our coalition team attended the Chamber of Commerce mid-January 2017 infrastructure kickoff, thanks to team member Ed Mortimer. It was very well done, with a large attendance and an emphasis on the following four points that we had helped develop:

1. Surface Transportation: To rebuild and expand our roads, bridges, and transit systems, it is time for a modest increase in the federal motor vehicle fuel user fee. Since 1993, thirty-nine states have raised their own state motor fuel user fees. Specifically, we called on Congress to raise the user fee by 5 cents a year for five years for a total of 25 cents and adjust the fee for inflation thereafter.
2. Critical Infrastructure: Rebuilding and modernizing our airports, ports, waterways, water systems, dams, rail systems, utilities, and other core infrastructure requires a multi-faceted financial approach that includes leveraging private-sector resources by:
    a. Creating a new loan program to finance a broad array of infrastructure projects with loans to be repaid through a dedicated public or private funding stream;
    b. Removing statutory and regulatory barriers to public-private partnerships;
    c. Creating a discretionary grant program to stimulate competition and leverage state, local, and private sector funds for projects of national significance; and
    d. Expanding private activity bonds.

3. Permit Streamlining: The permitting process for major infrastructure projects was broken. It can take longer to get government permits than it takes to construct a project. On average, it takes on average approximately five years to complete an environmental impact statement, a federal requirement for many large projects. Depending on the type of project, permitting can involve state and local approvals in addition to a myriad of federal permits. Congress and the administration in recent years have taken steps to improve the federal permitting process, but more must be done.
4. The Workforce Necessary to Rebuild Our Infrastructure: Rebuilding America's infrastructure will require skilled workers ready and able to take on new projects. Yet today—before any major new investment in our infrastructure, 78 percent of construction firms report that they are having a hard time finding qualified workers. If we do not expand the workforce, it will be impossible to move ahead with the projects that need to be undertaken. Policymakers should expand apprenticeship programs and the network of sector-based construction partnerships under federal workforce programs. And we must keep the skilled workers currently in the workforce thanks to programs like DACA and TPS. Ultimately, Congress needs to enact immigration reform so that we can attract and admit the skilled workers our nation needs.

I was very impressed with the Chamber's inclusion of DACA and, in fact, they had a large sign standing outside their entrance across from the White House exhorting the need for DACA, underscoring the important role of immigrants in our graying workforce and low fertility demographics. DACA stands for the Deferred Action for Childhood Arrivals immigration policy that allows some individuals who were brought to the United States illegally as children to receive a renewable two-year period of deferred action from deportation and become eligible for a work permit in the United States.

Amidst the infrastructure legislative effort in the 2017–2018 Congress, it did not help when President Trump met with the House Ways and Means Committee Democrats and unexpectedly criticized public-private partnerships.

Fortunately, I had a meeting already scheduled with the House Ways and Means Committee staff and would clarify that public-private partnerships (PPPs) are a very important option for project planning. They are all different, allow the leverage of federal dollars, and belong in whatever larger plan Congress may have for infrastructure investment. They are a conduit for bringing all the facets of a major infrastructure project together, particularly additional capital from both federal loans and private investment and development expertise.

PPPs are project-oriented and can have different characteristics. However, the key element is that the private sector takes the design/construction risk and additional equity investment risk. The public sector must do its part by working efficiently to perform what it is best suited for, including eminent domain, environmental impact statements, and the like.

In the infrastructure sector, energy and telecom have been deregulated for years and do not use the PPP concept for attracting infrastructure investment. However, the other three infrastructure sectors—water, transportation, and social (educational facilities, hospitals, public buildings)—have different histories with long-term governmental support, so the PPP is needed.

The public-private partnership is essentially an enabler for them, an infrastructure project development concept wherein the public sector takes on the project requirements for permitting, eminent domain, environmental impact statements, and other responsibilities relative to their expertise. They determine, for strategic reasons, to engage in a public-private partnership arrangement for a variety of purposes: Design/construction risk transfer, time value of money, project finance expertise, new technology, etc.

Each public-private partnership is somewhat unique. Granted, there are lessons learned from other successful projects, but each project has certain characteristics that must be addressed by the sponsors. All parties must have the contractual knowledge, expertise, and experience to assemble a thorough, successful public-private partnership agreement.

Unfortunately, that is not always the case, as witness the 16-mile Purple Line (Maryland) under construction between Montgomery and Prince George's counties, Maryland. A variety of lawsuits and a sympathetic judge led to cost escalations, and other mistakes had led to the private sector team threatening to leave the project in the spring of 2020 after years of work.

And then the 2024 collapse of Baltimore's Francis Scott Key Bridge occurred as an enormous container ship lost power and rammed into the bridge supports. If ever there was a time for engineering and infrastructure finance expertise, this was it. But the politicians were all over the media, with press conference after press conference featuring the new governor and the ten-member congressional delegation calling for 100 percent federal funding as a bipartisan imperative. They were determined to own this bridge disaster rebuild no matter the cost or the time. Political infrastructure posturing was crowding out the expertise needed.

President Biden announced, without precedent, that the federal government would be 100 percent responsible for funding its replacement; and Congress cemented this decision in its December 2024 continuing resolution.

The public private partnership was readily available with today's best-in-class experience, project finance expertise, and corporate engineering track records. However, the public sector must do its part and call on a US private infrastructure sector that has been very focused on the PPP process for the last decade here in the United States. Sure, they recognize its value to their business opportunities, but they are prepared to commit risk capital balanced with public sector credit enhancement.

As a successful PPP example, the sponsoring New York New Jersey Port Authority pursued a design, build, finance, maintain PPP approach (DBFM) for the new Goethals Bridge while the Authority continued to own and manage the bridge operations.

Implicit is the fact that all parties must have the contractual knowledge and experience to assemble such an agreement. In this case, Kiewit Infrastructure Co., a unit of the Omaha, Nebraska-based mining/construction company, successfully led the design and construction of the new bridge, while Macquarie Infrastructure and Real Assets Inc., a unit of the Sydney-based company, headed up the financing. Other members of the consortium included Washington-based Parsons Transportation Group, Cranford, New Jersey-based Weeks Marine Inc., and Kansas City, Missouri based Massman Construction Co. The financing consisted of $100 million in equity, a $500 million federal TIFIA loan, tax-exempt bonds, and a bank loan. The Port Authority would pay back the consortium over forty years, making annual availability payments that started at $60 million. Importantly, the Port Authority had said it would not start paying the developers' availability payments until seventy percent of the bridge was constructed, minimizing the risk that deadline had been achieved.

I included this example in my 2016 Stanford lecture on a variety of different bridge design construction projects. A personal goal of mine had been trying for years to establish a first-class university infrastructure/project finance program, starting first with USC, then UCSD in the West, and then Johns Hopkins Carey Business School and Georgetown the latter two because Washington, DC, is very much the infrastructure policy capitol of the country with virtually every infrastructure trade association headquartered there. Lecturing at both schools, the classes were all well attended and engaged. But Stanford's Global Projects Center (GPC) clearly had the dedication and expertise needed for this important opportunity, emphasizing their role as an interdisciplinary research center at Stanford University that seeks to facilitate understanding of the financing, development, and governance of strategic assets that underpin dynamism and competitiveness in today's global economy.

The GPC had outstanding relationships with the global infrastructure fund community, including the increasing number of US pension/infrastructure funds. I was very impressed with the participating graduate students, who were from all over the globe and represented a blend of the civil engineering and business schools at Stanford.

I had enjoyed being on the Stanford GPC Board of Advisors and lecturing twice a year. In that 2015 lecture, which featured a comparison of major bridge infrastructure projects, particularly their financing either through the public-private partnership (PPP) process or not, Goethals was certainly the winner compared to the ill-fated Caltrans San Francisco-Oakland Bay Bridge replacement project.

Today, public and private pension funds in the United States have approximately $5.14 trillion in assets with a long-term challenge to honor promises made to workers and retirees. Virtually all have recognized the infrastructure asset class as an excellent investment vehicle for long-term, stable investment yields.

Debated in the United States for the last twenty years (I was giving speeches on the topic and testifying particularly during my 1999–2004 USC tour), it had become clear that revenue-generating infrastructure is an ideal investment category for pension plans because these projects offer a stream of relatively predictable cash flows over a long period, with returns that can exceed those of most fixed-income investments.

Moreover, these types of infrastructure projects can act as an inflation hedge, which traditional investment options do not do as readily.

In the early stages around the year 2000, US pension plans in the aggregate allocated 2.5–3 percent of their portfolios to infrastructure; but this percentage has trended significantly upward to 5 percent as there is a growing consensus in today's pension fund market that long term yield infrastructure investments are a very effective balance to the pension fund actuarial profile.

When CalSTRS made a 2012 $500 million commitment to Australia's Industry Fund Management, and more US pension funds followed, the attraction of a low management fee, open-ended, well-staffed US infrastructure investment platform was obvious.

We devoted a good deal of time to what we labeled the Fiduciary Infrastructure Initiative project, via the Milken Institute, but the attorneys for the various state pension funds indicated their state laws would interfere. We actually had a full-day seminar with a dozen state pension fund chief investment officers in 2015 in Washington, DC, at the Federal Reserve headquarters. They were very interested!

The fact is that US institutional investors (pension funds) have been steadily increasing allocations to infrastructure as a stand-alone asset class since 2006. US investors are becoming more open to investment in the infrastructure asset class. Public employee and multi-employer funds have made major commitments to infrastructure fund managers such as Macquarie, High-Star (now part of Oaktree Capital), Carlyle, Global Infrastructure Partners, Alinda, First Reserve (now in BlackRock), Meridiam, Brookfield, and ULLICO.

In 2013, ULLICO launched its infrastructure fund, with my assistance, focused on the multi-employer fund community; and in late 2024, it was over $6 billion in commitments. It all started back in the spring of 2006 when I had a call from the lobbyists for the Laborers and the Operating Engineers national unions. They were concerned about the success that Macquarie was having in raising infrastructure commitments from their multi-employer funds. This was not the first time that this topic had come up. Actually, John Sweeney was the President of the AFL-CIO until 2009; and around 2001 or so, when I was at USC (commuting to Washington on a regular basis), he asked me to meet with the AFL-CIO Building Investment Trust (BIT).

My colleagues, including David Seltzer, had several meetings with the BIT executives introducing concepts such as concessions, social sector (real estate), etc. At the end of the day, they demurred, saying they would stay exclusively with real estate equity investing in union labor building projects, etc. So, in 2006, at the Laborers International conference room in Washington, DC, at 16th and I Streets, there was broad agreement that the multi-employer unions should consider launching their own infrastructure fund, as we had recommended in our memorandum. Attendees included the Operating Engineers, the Carpenters, Iron Workers, the Laborers, and others. But the question was, what organization would be the sponsor?

As it happened, Ed Smith was on the conference call from his Illinois Laborer's office. Ed had been a trustee on several Laborers' multi-employer pension funds, and when he moved to ULLICO, ultimately to be their president, he indicated to me in 2010 that they would begin the structuring of what became the successful ULLICO Infrastructure Fund to join the approximately $200 billion that had been raised by global infrastructure fund managers.

Many of these funds that have had success focused on an energy component to their strategy, which investors have found to be attractive due to the deregulated open market activity from our effort in passing Title VII of the 1992 Energy Policy Act (PUHCA Reform), which launched the independent power industry and project finance.

Here in the United States, it was the global trend of deregulation that I describe in this book, beginning in the 1970s through the 1990s, that served as a critical catalyst for the infrastructure investment opportunity that exists today.

Twenty-five years ago, in February 1993, our US Infrastructure Investment Commission recommendations were promulgated, and twenty-five years later had been duly recognized. I presented this paper entitled the White House Build America Infrastructure Initiative to the Treasury Department infrastructure team prior to meeting with them in 2014, as they were to launch their Build America Infrastructure Initiative:

As you know, the pace of official attention to the issue of America's deteriorating infrastructure has been picking up at the White House level during the last few months. There is a growing awareness and urgency that the need to restore our national infrastructure to the world-class levels we once took for granted is a critical national issue, as demonstrated at the Treasury Summit outbreak session on September 9, the launch pad for the President's Build America Infrastructure Initiative. A recurring theme seems to be the need for a national interagency infrastructure financing office (or a national infrastructure bank, as President Obama has called for since his 2008 campaign) with project finance expertise to be available to the dozen or so federal credit/lending infrastructure programs, including the TIFIA and newly established WIFIA programs, to enhance project development and infrastructure investment on a "best practices" manner. The Build America Interagency Working Group is preparing its recommendations to the President by November 14, 2014. Based on my long experience with the various infrastructure sectors, I am convinced of the ultimate need for a National Infrastructure Bank (NIB). I recognize, however, that the current political environment makes this exceedingly difficult.

I continued outlining in Treasury staff meetings that a national infrastructure financing platform would:

1. Serve as an interagency infrastructure financing office with project finance expertise to be available to the dozen or so federal credit/lending infrastructure programs to enhance project development and infrastructure investment on a "best practices" manner.
2. Provide private sector developers and infrastructure investors with credit enhancement tools and resources to identify and execute successful PPPs.
3. Work to popularize PPPs and remove the numerous state and local impediments to public-private partnerships.
4. Support project development in the pre-construction phase, which the private sector is very uncomfortable funding.
5. Smooth out the refinancing risk to cover the long-term nature of infrastructure projects.
6. Help work out the problems associated with appropriation risk.

As I read this list again, what impressed me is how well the project finance-oriented sponsors had addressed these issues, and billions were now being invested in US infrastructure projects.

Within the Federal Government, there are numerous entities that were already actively engaged in infrastructure—but in most cases, they lacked the project finance skill sets. An exception would be the Department of Energy's Loan Programs Office (LPO), created by Congress in 2005 to help American innovative energy and advanced auto manufacturing projects overcome hurdles in obtaining loans to help bring new technologies to commercial deployment. This office was to be a critical asset within the global climate energy transition, as was the TIFIA DoT office earlier in 1998 and the WIFIA EPA office in 2014.

It would have been very easy to have the LPO act as the core of a NIB-type platform servicing the operating needs of the other departments across the government on a fee-for-service basis. Not only would this have been an efficient move, but it would free up the other departments from having to recreate the operating infrastructures.

At the same time, it would facilitate hiring, planning, and execution of projects. Federal agencies are precluded from PPP-type private financing, and that would be an important reform to facilitate projects like the build-out of rural broadband and the rebuilding of our nation's locks and dams system of navigation, logistics, and commerce.

Much needed to be done, and the Obama White House and Treasury responded, with both Secretaries of Transportation Foxx and Treasury Lew taking the lead in creating the Build America Bureau at the Department of Transportation. Still, some form of a national infrastructure financing platform for all infrastructure sectors would be very helpful, allowing the TIFIAs and WIFIAs to do "the paperwork" and the "national infrastructure bank" to approve and administer.

We continued to advocate with both camps during the Trump/Clinton presidential campaign period and were pleased to read the following excerpt that was printed in a special edition of Public Works Financing for the May 2017 National Infrastructure Week panel that I was to lead before a full audience in one of the largest US Senate hearing rooms, located within the Dirksen Senate Office Building. It started out with "The Time is Right for Flanagan Bonds" and went on to note that for my lifelong work to promote private investment in public works infrastructure, they had elected to name a new investment credit bond, the Flanagan Bond. We were off to a good start, and this was the this was the title of my remarks: "Reinventing Federal Infrastructure Policy: A 25-Year Personal Perspective."

And I organized this program outline and chaired the following event during the 2017 National Infrastructure Week on behalf of the National Academy of Public Administration in Washington, DC, entitled Optimizing US Infrastructure Investment Policy Options. The event was held in that large Dirksen Senate Office Building auditorium, which was packed.

The discussion theme was as follows: With the 2015 passage of the FAST Act completed, what and how can the Federal Government, working with regional, state, and local governments, go even further to maximize their collegial effectiveness in responding to the national consensus for new and innovative thinking in spurring "best of class" infrastructure investment practices in partnership with private capital? And thereby, set a global example for infrastructure excellence.

Going forward, the role of project finance, institutional pension/infrastructure investment, and pending public policy proposals will be necessary ingredients in the process to open the infrastructure market in the United States in tandem with the establishment of a recognized long-term infrastructure investment asset class.

Discussion topics included:

1. Outlining and maximizing how revenues from repatriation tax policy can best be channeled toward investing in the nation's infrastructure.
2. Treasury's 2017 Budget Infrastructure Proposal: Expanding Public Private Collaboration on Infrastructure.
3. A review of pension fund/infrastructure asset class activity, performance, and size in the United States and globally.
4. Optimizing the US government's infrastructure departments' efforts to coordinate and achieve desired, tangible results regarding cost-effective infrastructure investment and the time value of money.
5. Federal role in incentivizing regional, state, and local infrastructure project development addressing the issues of project development and financing market risk.
6. Outlining the advantages/roles of federal lending/credit enhancement and regional/state/local project development.
7. Impediments to federal assets infrastructure investment, for example, FAA Next Gen, Corps Locks and Dams Rebuilding, and federal impediments to project delivery.

8. Optimizing the effectiveness of federal infrastructure credit programs along with TIFIA/WIFIA
9. The issues related to budget scoring and federal infrastructure investment.
10. A review of the US infrastructure market and its five sectors: energy, telecom, water, transportation and social.

One of our panelists was DJ Gribbin, who had served as General Counsel at both the FHWA and DoT and then worked at McQuarrie for a decade and really knew the public-private partnership world. As noted earlier, a few months later, DJ was one of the early appointments to President Trump's White House staff as Special Assistant to the President for Infrastructure Policy, a new position.

Another panelist was Tyler Duval, a McKinsey Partner and former Under-Secretary of Transportation; David Seltzer, Bryan Grote; the AFL-CIO Building and Construction Trades Council; and the US Chamber of Commerce.

We were fully engaged in 2017 and recommended to the White House infrastructure team, now led by D. J. Gribbin, these five new infrastructure investment policy tools:

1. Critical Asset Procurement Reform (CAPR) Program, Federal public-private partnerships.
2. Tax Credit Bonds for Public Infrastructure, Project Finance.
3. P3 Performance Incentive Grants, public equity for both planning and development.
4. Rationalizing the tax code provisions for Private Activity Bonds (revenue projects).
5. Enhancing Federal Credit Assistance provided for public infrastructure via some form of a National Infrastructure Authority (lending/leverage).

Other performance-based infrastructure ideas were: (1) establishing regional public finance authorities, (2) providing federal backstopping of state maintenance reserve funds, (3) creating environmental mitigation "banks," (4) encouraging pooled loans-to-lenders programs, and (5) modifying the tax rules for pension funds and sovereign wealth funds investing in US infrastructure projects.

While congressional infrastructure legislation and targeted program funding of our recommendations would be very effective and timely, the infrastructure asset class itself in the United States is moving forward and making outstanding progress.

In 2017, I was pleased to see that those hospitals, student housing, and other social infrastructure deals were the most popular among infrastructure investors, albeit most of the funding they invested went into energy and utilities. The latter had been the case for the last ten years.

At that time, a little more than half of all US infrastructure deals fell into the category of social infrastructure, which covers assets from clinics and assisted-living facilities to government buildings and apartment complexes near colleges, according to the research firm Preqin.

Preqin also reported that global infrastructure funds now had a record $150 billion ready to invest in infrastructure projects and also noted that the median annual return for infrastructure funds that began investing between 2000 and 2005 is 17 percent. For those that started making infrastructure deals since the financial crisis, it was about 10 percent. Some politicians tried to score points on this rate of return issue, but over time the benefits in terms of project completion on time and under budget won the day. Plus, those returns went to the pension fund and retirees.

At the start, traditional US public works like roads, train stations, and sewage-treatment plant projects had been in short supply for infrastructure investors due to the availability of municipal bonds and the bureaucratic nature of public projects.

Most projects that moved forward had been public-private partnerships. Bill Reinhardt, noted earlier as the publisher of Public Works Financing, dropped me a note in early 2018 reporting there were eighty-seven active procurements and 100 P3 projects in planning. So, the tide was turning.

I had mentioned several times that most early US infrastructure investment targeted the deregulated energy generation sector from wind farms, solar, natural gas, and utilities as reviewed in the earlier chapter. Such assets have been privately held in the United States since our 1992 Energy Policy Act and are easier to invest in; but there is much competition.

Private equity firms do sometimes delve into traditional public works. For example, KKR & Co. sold a concession it struck in New Jersey and Pennsylvania to repair and maintain municipal water systems in exchange for a percentage of billing revenue.

And there are a few firms that specialize in public-private projects, such as Meridiam, which is revamping the central terminal at New York City's LaGuardia Airport, built a California courthouse, and invested in Maryland's Purple commuter rail line. Plenary is another. And the ULLICO Infrastructure Fund was an equity investor in the Kennedy Airport terminal #1 renovation.

The Blackstone Group LP infrastructure fund, taking a hint from Warren Buffett's Berkshire Hathaway, is perpetual, meaning there will never be a deadline to liquidate investments. This aligns with pension fund principles of long-term investment holds with stable yields, unlike hedge/private equity funds. Both KKR and Blackstone have purchased insurance companies (a la Buffett) to manage their investments, many of which are in the infrastructure category.

Interestingly, in the early 1990s, Bill Crist was the president of CalPERS, the largest pension fund in the United States. Bill was very well respected and had a keen interest in our Infrastructure Investment Commission recommendations. After a speech I gave in Washington, DC, he contacted me, and we had several discussions both in Washington, DC, and Sacramento.

I suggested electric transmission (the grid) as a new opportunity, and he introduced me to some members of the CalPERS investment staff. They did not have their infrastructure staff at the time; it was early. Later, in 2023–4, the electric grid topic was constantly in public discussion in order to transport renewable energy and in 2024 itself to meet the AI challenge for needed electricity generation to power an avalanche of new data centers.

In February 2018, I received my invitation to the sixth annual National Infrastructure Week. Some personal history here: policy guru Dan Carol (in our coalition) had the initial Infrastructure Week idea, and I suggested it be every year as an annual event. I hosted the initial organizational meeting at the Army Navy Club back in 2012.

And in the same month of 2018, I was particularly pleased to read the excellent report published by The Brattle Group entitled Rising Tide of Next Generation US P3s and How to Sustain It. I knew the authors quite well, particularly Elaine Buckberg from our earlier Treasury meetings and before she joined General Motors. She and her team outlined that infrastructure public-private partnership (P3) activity in the United States has taken off since 2015, with more than thirty states procuring at least one project as a P3 and over 200 projects in the pipeline—well above prior levels of activity.

They went on to say that P3 projects in the pipeline today are also much more diverse in asset class than the classic toll road P3. Road projects are now the minority, with social infrastructure accounting for 24 percent of the total, followed by broadband and water, with the tide turning in 2012. I particularly liked the point that state and local governments had long financed public infrastructure through the municipal bond market, using conventional design-bid-build procurement. Conventional procurement generally involves separate bond financing, design procurement, and construction procurement, followed by government-led operation and maintenance. In contrast, Europe has used P3s to attract private investment into infrastructure, bundle together financing and multiple project phases, thus expediting progress.

While an inventor of the term and advocate for public private partnerships for many years, the uptick in activity over recent years has been very gratifying. Public-Private Partnerships, or P3s, as I had pointed out, are primarily designed for the water, transportation, and social (medical centers, campus facilities, civic centers) infrastructure sectors. Energy generation and telecom were deregulated, and billions of infrastructure funding have been placed in those sectors. My personal role in these economic openings is a point of personal pride.

The oracle for public-private partnerships was Bill Reinhardt, a longtime friend and editor of Public Works Financing. After his retirement salute toward the end of 2018, we proposed to him that it be continued as an infrastructure journal published at Stanford, and that happened.

At about the same time, in 2018, a front-page Wall Street Journal article entitled Investment in Infrastructure Is Booming caught my attention and included observations that rhymed with my predictions years earlier that:

1. Private equity firms would raise a record amount for infrastructure investing in 2018.
2. Institutional investors such as pension funds would be allocating more money to infrastructure, attracted by its reputation for steady yield-like returns.

I was pleased to note that the United States was now the largest market for energy-infrastructure assets, which was a direct result of the 1992 energy deregulation described in the previous chapter.

Pat Moynihan was a good friend and noted to me that I had worked with other industries and their reform, and asked for my help with infrastructure as he was convinced that government could not do it all.

But in February 2019, reflecting the congressional approach for US infrastructure investment legislation, the House Transportation and Infrastructure Committee held their first infrastructure hearing under the new Democratic leadership with Nancy Pelosi returning as the speaker. It was in a hearing room in the new U.S. Capitol Visitors Center. It was an enormous room with four rows for members of Congress. It looked like a Politburo meeting! The testimony, as usual, was very generic and political grandstanding, with the earmark message loud and clear.

Meanwhile, on the GOP side, as we approached the 2020 elections, a major funding shift championed by Transportation Secretary Elaine Chao revealed that rural areas, which had received 21 percent of the $7–$8 billion in infrastructure grants and loans in past years, had now received up to 70 percent in their 2018–19 campaign to improve transportation safety and capacity. Going forward, rural would now get 50 percent, which indicated to me that rural was code for red states where the GOP now prevailed.

While rural America comprises nearly 70 percent of roadways and those carry 47 percent of America's truck traffic, only 20 percent of Americans reside in rural areas, and 46 percent of traffic fatalities occur on rural roads, according to the secretary.

The point was made that the federal government was not pushing this on these rural areas or telling them what to do, according to a Chao adviser. But it sounded like you just needed to vote for the Republicans. The fact is these were grants, for the most part; and you cannot project finance these less populated regions. However, lending to urban projects can leverage federal dollars, thus benefiting rural projects with grants; and both approaches make sense, but in a coordinated way.

I was on a North American Infrastructure Leadership Forum panel in Washington, DC, on October 22, 2019, preceding Trump White House Economic Adviser Larry Kudlow and his remarks. When he spoke to my panel, it was a direct message for states and business leaders planning the nation's infrastructure projects, and he made the following points:

1. We'll cut red tape for you, but don't expect a check from us.
2. We will give you the permits if you can figure out how to pay for it.
3. Don't expect too much federal financial assistance; you can raise the money privately.

In a way, his comments synchronized with our 1993 commission recommendations and represented a new agenda in the infrastructure marketplace, such as project finance versus political finance, public-private partnerships, and the like. This marketplace will expand after the five-year bipartisan infrastructure law funding expires in 2025–6.

I had long argued in various USAID, World Bank, and various foundation panels that some percentage of cellular spectrum auction proceeds (US, India, etc.) should be focused on the funding of national infrastructure banks (including the US), in effect marrying the new economy with the old and using "customer infrastructure/project finance" to take advantage of the time value of money by building out the needed infrastructure and paying for it over many years.

India had become the "call center" of the world and was among the early adopters of new economic value spectrum auctions beginning in 1991; however, there were many bureaucratic hurdles. By March 2015, the government had earned revenue of $13 billion from these new economy spectrum auctions.

But again, none of this revenue was plowed back into an Indian Infrastructure bank at the time that could have focused on the social development of customer infrastructure and long-term financing. Rather, the Ambani family and their Reliance Industries were to be the major beneficiaries.

I was on a World Bank panel years back with an Indian professor at the Kellogg School who had been on India's telecom board, and his response to my proposal was that it will never happen. What I had suggested to that Kellogg School professor seemed, now thirty years later, to be happening.

But some bad news! In July 2023, numerous articles appeared about how the now-ruling Taliban would benefit from the extraordinary mineral riches embedded in Afghanistan. We had been in that country since 2001 and had been generally aware of these vast mineral holdings. I remember going to see the US Agency for International Development (State Department) and suggesting a public private partnership and even a willingness to go to Afghanistan to help set this up.

But this was long before the US International Development Finance Corporation launched in 2019. Absolutely nothing was done to developing that mining infrastructure during the twenty years of US engagement. Now, with the electric vehicle industry, Afghanistan has the largest lithium deposits in the world.

Here in the United States, we had been weak on this global infrastructure finance vocabulary, getting caught up by our US political adversaries who claimed privatization.

Since the millennium year 2000, we have made progress in developing successful infrastructure projects in the United States, many of which are public-private partnerships. There are now billions of dollars in US infrastructure (pension) funds making equity investments in much needed investment grade infrastructure projects.

In short, it is indeed all about the projects, and not the politics. The latter has plagued infrastructure strategy for years in the United States. I have to repeat this often—the emphasis needs to be on project finance, not political finance. Is the project investment-grade and can it be financed or does it need federal lending or even grants to get there?

As we predicted years earlier, investors had been flocking to infrastructure in droves (private infrastructure funds raised a record $95.7 billion in 2018 and a similar amount in 2019) as money managers bet on the growing need to upgrade and expand the world's railroads, natural gas pipelines, and data centers, not to mention the impressive rates of return for these infrastructure funds.

Infrastructure funds have readily gone into energy and telecom infrastructure because they were open and deregulated, as I had pointed out. They are now doing water, social, and transportation but it requires a PPP approach. State Departments of Transportation only do transportation. Therefore, you need a five-pronged infrastructure finance platform. Not a bureaucracy, but just a few young MBAs who have experience and can be public sector developers, working with the state Department of Transportation, Education, Health Care, Universities, etc., in issuing the RFPs for the various PPP projects.

Actually, Governors should require comparators in these state departments on projects above some size to determine the best way to finance a project. In our PIRC recommendations, we laid out many infrastructure finance tools that are focused on project development (and leverage federal dollars). The Governor's offices (and State

Treasurers) are best positioned to manage that coordination. But the 2020 pandemic arrived, and the coronavirus was having a severe economic impact, suggesting the importance of a national infrastructure investment strategy to finally include a national infrastructure corp., innovative finance tools, and infrastructure fund capital.

All three agencies had excellent project finance staffs with generic infrastructure investment expertise, and bringing them all together, while continuing their US transportation, water, and energy infrastructure activities, could easily add professional focus quickly on the financing of these other US infrastructure needs amidst the pandemic.

With the pandemic upon us, I wrote an op-ed with this proviso: Congress could mandate that the existing Build America Bureau (DOT, TIFIA, etc.), the WIFIA Program Office (EPA), and the Energy Loan Program Office (DOE) would all be transferred immediately to this new National Infrastructure Corporation (Treasury's Federal Financing Bank).

Having one infrastructure credit enhancement/lending agency to encourage additional private infrastructure to expedite getting this infrastructure investment program up and running immediately, investment (public-private partnerships) would be a powerful signal and a great rallying point.

Realistically, it was the only way we could get these various sector projects done (health care, rural broadband, etc.) as it included the needed project finance expertise to assist the regional, state, metro, and rural sectors in successful project development.

State and local governments were in fiscal straitjackets, but they can get the projects organized, and every governor should have an infrastructure project finance office to assist in the development and financing of projects in their region, particularly public private partnerships.

Plus, they could quickly recruit other project finance practitioners to ramp up and execute large-scale, long-term lending commitments to qualified regional infrastructure projects, whatever they may be.

Another point, the US International Development Finance Corporation (DFC) provides financing for private development projects overseas with a $60 billion lending cap. As I was saying, "if Congress can do this for US overseas infrastructure investment, why not a National Infrastructure Investment Corporation for lending to our own US infrastructure projects?"

Having one infrastructure credit enhancement/lending agency to encourage additional US private sector infrastructure investment participation (public-private partnerships) was the original concept back in our 1993 Infrastructure Investment Commission days.

Infrastructure funds have been equity investors in hospitals, college campuses (UC Merced), and the like. They have worked with the TIFIA and WIFIA offices but a "National" platform would wave the flag and get projects like rural broadband going. Well, we were in an election year, and for the record, House Democrats passed a $1.5 trillion infrastructure plan that went nowhere. The legislation was approved in a largely party-line 233–188 vote after the Trump White House issued a veto threat, and Senate Majority Leader Mitch McConnell said that same week that the bill is dead on arrival in the upper chamber. It was now a political pandemic as well!

The Senate had a much smaller bipartisan infrastructure (highway bill) reported months earlier by the EPW Committee that waited on Senate Finance Committee funding. But Congress then went on its Fourth of July 2021 two-week recess.

The US Chamber of Commerce has been pressing Congress to pass an infrastructure bill for years—but it won't back the legislation on which House Democrats are preparing to vote this week.

At the time in 2021, a bipartisan Senate group, led by Ohio Republican Rob Portman, finally released the draft outline of their tentative agreement on infrastructure. The plan included $579 billion in new spending over five years, including $110 billion for roads, bridges, and major projects; $66 billion for passenger and freight rail; $48.5 billion for transit; and $25 billion for airports.

The group listed eleven potential financing mechanisms. I was very pleased to note that the list included an infrastructure financing authority to leverage private investment, direct-pay municipal bonds for infrastructure investment, public-private partnerships, and an annual surcharge on electric vehicles.

Unfortunately, this infrastructure financing authority provision was deleted at the last minute when labor lobbyists ignorantly insisted on a Davis-Bacon inclusion (prevailing wage provisions), totally misunderstanding how project finance works in practice and that existing law already mandated that any federal lending or grants to construction projects must adhere to prevailing wages. It was very disappointing after all that work and the progress made.

The House, late on the night of November 5, approved the Senate-passed bipartisan bill; thus, those House earmarks were now in the wastebasket. This noble infrastructure effort was captured by the Biden White House political infrastructure czar process regarding how much grant funding could be delivered.

In January 2022, the newly assigned White House US infrastructure implementation czar, Mitch Landrieu, urged every community to establish their own infrastructure czar. They also released a Biden White House 465-page guidebook on how to obtain funding from the BIL.

As the thousands of attendees attended the global climate change forum in Glasgow, Scotland, in the first week of November 2021, I submitted this op-ed to the Washington Post as the global climate solution was inextricably tied to clean energy infrastructure investment.

Customer Infrastructure, Climate Change, and the Green Climate Fund

Early on in my infrastructure-related work in the 1990s, after our 1993 Infrastructure Investment Commission report that I chaired for Senator Daniel Patrick Moynihan was released, I gave several lectures at Georgetown University and at the World Bank and related symposiums about our findings, including a national infrastructure bank that could leverage federal dollars via lending to provide credit enhancement to investment-grade projects, many of which would be public-private partnerships.

Unfortunately, the typical World Bank lending/grant programs of that era emphasized the financing of large-scale generation facilities, which are very expensive and nurtured a culture of corruption overseas, as well as the vectoring of generation to favored industrialists.

Hearing the testimony during our commission hearings about the importance of the project finance discipline and learning that, with customers, you can finance the upstream transmission and generation facilities, it seemed logical that all US and World Bank type infrastructure finance activities should focus on what I began to call "Customer Infrastructure." By that I meant that any development project should start with investing in the social infrastructure aspects of the project, that is, installing the local wastewater piping and/or electricity distribution grid. In doing so, you are creating a retail utility with a paying customer base and revenue stream. It may be that there must be subsidies to ensure customer payments are realistic and reasonable, but it creates a discipline not only of pride in the community but a platform to then seek proposals from private developers for the more expensive upstream infrastructure.

I was pleased to read Bank of America CEO Brian Moynihan's excellent point that, within this global climate financing discussion, if there is a revenue stream, then the funding is infinite. Senator Daniel Patrick Moynihan had been the early catalyst, and now another Moynihan was batting cleanup.

6

Health Care Reform in 1993 (Clinton) and 2010 (Obama)

I received a 1993 call from Bernard Tresnowski, then CEO of Blue Cross Blue Shield (national) headquartered in Chicago, home also to the American Medical Association and the American Hospital Association. His call went something like this: Mr. Flanagan, I understand you are a close friend and advisor to the Senate Finance Committee Chairman, Senator Moynihan, and I would like to come and see you to discuss Blue Cross and the current health care debate (his Washington office had suggested this call, as it turned out).

I was very interested in the health care reform subject and welcomed his visit, particularly as the Moynihan's had been asking for my advice since Hillary Clinton was the health care lead for the Clinton administration, meeting with them and seeking their support. Later that week, Mr. Tresnowski came by my office and we chatted for half hour. I asked him, "What is your vision, your plan for health care?" and he responded to me, "I don't want to talk about a vision, a plan; I want to be at the table." I explained that he needed some sort of plan to match Senator Moynihan's expectations for a meeting. So, there was no meeting! He left my office!

But that being at the table became the mantra in 2009 and 2010 when President Obama took on the health care challenge and advocated universal coverage, making it up on volume. This time, the insurance companies supported the Obama effort and emphasized that they were at the table, and the Affordable Care Act passed into law, unfortunately focusing solely on universal coverage and not including cost containment. You needed both, in tandem, to make the system work based on my earlier experience. The Obama coalition assumed volume would bring costs down, and there was some truth to that in the insurance company bids. However, the prescription drug industry had other ideas.

The Supreme Court had heard arguments in early March 2015 over whether the new health law, the Affordable Care Act, allowed people in states without their own insurance markets to receive federal tax credits that reduced coverage costs. The number of uninsured would have risen by 8 million if the subsidies had disappeared, according to the experts.

The Court's ruling held that the Affordable Care Act authorized federal tax credits for eligible Americans living not only in states with their own exchanges but also in the thirty-four states with federal marketplaces. The ruling avoided both a major political showdown and confusion in states that would have needed to act on coverage.

In a moment of high drama, Chief Justice John Roberts announced that he would issue the majority opinion in the case. About two-thirds of the way through his reading, it became clear that he would be responsible for saving Obamacare.

Congress passed the Affordable Care Act to improve health insurance markets, not to destroy them, Roberts wrote in the majority opinion. If possible, we must interpret the Act in a way that is consistent with the former and avoids the latter.

And then in early 2020, the coronavirus had arrived in earnest in the United States, and as of early May there had been 1,249,846 confirmed cases and 75,197 deaths in the United States. By May 21, there were 92,000 deaths and climbing, and over 100,000 deaths on Memorial Day weekend.

To give some sense of the global magnitude, Spain had 221,447 confirmed cases and 26,070 deaths at that time. Italy and the United Kingdom each had suffered around 30,000 deaths and France had approximately 26,000 deaths from the resultant Covid-19. China, where the coronavirus began in late 2019, reported 84,409 confirmed cases and 4,643 deaths and announced that they had stopped the virus in their country by the end of April 2020. Over thirty countries had confirmed cases and deaths, and roughly ten countries indicated they had it under control.

With the constant rhetoric about the United States having the finest (and most expensive) medical care in the world, you really had to question the leadership of the Trump administration when viewing the deplorable number of US confirmed cases and deaths amidst the constant political infighting that continued into the summer of 2020. Having worked with Francis Fukuyama at Stanford, I found his 2020 analysis that President Donald Trump used the crisis to pick fights and increase social cleavages to be right on point and consistent with Mary Trump's description of her uncle as well. The divide-and-conquer mayhem of wearing or not wearing masks, for example caused great damage, including fights on airplanes, etc. And in 2022, the Biden administration reported that 93.6 million Covid cases and 1.04 million Covid deaths in the United States had occurred since early 2020.

By then, the majority of Americans were vaccinated, and that seemed to be the answer. Dr. Anthony Fauci was nationally recognized and announced he would retire in December 2023 at age eighty-one from his important national leadership role heading up the National Institute of Allergy and Infectious Diseases.

The Covid-19 pandemic had put hospitals and health care workers under enormous pressure. It also strained the US health insurance system. In 2019, roughly 160 million American workers and their dependents were insured through employers; but the Kaiser Family Foundation estimated that some 50 million American workers and their dependents utilizing the Affordable Care Act could lose their health insurance if the Republican siege on that law continued.

So, it was very fortunate that the Affordable Care Act (ACA) had been passed by Congress under regular order with numerous committee hearings and signed into law by President Obama on March 23, 2010, and the ACA's major provisions came into force in 2014. There were some GOP accusations regarding the partisan legislative track of the legislation, but I was closely monitoring and was impressed by the regular order being adhered to for passage.

In the years after President Obama had signed the Affordable Care Act into law, 20 million adults had gained health coverage. Now, for the first time ever, more than 90 percent of Americans had health insurance. The Affordable Care Act improved coverage and lowered costs for the more than 80 percent of Americans who had insurance before the law was passed. In California, for example, only 7 percent of citizens did not have health care insurance in 2016, down from 17 percent without coverage in 2013.

The increased coverage was due equally to an expansion of Medicaid eligibility and to major changes to individual insurance markets. Both involved new spending, funded through a combination of new taxes and cuts to Medicare provider rates and Medicare Advantage. In 2018, Oregon was to pass a law establishing health care as a right, as in the United Kingdom.

But there was unrelenting opposition to Obamacare from congressional Republicans, only to reach a higher decibel level after the Trump inauguration. It seemed they did not want the Affordable Care Act to work (similar to Social Security years earlier under FDR) and began a rear-guard action to throw roadblocks in its way! Repeal and replace was the original GOP strategy, but they could never agree on the replacement part!

In early 2016, I hoped that there would be a press conference by HHS Secretary Sylvia Burwell responding to reports that health exchange premiums could be increasing by as much as 25 percent the following year. These rumors were confusing to the layperson, that is, the voter in that election year, and the Republicans exaggerated the situation. The fact was that most health coverage is with employer health plans in the United States, and those premiums were going down.

But she did say that, while there are problems with the Affordable Care Act, they can be fixed. The alternative we have is to work together and improve the things that aren't working well. Well, the GOP was not interested; no, their plan was to attack incessantly, and I never understood why!

Secretary Burwell did lay the blame for the increases with health insurers, not on the program itself. Burwell did say, however, that most people seeing increased premiums would be eligible for tax subsidies.

Fast forward to the 2024 election year, and there was zero partisan political talk about the Affordable Care Act. As they say, time heals all wounds—Obamacare had survived.

Now back to 1993, when new President Bill Clinton launched a health care reform effort, putting his wife, Hillary, in charge. I assisted this effort by coordinating between the Clinton White House and the Moynihan's, as Senator Moynihan was now the powerful Chairman of the Senate Finance Committee. Ultimately, Hillary Clinton's inflexibility, a reluctant Congress, and the insurance lobby, in this case, brought the process to a halt.

The way it worked was the Moynihan's would call me, particularly Liz Moynihan, with their concerns prompted by Hillary Clinton's visits to their Navy Memorial condominium for discussions. After their call, I would then go and visit with the

Clinton White House's Ira Magaziner. Ira was a Brown University valedictorian, as well as a Rhodes Scholar along with Bill Clinton. He was the senior advisor for policy development for President Clinton and served as the chief healthcare policy advisor.

In our meetings, Ira and I were looking for a cost containment model that would foster transparency, competition, new technology, and consumer benefit, as was the model for the other industry reform sectors that I had worked on previously. We would get a blackboard out and hash away!

Universal coverage was a Clinton objective even then as it had political value; but the Moynihan's were telling me that it would be politically complicated. I did believe at the time that a successful cost containment strategy would ultimately lead to some form of universal coverage.

But the Clinton effort was not to succeed, particularly with the opposition of both the insurance and pharmaceutical industries. Hillary Clinton gave up eventually and was quite chastened. Plus, Senator Moynihan's policy preference at the time was to do welfare reform in a Democratic Congress first and then health care reform.

I will go into this 1993-4 effort in more detail, but suffice it to say it was an expensive learning experience as the GOP took over both houses in the 1994 elections, a major disappointment for Pat Moynihan as he had been chairman of the Senate Finance Committee for only two years.

Lawrence O'Donnell was the Staff Director for the Senate Finance Committee. He was a real character parking his motorcycle outside of the Russel Senate Office Building. We were good friends! He went on to become an American television pundit, actor, and host of The Last Word with Lawrence O'Donnell, an MSNBC opinion and news program.

Lawrence was also a producer and writer for the NBC series The West Wing, and creator and executive producer of the NBC series Mister Sterling. At the same time, Tim Russert was serving as the Senator's Chief of Staff, a very talented duo indeed, as Tim later on became the moderator of NBC's Meet the Press, head of their Washington Bureau, and the evening news anchor slot.

It wasn't until President Obama took up the health care challenge in 2009-10 as a millennium issue to be addressed once again in a Democratic Congress that universal coverage became the bow of the ship! I had my concerns as cost containment had to be addressed, plus we were still in the Great Recession, and there were other priorities, like saving the country from financial ruin.

My perspective on these issues, at the time, was a holdover from my earlier health care policy history. Also, it was the only major regulatory reform measure passed by Congress since the Millennium year 2000, and regular order being observed was the primary reason for its passage.

By January 24, 2024, the good news was that more than 21 million people had now signed up for health plans through the Affordable Care Act's health insurance marketplaces. I was somewhat perplexed by how silent the Biden administration was on this momentous accomplishment. After all, he had been the vice president at its passage, and the enrollment figures reflected a roughly eighty percent surge in sign-ups for the ACA since President Biden took office in 2021 and expanded the subsidies available to consumers. It was quite a Democratic Party victory, albeit the Biden White House was relatively silent on the ACA topic, as was their strategy, it seemed.

This record level of enrollment came as former president Donald Trump was again seeking the GOP nomination and again vowing to repeal the program if elected. But he was the Lone Ranger on this now, as most elected officials had accepted the ACA and the repeal and replace chorus was a distant memory.

Some personal history, early in my post-Navy career in San Francisco with the Martin Segal Company (owned then by the Wall Street firm, Wertheim), a 1975 Ford Foundation grant enabled me to guide Alameda County, California, to the first competitive bidding for its public employee health care system. This was also a first for California. Blue Cross had a virtual monopoly on these local municipal plans, and the goal of the grant was competition and economies of scale.

The Martin Segal Company was a nationwide consulting organization headquartered in New York that provided tailored consulting services, including actuarial services, to pension and health plans, particularly the multi-employer/union-trusteed plans. They were excited!

Jim Marshall was the Alameda County Human Resources director, and we worked very closely together. We first designed the basic plan and then put on several dog and pony shows to the dozens of cities in Alameda County. Blue Cross was out to get us, for sure! It was very challenging and ahead of its time—I am proud to say! We did release an RFP for the County, and Aetna miraculously bid and won! It was a big deal!

In 1977, having accepted Southern Pacific's offer to run their Washington office and knowing that railroad deregulation was my immediate task, I was transitioning to Washington, DC. Having landed at Dulles Airport, I shared a cab, as it turned out, with Dr. Alain C. Einthoven, a Stanford economist. He had been a Deputy Assistant Secretary of Defense from 1961 to 1965, and from 1965 to 1969 he was the Assistant Secretary of Defense for Systems Analysis. At the time, he was a professor of public and private management at Stanford Graduate School of Business.

We talked for an hour all the way into Washington, DC, about the economics of the health care system; and I emphasized the need for competition and transparency in hospital costs based on what I had seen at the Segal Company, an argument that continues to this day (albeit the Trump administration and GOP Congress called for just that). We were in the public policy groove, as you would say!

Looking at Dr. Einthoven's bibliography today, those issues have been his continued legacy in his many publications, and here are just four examples:

1. 1980 Health plan: The only practical solution to the soaring cost of medical care.
2. 1988 Theory and practice of managed competition in health care finance.
3. 1993 The history and principles of managed competition.
4. 2005 Competition in health care: It takes systems to pursue quality and efficiency.

Remember this conversation was in 1977, so maybe that cab ride was just too early!

In the early 1990s, Richmond, Virginia, super lawyer Justin Moore telephoned me with a tobacco question. Justin had been the Chairman of the Board of Dominion

Resources (a client) and on the Board of Philip Morris. He wanted my advice on the pending state attorney general tobacco lawsuits and what Congress might do.

President Clinton's health reform initiative was still alive then, and I suggested that Philip Morris set up an insurance program that cigarette smokers could join and pay a monthly (subsidized) premium. You could argue that the cigarette industry action would suppress any lawsuits! I was not a smoker and disapproved of the industry's advertising, but was giving my impartial opinion based on my own analysis.

Justin sent the memorandum I prepared to the CEO of Philip Morris, who responded to me in a personal note that they were not equipped for the health care insurance business. The rest is history, as state attorney generals banded together and won enormous penalties that tobacco will be paying to states (supposedly for anti-smoking initiatives) for decades to come in the billions of dollars.

As noted, since the states finally settled their lawsuits against the tobacco companies in November 1998, annual reports are issued assessing whether the states are keeping their promise to use settlement funds—estimated at $246 billion over the first twenty five years—to tackle the enormous public health problems posed by tobacco use in the United States. The states also collect billions more in tobacco taxes.

In Fiscal Year 2014, the states collected some $25 billion in revenue from the tobacco settlement and tobacco taxes, but will spend only 1.9 percent of it—$481.2 million—on programs to prevent kids from smoking and help smokers quit. This meant the states were spending less than two cents of every dollar in tobacco revenue to fight tobacco use.

In retrospect, my advice to Philip Morris in the early 1990s to set up a health care customer-oriented health insurance strategy for tobacco users was probably on the mark as far as a business public policy strategy is concerned. They spent some $3 million on lobbying in 2018 in that continuing spiral to nowhere, eventually succumbing to the multi-billion-dollar settlement with various state attorney generals.

But back to the Moynihan's and the Clintons in those early months of 1993. Hillary Clinton had visited with both the Senator and Liz Moynihan on several occasions at their seventh-floor condominium in the United States Navy Memorial complex at 801 Pennsylvania Avenue. Liz had cleverly purchased two moderately priced condo units then under construction in 1991 and had them merged into one very nice, roomy home overlooking the National Archives on Pennsylvania Avenue. Howard Baker bought the top floor unit above for $2–3 million. I was on the Board of the Navy Memorial Foundation itself, so it was fun to have them there as residents.

The Navy Memorial was to transform Pennsylvania Avenue and the adjacent neighborhoods. Pat Moynihan was the leader of that urban renaissance, and it was fitting that they were to live there until his untimely death in 2003. He had retired from the Senate at the end of the Millennium year 2000. I visited them many times, and it was the perfect spot for them.

I had been an original founder and board member of the Navy Memorial Foundation, along with several Naval Academy classmates (Class of 1965), and was very proud of our accomplishment in seeing the Navy Memorial completed as it truly transformed Pennsylvania Avenue!

Pat had begun his work on Pennsylvania Avenue shortly after John F. Kennedy took note of the street's shortcomings during his inaugural parade, as Moynihan described in a 1985 letter to The Washington Post that Kennedy would be waving first to the left and then to the right, and looking hard at downtown Washington for what was most likely the first time in his life. He saw that the area was all but derelict; it was simply a setting of used-up buildings that had been or were being abandoned, as downtown floated out Connecticut Avenue, leaving the Capitol behind.

Pat Moynihan served as an Assistant Secretary of Labor in the Kennedy administration and spent the next forty years, including four terms in the Senate, working to elevate the avenue into something that America could take pride in. He recommended the establishment of the Pennsylvania Avenue Development Corp. in 1973, and among the improvements that followed were the preservation of the Old Post Office Pavilion (for a time the Trump Hotel), the opening of the East Building of the National Gallery of Art, and the construction of the Canadian Embassy, Market Square, and the Ronald Reagan Building.

Liz and Pat Moynihan were good friends, and I would serve on their political steering committee for many years. When Pat became the chairman of the Senate Finance Committee in 1993, he would repeatedly tell me that he was skeptical both about the timing of President Clinton's health care proposal and its universal coverage provision. Focused on the financing of health care, he stated that there was no health care crisis in this country. Again, Pat felt strongly that welfare reform should go first, and then we should move to health care, building on that success. Liz Moynihan would call me up and say that Hillary came by again, but she just would not listen. Pat told her, "Let's do welfare reform first, then health care," but she will not agree. And years later, Hillary would succeed Pat representing New York in the Senate. How the world turns!

Despite his earlier writings on the negative effects of the welfare state, Pat surprised many people later by voting against the Clinton-backed welfare reform proposal as drafted in 1996 in the GOP-controlled Congress focused on workfare, a GOP recipe. He was sharply critical of the GOP bill and certain Democrats who crossed party lines to support it. This was also a reaction, some felt, to Clinton's pushing aside his 1993 welfare reform proposals in favor of Hillary's health care reform effort.

At the time in 1993, as the chairman of the Senate Finance Committee, Pat had offered strategists at the Clinton White House a suggestion. He knew many Democrats were pressuring the president to pursue universal health care, but Moynihan believed nearly total Republican opposition would be difficult to overcome. He suggested to me, as he had to Hillary, that instead the president should focus on another promise he had made, to end welfare as we know it, as Republicans could be convinced to back that.

Pat believed the nation's welfare system was in a more acute crisis than its health care system. He also believed that major reforms rarely passed Congress with the support of only one party. They pass 70–30, he explained, or they fail. Anything big has to be bipartisan, he would tell me.

Hillary Clinton continued her visits, and Pat Moynihan would repeat his idea for welfare reform first, then health care, and explained that to the first lady, but she was determined; and that is what happened. I would get Liz Moynihan's calls and would brief Ira Magaziner on this situation, but there was nothing he could do inside the White House.

Pat's recommendation of Ruth Bader Ginsburg to President Clinton to serve as an associate justice of the Supreme Court of the United States from 1993 until her death in 2020 was part of that drama. She was nominated by President Bill Clinton to replace retiring justice Byron White, and the Clintons thought that might sway Pat regarding health care first at the time.

The White House vigorously pursued the health-care-reform agenda crafted by the First Lady and her team. They presumed most Republicans would line up against them but figured the Democrats would back them. The Moynihan's told me in one of their 1993 calls that Senate Minority Leader Robert J. Dole (R-Kan.) had handed a note to Pat, the Senate Finance Committee chairman, suggesting that they map out a compromise. So, they called Dave Gergen, urging the White House to loosen its insistence on achieving universal coverage right away. Moynihan reminded Gergen that great advances in the nation's social safety net—including Social Security and Medicare—had been passed by large congressional majorities of a kind the Clinton plan simply did not have. Gergen, later, was in the White House Map Room with the president, first lady, and other aides to decide whether the president should signal that he was open to a gradual phase-in of universal coverage. The question was put to the president and first lady, and she was very opposed to incrementalism. Gergen looked at his watch and jotted down: At 10:22 p.m. tonight, health care died and called Pat Moynihan.

Republicans won resoundingly in the 1994 midterm elections, and President Clinton learned from the experience. The White House reverted to the approach Moynihan had initially suggested, that is, welfare reform except now with a GOP Congress, so it was workfare.

The so-called Personal Responsibility and Work Opportunity Reconciliation Act of 1996 was passed by the 104th United States GOP Congress with Newt Gingrich as Speaker and signed by President Bill Clinton on August 22, 1996. The bill implemented major changes to US social welfare policy:

1. Replacing the Aid to Families with Dependent Children (AFDC) program with the Temporary Assistance for Needy Families (TANF) program.
2. Granting states greater latitude in administering social welfare programs.
3. Implementing new requirements on welfare recipients, including a five-year lifetime limit on benefits.
4. Implementing work requirements.

After the passage of the law, the number of individuals receiving federal welfare dramatically declined.

The law was heralded as a reassertion of America's work ethic by the US Chamber of Commerce, largely in response to the bill's workfare component. The law was a cornerstone of the Republican Party's Contract with America and also fulfilled Clinton's campaign promise to end welfare as we know it. But Pat Moynihan disagreed with the approach and voted against it. This was not a fender-bender; no, it was a real political pile-up!

When Bernard Tresnowski visited me in my office wanting to be at the table, I should have told him my often-repeated theory; that is, you are much better off in the public policy process if you state that you will support the proposal if it is modified versus saying we will oppose the proposal unless it is changed. You need to go beyond being at the table. That was how we completed electricity deregulation in 1992 just before his visit.

But my earlier experience with Blue Cross Blue Shield, in Alameda County, did influence my thinking. I felt they were just going to oppose reform, as Mr. Tresnowski (president of the Association from 1981 until his retirement in 1995) had publicly stated around that time:

But he said nothing to me about consumers, cost containment, competition, transparency, and technology: All essential ingredients for a policy focused on the health of the American citizen.

Reviewing my files, I came across an October 21, 1994 letter that I sent to Dr. Steve Schroder, then the President of the Robert Wood Foundation in Princeton, New Jersey. I noted having attended a recent luncheon with Dr. Phil Lee (HHS) wherein he offered the thought that the recent health care reform debate had drifted from the subject of health to the topic of health care insurance. He was right, and at a subsequent event I attended, Senator Ted Kennedy predicted it would be another twenty years before we finished the job of health care reform. And he was close to the mark!

I was saddened to read that old friend Michael Bromberg had passed away in August 2016. Mike led the for-profit Federation of American Hospitals from 1969 to 1994 and was greatly admired for his consummate bipartisan skills in the health care policy sector. His focus on cost containment fit well. He had some good ideas for reform, but in 1994, with the failed Clinton effort, it was time to move on.

Also at that time, Karen Ignagni, the CEO of the American Association of Health Plans (AAHP) from 1993 to 2003, was in our discussion groups. She was to run the successor Health Insurance Association of America through 2015. Karen opted to be at the table after initially being in opposition. And she did so, in June 2009, by telling President Barack Obama: "You have our commitment (HIA's) to play, to contribute, and to help pass health care reform this year." By being at the table, she was supporting the proposal if it contained some of their suggestions.

Before joining AAHP, Karen was a director of the AFL-CIO's Department of Employee Benefits. Previously, she worked as a staffer for Senator Claiborne Pell from Rhode Island, having graduated from Providence College.

At the suggestion of AFL-CIO President John Sweeney (also a good Moynihan friend), Karen and I had lunch when she was still at the AFL-CIO on this health care strategy topic. She wrote many articles on various aspects of health care policy issues. But most importantly, I may have convinced her to be at the table with policy commitments in 2009, working with the White House Office of Health Reform and a Democratic Congress. We had talked about my earlier legislative efforts and how it was a much better legislative strategy to say we will support this if versus we will oppose unless!

In 2021, I was working my way through former President Barack Obama's first volume biography, A Promised Land, and early in 2009, he was holding an Oval Office health care strategy session with his two key aides from his Chicago days, Rahm Emmanuel and David Axe Axelrod. They were not very encouraging about pursuing the health care reform effort, noting how little credit President Obama was getting for his economic policy efforts to bring the country out of the great 2007–2009 recession.

Obama rightly notes his Democratic Party's lack of an effective economic management image despite their Herculean White House efforts. This inability of Democrats to talk about their economic achievements has been and will continue to be a political liability, allowing the GOP to take undeserved credit, with polls consistently favoring the Republicans on the economy since the millennium year 2000.

In earlier pages, Obama talks about Ted Kennedy's 2009 visit to a White House seminar on the health care topic. In ill health, Kennedy still exhorts the crowd to move forward; and the applause is deafening. Remember, Ted Kennedy and Caroline had endorsed Obama's presidential candidacy (against Hillary Clinton). As I read that paragraph, it seemed that was the moment when Obama decided to get health care reform done in honor of his hero, Senator Kennedy.

The House passed their health care legislation on November 11, 2009, and the full Senate debated the health care bill for twenty-five straight days before passing it on December 24, 2009. Again, importantly, this was regular order at its best, with partisan debates taking place and Democratic and GOP amendments offered. Universal coverage was the major theme.

For historical reference, earlier in June and July 2009 with Democrats in the majority, the Senate Health, Education, Labor and Pensions (HELP) Committee spent nearly sixty hours over thirteen days marking up the bill that became the Affordable Care Act. That September and October, the Senate Finance Committee worked on the legislation for eight days, its longest markup in two decades. It considered more than 130 amendments and held seventy-nine roll-call votes. This was classic regular order in the bipartisan tradition.

While several bills eventually coalesced into what became the ACA, and the Congressional Budget Office (CBO) provided numerous reports and scoring on multiple aspects of the law ahead of its vote in the Senate, the ACA passed without a single Republican vote. They argued that they were ignored and uninvited to the policy process, which was simply not the case.

On February 25, 2010, in the so-called White House Health Care Summit, even though Congress had acted, President Obama held a seven-hour bipartisan meeting at Blair House on the health reform legislation to see if there was still a chance for a bipartisan approach.

Attendees included House and Senate leadership, chairs and ranking members of committees overseeing health insurance legislation, Vice President Joe Biden, Health and Human Services Secretary Kathleen Sebelius, and Nancy-Ann DeParle from the White House. I watched it on C-SPAN.

The discussions included cost containment, insurance reforms, eliminating waste, reducing the deficit, and the central theme of universal coverage; however, there was no bipartisan agreement.

The final Affordable Care Act referred to two separate pieces of legislation—the Patient Protection and Affordable Care Act (P. L. 111–148) and the Health Care and Education Reconciliation Act of 2010 (P. L. 111–152)—and was finally signed into law by President Obama the following month on March 23, 2010. The contents of the bill had been made available to both parties' multiple times throughout its development and to the press.

The Democrats' in-depth health care legislative process is important to remember, as the GOP, once in the majority, defended their partisan attacks on Obamacare, claiming that they were not included in the original Affordable Care Act process, which was not true. Later, the GOP would claim that they were ignored. But it was their unfortunate story to back up their hard-right partisan attacks when they returned to the majority.

The GOP repeal and replace strategy in 2017 was closed-door, highly partisan effort and bereft of any policy suggestions other than repeal. GOP Senator John McCain noted this posturing in his book, *The Restless Wave*, as he cast the deciding Senate floor vote to oppose repeal, as there was no GOP replacement.

It is amazing to me how President Obama's major legislation was so little understood. With its complications, lack of cost containment, and general confusion, it became a third rail leading up to the 2014 midterm elections debacle for the Democrats, just as it had happened in 1994 ten years before, when Newt Gingrich became the Speaker amidst the health care confusion at that time.

In the 2018 Democratic primaries, the so-called progressives were calling for universal Medicare, which, in many ways, was the Affordable Care Act, which actually was designed to pay for itself and provided universal coverage. While the 2017 GOP tax cut raised the indebtedness of the country, I found the progressive advocacy to be naïve, ill-informed, and ill timed.

In reflection, the supporting segments of the US health care industry were relatively quiet. It would have been helpful if the medical profession had been more outspoken publicly in support beginning in 2010; however, the partisan nature of the congressional process probably scared them away.

It was unfortunate that the health care enrollment roll-out turned into a Health and Human Services Department Information Technology (IT) debacle in October 2013. But it did wake up the policymakers that government IT procurement was a real problem. I talk more about this in Chapter 10 in this book.

One innocent victim was Maryland governor Martin O'Malley, who was gearing up to run for President of the United States as an experienced and competent manager, and had to watch his state health exchange blow up in smoke due to IT failures while his Lt. Governor, Anthony Brown, who was running to succeed him, was nominally in charge. They both were damaged!

Several years later, now a resident of Annapolis, Maryland, I noticed that the Maryland Health Care Commission created the campaign, WearTheCost.org, and distributed black T-shirts that said HIP REPLACEMENT $30,067 in big type from the commission's database or HYSTERECTOMY $16,138. Other shirts featured prices for a knee replacement or baby delivery, showing the huge differences in what the same procedures cost at different Maryland hospitals.

The hysterectomy expense of $16,138 on the T-shirt was just an average. In recent years, the operation cost as much as $20,635 at Johns Hopkins Hospital in Baltimore and as little as $12,798 at Anne Arundel Medical Center in Annapolis, which happened to be our family hospital; but it is now entitled Luminis Health System, which is like going into the major leagues for executive compensation. All the employees seemed disgruntled.

Hopkins was also the most expensive hospital in which to have a baby, at $14,578, compared with the average Maryland cost of $11,590. The commission website's price quotes applied to commercial insurance rates and included hospital care as well as non-hospital spending, such as doctors' fees and prescription drugs. Hospital-to-hospital results vary sharply even under Maryland's unique health care finance system, which regulates what hospitals are paid.

Interestingly, a $4 million federal grant financed the Wear-the-Cost campaign. Price transparency has been a laudable cost containment goal for decades, even in the 1970s when I was at the Segal company. Even back then, we were arguing for hospital cost transparency. If patients can give more business to lower-cost institutions with fewer complications, hospitals will work harder to contain costs and improve outcomes, slowing the increase in insurance premiums and government health expenses. But customers, that is, patients, need to understand the product first and know what it costs.

After the passage of the Affordable Care Act in 2010, the following year the new House GOP majority repeatedly voted to repeal it; but they were now on a tenuous limb with the President's initial announcement in early 2014 that 8 million people had signed up for health care through the new insurance exchange.

There was much GOP political criticism, but the health care industry, the hospitals, doctors, and insurers were going to quietly make it work.

This thing is working, Obama said of the Affordable Care Act, his signature domestic achievement. And just before Christmas, HHS Secretary Sylvia Matthews Burwell (who had done a masterful in-house job since her arrival) announced updated health care enrollment numbers as 6.4 million people had signed up for 2015 health insurance plans sold on HealthCare.gov, the federal Obamacare exchange that was now serving thirty-seven states.

That big number included about 1.9 million new customers, existing Obamacare customers who actively re-enrolled since sign-ups began November 15, and people who were automatically re-enrolled in their current health coverage, per the Health and Human Services Department. Experts were encouraged and indicated they would achieve the targeted 9.1 million enrollees.

This good news seemed to indicate that there would be no wholesale repeal of President Obama's Affordable Care Act, as the Senate could not pass the House health repeal bill or their GOP Senate version either.

It was an ugly time, and amidst all this political theater, the GOP Tea Party was sowing confusion in the marketplace and preventing progress, which seemed to be the GOP objective. It reminded me of the GOP objections to FDR's Social Security proposal.

The medical/health care sector continued to be supportive of the Affordable Care Act; however, for some reason, the GOP ignored them, calling instead for the repeal the legislation from the first day of its enactment. Once they controlled their respective chambers, they began in earnest. The GOP health care legislative effort, following the Trump 2016 election, was conducted behind closed doors with little transparency or bipartisan accord.

My prediction was that the 2017–18 GOP Congress would, at some point, try to pass their version of the Affordable Care Act, with the first sentence being the repeal of the Obama Affordable Care Act, and then the next section would be the "Affordable Care Act" by another name, with their incremental revisions to the original Obama version.

But I thought they would wait and get in the legislative rhythm by doing a bipartisan infrastructure bill first, as I talked about in the previous chapter. Infrastructure would hinge on tax reform (tax cuts), which we thought would have to be the first item on the 2017 GOP post-election calendar.

But I was surprised that the House conservatives could not wait; health care went first in the Trump presidency with a repeal and replace effort. Apparently, the Trump team wanted to do infrastructure first, I am told, to generate some bipartisan momentum; but the GOP leadership said no, they mistakenly wanted to go after health care as that is where the money is for infrastructure.

The Senate opposition began the next day when, finally, influential hospitals led by the American Hospital Association, doctor groups led by the American Medical Association, and seniors led by the powerful American Association of Retired Persons came out against the House health-care proposal.

In 2017, virtually every major medical care and health care delivery organization signed letters of opposition to the Republicans' American Health Care Act, and the town halls around the country were the scene of very crowded and vocal protests by the constituents of the host congressman.

At the same time, as this rhetorical combat was happening in the US Capitol, a study came out indicating a Canadian born with the fatal lung disease cystic fibrosis can expect to live a decade longer than an American with the same disease, which accentuated the debate over the quality/cost of US healthcare.

And that is what the Congressional debate should have been about! Here in the United States, we spent about $9,400 per capita on health care in 2014, versus about $5,300 in Canada, according to the World Health Organization. Yet the US fares worse than Canada on broad measures including life expectancy and infant mortality, according to World Bank data. We seem to pay the most for the least!

Cost containment indeed was not adequately addressed in the Affordable Care Act, theorizing on economies of scale under universal coverage. Major employers noted that the cost of their health care plans would grow five percent in 2018, to an average cost of more than $14,000 per employee based on a 2017 survey of 148 large companies; the increase was attributed largely to expensive specialty drugs and individuals with high medical costs. Employers can, since after the Second World War, deduct their expenditures for employee health and pension fund coverage, and it is significant!

It was hard to fathom why Congress would pass earlier legislation that prevented Medicare from negotiating rates for drugs; but that is what happened. And while Medicare had a significant impact on negotiating rates for all other facets of health care, the highly paid pharmaceutical lobby displayed an amazing arrogance that came back to haunt them. Here is that history:

Pharmaceutical misbehavior began with former Louisiana Congressman Billy Tauzin, originally a southern Democrat who served as GOP Chairman of the House Energy and Commerce, with jurisdiction over our nation's drug policy.

Two months before resigning as chairman of the House Energy and Commerce Committee, which oversees the drug industry, Tauzin had played a key role in shepherding the Medicare Prescription Drug Bill through Congress. Democrats said that the bill was a giveaway to the drug makers because it prohibited the government from negotiating lower drug prices and banned the importation of identical, cheaper drugs from Canada and elsewhere. In January 2005, the day after his term in Congress ended, he began work as the CEO of the Pharmaceutical Research and Manufacturers of America (PhRMA), a trade group for pharmaceutical companies. Tauzin was hired at a salary estimated at $2 million a year.

Five years later, he announced his retirement from the association at the end of June 2010 after President Barack Obama on March 23, 2010, signed into law the Affordable Care Act which unbelievably failed to address the pharmaceutical industry and its escalating drug costs. Tauzin had performed well!

I knew Billy Tauzin as this was the same committee that passed our electricity deregulation bill (PUHCA Reform) in 1992. Louisiana politicians, I had learned, were in a class by themselves when it came to wheeling and dealing. For example, in 2003 Mr. Tauzin, then chairman of the House Energy and Commerce Committee, made an unusual real estate deal when he paid more than $1 million for a 1,500-acre ranch in Texas. And he invited a dozen friends—mostly executives and lobbyists with interests before his committee—to cover its mortgage by paying dues as members of a new hunting club.

As head of PhRMA, Tauzin was a key player in the 2009–10 health care reform negotiations that produced pharmaceutical industry support. He received $11.6 million from PhRMA in 2010, making him the highest-paid health care lobbyist. Over the course of 2009, the drug industry trade group spent over $28 million on lobbyists.

Aside from PhRMA's massive in-house lobbying operation, the trade group hired forty-eight outside lobbying firms. The total number of lobbyists working for PhRMA in 2009 reached 165. Some 137 of those 165 lobbyists representing PhRMA were former employees of either the legislative or executive branches. Of these, dozens were former congressional staffers, including two former chiefs of staff to Senate Finance Committee Chairman Max Baucus.

Then add the Biotechnology Innovation Organization (BIO), a lobbying group for the biotech industry, which spent $9.9 million, while individual companies spent comparable amounts, including $11.4 million for Pfizer Inc. and $6.8 million each for Merck and Eli Lilly.

According to data compiled by the Center for Responsive Politics, drug makers contributed huge sums to congressional campaign committees during the same period.

On March 5, 2009, the Obama White House held a meeting with industry leaders to try to bring them to the table and see what could be done to gain their assistance. Two months later, PhRMA and other trade industry groups pledged cost-cutting measures to the White House that would save, they claimed, upwards of $2 trillion over the next decade.

President Obama announced the deal in the State Dining Room, flanked by leaders of the various trade groups; the administration followed up with a media blitz in the press and on the White House website. But the cost-cutting never happened!

Fast forward to early 2018, and there was broad bipartisan support for the so-called CREATES Act, which would assist generic drug developers against opposition from branded pharmaceutical companies seeking to keep their competition at bay.

Conservatives such as Sens. Ted Cruz of Texas and Mike Lee of Utah, along with liberals such as Sens. Dianne Feinstein of California and Sheldon Whitehouse of Rhode Island, were co-sponsors of the bill. Heritage Action and FreedomWorks on the right, as well as Families USA and Public Citizen on the left, were supporting it, as were the American Hospital Association and America's Health Insurance Plans.

It allowed generic companies to sue branded companies for failing to provide them with samples needed for testing and gave the Food and Drug Administration more authority in approving alternative safety protocols if the branded company refuses to allow generic competitors to participate in a medication's safety protocol. The FDA supported the proposal.

Yet the bill was opposed by the Pharmaceutical Researchers and Manufacturers of America and never made it into the two-year budget agreement signed by President Trump in February 2018. Under congressional Regular Order, this provision, with its political support, normally would have been reported from the House and Senate committees to their respective floors for voting.

At the same time, in the courts, a February 2018 trial was underway in federal court in Philadelphia, testing the power of the Federal Trade Commission to punish drug makers' alleged moves to thwart the sale of low-cost generics.

When it comes to transparency, from my experience, health insurers receive a report card grade of C. The contracts between insurers and medical providers prevent either party from disclosing negotiated prices. Both sides insist on price secrecy! And then there were the pharmaceutical benefit managers (PBMs) that maneuvered their way to being the "middlemen."

In 2016, my grandson living with his family in Petaluma, California, had a bike accident (hit by a moving vehicle), and while there was a local hospital, the ambulance service arbitrarily drove him some thirty miles to the larger and better-equipped Santa Rosa hospital for an MRI. His parents received a bill for about $45,000 for that ambulance ride and hospital visit. Fortunately, they had a very good employer-provided health plan that was ultimately responsible, but it is a good example of the practices that occur.

In 2019, the Trump administration (and in particular HHS Secretary Alex Azar, June 17, 1967) spoke out on new policies that would require pricing information on drug advertising on television. Azar was a lawyer and pharmaceutical lobbyist and was formerly the United States Deputy Secretary of Health and Human Services under George W. Bush from 2005 to 2007. He knew the issues and was quite smooth in his presentations.

From 2012 to 2017, Azar was President of the US division of Eli Lilly and Company, a major pharmaceutical drug company, and was a member of the board of directors of the Biotechnology Innovation Organization, a pharmaceutical lobby. They deserve credit for the November announcement that, beginning in 2021, all hospital and related medical pricing must be publicly disclosed, which caused great alarm in the sector.

Americans now have the right to upfront healthcare prices due to this federal hospital price transparency rule that took effect in January 2021. Unfortunately, most hospitals have not followed that rule. According to one recent study, only a quarter of hospitals nationwide are fully compliant, including posting discounted cash prices and all health insurance plan rates.

This figure was only 28 percent in Virginia; but in 2023, these federal rules were codified in Virginia state law. This added an important layer of enforcement to ensure hospitals comply with all pricing requirements.

The US Department of Health and Human Services had only fined four hospitals nationwide for violating the rule. Now Virginia's regulators could do a much better job of enforcement. Still, the elephant in the room, prescription drug pricing reform, remained static despite efforts to break open the generic market.

Congress created the 340B Drug Pricing Program in 1992 with the goal of helping providers by requiring manufacturers to offer steep drug discounts to certain safety net hospitals. However, the program included no clear mandate on how the rebates should be spent. The good intentions had been effectively derailed by pharmacy benefit managers (PBMs) that occupied a central role in the drug price supply chain as

Profit margins of up to 100 percent allowed hospitals to pay inflated fees to these pharmacy partners, which could earn margins well above what the patient's insurance company usually pays.

Public companies such as Walgreens, CVS, and Cigna (now merged), UnitedHealth Group, Walmart, and Kroger rushed into the 340B business with an industry of consultants and technology companies helping hospitals and commercial pharmacies profit from this aspect of the 340B program.

Patients don't benefit from these discounts. Instead, they are expected to pay their health plans' full out-of-pocket costs. A patient with a high-deductible health plan must pay the full list price for his medication.

Looking back, the Affordable Care Act seemed to be working out even if done the hard way; and its two separate pieces of legislation—the Patient Protection and Affordable Care Act (P. L. 111–148) and the Health Care and Education Reconciliation Act of 2010 (P. L. 111–152) had gained market traction. GOP congressmen were reminded of that daily in their district offices and town hall meetings.

Incredibly, the House of Representatives held more than fifty anti-Obamacare votes beginning when Republicans took control in 2011. In all my years in Washington, DC, this was unique. Those GOP members were truly myopic! And it hurt them and the nation! And yet the fastest week-to-week growth rates were in Louisiana, Nevada, Mississippi, Texas, and South Carolina, ironically where political opposition was the loudest but the need was the greatest.

Surprisingly, out of nowhere, congressional leaders stated during the 2016 campaign that legislation to add billions of dollars to federal biomedical research and ease drug approvals was a main priority for the lame-duck session after the November elections, and pass it they did. It turned out that some of our major political leaders had a real interest in some of the initiatives likely to be funded under the so-called 21st Century Cures legislation.

President Barack Obama was interested in funding for precision medicine, which was aimed at discovering genetic causes of disease. Vice President Joe Biden, whose son Beau died the prior year of brain cancer, had been heading up the cancer moonshot effort to speed up research, and Senate Majority Leader Mitch McConnell, who spent part of his childhood confined to a bed because he was stricken with polio, said he was interested in regenerative medicine.

But on November 29, after the 2016 general election and Trump's victory, in what was turning out to be the fastest cabinet named in a long time, the president-elect picked House Budget Committee Chairman Tom Price (R., Ga.) to be Secretary of the Health and Human Services Department. A sixty-two-year-old former orthopedic surgeon, Price was one of several GOP physicians who sought to draft the party's alternative vision to the Democrats' Affordable Care Act.

Earlier in his congressional career, he sponsored legislation in the House to restrict a national database from compiling information about malpractice judgments and hospital disciplinary actions against individual doctors. Price had also championed his own legislation, the Empowering Patients First Act, since 2009, taking a position on several issues for conservative health policy thinkers. In its latest version, the proposal included refundable, age-adjusted tax credits for people to buy insurance if they did not have access to coverage through an employer or government program.

The plan offered a one-time credit aimed at boosting health-savings accounts, long described by supporters as a way of bringing down medical spending, and derived part of its funding from capping how much employers can spend on providing employee health care before being taxed. Price's plan sought to make health insurance available to individuals with pre-existing medical conditions by helping states set up new high risk pools or other programs for such enrollees and set new rules allowing insurers to sell policies across state lines. I had to hand it to him; at least he had a plan! But he was gone by early October with his resignation due to abusing government corporate jet travel!

Democratic and Republican states were moving in opposite directions on health policy, leaving different options for care depending on which state you lived in.

Increasingly, state health-care policy reflected the ruling party's goals. President Obama's ACA sought to have a national approach where the healthy help cover the costs of the sick and the wealthy help cover the poor, and it led to about 20 million people gaining health coverage.

Under the Trump administration's proposals, states were to get more flexibility in waiving ACA requirements and oversight of plans that don't comply with the ACA. In summary, blue states would have better health care coverage than red states, which would breed more political dissonance.

As to cost-containment, US health care spending grew 4.8 percent in 2016, the bulk of that increase due to pharmaceutical spending. The country spent $3.4 trillion on health care in 2016, a number that was projected to grow to $5.5 trillion by 2025.

Hospital care made up 32 percent of US budget expenditures, and roughly, one third of the $3.3 trillion the United States spent on health care in 2016 was poured into hospitals. Doctors and clinical services totaled about 20 percent and prescription drugs were at 10 percent. Still, growth in prescription drug spending was faster than that of any other service in 2015.

The spending projections put health care on track to make up about a fifth of the economy by 2025, based on what would happen if the Affordable Care Act remained in place with a 5.8 percent annual growth rate through 2025.

And in the big picture, if you will, health care cost containment was more than just prescription drugs. The nation's deficits were mounting, certainly from the pandemic but even afterwards, and just the stability of Social Security and Medicare seemed to be a political Orphan Annie.

In a broad sense, the good news was that the ACA accomplished what lawmakers set out to do: dramatically reduce the US uninsured rate and make comprehensive coverage available to people no matter what their health condition. But Medicare spending was expected to grow at an average of 7.1 percent per year over the ten-year period, while Medicaid spending is expected to grow at an average rate of 5.7 percent annually between 2017 and 2025.

These two programs do need reform, but neither political party seems capable of addressing the topic equitably. Simply turning Medicaid over to the states was not a solution. The sad but widely known fact was that we spend more on health care than any other nation, and yet our life expectancy of 78.8 years ranks the United States in twenty-seventh place among the thirty-five industrial economies in the Organization for Economic Cooperation and Development (OECD).

In 2018, I watched on CSPAN as the Senate Health, Education, Labor, and Pensions—aptly named the HELP committee—held the first of a series of planned hearings on the rising costs of healthcare in the United States. Testimony was provided about the increasing costs of healthcare in the United States and what was causing that rapid growth. Several points were made that I found interesting, including, for example: In 2016, the United States spent about $3.3 trillion on healthcare, which averages to about $10,000 per person in an aging population. Additionally, prices on healthcare services had grown faster than other prices in the economy due to complexity in the system and increased consolidation of hospitals, which can lead to a lack of competition.

Now let's back up for a moment and reflect on some past medical history. In 1993, President Bill Clinton proposed Hillary's healthcare reform bill that I worked on; and it included a mandate for employers to provide health insurance to all employees through a regulated marketplace of health maintenance organizations.

The 1993 Republican alternative, introduced by Senator John Chafee as the ranking Republican on the Senate Finance Committee and Pat Moynihan's good friend, was entitled the Health Equity and Access Reform Today Act. It contained a universal coverage requirement with a penalty for noncompliance—an individual mandate—as well as subsidies to be used in state-based "purchasing groups."

The advocates for the 1993 bill included prominent Republican Senators Orrin Hatch, Chuck Grassley, Bob Bennett, and Kit Bond. Of 1993's forty-three Republican

Senators, twenty supported the HEART Act. Another Republican proposal, introduced in 1994 by Senator Don Nickels (R-OK), whom I knew well, was the Consumer Choice Health Security Act, which contained an individual mandate with a penalty provision. Thus, there had been bipartisan precedent in the Senate.

But the House was different after 1994, as the Newt Gingrich opposed all Democratic Party measures; dogma had taken hold, and they had won the elections in both Houses, so amazingly nothing happened. The main reason was that in 1994, two ads, paid for by the Coalition for Health Care Choices, opposed President Clinton's health care plan. The insurance ads portrayed a couple named Harry and Louise asking questions, and they were very effective.

Health Savings Accounts (HSAs) were established as part of the Medicare Prescription Drug, Improvement, and Modernization Act, signed into law by President George W. Bush on December 8, 2003. They were developed to replace the medical savings account system.

Individuals now have health tax-exempt savings accounts that allowed them to contribute and withdraw funds for their medical expenses. The money that they contribute is tax-exempt because the IRS considers HSAs to be health insurance plans for tax purposes, and therefore, any income received from a health insurance plan is tax-free.

One of the main reasons that HSAs are attractive is the employer contributions as an additional benefit. Your employer can match (tax-deductible) your HSA contributions up to a certain amount.

In 2006, an insurance expansion bill was enacted at the state level in Massachusetts. The bill contained both an individual mandate and an insurance exchange. Republican Governor Mitt Romney vetoed the mandate, but after Democrats overrode his veto, he signed it into law.

Romney's implementation of the Health Connector exchange and individual mandate in Massachusetts was at first lauded by Republicans. During Romney's 2008 presidential campaign, Senator Jim DeMint (later President of the Heritage Foundation) praised Romney's ability to take some good conservative ideas, like private health insurance, and apply them to the need to have everyone insured.

In 2007, a year after the Massachusetts reform, Republican Senator Bob Bennett and Democratic Senator Ron Wyden introduced the Healthy Americans Act, which featured an individual mandate and state-based, regulated insurance markets called State Health Help Agencies. The bill initially attracted bipartisan support but died in the Senate Finance Committee.

The healthcare legislation that eventually emerged from Congress in 2009 and 2010 bore similarities to the 2007 bill in that it was patterned after Romney's state healthcare plan.

So, there had been a bipartisan history for health care reform, and President Obama had brought representatives of the two parties together at the 2010 televised meeting at the Blair House aimed at jump-starting the overhaul and picking up on this history that led to the Affordable Care Act in March 2010.

The law had three primary goals:

1. Make affordable health insurance available to more people. The law provided consumers with subsidies ("premium tax credits") that lower costs for households with incomes between 100 percent and 400 percent of the federal poverty level (FPL).
2. Expand the Medicaid program to cover all adults with income below 138 percent of the FPL. Not all states have expanded their Medicaid programs.
3. Support innovative medical care delivery methods designed to lower the costs of health care generally.

Interestingly, most physicians serving in Congress are Republicans, as outlined below:

1. 113th Congress (2013—15)— From 2013 to 2015 there were twenty-one physicians in Congress, twenty of whom were male and seventeen were members of the Republican Party.
2. 114th Congress (2015—17)—From 2015 to 2017, there were eighteen physicians in Congress. All were male and fifteen were members of the Republican Party.
3. 115th Congress (2017—19)— From 2017 to 2019 there were fifteen physicians in Congress; all were male, and thirteen were members of the Republican Party.

You would think they would be very sensitive to these nuances in healthcare policy. And sure enough, ten Democratic doctors were running for Congress in 2018, much of this interest in reaction to the GOP attacks on Obamacare. Like many other Democrats, they were campaigning hard on the need to overhaul the nation's health care system and would dramatically alter the earlier physician makeup in Congress.

From 2000 on, thirteen of the fifteen doctors in Congress were Republicans. Three were senators, including Louisiana's Bill Cassidy, a gastroenterologist who had a public health background. His medical colleagues in the Senate came from fields such as orthopedic surgery, urology, and anesthesiology.

By contrast, the insurgent Democrats hail predominantly from specialties such as emergency medicine, pediatrics, and internal medicine.

As a profession, physicians once tended to be Republican. The infusion of female and minority doctors has changed this, and more than 50 percent of party-affiliated doctors are now Democrats, according to research published by the National Academy of Sciences, and the medical establishment has emerged as a staunch Affordable Care Act (ACA) defender. The majority of medical students today are women.

In mid-2018, hospitals, doctors, medical schools, patient-advocacy groups, the health insurance industry, and others filed briefs in a federal court in Texas, disputing the argument of twenty Republican-led states and the Trump Justice Department that all or part of the 2010 Affordable Care Act was unconstitutional.

Three hospital trade groups, the Association of American Medical Colleges, and five major groups advocating for patients with diseases, including the American Cancer Society, the American Heart Association, and the American Lung Association, filed their briefs. The liberal consumer health lobby Families USA, the Small Business Majority, a group of law professors, and a separate group of healthcare and economic researchers also filed briefs.

In all, eleven friend-of-the-court briefs were filed, each making the case that a ruling in favor of this latest challenge to the ACA's constitutionality would have a devastating impact on doctors, patients, and the American health care system as a whole.

Instead, the Trump Department of Justice contended that ending the penalty at the start of 2019 would make the ACA's insurance requirement unconstitutional. This refusal of the Justice Department to defend an existing statute was without precedent, prompting the lead Justice Department lawyer to resign. And the attacks on Obamacare continued, as the Trump administration had been taking steps to dismantle the ACA through executive powers:

Both the Blue Cross Blue Shield Association and America's Health Insurance Plans Association noted their concern and alarm as they would have to increase rates at a critical time in the next sign-up period. These attacks seem unrelenting, unfair, and unwise as American consumers consistently signed up and supported the ACA. The Affordable Care Act allowed states to expand their Medicaid programs to include people earning around $16,000 a year, which was previously too much to qualify for the social safety net but often too little to pay for health insurance out of their own pockets.

And a majority of states chose to expand their Medicaid programs, a move that was initially fully funded by the federal government.

It was implausible, but the rural poor seemed impressed with the Trump rhetoric and not the reality.

Importantly, in states that did expand Medicaid, those geographic disparities were almost nonexistent. There were several reasons cited in the report that Medicaid expansion could be part of the solution:

1. It's difficult to get insurance company to offer plans in sparsely populated rural towns.
2. Areas with more insured residents attract clinics and providers to operate there; and
3. Rural hospitals are less likely to close in places where they can depend on Medicaid payments.

In late July 2018, I was to watch a House Energy and Commerce Committee hearing on the 21st Century Cures Act, signed into law on December 13, 2016, to accelerate medical product development and bring new innovations and advances to patients who need them faster and more efficiently. Both the heads of the National Institutes of Health and the Food and Drug Administration were the lead witnesses.

It was a remarkable bipartisan hearing, with accolades being tossed about and personal family medical stories told. It seemed everyone in the hearing room was concerned about medical care. It caused me to wonder why the incessant GOP attacks on the Affordable Care Act and Medicaid expansion.

It was a true shock to our health care system when the coronavirus arrived in late 2019, as we were not ready. This rash of headlines in 2018 and 2019 about costs for newly approved drugs illustrates the point:

1. At $2 million, the new Novartis drug is the priciest ever (May 24, 2019).
2. Restrictions on $2 Million Drug Highlight Challenge for Gene Therapies (July 28, 2019).

3. Biotech Proposes Paying for Pricey Drugs by Installment (January 8, 2019).
4. New Gene Therapy Priced at $1.8 Million in Europe (June 14, 2019).
5. Drug Firm Spark Therapeutics Will Charge $850,000 for Vision Loss Gene Therapy (January 3, 2018).
6. High Hopes for a Gene Therapy Come with Fears Over Cost (September 24, 2018).
7. The Million-Dollar Cancer Treatment: Who Will Pay? (April 26, 2018).

In the face of these discouraging headlines, I was pleased to read that insurers were offering new plans aimed at making the cost of gene therapies more manageable for employers.

Other ideas were being reported, and it all reminded me of some of my 1992 Clinton White House conversations with Ira Magaziner.

One idea among large corporations like Walmart was to switch their employee coverage from the traditional fee-for-service model to what was being called direct contracting, where providers/carriers would guarantee health care services at a fixed rate for a very large volume of employees.

But health care experts noted the markets were stabilizing for different reasons. In fact, these experts stated premiums would likely be going down much more if not for the GOP constantly attacking the ACA and raising uncertainty about the ACA's future.

The midterm 2018 election results, with the Democrats taking over the House, showed the importance of health care to the voters and caused some GOP reflection. Then, the Department of Health and Human Services announced its new regulatory proposal to require pharmaceutical ads to include the pricing of the advertised product. It was almost comical to witness GOP congressmen who had voted many times to repeal Obamacare, now saying they had always been supporting coverage for pre-existing conditions.

What I did not understand was that the liberal Democrats, after their party regained control of the House of Representatives in 2019, were not working to repair the GOP damage to Obamacare. Instead, over a hundred signed on for their Medicare for All legislation, which would dramatically alter the medical infrastructure of the United States while not addressing how this "dream" would be funded. They were lambasted and continually panned as socialists, an unfortunate political burden for centrist Democrats.

As the disastrous 2019 Democratic Party Presidential TV Debates continued, health care proposals proliferated; but already, interest groups were mobilizing and pooling resources to undermine most of these Democrats' plans.

The Partnership (Coalition) for America's Health Care Future—insurance companies, pharma, hospitals, and other industry participants—was already running TV ads and commissioning polls to diminish support for any expansion of government provided coverage, particularly Medicare for All.

A July poll commissioned by NPR and Marist found that 41 percent of Americans favored Medicare for All plans that replaced private insurance, while 70 percent said they supported having the choice of being covered by a government-run plan (public option) or private insurance. These polls were worthless, but when you have over twenty Democratic candidates vying, they will support just about anything to win percentage points.

The industry coalition argued in 2019 that Medicare for All could hurt rural physicians and cause many hospitals to close. Supporters responded that only insurance would be centralized and that the program would allow all Americans to go to doctors and hospitals of their choice. The cost estimates were prohibitive. Having been engaged in other regulatory initiatives, it seemed there just wasn't the intellectual breadth—nor White House leadership—needed to bring moderates together.

On June 18, 2019, I was to watch the Senate testimony of the American Hospital Association (AHA) before the Committee on Health, Education, Labor and Pensions (HELP) on the "Lower Health Care Costs Act" topic. Tom Nickels was the Executive Vice President for Government Relations and Public Policy in their large Washington, DC, office (Chicago was their long-time home base).

It is a challenge to be testifying on behalf of nearly 1,500 hospital and health system leaders who had just met in San Diego for their 2019 AHA Leadership Summit, where they announced strategies for enhancing the affordability and value of health care; opportunities for advancing quality, patient safety, and community health improvement; models for creating cultures of innovation that drive delivery system transformation; leadership competencies and workforce strategies for positive change; and governance excellence.

Chances are they were never able to agree on a proactive agenda, so typically, in these large public policy organizations, taking the easier tack of either these grandiose statements or opposing specific issues is the only way out. The net result is that no senator or staff person is impressed, as they are looking for solutions.

As I have often said, it is better to say we will support if, versus we are opposed unless. Well, Mr. Nickels, a long-time AHA executive did not surprise me as he arbitrarily went through a long list of criticisms and no solutions.

The Obama administration was able to win over the health care industry only by killing the so-called public option, which some moderate Democratic candidates were supporting in 2019. The public option is essentially a proposal to create a government run health insurance agency that would compete with other private health insurance companies within the United States.

Most Americans don't understand this concept, which was initially proposed for the Affordable Care Act but was removed after Sen. Joe Lieberman threatened a filibuster. His state of Connecticut is home to several large insurance companies.

As a Democrat and one of three founders of the Democratic National Committee party headquarters building on the House side of the Capitol, I felt a duty to monitor the disastrous Democratic television debates in the summer and fall months of 2019. Health care in many flavors seemed to be the main topic. Medicare for All was hot in the first debate but then cooled to the public option and finally maybe Obama's Affordable Care Act just needs some fixing after the GOP attacks, which was Joe Biden's position.

So maybe the Democratic Party debates were a learning process. Following the September debate, the Washington Post had an article focused on the veterans of the ill-fated 1992 Clinton and successful 2010 Obama health care legislative efforts.

The article featured White House and HHS staffers from those episodes now serving as health care advisors to various presidential campaigns. Instead of simply committing to the "correction of the GOP attacks on the Affordable Care Act," now each candidate would have their own recipe adding to the noise.

Within the large 2019 Democratic presidential primary field, moderate Democrats, including former vice president Joe Biden, preferred to build on insurance expansions introduced by the 2010 Affordable Care Act, while giving people the choice of buying into a new government insurance plan.

Unfortunately, during the 2019 Democratic debates, the candidates rarely brought up the ACA (except for Biden), instead preferring to discuss ways of expanding affordable coverage either via Medicare-for-all or by adding a government-sponsored "public option" plan to the marketplace.

By early March, it appeared Joe Biden would be the Democratic Party candidate for president.

But that same month in 2020, the coronavirus had truly arrived in the United States, shaking our health care system to its roots, whether it was New York City or Phoenix, Arizona. There were traumatic stories, data about deaths, and chaos at the Trump White House.

The United States reported on April 2 that more than 1,000 deaths from the coronavirus had occurred in a twenty-four-hour period, moving its total death count to more than 5,000 as of Thursday morning, according to a Johns Hopkins University database. It would continue to climb that month, according to the experts.

The US Congress passed three major legislative packages in response as follows:

1. Phase one, signed by President Trump on March 3, provided $8.3 billion in fresh funds for health agencies, testing, and small-business loan subsidies.
2. Phase two, enacted March 18 and worth about $100 billion, included tax credits for employers offering paid sick leave, as well as increases to unemployment benefits and food assistance.
3. Phase three, enacted March 27, provided some $2 trillion and included checks to households, grants and loans for airlines and other distressed industries, and loans and grants for small businesses.
4. Phase four was expected to include infrastructure, but it later appeared that it would be more focused on phase three; therefore, there would be a phase five for infrastructure.

President Trump had appointed a coronavirus task force with the Vice President now as its lead and Dr. Anthony Fauci, who had served as the director of the National Institute of Allergy and Infectious Diseases (NIAID) since 1984, as its brains. He was to announce his retirement for December 2022.

An interview Dr. Anthony Fauci gave with Science Magazine in late March after dozens of televised task force briefings from the Oval Office expressed some of the tensions in working with the president who would monopolize the stage. As the coronavirus continued to lay siege to the US and global economies, lessons learned would already be evident in early April.

And on April 12, the United States had again over 2,000 Covid-19 deaths in a single day, according to figures maintained by Johns Hopkins University. The figure increased the national death count to over 20,000 days later, with almost 400,000 cases, and it continued at that pace. There were 1,446,242 cases worldwide and 83,424 deaths. Nursing homes in the United States were emerging as serious problems.

Americans filed for unemployment in the last week of March; the pandemic total was over 17 million, and it was at 26 million on April 23. Watching the returning House of Representatives with their bandanas on to vote for the fourth Covid legislative package was somewhat nerve-wracking. They were in full panic mode! It was like the country was in a trance!

Congressional Democrats were also were pressuring the administration and insurers to waive treatment costs for the growing number of Americans who were losing employer-provided health coverage as job losses mounted.

Hospitals were eager to get funding, many facing bankruptcy as they were restricted to Covid-19 patients and no elective surgery; and administration officials were working on how it would go toward revenue assistance, covering the costs of the uninsured, and the needs of hospitals. Indeed, the Coronavirus pandemic underscored health care reform in the supply chain sector.

Amidst this 2020 pandemic pandemonium, the first responders were very impressive. Doctors, nurses, and orderlies were real heroes. It was heartbreaking to read how Chinese American first responders were being yelled at as responsible for this Wuhan virus!

Chinese Americans make up only 6 percent of the US population but are 18 percent of doctors and 10 percent of nurses.

But the educational sector, with teacher unions becoming the last responders, was disheartening.

On June 1, 2020, the Johns Hopkins reports indicated that close to 103,000 Americans had died in the 2020 coronavirus pandemic up until that point, more than any other country. More than 25,000 elderly residents had died in nursing homes, along with some 400 nurses, aides, and other staff.

And the National Institutes of Health reported that while it spends close to $36 billion on medical research annually, much of it is on hold right now. Congress had bequeathed billions of dollars to government labs, universities, and other agencies to develop vaccines to stop the coronavirus/Covid-19 pandemic. Much of that would find its way to the pharmaceutical industry as these drug makers invested billions of dollars and dedicated their top scientists to virus research, and it worked.

Having taken my granddaughter and her mother to an oral argument at the Supreme Court several years earlier, Chief Justice Roberts had turned out to be a man of the Millennium! In 2020, the Supreme Court pushed the slow button on a filing to expedite hearing the Texas/GOP state attorney general's case regarding the ACA's constitutionality.

And by March 2020, former Vice President Joe Biden had virtually won the Democratic Party's 2020 presidential nomination. I was pleased for the Biden family, whom we had known for many years. I was also pleased for the Affordable Care Act, as he ran in favor of strengthening it.

On Friday evening, September 18, 2020, Supreme Court Justice Ruth Bader Ginsburg passed away after battling cancer-related medical issues for several years. I sent this note to Marcia Coyle, an Annapolis friend, who covered the Supreme Court for the PBS NewsHour program:

> Marcia… I hope you are well! Here is some history that might be helpful! President Bill Clinton had nominated Judge Ruth Bader Ginsburg to the Supreme Court on June 14th 1993. It happened that I was a good friend of New York Senator Daniel Patrick Moynihan and his wife, Liz.
>
> Pat, at the time, was chairman of the Senate Finance Committee; and the Hillary Clinton health care debate was at its zenith. She was meeting periodically with the Moynihan's at their condominium in the Navy Memorial complex (801 Pennsylvania). Coincidentally I had been one of the original founders of that memorial (Naval Academy grad).
>
> Liz Moynihan would call me up and note that Hillary had stopped by to see Pat on the health care reform versus welfare reform topic once again. I had been very involved in other regulatory reform efforts; and was serving as sort of a go between for them with the White House's health policy advisor, Ira Magaziner,
>
> On one of those calls, probably late May or early June of 1993, she excitedly told me that Pat had talked to President Bill Clinton and recommended that he nominate Ruth Bader Ginsburg (New Yorker serving as a judge on the US Court of Appeals for the DC Circuit.) to succeed the retiring Supreme Court Justice Byron White.
>
> President Clinton, from what I recall Liz Moynihan telling me, told Pat that he liked the idea and would do it. The rest was wonderful Supreme Court history!
> Dan

Following my note to Marcia, I had a nice chat with Liz Moynihan in New York that afternoon and reminisced (coincidentally, that was her ninety-first birthday, and she was to pass away three years later—a real loss).

Liz explained that President Clinton was flying to New York (Air Force One) back in that May/June 1993 period and invited Pat along as the senator from New York. She went on to say that President Clinton told Senator Moynihan that he was having a tough time finding his nominee for that current Supreme Court vacancy. And that is when Pat Moynihan suggested Judge Ruth Bader Ginsburg, whom the Moynihan's knew well. President Clinton liked the idea and followed up. He called Pat Moynihan days later and said he had called Judge Ginsburg, and she had accepted. They had fun calling Judge Ginsberg themselves to congratulate her. And Liz then called me just before it was formally announced by the White House. Yes, it was wonderful history!

In reflection, I suspect that the Clintons made that choice not only due to their appreciation for Judge Ginsberg, but Hillary, at the time, was deeply engrossed in her 1993 health care reform initiative and needed Pat Moynihan's support as Chairman of the Senate Finance Committee.

And on June 17, 2021, the Supreme Court again upheld the Affordable Care Act in the third major case from Republican challengers to reach the high court. So, at last, the ACA was real.

But I was frustrated to read on July 30, 2024, that a new US study by physician researchers had found that when private-equity firms buy hospitals (systems)—and they frequently do—they sell off assets, challenging longtime industry claims that the purchases lead to investment in patient care. The study, which examined 156 purchases over the past decade, was published in JAMA, the journal of the American Medical Association. In July 2024, a new study by physician researchers at the University of California at San Francisco found that when private-equity firms buy hospitals, they sell off assets. It reminded me of similar tactics with newspapers.

And finally, some personal health care reform history and this note to my niece (and hospice nurse in Marin County) Alia Berlin in January 2023 following up on our internment of her grandfather, my brother-in-law, Neal McNamara at Arlington National Cemetery.

> Alia, You will remember my story of your grandfather Neal McNamara, as a San Francisco Home Health Care Board member, calling me in Washington DC around 1978 to meet their Director Hadley Hall. We had a very good meeting here at my Washington office as I found Hadley's cost-effective argument for Medicare coverage of home health and hospice care to be persuasive. Fortunately, at that time, good friend Senator Frank Church (D. Idaho) was then Chairman of the Senate Committee on Aging. I called him and he set up an appointment for us to meet with the Staff Director, Val Halamandaris. I am convinced our 1978–79 visit had a big impact on his commitment to including home health care in Medicare. Coincidentally, Val was in our Annapolis area hospital in his last days: I happened to be the duty Eucharistic minister and gave his wife communion. Uncle Dan

Part Two

Follow-On Efforts

7

NAFTA 1993, Mexican Energy Reform 2014, and Retreat 2022

Mexican Energy Reform 2013–14 and Retreat 2024

In April 1994, I received a letter from Hermann von Bertrab, on Mexican Embassy stationary, that was very gratifying. Hermann had served as the Mexican ambassador in Washington, DC, for the NAFTA negotiations and had retained my firm. We were to work together for the next two decades, until Mexican energy and electricity reforms were enacted in 2014. We had become close friends.

I was overwhelmed to read Mexican Ambassador Hermann von Bertrab's farewell note to me as he returned to Mexico, expressing his deep appreciation and profound gratitude for my advice and steadfast support during the North American Free Trade Agreement negotiations and approval processes.

From a historical perspective, Mexico did not enter the global marketplace until the mid-1980s. Before then, most major industries were state-owned and international competition in Mexico's domestic market was insignificant due to prohibitive tariffs. The privatization of most government industries and NAFTA itself revolutionized Mexico's economy, much to the advantage of both Mexico and the United States.

NAFTA was the proverbial win-win as regional trade surged over the treaty's first two decades, from roughly $290 billion in 1993 to more than $1.1 trillion in 2016 before the presidential election. Canada and Mexico were the two largest destinations for US exports, accounting for more than a third of the total. US foreign direct investment in Mexico increased during that period from $15 billion to more than $100 billion, according to the US State Department. And yes, some US manufacturing jobs had moved to Mexico.

The Government of Mexico's SECOFI ministry had retained my firm in 1992 to research the benefits that would accrue from a NAFTA infrastructure/environmental/energy reform investment perspective. The Mexican president at the time was Carlos Salinas de Gortari, a true reformer. He was one of the many bright Mexicans of his generation who studied at US universities and had earned a master's degree in public administration from Harvard University in 1973 and went on to earn a PhD from Harvard's Kennedy School of Government in 1978.

Until 2000, this Office for Commerce and Industrial Development (SECOFI) was the lead agency for initiatives like NAFTA, but that name was changed when Vicente Fox, an ex-Coca-Cola executive, became President in 2000 representing the PAN party and wanted to enhance the agency's commercial role.

The successor Office of Economic Affairs now houses: the National Meteorological Center, the Federal Competition Board, the Federal Commission on Regulatory Reform, the Mining Development Trust Fund, the Mexican Industrial Property Board, the Federal Consumer's Advocate, Pro-México (travel/tourism), and the Mexican Geological Service. It is very similar to the US Department of Commerce.

A recent Director of Economic Affairs was Ildefonso Guajardo Villarreal, who worked for Hermann von Bertrab during the 1991–2 NAFTA negotiations and played a key role in the 2018 negotiations for what some were calling the new NAFTA in 2020. Much of my consulting included coordinating with Ildefonso and his colleagues. In fact, many friendships evolved from that endeavor.

As to NAFTA history, initially there was the US-Canada Free Trade Agreement, which entered into force on January 1, 1989. Shortly afterward, Mexican President Carlos Salinas approached US president George H. W. Bush to propose a similar US-Mexico agreement to bring in foreign investment following the Latin American debt crisis.

As those two leaders began negotiating, the Canadian government under Prime Minister Brian Mulroney feared that the advantages Canada had gained through the US-Canada Free Trade Agreement would be undermined by a US-Mexican bilateral agreement and asked to become a party to the US-Mexican talks.

The three leaders signed NAFTA in their respective capitals on December 17, 1992. The signed agreement was then to be ratified by each nation's legislative or parliamentary branch. This responsibility then fell to the new Congress and newly inaugurated President Bill Clinton, who had defeated President Bush the previous November.

Before sending the NAFTA to the United States Congress, President Clinton added two side agreements, the North American Agreement on Labor Cooperation (NAALC) and the North American Agreement on Environmental Cooperation (NAAEC), to protect workers and the environment, and also to allay the concerns of many House members. As it happened, I had advised the Mexican team on the environmental side agreement.

And shortly thereafter, I was to watch with my son Clay from the Speaker's Gallery, as the US House of Representatives passed the North American Free Trade Agreement Implementation Act on November 17, 1993, 234–200 after much consideration and discussion. The agreement's bipartisan supporters included 132 Republicans and 102 Democrats.

The bill passed the Senate on November 20, 1993, 61–38. Senate supporters were thirty-four Republicans and twenty-seven Democrats. President Clinton signed it into law on December 8, 1993; the agreement went into effect on January 1, 1994, and was to eliminate barriers to trade and investment between the United States, Canada, and Mexico.

From my Washington, DC, Capitol Hill experience, I knew that so-called blue line copies of the new law could be obtained from the Government Printing Office as the

Archivist of the United States must furnish to the Public Printer a copy of every Act and joint resolution, as soon as possible after its approval by the President, or after it has become a law under the Constitution without his approval. I ordered a dozen of the NAFTA Proclamations signed by President Clinton and distributed them to the Mexican Embassy NAFTA staff. They were very appreciative.

President Clinton, while signing the NAFTA legislation, remarked to the attendees and press that NAFTA meant good-paying American jobs. If he didn't believe that, he wouldn't have signed.

The North American Free Trade Agreement (NAFTA), which came into effect on January 1, 1994, superseded the initial Canada–United States Free Trade Agreement and brought the immediate elimination of tariffs on more than one-half of Mexico's exports to the United States and more than one-third of US exports to Mexico.

Within ten years of the implementation of the agreement, all US-Mexico tariffs were eliminated except for some US agricultural exports to Mexico, which were phased out within five years. Most US-Canada trade was already duty-free. NAFTA also sought to eliminate non-tariff trade barriers and to protect the intellectual property rights of traded products.

NAFTA also included chapters covering rules of origin, customs procedures, agriculture and sanitary measures, government procurement, investment, trade in services, protection of intellectual property rights, and dispute settlement procedures.

And it worked; I was very proud of the results. In 2000, at the peak of Mexican migration to the United States, 1.5 million Mexicans were apprehended at the border. Back then, critics of illegal immigration talked about a flood of Mexicans overwhelming the United States. Many still do.

But by 2019, the North American Free Trade Agreement had produced an increase in economic opportunity. Over the past two decades, average income in Mexico had risen by roughly 20 percent. Educational attainment had gone up by 50 percent. Public services such as health care had dramatically improved. Immigrants in the United States sent billions in remittances back to Mexico, which paid for university educations and provided capital for small businesses. Senator Pete Wilson, later the California governor, had made a similar projection to me.

Migration from Mexico had dropped 90 percent over the past twenty years following the millennium year 2020. In 2019, for the first time ever, Guatemala and Honduras were on pace to surpass it as the leading sources of illegal immigration to the United States. The dramatic collapse of migration from Mexico has received almost no public attention.

Mexicans now had greater access to US visa programs (agriculture/temporary workers). On the other hand, relatively few of those same visa categories were awarded to Guatemalans and Hondurans, in part because those countries are farther from the border and transporting those workers costs more. But beginning in 2018, immigration apprehension at the border began to reach that 1,500,000 figure once again; however, this time it was made up not so much of Mexicans, but of individuals and families from Central America, Venezuela, and Cuba via Nicaragua.

The demographic story is also important. In 1995, Mexico's median age was twenty-one. In 2020, it would be about thirty. Mexico's baby boom was over, due to a combination of economic growth and cheaper contraception, thanks in part to the Mexican government's family planning policy.

A very interesting feature of NAFTA is that there was the initial 1992 agreement; and under our US trade laws, the president had significant unilateral authority regarding its execution but not termination. Additionally, Congress voted to ratify NAFTA, and I have a copy on my office wall.

While the US Constitution explicitly gives Congress the power to regulate commerce with foreign nations, over the years Congress has delegated much of that power to the president. Here is a brief resume of those important US trade policy covenants:

Nearly all US free trade agreements, including NAFTA, allow the president a withdrawal privilege. For NAFTA, withdrawal from the pact can be done after giving six months' notice in writing to the other parties. But Congress can intercede, particularly on agricultural issues. Similar escape clauses would also allow the president to withdraw the United States from other free trade agreements with other nations, and even from the World Trade Organization, which would allow other countries to raise the tariffs they charge on American exports.

The trend toward presidential primacy had a long history. Congress passed the Trading with the Enemy Act, as the First World War threatened, which gave the president the power to regulate all international trade and financial flows, and even to freeze or seize foreign assets.

And under the Trade Expansion Act of 1962, the president could now raise tariffs as necessary to strengthen national security. Congress delegated extensive trade authority to the President, in particular under the Trade Act of 1974.

The president also has the International Emergency Economic Powers Act of 1977, originally written to give the president the tools to impose economic sanctions on America's enemies.

But, with Congress having passed the 1993 NAFTA implementation statute, the president's authorities were limited in some ways. Congress would have to ratify changes. Additionally, Congress in 2018 was quite vocal in asserting its concerns regarding President Trump's anti-NAFTA and anti-free trade rhetoric, which had been one of his campaign trademarks.

Still, Trump quickly exited three major treaties—the Trans-Pacific Partnership, the Paris climate accord, and the Iran nuclear accord—and then called for drastic changes to the North American Free Trade Agreement. Just over a year into office, he was launching trade wars against our closest G-7 allies as well as China. The GOP Senate leadership was vocally alarmed, but no remedial legislation regarding trade and presidential powers was enacted albeit introduced.

The first three treaties noted earlier had not been ratified by Congress, so Trump was able to terminate them, but NAFTA was ratified by Congress. And while Congress had delegated extensive trade authority to the President, in particular under the Trade Act of 1974 and under the implementing statutes for each of the US international trade agreements, it had never delegated to the President the power to withdraw the US from any ratified treaty.

As long as there are tariffs, Senators had told Trump they would not pass his new NAFTA, and instead old NAFTA would stay in place despite his threats to terminate

NAFTA without Congress. However, they did pass the new NAFTA while the tariffs stayed in place as President Biden entered office on January 20, 2021.

Biden administration officials said they wanted to take their time in developing a new trade approach, rather than move precipitously to mollify business, and basically left the Trump tariffs in place. The economy's robust growth in the first half of that pandemic year, including the addition of more than 4.3 million jobs, eased the pressure to act.

Mexican energy reform was really important. Looking back, NAFTA itself had been signed originally into law in 1993, just one year after we had opened up the US wholesale electricity power market in the Energy Policy Act of 1992 discussed in Chapter 4. The eventual Mexican energy reform actions in 2014 hinged, in many ways, on the 1992 US example of reform and the availability of this new US independent power sector.

It was very helpful that I had been a leader in this 1992 US energy reform effort as it gave me standing in making my recommendations later in Mexico City. The Mexican energy reform effort was to ensue over those twenty years following the passage of NAFTA, and I was pleased to provide some policy leadership based on our own US experience. In the years immediately following the 1993–4 NAFTA agreement, I remember many meetings at the Hacienda (Mexico's equivalent of OMB) to review potential electricity reforms with Hermann's senior-level contacts there.

We also met often with the management of the Federal Electricity Commission (CFE), the national electric utility company, owned by the Mexican government, which generated, distributed, and marketed electric power for most of Mexico in a very inefficient manner.

I explained the new US Energy Policy Act, particularly Title VII, and how the independent power industry would bring about a very important realignment of investment, technology, risk transfer, and consumer benefit. This would be a credible path for Mexico's electricity sector to follow.

The CFE is where I first met their CEO, Dr. Rogelio Gasca Neri, who was very receptive to our recommendations. Rogelio was one of the country's most accomplished energy leaders and public servants. During his decades-long career, Rogelio had served on the board of directors of Pemex, as the top executive of Mexico's national electric utility, CFE (as I mentioned) and as an undersecretary in four different cabinet departments. Rogelio had an MBA and a PhD in Engineering from Stanford University.

I remember visiting with Hector Olea many times in Mexico City during the NAFTA negotiations. After earning his doctorate at Rice University, Hector was a member of the negotiating team (electricity) that represented Mexico in the NAFTA negotiations when I first met him.

In 1995, he was appointed Chairman of the new Energy Regulatory Commission in Mexico, very similar to our US Federal Energy Regulatory Commission (the FERC). During his tenure, he led the design of a regulatory and institutional framework for the power and gas sector that encouraged the private sector, creating a more open regulatory process for project development. It was the beginning of opening up the electricity market, but much more reform would be required in all three utility modes: generation, transmission, and distribution.

Our first meeting was at his headquarters, a brand-new building still awaiting electricity for the elevators, so we walked up the stairs five floors.

This is where I first coined the phrase, customer infrastructure, wherein Mexico should focus on the build-out of metro area customer utility distribution systems, with customer subsidies as necessary.

With customers you were then enabled, with that relatively modest investment, to issue competitive solicitations for new wholesale transmission networks and new generation, which is the more capital-intensive sectors (75%) of the three: generation, transmission, and distribution.

Knowing that generation and transmission made up roughly 75 percent of a typical US electric utility cost, the leverage of focusing federal dollars in Mexico on the distribution system would be a good fiscal strategy with significant economic benefits. Furthermore, that social development would be good politics. In short, good policy results in good politics!

As with the United States, natural gas generation would be the first mover, but renewable energy would also be enabled as well with these sectors winning utility procurement bidders making large-scale investments based on the distribution utility (CFE plus) long-term customer payment stream.

Hector understood this strategy and was very effective, even without the 2014 statute at the time.

As the years went by, and after a number of trips to Mexico City, it dawned on me one day that there was no private sector energy company in Mexico, so our arguments lacked allies. As a result, Hermann set up a meeting with Luiz Tellez, a former student of his and a recent Secretary of Energy in the cabinet of President Ernesto Zedillo. Luiz later served as Secretary of Communications and Transportation in the cabinet of President Felipe Calderon until 2009, again to deregulate another Mexican sector, telecommunications.

When the PRI lost the Mexican presidency in 2000 to the PAN's Vincente Fox, Luiz joined the private sector as Executive Vice President and CEO of DESC, S. A. de C. V. Later, he joined The Carlyle Group as Managing Director, focusing on buyout investment opportunities in Mexico.

Hermann von Bertrab and I met with Luiz in 1999 at DESC, and he really liked our Energy Company of Mexico idea, noting the need to train young Mexicans in these energy/business disciplines. Luiz had received a doctorate's degree in economics from the Massachusetts Institute of Technology and was one of several MIT economists I was to meet in the PRI governments. They were all change agents!

But unfortunately, the Enron bankruptcy occurred on December 2, 2001, under Chapter 11 of the United States Bankruptcy Code. Enron's $63.4 billion in assets made it the largest corporate bankruptcy in US history until WorldCom's bankruptcy the next year. As a result, we would have to wait as the energy markets were in disarray, and raising capital for Mexican energy investment was not practical.

But in 2004, Hector Olea founded and was the president and CEO of Gauss Energia, an energy development firm that specialized in Mexico's energy sector. After the 2014 passage of the new electricity law encouraging renewable energy, he became the president of ASOLMEX (Asociacion Mexicana de Energia Solar Fotovoltaica), their solar industry trade group.

On December 1, 2012, Peña Nieto was inaugurated as the new president of Mexico for the traditional one six-year term. He defeated Lopez Obrador in a close race, and during his first four years, he led a breakup of monopolies, liberalized Mexico's energy sector, reformed public education, and modernized the country's financial regulations. I was impressed!

Energy reform was one of the first issues he was to champion. Finally, on August 11, 2014, President Peña Nieto signed into law the twenty-one secondary component parts of comprehensive energy reform. This was eight months after passing the 2013 constitutional amendments to radically transform Mexico's hydrocarbon and electricity sectors.

President Nieto also announced that he would speed up the creation of a new electric power grid and advance the date for declaring which oil fields would be available for bidding by private and foreign companies.

In 2013, I had told my Mexican friends it was now time to finally create the Energy Company of Mexico, hire top-notch young MBAs, and be ready when the 2014 reform laws were passed. They knew Rogelio and had several meetings with him at my suggestion, but it was a challenge for them. Nonetheless, US energy firms like Sempra in San Diego actively engaged (and Luiz Tellez was now on their board).

Mexico's 2013 energy reforms were based on opening the energy markets to private energy sources coupled with a modernization of the two state-owned monopolies, Pemex (oil and gas) and CFE (electricity). There has been considerable activity, including independent power producers and now transmission in 2018.

Another area for private capital was natural gas storage, which was critical for Mexico as it moved to replace overused fuel oil and reduce carbon emissions to meet climate change goals.

Mexico is one of the most natural gas-dependent nations, with gas dependent nations with gas, from Texas supplying 45 percent of all energy and 60 percent of electricity. Mexico has depended on piped natural gas imports from the United States, which accounted for about 55 percent of Mexico's total gas usage. Much more gas would be required even as the global climate challenge arrived two decades later.

On a per capita basis, Mexico's 130 million citizens consume just a third of the electricity that other OECD nations do. However, as a result of the 1993 NAFTA and the 2018 new NAFTA, there was a manufacturing boom in Mexico, primarily in the automotive industry, which would require increasing amounts of natural gas.

Mexico would now use three LNG import terminals, but this relatively expensive supply is a challenge for a nation where 50 percent of the people live below the poverty line. Gas storage in Mexico would help stabilize the market. Renewable energy would also be very important, and there are independent power producers in Mexico now building wind and solar farms.

Two years later in 2020, I told an infrastructure fund client that Mexico was a client during the 1993 NAFTA process on the issue of infrastructure development, particularly energy. I noted that it took a while for the 2014 law, but SEMPRA was there much earlier with their Inova investment and had done well. Headquartered in San Diego, they had enjoyed a very good relationship with the Mexican business leadership, particularly Luiz Tellez, who was the Secretary of Energy in the cabinet of President Ernesto Zedillo. He was indeed an outstanding leader and the epitome of the new PRI leadership at the time. I pointed out that the new President Lopez Obrador seemed to be favoring the state-owned CFE electric utility once again. But they still need private sector energy capital and expertise.

The first Mexican presidential election considered open and democratic was the 1994 contest after NAFTA, when the PRI's Ernesto Zedillo took office. During his term, several reforms were enacted to ensure fairness and transparency in elections. As a result of these reforms, the 1997 federal congressional election saw the first opposition Chamber of Deputies ever, and the 2000 elections saw Vicente Fox of a PAN/PVEM alliance become the first opposition candidate to win an election since 1911.

This historical defeat was accepted on election night by the PRI in the voice of President Zedillo. While this calmed fears of violence, it also fueled questions about the role of the president in the electoral process and to whom the responsibility of conceding election defeat should fall.

Former President Felipe Calderón won with 36.38 percent of the votes in the 2006 general election, finishing only 0.56 percent above his nearest rival, Andrés Manuel López Obrador (who contested the official results as he did again in 2012).

Former President Vicente Fox had been elected with a plurality of 43 percent of the popular vote; Ernesto Zedillo had won with 48 percent of the vote, and his NAFTA predecessor Carlos Salinas had won with a margin of 50 percent. Enrique Peña Nieto had won only 38 percent of the popular vote in 2012, and his six-year term would expire in 2018.

After his two prior attempts, Andrés Manuel López Obrador finally won with a majority (53%) on July 1, 2018. He was the national leader of the PRD between 1996 and 1999, and in 2000, he was elected Head of Government of Mexico City. He left the PRD in 2012 and in 2014 founded the National Regeneration Movement (MORENA), which he led until his election as president.

A traditionalist, old-style candidate, he benefited politically from the 2016–18 Trump attacks on Mexico; but his early NAFTA reform pronouncements and general economic approach were initially encouraging, particularly regarding the 2013–14 energy reform process. However, that would change as he was a populist and true nationalist, unfortunately. He stumbled in his response to the Covid-19 pandemic in Mexico, his attempts to deal with drug cartels, and the economy even prior to the pandemic.

This political history emphasizes that the vast majority of the Mexican public officials that I met and worked with were from the PRI. They were impressive, a new generation, many with advanced degrees, including PhDs from the best US universities: Stanford, Harvard, Rice, MIT, and Yale. They wanted to modernize and reform their country, and NAFTA, in 1992-3 was their critical path.

In many ways, they sought to mimic the US economic regulatory reforms during the preceding two decades, and that was my role. Those reforms seem to be embedded now, as the PRI's laudatory efforts to reform the justice system were well placed.

Even with his two failed presidential bids, López Obrador still emphasized the fight against extreme poverty, saying it would lead to less violence and a stronger economy. In 2018, he portrayed himself as more pro-business and pro-American than in the past. While he was a critic of NAFTA in the past, he and his team insisted that they wanted to preserve it. The PRI's economic reforms were recognized; however, more was needed in how they explained them.

López Obrador had received more than 53 percent of the 2018 presidential vote, according to Mexico's election agency. That was thirty percentage points more than his closest rival. Conversely, the PRI, despite its economic accomplishments, had collapsed as a result of perceived corruption and cartel crime. It was its worst result since its founding in the late 1920s and was projected to win only forty-three seats in the 500-member lower house compared with 204 beforehand. Thirty percent of voters were millennials who wanted change, the themes of the Obama presidential campaigns as well.

López Obrador's party also won overwhelming majorities in both houses of Mexico's Congress, several key gubernatorial races as well as the Mexico City mayor's office. Female candidates made major gains, securing 49.2 percent of Mexico's 128-member Senate—a 50 percent rise—and 47.8 percent of the lower house of Congress, both the nation's highest-ever levels of female representation. In Mexico City, voters among the capital's 8.9 million inhabitants elected their first female mayor.

The results made Mexico's Senate the second-largest female representation in the world after Belgium. By contrast, the US Senate is 23 percent female and the House is 19.3 percent. The female momentum occurred after Mexico changed its constitution in 2014, requiring political parties to field male and female candidates in equal numbers at the federal, state, and local levels.

It all sounded like Title IX here in the United States for educational programs, including male and female athletics. Or even our failed Equal Rights Amendment!

The Mexican press reported that of the more than 83,000 candidates seeking office nationwide, 50.4 percent were women. More than 89 million Mexicans registered to vote in that year's election, making it the largest democratic contest in the country's history. Female voters represented 51.9 percent of the total, one of the highest ever tallies. I was impressed!

Claudia Sheinbaum, then a fifty-six-year-old environmental engineer, won Mexico City's mayoralty by a landslide (She was to succeed him as Mexico's president in 2024). She served as environmental chief when López Obrador was mayor of Mexico City from 2000 to 2005. She ran on a platform of improving drinking water and transportation infrastructure services. I remember well meeting with the water services back in 1993, and we talked about the concession model to encourage new private capital infrastructure investment. In 2024, Mexico City's two large dams were drying up due to drought and the city was in dire water supply straits.

The López Obrador proposals centered on increased social spending and public investment, including a public works/infrastructure program to employ 2.3 million young people, grants to 300,000 university students, and a plan to double the amount of money older people receive as retirement pensions. He compared his plan to the New Deal under US president Franklin Delano Roosevelt.

The 2018 Mexican election turned into a referendum on mainstream political parties' efforts in prior years to eliminate corruption and improve security. Yet those efforts failed, corruption had deepened, security worsened, and the attempts at judicial reform foundered.

Normally, in my experience, the economy steers political voting, but not this time! Addressing the corruption and security topics successfully was key to the economy retaining its impressive post-NAFTA momentum.

The PRI reforms in energy, telecommunications, education, transportation, and manufacturing are a legacy that we all worked hard to achieve, beginning with NAFTA in 1993. Left alone, they would buttress the efforts toward security and judicial reform!

The economy, via NAFTA, had made impressive progress, and economic and energy reform would continue. Those were the two issues I had worked on for many years and noted there were no campaign attacks on those reforms.

I had met with Antonio Ortiz, Economics Minister in the Mexican Embassy in Washington, DC, on September 12, 2013, to discuss the lessons learned from our 1992 Energy Policy Act. Title VII on Electricity had restructured the US electrical utility industry and launched the independent power industry worldwide, and how that could apply to President Enrique Peña Nieto's plan to finally open the Mexican energy sector to new investment.

We also reviewed the NAFTA history, and I sent this note shortly thereafter:

> Antonio . . . I had time today to research the 1993 House NAFTA vote which passed 234 to 200 with 102 Democrats and 132 Republicans in support. California voted 31 to 21 in support including Nancy Pelosi. However, all three San Diego members of Congress voted "no" including Bob Filner, Lynn Schenk and Duncan Hunter. Today, that vote would be very different I believe. Dan

These political winds of change reminded me of my 1994 advice to John Sweeney, President of the AFL-CIO, to not complain about the recently passed NAFTA but use it! Go to Mexico and help the honest unions organize and lift wages! And he did.

In summary, NAFTA was negotiated by President George H. W. Bush and signed into law by President Bill Clinton in late 1993, spurring trade between the three countries by reducing Mexico's high tariffs on goods from Canada and the United States. It worked and was a true success story despite the Trump administration 2017–18 accusations about it being the worst trade deal ever. Maybe this is the way you negotiate real estate deals, but not international trade.

NAFTA presented new opportunities for US companies and their workers, and it spurred innovation and investment, logistics, and supply networks. Rail investment was very significant, with US carriers like Kansas City Southern investing in new track networks, particularly for automobiles. The state of Texas now has a very significant NAFTA supply chain economy.

NAFTA allowed the purchase of a wider variety of products at lower prices. Contrary to the political rhetoric, NAFTA generated higher US national output, and a number of reports indicate that the US gross domestic product is now 0.2 percent to 0.3 percent larger than it would be without NAFTA, a yearly boost of about $50 billion.

There was consensus that NAFTA could be updated in a lesson-learned way. I was impressed to see proposals in 2017 by labor and others that appeared very reasonable. The New NAFTA would work fine. With all of this positive interaction with Mexico, why did President Trump continue to demand his Border Wall and create diplomatic confusion in this critical transition period?

Ildefonso Guajardo Villarreal, the Mexican economic secretary, was to indicate that the three countries were at a good moment in the negotiation process, and that progress made so far had put the countries on the right track to conclude the negotiation before the July 2018 Mexican presidential elections.

As I mentioned, Ildefonso was on the Mexican NAFTA negotiation team staff back in 1992–3. I had enjoyed working with him and was very pleased to see his role today. His arguments were sound. Also, on that 1992–3 team was Luis de la Calle, a very good economist.

In 2014, more than 125,000 small US businesses exported $136 billion in goods and services to Canada or Mexico. That is 25 percent of all US small-business exports. American consumers saved $10.5 billion a year from lower tariffs under NAFTA, with most of the benefits going to households with annual incomes below $70,000.

I, like most American consumers, enjoy avocados; yet before NAFTA, the United States banned all imports of Mexican avocados. The ban was lifted altogether in 2007; and while US avocado imports surged 2,214 percent from 1992 to 2012, overall US avocado production rose. In California, the number of avocado orchards increased from 4,801 in 2002 to 5,602 in 2012. US shoppers see this bounty every day in our markets!

I noticed a 2018 Business Roundtable study estimating that NAFTA withdrawal would prompt US GDP to shrink by at least 0.6 percent—about $120 billion a year—in the initial post-exit years, with US exports down more than 2 percent. This drop in output and exports would initially destroy more than a million US jobs across all fifty states. So, I thought it was a relief to see the NAFTA reform negotiations turning in a positive direction.

I wrote on October 1, 2018, to Hermann von Bertrab that I had been watching the NAFTA news conference in the Rose Garden at the White House that morning, and there was much goodwill! Canada had agreed, in late-night negotiations, to join the trade deal that the United States and Mexico reached the prior month, meeting negotiators' self-imposed midnight deadline to allow Mexican president Peña Nieto to sign the new NAFTA accord on his final day in office.

I stated that the new treaty, preserving the three-country format of the original North American Free Trade Agreement favored by business groups and congressional Republicans, was expected to be signed by President Trump and his Canadian and Mexican counterparts in sixty days, with Congress likely to act on it next year. The truth is, I am sure we could have updated the NAFTA with these same changes without all the Trump bravado! I noted my idea for a new Mexican Embassy here in Washington, DC, after NAFTA.

Since the 2012 elections, I have expressed my optimism about Mexico based on my own intimate experience representing their government (SECOFI) during the NAFTA debate in 1993. As I said, the PRI was then being led by very well-educated PhDs from Harvard, MIT, and Chicago; and they were determined to modernize their country.

Hermann von Bertrab had been a mentor to many of them and was a great leader for his country as the Mexican Ambassador to the United States during the 1993 NAFTA negotiations. It was an honor for our firm to research and "make the case" for how NAFTA would benefit both countries and Canada from an infrastructure investment and environmental perspective. I traveled extensively in Mexico for that purpose!

NAFTA was a big vote, as I have said, with lines extending throughout the capital to the outside hoping to witness the vote. Before Hermann returned to Mexico City in 1994, there was a dinner in their honor that Fonny and I both attended. As he went around the room saluting each invitee, when he came to me, he said, "And here's to Dan Flanagan, the man with the ideas!" It was much appreciated.

The NAFTA pact has clearly been an economic success. Over the past twenty years, US trade with Mexico and Canada has nearly doubled to $1.2 trillion in 2014, from $737 billion. While the immigration issue often gets erroneously conflated with NAFTA, the economic numbers tell a clear story. Ironically, Trump called NAFTA a disaster during the campaign; but since then, even the Heritage Foundation has stated that it has been good for both sides.

Then why were there attacks during the campaign? Well, the answer would be the tactics of divide and conquer. Mexico and NAFTA were pawns in the Trump political campaign to win certain rust belt states and essentially took the electorate there for a ride that they would regret.

The new NAFTA had improvements that were long recognized as necessary to update or modernize the original agreement.

In 2015, Hermann and his wife Ibone visited us in Annapolis, Maryland. We had lunch looking out on the Severn River, visited the Naval Academy Museum, saw the Mexican cannons taken by the US Navy, and watched the Brigade of Midshipmen parade. They were very happy! They visited again in 2019.

Hermann had been a priest and Ibone a nun in Mexico; although interestingly, she was also a champion diver for the Mexican Olympic team and was still competing in international senior diving competitions. We visited with them many times in Mexico City; went to their weekend home at Valle de Bravo, described as Mexico's ritziest weekend getaway resort town; and sailed in Zihuantanejo with her brother Xeneko on his fleet of vintage former America's Cup sail boats.

I sent a note to Hermann as he introduced us to Tania Elias Calles, whose great grandfather, Plutarco Elias Calles, was the President of Mexico and founder of the PRI Party. She lives in Puerto Vallarta, where we were visiting and where she pursued her international sailing activity.

I told her of my very positive impression of the young PRI leadership, all with Harvard, MIT, or University of Chicago PhDs who are devoted to modernizing their country. She was pleased as the PRI has had a checkered history; but we agreed they were trying to change that in what you might say is a millennial way. This is the same message I had conveyed to then-Senator Pat Moynihan and John Sweeney, president of the AFL-CIO, in the 1990s.

Today, I feel vindicated as it has worked, not 100 percent but maybe give it 80 percent. Mexican immigration to the United States is no longer an alarming issue despite the Trump declaration of a National Emergency and his hopes that there will be pandemonium. Indeed, Mexican-origin illegal border crossings had been greatly reduced beginning around the year 2000 as the NAFTA economy began to gain momentum, and there were jobs now in Mexico.

But we were not paying attention to the problems of Central America, and illegal immigration to the United States from those countries grew considerably. Albeit, finally, the Biden administration modernized its immigration/asylum process, allowing for a reservation system; and it worked. Still, it was very difficult for anyone to emigrate to the United States, as the relevant agencies, including the State Department, seemed understaffed and ineffective, with numerous delays.

Unfortunately, the invitation by PRI Mexican President Pena Nieto to Donald Trump during the 2016 US presidential campaign, which Trump cleverly accepted and visited for a few hours, backfired on the Mexican president and was an enormous faux pas on both sides of the border.

It appeared that saner minds were taking charge in the United States, and a very reasonable letter to Mexico emerged from the US Trade Representative's Office regarding NAFTA negotiations.

On Wednesday, April 19, 2017, Hermann von Bertrab sent me a note saying that the problem is that your dear President says one thing one day and contradicts himself the following day, obviously not only about NAFTA. Will his personnel be able to restrain him and teach him what strategy means, or else?

He asked how all this came about. Certainly, the American electioneering system with its primaries and state voting is liable to generate radicalism and unfairness. Is there any way it could be changed?

And I respond that you have it analyzed perfectly. President Trump will continue his ways, I am sure, until there is a backlash, which is still months away; and he is forced to recruit a first-class team at the White House to control him. His behavior during the first 100 days has been a concern to Republicans; and they are starting to publicly criticize him on tax returns, excessive weekend travel, etc. His budget goes to Congress next month, and that will be the beginning of reality! As for elections, there are congressional elections next year, and that will be the next stage! The Democrats are encouraged; the more tweets, the better from their perspective to overcome the local advantage that incumbents enjoy. Months later, on October 9, 2017, I sent Hermann von Bertrab a note telling him that Senator Corker, as chairman of the Foreign Relations Committee, could schedule some very tough hearings and stated his concern that the White House had devolved into an adult day care center and warned that President Trump's behavior is setting the nation on the path to the Third World War.

American businesses were concerned. In a sharp critique of Trump administration trade policies, the president and CEO of the Union Pacific Railroad, Lance Fritz, said in late July that withdrawal from the North American Free Trade Agreement would have a disastrous impact on the economy and that President Trump's trade war with allies diverts the United States from a more pressing trade imbalance with China.

He added, at a National Press Club luncheon I watched in Washington, DC, that new tariffs on steel had driven up the cost of a new mile of railroad track from $3 million to $3.75 million, and that tariff-caused uncertainty at US ports is leaving ships sitting in docks, unloaded, for weeks at a time. He said he is worried that a withdrawal from NAFTA would be an unnecessary shock to an economy that is booming.

And we had forgotten that while the US economy made up 23 percent of the global GDP, China was not far behind at 16 percent, with Japan at 5.9 percent. What were we doing but shooting ourselves in the foot! Mexico was at 1.4 percent based on its 2.4 percent annual growth rate during the six-year Pena Nieto presidency; and those numbers had stemmed Mexican immigration to the United States as jobs were now a growing facet of the Mexican economy. Leave well enough alone, you would think!

The Canadian Prime Minister also said he had offered to travel to Washington to meet with Mr. Trump and complete a new NAFTA pact because he believed the outlines of a deal were in place. He said he was told by Vice President Pence that Canada would need to agree to a sunset clause—a provision that would end the deal every five years unless explicitly renewed. That was a condition Mr. Trudeau told the Vice President he would not accept, and rightly so.

The Canadian Foreign Minister Chrystia Freeland also spoke and accurately pointed out that the US tariffs, claiming "national security," actually violated NAFTA and World Trade Organization rules, and that the country planned to begin trade litigation.

Invoking "national security" has been a very much abused principle in the US over the years. I remember how the Defense Department opposed the 1982 breakup of AT&T for these same "national security" reasons.

Rather than forcing Canada and Mexico into concessions on a new NAFTA, my perspective was that the tariff move was likely to strengthen Canada's and Mexico's resolve to not back down to US NAFTA demands. Our European allies also seemed to be united in their opposition.

All this goodwill built up over decades had been slowly decimated beginning from the very day Trump was sworn into office, reiterating his campaign rhetoric. And then the debilitating G-7 conference in Quebec on June 9 and 10, 2018, where Trump attempted to destroy the US role in the Atlantic Alliance. At the Group of Seven summit, Trump complained that we're like the piggy bank that everybody is robbing, and that ends.

The president's outbursts turned the summit into the 2018 G-6 vs. G-1, according to all the media reports. A photograph showed Trump sitting, his arms crossed in a defensive posture, while German Chancellor Angela Merkel, surrounded by the other leaders, leans across the table glaring at him. Trump looks like a defendant who has just been found guilty by a jury of his peers. After the meeting, Canadian Prime Minister Justin Trudeau, responding to a press question, said that the US national security tariffs were insulting and noted that Canadians were polite and reasonable but would not be pushed around.

There have been transatlantic disagreements, but none of those disputes called into question the fundamental unity of the West in the way that Trump's self-destructive actions had done. The Atlantic alliance was born in Canada in 1941 (Newfoundland—Churchill and Roosevelt) and may well have died there in 2018.

It was encouraging to see in the week before the G-7 gathering that a bipartisan coalition in the Senate was finally rebelling against the Trump administration's unilateral trade war. Senator Bob Corker of Tennessee, Chairman of the Senate Foreign

Relations Committee, introduced a bipartisan bill to curtail the President's power to impose tariffs and other trade restrictions.

The bill would amend the Trade Expansion Act of 1962, which under Section 232 allows the President to impose tariffs or restrictions in the name of national security. The legislation would require the President to submit 232 restrictions to Congress for approval under an expedited process.

And finally, on Monday, August 27, 2018, the United States reached a handshake agreement with Mexico amid the month-long contentious talks on revamping the North American Free Trade Agreement (NAFTA). Canada would now review that agreement and probably join all three parties, according to press reports at the time.

Unfortunately, amidst this hard work and goodwill, President Trump reportedly made these points to reporters in the Oval Office, who were summoned to watch him speak by phone with outgoing Mexican President Enrique Peña Nieto, that the name NAFTA would be scrapped for an updated North American agreement, saying it had bad connotations. He expressed doubt on whether Canada would be party to a new trade agreement, noting that the two nations would begin talking relatively soon. He also added his plans to "terminate" the existing NAFTA agreement and move forward with the new emerging deal called the United States-Mexico Trade Agreement.

But Trump would need Congress to approve the breakup of the three-nation agreement, a move that most on Capitol Hill would oppose; in the end, the "new NAFTA" had all three nations as signatories, and there were very positive provisions included.

As for a new embassy, years ago, after the passage of NAFTA, the Mexican Ambassador and his staff indicated to me that they were not happy with their current embassy building on Pennsylvania Ave., beyond the White House.

There was a federal court building then, next to the Canadian Embassy, slated to close; and my vision was to sell the current Mexican Embassy and establish a new embassy (Design Build Lease Transfer) on that courthouse property next to Canada and call it the Plaza of the Americas.

The State Department, the Mexican Ambassador Jesus Silva Herzog (1995–7), our US ambassador to Mexico Jim Jones, Senator Moynihan (Chairman of the Committee overseeing federal buildings), and many others all thought it was a great idea.

Then the Mexican peso collapsed, and an article about a "Palace on the Potomac" appeared in a Mexico City newspaper.

Unfortunately, I was not aware that the Freedom Forum chaired by Al Neuharth, CEO of the Gannett/USA newspaper chain, was interested in the property as well, and there could have been a discussion about a dual-use strategy for the property. Living by Arlington at one time, I was well aware of their Roslyn facility. However, they were to purchase the federal court property and build the enormous (and, in my opinion, unneeded) Newseum, which became the home of the TV media while the National Press Club continued to represent journalists and their professional trade.

The Newseum's finances became unstable when it took on $300 million in debt to open the 250,000-square-foot steel and glass building between the Capitol and the White House. The operation had posted an annual deficit every year since, despite a large subsidy from the Freedom Forum. It charged almost $25 for entry, making it one of the most expensive attractions in a city that boasts of many free cultural institutions.

Reading the article that described this situation while I was in California in August 2018, I wrote to Jan Neuharth, the CEO and Chairman of the Freedom Forum at the time (daughter of the founder) about my original idea for the Mexican Embassy and a Plaza of the Americas, and maybe there was a way to make this happen.

They were very interested, and her advisors, including Nick Pappas for real estate, agreed to meet as soon as the new NAFTA agreement was signed and use that political momentum to move the exploratory effort forward.

I pointed out that their building could be modified (dual use) as it does look like an embassy and fits with the Canadian next door. Plus, I was to learn that the current Mexican ambassador wanted to move from the current embassy just as his predecessor did back in 1993.

So, the New NAFTA was agreed to on September 30, 2018, and the politics should have been in place as well. So, I thought! Nick Pappas, the real estate advisor, and I decided to wait until the politics of the New NAFTA settled down. A few months later, I wrote to Nick in response to the January 25, 2019, public announcement that Johns Hopkins University is acquiring the building that houses the Newseum in Washington, DC, where it plans to consolidate its presence in the nation's capital, provide more opportunities for students, and better inform policymakers.

> Nick, while disappointed the Mexican embassy idea has been replaced, this is a wonderful move for all of the JHU activities in Washington—including SAIS. I have lectured quite a bit at both their Carey and SAIS campuses (infrastructure); and those old buildings can be added to the other think tanks in that neighborhood.
>
> I am already looking at bringing an infrastructure finance study center there (JHU/SAIS and Stanford). It is the perfect location. As I mentioned, I was a founder of the Navy Memorial complex up the avenue and this location is unique!

The Plaza of the Americas' idea has once again come and gone; and as it turned out, Nick had done the Johns Hopkins deal, and we had a good chat.

This was a victory, in a way, for the National Press Club where the real reporters hang out on 14th Street just up from Pennsylvania Avenue! Not the TV mavens! Meanwhile, despite Trump's bantering, Mexican President Peña Nieto told Trump that he looked forward to adding Canada to the deal; and US Trade Representative Robert Lighthizer said if they could get a deal with Canada by the end of that week, he would notify Congress that an updated deal was complete, starting the clock in which the three nations would need to sign the new deal by the end of November before the new President Lopez Obrador was sworn in.

The new US-Mexico deal would require 75 percent of auto content to be made in the United States and Mexico, up from 62.5 percent, and would require that 40–45 percent of auto content be made by workers earning a competitive wage. Canadian officials said they were eager to begin talks with the United States.

But Trump, wanting to salvage his role in the collapsing White House global trade strategy, said publicly that he would punish Canada with car tariffs if they played hardball on a final deal. The president said that with Canada, the easiest thing we could do is tariff their cars coming in.

Canada was insisting on retaining the original NAFTA arbitration provisions; and ironically, while Trump complained vociferously about US dairy exports, there had been an agreement on that contained in the proposed Trans-Pacific Partnership agreement that Trump had abandoned.

By leaving that proposed agreement, assembled under President Obama, President Trump severely hindered the United States' position with respect to those same countries, with China the beneficiary.

The Trump trade negotiators had been pushing Canada to join a new NAFTA framework set that month between the United States and Mexico by September 30. However, talks with Ottawa broke down on a number of points. Congress had made it clear that it insisted on a three-partner NAFTA approach.

Mr. Trump took office vowing to shake up the global free-trading system and put his stamp on it. He'd done so in many ways, with threats to rip up existing trade deals and pull out of the World Trade Organization (WTO). To me, he seemed to be "shooting from the hip" as reports show that he doesn't read memos and just wings it! The world had prospered under the WTO, and China has been a credible member since its joining.

And he has faced a backlash from US business and farm groups worried about the costs to consumers and exporters, and from lawmakers in his Republican Party. US farm income was now slated to drop 13 percent in 2018, which the Department of Agriculture was addressing through farm payments that would only make up a portion of the lost income. This payment approach would continue in 2019 albeit I wondered where the dollars that the Department of Agriculture sent out came from!

How they would vote in the 2018 midterm elections was front and center in the minds of members of Congress. And while the farmers hurt, they went along; but the Democrats surged and won forty seats, and my long time San Francisco friend, Nancy Pelosi, was now reelected as the Speaker of the House.

And this Trump trade chaos was occurring while thousands of US flags around the country were at half-staff in honor of the death days earlier of Senator John McCain, except for the White House flag. Finally, at his staff's urging, President Trump's White House late that same Monday issued this statement recognizing the death of Sen. John McCain (R-Ariz.), following criticism of his earlier response to the Senator's passing, and that he respected Senator John McCain's service to our country and, in his honor, had signed a proclamation to fly the flag of the United States at half-staff until the day of his interment.

No one believed him, as he had said earlier that McCain was not a war hero. He was a war hero because he was captured. I like people who weren't captured.

McCain, a former Navy pilot, spent roughly five and a half years in a notorious North Vietnamese prison known as the Hanoi Hilton, where he was repeatedly tortured. He was to be buried that following weekend at our mutual alma mater, the US Naval Academy in a very impressive ceremony—practically a rebuttal to the President. We visited the McCain burial site at the Naval Academy before the 2020 pandemic several times with friends.

McCain's father and grandfather, both admirals, are buried at Arlington National Cemetery. The US senator from Arizona chose to be buried looking out at the Severn

River alongside longtime friend and Naval Academy roommate Chuck Larson, a former academy superintendent.

In October 2018, I watched a labor-sponsored Economic Policy Institute/Notre Dame New NAFTA panel on CSPAN and was impressed with the participants and the positive points made regarding NAFTA and the New NAFTA, as well as the encouraging opinion poll overview. Free trade had won! The panel went on to summarize that earlier on Sunday, September 30, the United States, Canada, and Mexico reached an agreement to update the North American Free Trade Agreement, the 1994 pact that governs more than $1.2 trillion worth of trade among the three nations. This met the deadline for Mexican President Pena Nieto to sign the agreement before he would leave office on November 30. Most of the key provisions, which were quite reasonable according to these experts, don't start until 2020 because leaders from the three countries had to sign it; then Congress and the legislatures in Canada and Mexico have to approve it, a process that is expected to take months. But ultimately, it should happen. The key provisions for this new NAFTA included a new name: the United States-Mexico-Canada Agreement, or USMCA, and added that:

1. Starting in 2020, to qualify for zero tariffs, a car or truck must have 75 percent of its components manufactured in Canada, Mexico, or the USA.
2. Starting in 2020, cars and trucks should have at least 30 percent of the work on the vehicle done by workers earning $16 an hour. That gradually moves up to 40 percent by 2023.
3. Mexican workers must have more ability to organize and form unions.
4. More stringent protections for patents and trademarks, including for biotech, financial services, and even domain names. Canada will extend the term of copyright to seventy years after the copyright holder's death.
5. US drug companies will now be able to sell pharmaceuticals in Canada for ten years before facing generic competition, up from eight years of "market protection."
6. Provisions for private companies to be able to challenge the Mexican government if it changes the rules and tries to nationalize its energy sector again.

The Pena Nieto energy reforms were critical for Mexico's future, and I was pleased. This proviso also included other Mexican infrastructure sectors such as telecommunications and I watched the White House Rose Garden press conference, and US Trade Representative Robert Lighthizer bestowed much praise on White House aide Jerod Kushner, Trump's son-in-law, as well as his 250-person USTR staff. It became increasingly clear that Kushner's White House role was not as a doer but rather as the caretaker of the president.

The truth is I am sure we could have updated the NAFTA with these same changes without all the Trump bravado. Many of them had been under discussion for some time.

I happened to have meetings with senior staff of both the House Ways and Means Committee and the Senate Finance Committee on infrastructure finance during the January 2019, Trump-inspired government shutdown. The mood was bleak, and it was clear that the new NAFTA had faced uncertain prospects at the time in Congress, allowing the old NAFTA to stay in place in the interim.

Some analysts suggested the new NAFTA agreement might allow the United States to find its way back in with the Transpacific Partnership nations, making the calculation that these concessions are worth it to gain access to the huge US market and are a counterweight to China's regional influence. I was surprised that the Biden administration did not pursue that course. They were betting on an overhaul of domestic US manufacturing, which was a carryover from Trump's theme.

I am very proud of the various Mexican reforms, particularly in energy, to which I was a party during the 1994–2014 time period, and how both the United States and Mexico have prospered.

I was also impressed, initially, with the long-overdue labor reforms in 2019 after new President López Obrador raised Mexico's national minimum wage by 16 percent in December, while doubling it along the border with the United States to around $9.30 a day.

His proposed labor legislation would require unions to prove they represent a majority of workers before signing a collective bargaining contract. It had been the practice that union leaders and company executives frequently signed contracts without worker consent—contracts known as protection agreements—and most workers weren't allowed to elect union leaders through secret ballots.

The proposed new laws would mean protection agreements already in force would have to be ratified through secret ballots among workers, and union leaders would also have to be elected through secret ballots.

The country's corrupt labor movement, long dominated by the Confederation of Mexican Workers, had finally been effectively challenged.

It reminded me once again of my 1994 advice to John Sweeney, President of the AFL-CIO, to not complain about the recently passed NAFTA but use it! Go to Mexico and help the honest unions organize and lift wages! And he did, met the new leadership, and was impressed.

I was pleased that the AFL-CIO and other US labor unions sent a delegation to Matamoros to support the Mexican workers in their strike demands there in early 2019. The AFL-CIO publicly called the settlements "a huge victory for the workers."

While Lopez Obrador was to turn back the clock on his predecessor's educational (union) reforms, I was pleased to read in May 2019 that Plenary, the Canadian infrastructure firm, had expanded its North American footprint with an investment in Canadian Towers and Fiber Optics (CT&FO), a company providing fiber optic solutions for Mexico's developing telecommunications sector, which was one of the NAFTA-inspired reforms.

They had successfully installed more than 311 miles of fiber optic cable across five cities in Central Mexico, including Queretaro, Leon, Guadalajara, Irapuato, and Aguascalientes. With one full-length long-term dark fiber lease agreement already in place, they were going to lease the remaining capacity, expand the network into other regions within Mexico, and advance into the tower and microcell segments.

In addition to promoting the expansion of telecommunications capacity, the Mexican government had also announced a six-year national infrastructure plan that contemplated new rail developments, modernization of existing roads, construction of new roads, and construction and rehabilitation of hospitals and schools across the country. Those were some of my NAFTA infrastructure assignments years ago.

Unfortunately, the nationalist AMLO pedigree returned in June 2019 focused on the energy sector just as construction crews finished work on a 500-mile, $2.5 billion natural-gas pipeline under the Gulf of Mexico from South Texas to the port of Tuxpan in northeastern Mexico. The pipeline would increase Mexico's capacity to import natural gas by 40 percent, fueling the power plants and industrial development.

But President López Obrador had instructed Mexico's state-owned power utility, the Federal Electricity Commission (CFE), to require the pipeline's builders, along with two other private operators, to enter into arbitration. As noted earlier, CFE had been the monopoly for many years and now wanted to regain that position by demanding some $900 million for alleged delays in the construction of this South Texas marine pipeline and around $2.7 billion more related to six other pipelines.

The CFE also wanted to reduce the capacity and usage rates it would charge under the contracts, a haircut as it might be termed. The bureaucrats had dealt a double blow to Mexico's economy by raising costs for industries that depend on natural-gas-fired electric power and creating uncertainty over whether the government would honor contracts.

It was termed a war on triple-A foreign investors and was very unfortunate, revealing an economic ignorance regarding the value of the reforms that the educated PhDs of earlier administrations had fought so hard to enact.

But with the recommendations of Mexican billionaire Carlos Slim, who owned one of the pipeline companies, there was a compromise on the fees, length, etc., allowing a win for all sides.

While Mexico had been a magnet for power sector investment since the implementation of the 2014 energy reforms, the government of Andrés Manuel López Obrador had different plans for private participation in the energy sector. In the month of May 2019 alone, the government (CFE) adopted three different regulations deeply impacting renewable projects and the wider market.

They were using the word "reliability" to disguise their nationalist strategies. (In the United States, they use the words "national security.") But I was pleased to read a few weeks later that Mexico's antitrust commission has turned to the Mexican Supreme Court to challenge these new government rules for the electricity sector, which would restrict competition in the market in violation of the constitution and energy laws, and there were the new NAFTA energy backsliding provisions.

As noted, the policy for network reliability and stability that the Energy Ministry published in May was seen by energy companies and industry groups as favoring state-owned electric utility CFE over private-sector generators. The grid operator would put energy from CFE plants onto the network before cheaper options from private generators that had invested billions of dollars in the country, especially in wind and solar stations. Obrador had benefited vote-wise from these Pena Nieto reforms; but I was alarmed to read in February 2020 that as president he was now curtailing some of the country's independent regulators that had served as a check on executive power since the country became a full democracy.

These attacks included the antitrust commission, as well as the Supreme Court, and then—to my consternation—the commission that oversees Mexico's electricity and gasoline sector. These independent regulatory agencies had helped to truly open up the governmental monopolies and had drawn billions in private investment to Mexico's energy, telecom, and other industries.

But despite this success, it seemed the López Obrador government wanted to get private companies out of Mexico's energy sector. Many officials at other agencies were alarmed as well. He had canceled the country's biggest public-works project—the new, $13.3 billion Mexico City airport that was one-third complete—and announced a series of public referendums to let voters make key public policy decisions. Other moves have also raised alarms, such as a proposed bill to outlaw many forms of banking fees on customers.

The Economic Competition Commission said that it considers the rules to violate the principles of free competition and market access set out in the constitution by limiting access to the transmission and distribution network and favoring some participants over others.

The government of President Andrés Manuel López Obrador had asserted that changes to the country's energy laws under the Pena administration hurt CFE, as they end up subsidizing private projects through artificially low transmission charges. Energy Minister Rocío Nahle said in a tweet later that network reliability is above any public or private economic interest and is considered strategic.

It was disappointing to read that the energy sector should be controlled by the state and by the national state companies themselves, as it was many years ago in Mexico. But it was heartening to read that the independent power generators had obtained various courts' stays against the new rules.

At the same time, the transportation industries pointed out in their press releases that North American trade now accounted for 42 percent of US freight railroads' carloads and intermodal units, and more than 35 percent of rail revenue is directly associated with this trade, as are 50,000 US rail jobs—worth more than $5.5 billion in annual wages and benefits.

And the majority of this trade moves by truck, with $772 billion worth of goods crossing our borders with Mexico and Canada every year, according to the American Trucking Association. Additionally, billions in border transportation infrastructure improvements have been made as well.

NAFTA, and this New NAFTA, were critical economic engines that, despite some speed bumps, had delivered on their promises.

As I said, I will never forget the extended line of visitors both inside and outside the US Capitol hoping to be in the House gallery for that 1993 NAFTA vote. The queue extended down the hallways and out the main door into the parking area on the East Side of the US Capitol. It was historic and deserves to be remembered as such.

My son was to send a text photo of Hermann visiting them in San Diego with his navy shirt inscribed, "Don't Give up the Ship," the perfect metaphor at just the right time.

On July 1, 2020, the US-Mexico-Canada Agreement (USMCA) was official; but the culmination of years of negotiations would not necessarily mean the end of trade tensions among the three North American nations.

Updating the twenty-five-year-old North American Free Trade Agreement (NAFTA) was a logical and timely goal. But the Trump administration had to turn it into a political circus. The fact is the New NAFTA (USMCA) largely preserved the duty-free trade and economic integration of North America that was begun in 1994 with the NAFTA but included a range of fresh provisions such as new rules covering digital trade and intellectual property.

Since the implementation of the North American Free Trade Agreement in 1994, Mexico's role in the US supply chain has grown, evolving from an exporter of textiles to a leading automobile and aerospace manufacturer.

In June 2020, Mexico's competition commission—an independent regulatory body that I knew well—went to the Supreme Court, alleging that a new federal electricity policy announced in May is anticompetitive because it doesn't treat CFE's rivals equally and that it oversteps executive authority. A high-court stay had been upheld on appeal, pending a ruling on the policy.

This was a setback for López Obrador, who had successfully purged several independent institutions and packed them with loyalists. He now controlled the energy regulator and the hydrocarbon commission.

According to press reports, on June 22, 2020, López Obrador met with about two dozen regulators and officials to present a seventeen-point plan for saving Pemex and CFE, including a proposal to end new permitting for competitors.

AMLO has also said publicly that he was ready to change the constitution to protect state control of energy, a rollback of Mexico's 2014 energy reform. The reforms were working, but his political cadre wanted control for jobs and corruption. It frustrated me that progress was the enemy of these populists.

At issue were recent amendments to the 2014 Mexican Electric Industry Law (LIE) that the López Obrador government put through Congress in March to reverse steps the Pena Nieto government had taken to allow private companies to engage in electric generation and supply.

Various independent power companies had developed projects in Mexico with the aim of selling electricity and other related products through a wholesale electricity market with open access and free competition rules. Long-term contracts were signed with the CFE and industrial customers to supply electricity. A number of projects secured financing on the basis of such contracts.

On February 3, 2021, Mexico's Supreme Court ruled 4–1 that changes in regulations for the country's electricity market, which gave priority to the state-owned utility over private power generators, were unconstitutional, stymying Amlo's plans.

When we successfully opened the US energy markets in the United States (Chapter 4), we labeled our opponents the just say no crowd, and it worked. In Mexico, AMLO was starting to look like an old-fashioned populist dictator, and corruption and violence were on the rise.

Sure enough, a bill to change the country's constitution to boost state control of the electricity industry was introduced on October 1, 2021, by President López Obrador (AMLO). It was a move that could jeopardize billions of dollars in investments by private power generators. However, it would face a difficult time in Mexico's Congress, where López Obrador's leftist party lacked the two-thirds majority needed to change the constitution. And the courts were to be heroes!

But the effort by AMLO and his economic team to roll back the historic 2013–14 opening of the country's energy industry that allowed far greater private investment in electricity and oil was very disappointing. The 2013–14 reform had worked well, ending decades of inefficient government monopolies and lowering electricity prices through competition and innovation.

When I went to meetings at CFE's headquarters in the mid-1990s to explain what we had done in the United States in 1992, there was a polite but cautious. But now, decades later, this statist government has criticized the opening of the energy market, suggesting that the changes favored private firms over state-run companies such as the electric utility CFE.

Private firms (independent power producers) were now producing some 62 percent of the country's power, according to the Mexican government's estimates. The 2013–14 act had forced the national electricity grid to distribute the least expensive power first, a move that ended up giving priority to cheaper privately produced power since most CFE plants were older and inefficient.

Very importantly, the Mexican courts had blocked as unconstitutional earlier moves by the AMLO administration to rewrite the rules governing the electricity industry.

Yet President Andrés Manuel López Obrador's desire to put the state in full control of the energy industry, as it was in the 1970s, continued. Constitutional amendments proposed by AMLO, as the president is known, and sent to Congress for approval in a bill later in August 2021 were labeled electricity reform.

Private companies would still be allowed to operate under the new law, but they would have to sell to the state-owned federal electricity company, or CFE, which would set prices as a monopsony and would run a monopoly in selling to users. The CFE would be in charge of dispatching supply and guaranteed a minimum of 54 percent of the market.

Since Mexico opened its energy markets to private investment in 2014, electricity generators selling power into the grid have enjoyed dispatch of supply according to price, with more cost-efficient plants, like those using renewables, natural gas, and modern technology, going first. Large consumers, including manufacturers, have been allowed to contract directly with private suppliers, which rent transmission lines at prices set by an independent regulator.

But it was clear that by giving the CFE constitutionally mandated control over the nation's supply and pricing of electricity, Mexico would dangerously centralize political and economic power in the state-owned company. There was an estimated $45 billion in private capital—foreign and domestic—in Mexico that would be affected by this new law.

Also, the bill violated the new US-Mexico-Canada Agreement as it abrogated contracts, eliminated market-based competition, discriminated against private capital, canceled access to activities not reserved as exclusive in the agreement, and also contravened environmental commitments. Mexico was already violating the rights of American energy companies. It had seized storage terminals and targeted private power generation companies for the cancellation of permits, including renewables.

Mexico's Supreme Court basically caved in politically to AMLO and ruled on April 7, 2022, that key components of legislation passed in 2021 to overhaul the country's electric industry law (known by its Spanish initials LIE) did not violate the Constitution.

It was very disappointing that Obrador had staked his presidency on what he called the fourth transformation of the country so that Mexico looked like it did in the 1970s. But Mexico's lower house rejected the constitutional amendments proposed by López Obrador to give the country's state-owned power company control over the electricity industry in a 275–223 vote, short of the two-thirds majority needed to change Mexico's constitution. All opposition parties, including the PRI and the PAN, voted against the amendment.

My Mexican colleagues had focused on building institutions. I hoped they would eventually would prevail as Mexico's existing electricity law, introduced in 2013, had brought market competition and progress to that sector. The cheaper alternatives often came from renewable energy plants owned by private companies. On January 31, 2024, Mexico's Supreme Court struck down the remaining provisions of President Andrés Manuel López Obrador's nationalist electricity policies.

Mexico voted in presidential and legislative elections on Sunday, June 2, 2024. Eight Mexican states, plus Mexico City, held gubernatorial contests.

Claudia Sheinbaum, a PhD in environmental science, former head of the Mexico City government, and a member of Mr. López Obrador's Morena party, was the victor and would inherit a stable economy where firms are profitable and manufacturing was expanding. Mexico has a rising middle class and enviable demographics. What the new President Sheinbaum would do in energy and infrastructure policy was the question. Mexico's economic gains in the past six years had come despite AMLO and his opposition to the free-market economic policies that my NAFTA friends had installed so brilliantly.

During the Obrador presidency, his so-called fourth transformation would have restored the Mexican state to a large role in the economy and consolidated power in the executive, as was the case fifty years ago. But it did not happen and is a credit to various institutions:

1. The Supreme Court and the National Electoral Institute defended pluralism and blocked AMLO's attempts to grab power.
2. It's also a credit to my Mexican friends who opened the economy, the establishment of the Federal Economic Competition Commission, and the National Institute for Transparency, Access to Information, and Protection of Personal Information.

I was very proud of the 1993 NAFTA victory vote and the 2014 Mexican energy reform.

8

Transportation Infrastructure Finance and Innovation Act (TIFIA), 1998

As noted earlier in Chapter 5, being appointed by the Speaker of the House of Representatives, Thomas Foley, to serve as Chairman of the 1992-3 Commission to Promote Investment in America's Infrastructure was an honor.

Our seven hearings, with a variety of expert witnesses from throughout the country, included testimony pointing out that we were the only nation to use the tax-exempt bond approach and, as a result, lacked private sector project finance expertise in providing public infrastructure.

Our report, entitled "Financing the Future," was issued in February 1993 and continues to receive considerable attention. Our recommendations are now seen as the critical path going forward in modernizing the nation's overall infrastructure investment effort, buttressed with private capital and project finance expertise. As Chairman, I testified before Congress on several occasions regarding our principal recommendations: new federal lending and credit enhancement programs, promoting project finance in the infrastructure sector, and establishing a National Infrastructure Corporation.

Our first legislative achievement passed into law was the Transportation Infrastructure and Innovative Finance Act of 1998, or TIFIA as it is commonly known throughout the country. In 2021, according to the US Department of Transportation, it had closed $34.5 billion in TIFIA financings, supporting more than $120 billion in infrastructure investment across the country for rail, highway, and transit since its 1998 passage into law.

In 2014, WIFIA was passed by Congress for water-related infrastructure, essentially the same law but "water" replacing "transportation." On a conference call in the spring of 2020, the staff director for the Senate Commerce, Transportation and Science Committee related how he was traveling across his home state of Mississippi and counted some 650 independent public water districts, all needing infrastructure replenishment, and to do that, consolidation incentives were needed.

And applause is due to the Obama administration's efforts in establishing the Build America Bureau within the Department of Transportation. I was very proud as the infrastructure asset class is now well established in the United States with large-scale pension fund interest. Additionally, my Infrastructure Investment Commission inspired phrase "public-private partnerships" is now in common use globally.

To begin, while the Infrastructure Investment Commission was taking quite a bit of my time in 1992, our firm was also representing all the utility companies that supported the passage of PUHCA Reform Title VII (Electricity) in the 1992 Energy Policy Act. With President Bush that year, when he signed the Energy Policy Act, we were launching the independent power industry; and it dawned on me that we were creating the US project finance industry as well, in tandem with our Infrastructure Investment Commission hearings and testimony.

I was very proud of our Commission report in 1993 and its recommendations; providing credit enhancement to project sponsors on favorable terms was the first to be acted upon by Congress. Here is some brief history in that regard.

After my annual testimony over a four-year period, federal lending to projects as a credit enhancement was proposed for transportation projects by the Clinton administration's Department of Transportation. I remember coming by and briefing Senator Moynihan in his Senate office before his meeting with Treasury Secretary Bob Rubin.

Secretary Rubin signed off and, despite OMB objections, we secured the provision in the 1998 Congressional transportation funding initiative known as TEA 21, signed by President Clinton on June 9, 1998. The provision was commonly referred to as TIFIA and stood for the Transportation Infrastructure Finance and Innovation Act.

Over the years since then, significant progress has been made through the advent of public-private partnerships, a phrase a group of colleagues and I launched that same year, 1993, at the Plaza Hotel in New York. Pension funds are now major investors in the infrastructure asset class, particularly in energy generation (natural gas and renewable) assets with long-term power purchase agreements with utilities throughout the country, along with social infrastructure assisting the development of a variety of campus facilities.

Following the 1998 Congressional passage of TIFIA, I joined the USC faculty for several years (1999–2004) to develop a project finance curriculum within the school's MPA program for public sector employees to be able to structure needed infrastructure projects as public-private partnerships. Enabling pension fund infrastructure investment in what became commonly known as the infrastructure asset class was another objective.

Our center was titled the National Center for Innovations in Public Finance. Chris Leslie (Macquarie) and his Australian colleagues were always available to serve on my USC project finance lecture team along with David Seltzer and Bryan Grote (Mercator), Geoff Yarema (Nossaman Law Firm), and Mike Schneider (Parsons Brinkerhoff). Our case study lectures were always well attended. We were the founders of the US infrastructure investment sector!

Years later, in early 2025, when wind-inspired wildfires broke out in Pacific Palisades and Altadena, destroying thousands of homes and infrastructure, I lamented the traditional public finance (bonds) curriculum of my fellow USC faculty members, as my infrastructure investment/project finance classes would have been very helpful in contributing to the rebuilding of these Los Angeles communities. But you have to remember that there are one hundred cities in Los Angeles County, and I would often say to leaders there that their very large LA community was flat; it needed to be vertical like my hometown of San Francisco.

TIFIA was the original infrastructure investment building block, and much credit goes to our commission consultant, David Seltzer, who joined the Department of Transportation as a consultant in 1997 (commuting from Philadelphia) and quietly authored TIFIA. He designed the Transportation Infrastructure Finance and Innovation Act (TIFIA) program to provide credit assistance via loans for qualified investment-grade projects of regional and national significance.

Many large-scale, surface transportation projects —highway, transit, railroad, intermodal freight, and port access—were eligible for assistance. Eligible applicants included state and local governments, transit agencies, railroad companies (intermodal), special authorities, special districts, and private entities. Prevailing wage provisions applied, and most importantly, a new emphasis was on project finance, that is, on projects that penciled out for financing.

The TIFIA credit program would fill market gaps and leverage substantial private co-investment by providing supplemental and subordinate capital plus leverage (by 11–12 times) the appropriated dollars it was to receive from Congress. TIFIA was a change agent forcing the public sector to open its projects to a new infrastructure financing opportunity and to become more innovative regarding project funding options and development.

There were many clever provisions in TIFIA, and David Seltzer deserves the credit. I particularly liked the investment-grade rating requirement.

In 2014, Congress authorized a TIFIA-type program for water projects under the auspices of both the EPA and the Corps of Engineers. It is entitled WIFIA, and the EPA took the lead in setting up a loan office with project finance expertise, with many of the new staff recruited from the Build America Bureau at the Department of Transportation.

There is a recognition that water infrastructure is very much in need of new financial tools, restructuring, and consolidation. There are simply too many small, underfunded public water utility districts in the United States that have, in fact, have been cited for years by the National Academy of Sciences for their dismal water safety standards.

WIFIA duplicates the TIFIA format with the exception that its funding comes from general revenue whereas TIFIA is funded from the Highway Trust Fund. The federal government subsidizes the payment of the interest on the loans. Congress was very impressed with its leverage multiplier; and ironically, Senators Boxer and Inhofe both said in 2014, "let's duplicate TIFIA (1998) for water" in their respective leadership roles on the Senate Environment and Public Works Committee.

So, a W was essentially superimposed on the TIFIA statute that had been authored by our commission consultant, David Seltzer. There is a five-year grace period in TIFIA wherein loan payments kick in after the project is in revenue service. Investment-grade ratings were importantly required in TIFIA and now WIFIA. Both are very popular programs. For example, WIFIA was only four years old, and the EPA received more than $9.1 billion in collective loan requests for 2018 Water Infrastructure Finance and Innovation Act program funding in sixty-two letters of interest (LOIs).

The more than $9 billion in WIFIA loans requested was nearly double EPA's lending capacity for 2018, demonstrating the critical need for investment in our nation's water infrastructure. Multiple LOIs were received from prospective borrowers located in twenty-four states, for a wide variety of projects, including wastewater, drinking water, water recycling, desalination, stormwater management, and combined approaches.

While the majority of prospective borrowers were municipal government agencies, other prospective borrowers included small communities, tribes, and public-private partnerships. Consolidation of the thousands of municipal water districts was identified as a critical need.

TIFIA, emanating from our 1993 Infrastructure Investment Commission report, was signed into law in 1998 under the Clinton administration; and it was the beginning of a project finance approach to infrastructure investment in the United States. TIFIA is funded via the Highway Trust Fund and WIFIA through general EPA agency budgeting.

Around the millennium year 2000, the US infrastructure fund concept began with continuing momentum, and billions now in many such funds investing in a variety of infrastructure platforms, including transportation, water, energy, telecommunications, and the social infrastructure sector.

I am particularly proud of my assistance at that time to the labor union community, resulting in the 2010 establishment of their own ULLICO Infrastructure Fund, which, in 2023, had close to 6 billion dollars in assets under management.

And project finance/infrastructure finance was recognized by the Obama administration, following the Great Recession when President Obama instructed his second-term Secretaries of the Treasury, Jack Lew and Transportation, Anthony Foxx in July 2016 to organize supportive initiatives, including the Build America Bureau and a legislative proposal for a national infrastructure bank, one of our original 1993 Infrastructure Commission Recommendations.

It was to be a government-wide initiative to increase infrastructure investment and economic growth by engaging with state and local governments and private sector investors to encourage collaboration, expand the market for public-private partnerships (PPPs) and put federal credit programs to harness the potential of private capital to complement government funding, with establishment of technical assistance efforts at the Environmental Protection Agency and the Department of Agriculture in expanding their work on pre-development funding, and promoting the US Infrastructure market more widely.

I was very gratified to read the 2016 President Obama Executive Order that noted the diverse opportunities for collaboration in developing, maintaining, upgrading, and financing infrastructure and to facilitate, as appropriate, greater public and private partnerships and collaboration, including with international investors.

And it was an over-the-top moment for me that year when President Barack Obama announced this government-wide initiative to increase infrastructure investment and economic growth by engaging with state and local governments and private sector investors to encourage collaboration, expand the market for public-private partnerships (PPPs) and put federal credit programs to greater use, expand our work on pre-development funding, and promoting the US Infrastructure market more widely.

This would be the Department of Transportation's Build America Bureau TIFIA Credit Program, and its basic purpose, processes, and history of the program are to leverage federal funds by attracting substantial private and other non-federal co-investment in critical improvements to the nation's surface transportation system by offering three distinct types of financial assistance: Secured (direct) loans, loan guarantees via full-faith-and-credit guarantees by the federal government, and standby lines of credit revenues, if needed, during the first ten years of project operations.

All of this had its genesis from our 1993 report, much of it the work of David Seltzer, who also suggested that the amount of federal credit assistance initially for TIFIA assistance should not to exceed thirty-three percent of total reasonably anticipated eligible project costs, and TIFIA interest rates on loans were equivalent to Treasury rates.

Congress initially funded TIFIA in 1998 at $125 million, which allowed lending out ten to eleven times that amount. Ultimately, Congress increased that appropriation to $1 billion (even $2 billion in one year) and increased the lending limit to forty-nine percent of a project's construction costs.

Some twenty years later in 2018, the TIFIA portfolio encompassed over $27 billion in federal credit assistance to intermodal, highway, transit, and rail projects totaling more than $92 billion in infrastructure investment in the United States. Over sixty major transportation projects had been financed and constructed because of the TIFIA program under the Department of Transportation's Build America Bureau, whose transparency coupled with expertise, encouraged quality projects that were completed, versus many grant programs that were never completed.

I have a copy of the official TIFIA authorization from 1998 signed by the Secretary of Transportation Rodney Slater, with a personal congratulatory note hanging on the wall in my Washington, DC, office.

To step back for just a moment, there had been numerous congressional infrastructure hearings, conferences, events, bipartisan legislative proposals, and national infrastructure weeks beginning in 2012. Our Performance Review Infrastructure Committee (PIRC) coalition worked closely with the Obama team and attempted to maintain the momentum and navigate the ensuing Hillary Clinton—Donald Trump campaign and early Trump administration infrastructure initiatives that failed to gain congressional support.

The coalition was composed of the top minds in this infrastructure investment sector, and our five recommendations had been received by the Trump infrastructure team as well as the Senate Finance Committee and House Ways and Means Committee.

The ensuing Trump administration proposal by D. J. Gribbin was delivered to Congress in February 2018 (really a year late); it was a disappointment, with complicated state and local provisions as well as rural programs causing confusion in Congress. In fact, the definition of rural became a central theme. As noted earlier in Chapter 5, Transportation Secretary Chao admitted she could not remember the definition of rural when asked in a Senate hearing. It was hopeless!

It seemed that the focus for infrastructure legislation was to be in the next Congress beginning in 2019, or so we thought but it did not happen. Finally, in August 2021—amidst the pandemic—the US Senate passed the bipartisan multi-year infrastructure bill totaling some $1 trillion (actually over $500 billion in new grant funding), with newly inaugurated President Biden's support.

I reached out in August 2021 to my old friend Polly Trottenberg from the 1993 Moynihan Infrastructure Investment Commission days, and the Deputy Secretary of Transportation in the Biden administration, and told her that I watched the Senate's 69–30 bipartisan vote on C-Span the other day as thirty Senate Republicans handed Joe Biden a political victory by voting for the historic $1 trillion infrastructure, eight-year package fulfilling his campaign pledge to restore bipartisanship in Washington and provide the most funding in decades for roads, airports, railroads, drinking water, rural broadband, and other priorities.

But unfortunately, it does not provide for a National Infrastructure Bank, or the similar Infrastructure Finance Authority (IFA) provision, with a $20 billion lending cap that had been included in all the earlier compromise proposals and the latest Bipartisan Infrastructure Agreement but was removed before final passage despite long-time bipartisan support.

Our coalition had long supported this federal lending platform. Ed Mortimer, the Chamber infrastructure VP who was chairing the bipartisan infrastructure lobbying coalition effort, told me that week that labor had insisted that Davis-Bacon be included in the Infrastructure Finance Authority (IFA) $20 billion lending provision. The GOP members of the Senate bipartisan group objected, and the provision was removed.

It was unfortunate that the Infrastructure Finance Authority (IFA) provision had not been included, as there were many new funding categories, such as rural broadband, where the expertise and credit enhancement of an IFA would have been very helpful to the public-private partnership in designing their project finance structure. Many of these projects could be public-private partnerships leveraging federal dollars in long-term, low-interest loans matched up with infrastructure fund equity investment. With the advent since 2000 of multiple infrastructure funds, many public employees' pension funds had "responsible contractor" provisions. Furthermore, it was very clear in existing law that federal grants and loans require prevailing wages.

Our earlier 1993 Infrastructure Investment Commission report included several provisions, including the need for US project finance expertise, credit enhancement for projects so that additional capital would come into projects, and to house this activity in a national infrastructure corporation.

Since 1993 and our Commission's work, plus the deregulation (opening) of the electric utility wholesale generation market, the United States has gradually implemented new, more cost-effective infrastructure investment/project finance practices. Billions of investment dollars in the open deregulated infrastructure markets of energy and telecom have ensued, much of this investment coming from US pension funds.

Yet far more of these private sector dollars were needed in our traditional, yet underinvested, transportation, water and social sectors. Private capital and life cycle asset performance are critical to making up that deficit; and project lending, credit enhancement, risk transfer, project finance expertise, private capital, and new technology are among the tools needed to close that gap. Remember that bond-funded infrastructure does not address maintenance requirements. But private/pension fund investors demand it as a prerequisite for their investment.

The public-private partnership (PPP) procurement process is the critical path for these three infrastructure sectors, unlike energy generation and telecom, which have been deregulated and are part of the private sector.

The success of the 1998 Transportation Infrastructure Financing and Innovation Act (TIFIA) has demonstrated the advantages of federal lending and leverage to stimulate private capital investment in projects developed with regional/state/metro leadership assistance in collaboration with the relevant federal department or agency.

Remember, for every appropriated dollar, TIFIA lending volume can approximate ten times that amount, while federal grants are dollar for dollar and have a modest success rate. WIFIA leverage is even higher with its existing customer base and a lower risk ratio.

There is a role for the federal grant, and that is to be available in some cases to assist with planning costs (a good investment of several million dollars can open the door to a multi-million-dollar project) or to be added to an investment tranche at the end of the financing, if it is needed to complete the transaction.

But in 2021, the emphasis was on political grant money, and the White House Infrastructure Czar approach was unfortunate. However, the Build America Bureau was able to manage projects amidst this five-year bounty.

As I noted, TIFIA will typically lend up to a third, or up to forty-nine percent possibly, of a project's construction cost for a thirty-five-year duration at Treasury rates with a five-year grace period for the beginning of payments. This lending/credit enhancement invites the remaining two thirds of the project to be financed by other means, particularly private equity investment per the projections of our 1993 Infrastructure Investment Commission. And these projects now must have two investment-grade opinion letters from major US rating agencies before loans are made.

In 2016, TIFIA committed loans of approximately $2.5 billion to seven transportation projects totaling approximately $8.2 billion. In the two-year period, 2012–2014, some $7.8 billion in loans went to nineteen projects totaling some $27 billion. So, it works!

Now, in my view, we needed to build out the project delivery system at the regional, state, and local/metro level to complete the infrastructure investment cycle. A key finding of the Obama Treasury Department was that, despite this progress, there was still a demand for an investable pipeline of PPP projects. Encouragingly, according to the 2018 Brattle report, the period of 2015–17 saw a remarkable upward trend in PPP project delivery, particularly in the social sector of hospital, university campus, and civic center/courthouse projects.

Still, it followed our 1993 Commission recommendations that the federal role is to leverage its financing advantages for projects while state and local agencies develop the projects themselves and their long-term funding schemes.

There is a friction between states and local/metro/regional/rural project development that the incentives are designed to address. If large, densely populated metro regions are willing to finance their infrastructure needs, then grant money is more readily available for rural projects. Unfortunately, Congress needed time to understand our Commission proposals and testimony. TIFIA, in my view, was actually just a starting point! WIFIA in 2014 was the next step.

And at the same time, institutional investors were engaged, and numerous public employee pension funds had identified long-term infrastructure investment as a highly desired asset class, noting their long-term retirement obligations and desiring a National Infrastructure Bank as both an imprimatur for this policy and a stimulant for project investment opportunities.

Other policy options that our coalition has suggested for Treasury consideration included the following:

1. Reorganize the Department of Transportation as the Department of Transportation and Infrastructure and add an Assistant Secretary for Infrastructure Project Development and a Deputy Assistant Secretary for Public-Private Partnership coordination.
2. Review tax policy regarding the realignment of infrastructure-related policies, particularly support for project-oriented municipal bonds, including private activity bonds.
3. Reforming federal procurement rules to allow federal public-private partnerships.
4. All federal infrastructure funding programs will require a "comparator" process to determine the superior procurement process, and recipient regions/states will be required to do likewise. Incentives for state governors to issue related executive orders will be provided.
5. Encourage governmental agencies (federal/regional/state/municipal) to place proceeds from PPP concessions in related infrastructure trusts for reinvestment in other projects.
6. Revise federal OMB scoring so that P3 projects are considered an "operating lease" transaction (House PPP Panel Recommendation) as opposed to an upfront scoring under a capital lease. This would have a significant positive benefit in any federal social (real estate) development project.
7. Revise the Federal Acquisition Regulations (FAR) to promote large-scale IT procurements as service leases (risk transfer), like the uniquely successful Navy Marine Corps Intranet procurement (2001).
8. Regional/State Project Planning Assistance program. Many large-scale PPP projects are stymied by the unavailability of modest funding for public agencies to do preliminary EIS work. Consider incentives for establishing regional infrastructure authorities, for example, Washington, DC, Metro region (not to be confused with MPOs).
9. Loans to Lenders (TIFIA) to enable State Infrastructure Banks or regional exchanges like the WCX to foster infrastructure investment in their respective areas.
10. Revise policies that will give federal agencies, for example, FAA, Corps of Engineers, more flexibility in financing major upgrades to federal assets such as Next Gen air control and locks and dams.
11. Include investments in natural infrastructure as essential parts of water systems, including funding of repair and maintenance as part of federal water projects (Central Valley, Bonneville, and Tennessee Valley Projects). Federal water and power contracts shall include the costs of such repairs in their pricing.

12. For disaster response and rebuilding infrastructure for optimal performance, reform the Stafford Act to allow loans to the private sector, particularly investor-owned utilities.
13. Review and reform all federal credit programs related to the infrastructure sector.
14. Consider establishing within the White House a National Infrastructure Investment Council akin to the National Economic Council, National Security Council, etc. to design and maintain a more comprehensive approach to infrastructure investment policy, incorporating private capital, under the guidance of an experienced expert experienced staff.

There is a National Infrastructure Advisory Council focused on critical infrastructure security coordinated by the Department of Homeland Security focused on crypto security. Crypto security is a component of communications security that deals with the creation and application of measures leading to secure ciphers and codes, which are used to protect encryption systems and methods from enemy discovery, decryption, interception, and tampering.

But it does not address the infrastructure investment topic.

Most infrastructure projects in the transportation, water, and social (educational/campus/medical) sectors will be public-private partnerships, and developers suggested that predevelopment costs of approximately 10 percent will be needed to jumpstart these public-private partnership projects.

Importantly, there is a need for federal government support to help fiscally strapped local governments make the shift from a procurement system that favors low-bid capital procurements, which have generated a $3 trillion deferred maintenance backlog—to one that rewards life cycle thinking, multi-modal integration, and investment in maintenance and, most importantly, municipal water district consolidation. The water utility crises in Flint, Michigan, and later in Jackson, Mississippi, underscore this point.

Performance-based life cycle cost agreements that cover long-term operations and maintenance are not only very important but private/pension fund investors require that O&M be built into the project, and public private partnerships (PPPs) do that!

Bottom line, from my perspective, is that investors demand long-term Operations and Maintenance (O&M) coverage if they are to invest in infrastructure projects. Bond covenants do not address life cycle or O&M issues.

There is no doubt that strides have been made in the project finance/innovative finance disciplines. The availability of pension fund capital, the acceptance of the infrastructure asset class, the Obama administration's Build America Initiative, and pension funds have become major investors in these long-term infrastructure assets and desire more available projects for investment or deal flow, as is commonly said. Our coalition continued to advocate:

1. Critical Asset Procurement Reform (CAPR) Program for Federal Assets/PPPs.
2. Public Benefit Infrastructure (PBI) Tax Credits.
3. Performance and Partnering Incentive (PPI) Grants.
4. Standardized Private Activity Bonds (QPIBs) with no federal volume cap.
5. Strengthened Platform for Federal Credit.

Somehow, the bipartisan private capital/public-private partnership policy momentum we had in both the Obama administration and in Congress had been paused by the 2021 pandemic emphasis on grant funding. However, the infrastructure fund community was able to gain its foothold and is doing well.

And I remain hopeful that a future innovative infrastructure investment legislative package will emphasize the following:

1. The federal government has the unique capability of providing project finance expertise, credit enhancement, lending (with 10:1 minimum leverage versus grants), project planning assistance, and tax-exempt privileges to project applicants.
2. Checks and balances in a major lending program are important. The approval and funding process could take place at the "national infrastructure bank" for all federal infrastructure credit programs, both existing and planned.
3. The state/regional/local infrastructure sector has the responsibility to develop the projects, more than likely as public-private partnerships in the transportation, water, and social (education/healthcare) infrastructure sectors, while energy and telecom infrastructure markets are already "open."

In 2018, I wrote this background memo sent out to my colleagues both in Washington, DC, and the Stanford Global Projects Center about US infrastructure deal flow:

1. The traditional 2 percent and 20 percent (five-year hold) model was the initial private equity strategy for infrastructure; around 2010 or so there was a revolt. I well remember the pension fund meeting at the AFL-CIO headquarters when speakers objected, saying they wanted a lower fee, long-term, stable yield approach to fit their actuarial assumptions. CalPERS, etc., were all there!
2. The private sector's reference to renewable energy, railroads, utilities, and pipelines (and adding telecom) is accurate as they are deregulated and open to private investment. Macquarie's funds have owned three different utilities in the United States for years. The other US infrastructure investment categories are water, transportation, and social; and those require more work compared to other countries. Concessions, Public-Private Partnerships, consolidation (water), etc. are all part of the process; and this is where the state/local emphasis could be useful.
3. Lastly, Congress needs to recognize that the infrastructure asset class is now an established and successful investment category. Pension funds are major investors, and this infrastructure investment opportunity deserves public support as it provides future pensioners with attractive, stable returns in their own pension funds.

In earlier Congresses, our Commission's recommendation for a National Infrastructure Corporation (nee "bank or authority") had been recognized as needed on a bipartisan basis; but the highway trust fund bill or some other issue seemed to always be the US political counterpoint, unlike our global neighbors.

The establishment of a national infrastructure lending platform, be it named an infrastructure bank, a corporation, an authority, a fund, or an office at Treasury, is not meant to be a large bureaucracy but rather a necessary project finance platform to consolidate federal credit and infrastructure lending to the state, local, and regional project sponsors.

It's funny how long-time colleague David Seltzer was the author of TIFIA in 1998. That would "morph" into WIFIA in the Senate Environment and Public Works Committee in 2014; clearly, the need is there.

Public sector water systems need scale and expertise; hence, some form of optimizing the infrastructure of these thousands of public US water systems is what our PIRC recommendations suggest.

Consolidation is critical, and large water distribution companies (public or private) would evolve with their downstream delivery infrastructure upgraded and modernized, while the upstream infrastructure, including drinking and wastewater treatment plants, would be spun off to launch the water sector equivalent of the independent power producers (IPPs) for electricity generation.

WIFIA (2014), modeled after TIFIA (1998), lending is available through the EPA as a credit enhancement to encourage water project related private/institutional capital investment. (It does need some changes to reflect water-based procurement as opposed to transportation.)

With customers, you can readily finance water infrastructure utilizing WIFIA, for example. The challenge for publicly owned systems is that rates are controlled by elected politicians, whereas for private sector water utilities rates approved by regulators. The latter works much better!

The Jackson, Mississippi Water Department had become the poster child for inept management and repeated water emergencies in recent years. Despite state and national assistance in grants, the consolidation solution of the state's water departments was ignored.

I was disappointed to read in the Academy report that repeat violations are prevalent in public water locations, indicating that water systems in these regions struggle with recurring issues.

These findings indicated to me the types of underperforming systems that might benefit from assistance in achieving consistent compliance. The National Academy of Sciences summary of failing public sector water districts suggested our water consolidation legislative proposal made good sense, particularly with public water systems. It seemed clear that consolidation of water infrastructure assets and private sector regulation of water companies was the way forward in terms of scale, new technology, and consumer benefit.

It was encouraging to me that there had been increased interest in alternative approaches to infrastructure funding. For example, a timely Journal of the American Water Resources Association article noted two of these approaches—public-private partnerships and loan guarantees—albeit hampered by existing federal budgetary policies.

This has been my infrastructure strategy for many years. However, these public municipal water utilities are their own worst enemies with elected officials as the board of directors. Once again, the bottom line is that these thousands of water districts need to be consolidated, and incentives for that infrastructure investment make sense.

And recognition that private utilities regulated by state public utility commissions have a far greater success rate in terms of safety and water quality through increased infrastructure investment.

But if a rural utility wants to keep its distribution customer identity, that is okay. However, the large-scale treatment and distribution infrastructure needs to be consolidated with some form of regional water authority to publish the request for proposal (RFP) as a public-private partnership.

These public water utilities need to spend $655 billion over the next twenty years to upgrade water and sewer systems; in the face of some 240,000 water main breaks a year, contributing to $2.6 billion in lost drinking water, according to the EPA.

Water utilities' funding comes almost entirely from their customers, with the US government providing just about 4 percent of the total. So, the customer funding stream is there for project financing! However, we need to scale up these systems. A new infrastructure financing strategy also needs to be adopted, along with consolidation to bring this needed scale to that financing.

The state revolving funds are not enough, prompting Congress, as pointed out, to launch the WIFIA program at the EPA in 2014, modeled after the 1998 TIFIA legislation. WIFIA is now available through the EPA as a credit enhancement to encourage water project related private/institutional capital investment. The time value of money suggests making the infrastructure investments now and amortizing the cost over many years so that rate increases are reasonable.

And infrastructure funds are the perfect investment vehicle for seeking long-term, stable yields.

In 2023, the EPA released a May WIFIA report highlighting its newest selected projects!

The WIFIA program also released its 2022 Annual Report, highlighting the incredible impact of WIFIA projects throughout the previous year and emphasizing the program's goals for the future.

In November 2019, our coalition was invited to meet with congressional staff to review other infrastructure finance proposals, including much-needed water utility consolidation incentives.

It is important to repeat that every dollar appropriated to these platforms would allow multiple dollars to be lent to a creditworthy project. So, if our national infrastructure policy is to scale up and invest billions in qualified infrastructure projects, then there is a need for this independent national lending platform with a cadre of dedicated project finance experts to oversee the analysis and approvals of such major loans to investment-grade projects on a checks-and-balances basis.

While the NIB/Infrastructure Financing Authority idea came close in the 2021 bipartisan infrastructure legislation, it wasn't to be. Nonetheless, several departments ranging from Transportation (Build America Bureau–TIFIA) to Energy (Loan Program Office) and the EPA now with WIFIA had some form of infrastructure financing platform.

And disappointingly, while the Senate 2021 bipartisan infrastructure legislation proposal had initially included the Infrastructure Financing Authority provision, when I learned of its inadvertent removal, I had just turned eighty years of age and surrendered.

In 2016, Cledan Mandri-Perrott joined me and several infrastructure colleagues in Washington, DC, for lunch. At the time, he was the head of infrastructure finance for the World Bank Public Private Partnership Group. Years earlier, Cledan had been assigned from the World Bank to open their infrastructure finance/project development office to be headquartered in Singapore. Initially, he told me there were two of them manning the project finance office there, but that day he said they had over 200 employees there now.

I noted to Cledan that, as Chairman of the 1992–3 Infrastructure Investment Commission, I spent many hours with World Bank senior executives in the 1995–2005 period urging them to move in scale into project finance and lending directly to good quality projects and not lending to governments. Coincidentally, it was some ten years ago, according to Cledan, that the World Bank did make this policy decision and also decided, interestingly, to have it based in Singapore.

Cledan wrote to me in March 2018 that, after his many years at the World Bank, he was leaving to join Partners, a very large infrastructure fund platform located in Switzerland.

In mid-2017, wearing my Stanford Global Projects Center Advisory Board hat, I sent this note to Professor Ray Levitt, the co-chair of Stanford's Civil Engineering Department, who agreed with its premise and asked me to participate in a Stanford ASCE conference call with their leadership.

> Ray, The ASCE published another of their report cards yesterday with the usual Cs and Ds for US infrastructure. They began this marketing/public policy tactic some five years ago and it always gets picked up and repeated by various outlets.
>
> I have been on panels with their senior staff; and have asked them "why don't they now change the message to what it will take to get an A". Get into the "solution" mode! Each time they demur with a sheepish smile as if their only solution is more government money. I personally find their tactics being harmful to the cause of infrastructure investment as it confuses/discourages policymakers.
>
> From an engineering profession point of view, I would think that they might want to join with those who are advocating greater emphasis on project finance, time value of money, risk transfer and the other important techniques such as credit enhancement, public private partnerships, national infrastructure bank etc. That is where the Trump Administration is going, and they ought to get in the parade.
>
> Instead, it comes across in Washington DC as a self-serving message. Dan

We did have our ASCE conference call, and the ASCE began attending our PIRC infrastructure coalition meetings.

As I noted in the earlier infrastructure investment commission chapter, the Chamber and AFL-CIO jointly participated in our PIRC effort, and we were optimistic. The Chamber infrastructure finance proposal, as it turned out, was very similar to our PIRC coalition recommendations.

After the 2017 tax cut bill passed, the Senate majority leader stated that a bipartisan infrastructure package was the Senate's next step; and the US Chamber of Commerce mounted a large-scale advocacy effort shortly thereafter in 2018.

I was pleased to assist the US Chamber of Commerce in preparing its policy, noting communities should have a large toolkit of funding and financing options available for infrastructure projects and calling on Congress to:

1. Expand and improve existing federal loan programs covering transportation, water, and rail (e.g., TIFIA, WIFIA, and RRIF) to make it easier for the private sector to participate in infrastructure projects and leverage an average of $40 for every dollar of federal funding;
2. Create a new loan/loan guarantee program to finance a broad array of infrastructure projects with loans to be repaid through dedicated public or private funding streams (the bipartisan proposal for a $50 billion fund leveraged 15:1 and thus supporting up to $750 billion in loans or guarantees is one possible model);
3. Remove statutory and regulatory barriers to public-private partnerships:
    a. For example, federal law currently limits the number of airports that could be practically sold or leased to the private sector to ten;
    b. The use of public-private partnerships should be specifically authorized and encouraged with respect to federal assets with significant maintenance backlogs and the means of generating revenue or their own dedicated funding stream (such as waterways and dams);
4. Create a discretionary grant program to stimulate competition and leverage state, local, and private sector funds for projects of national significance; and
5. Expand private activity bonds.

We were just glad to see the infrastructure proposal move to Congress in early 2018. It had been held hostage in 2017 for the tax cut legislation including, as noted, taking the overseas cash repatriation issue away from infrastructure.

And the Wall Street Journal deadpanned the 2018 Trump (DJ Gribbin) proposal, stating that the infrastructure plan fell flat for investors. DJ Gribbin resigned after its release, moving to the large infrastructure fund Stone Peak Partners.

But we went back to work, and that National Infrastructure Week program demonstrated real progress. For example, public-private partnerships were described in glowing terms by panelists based on specific project experience. Maybe we can finish the legislative effort with this public support, I thought. Having been one of the founders of National Infrastructure Week, the goal was to encourage large-scale infrastructure investment via a mix of public and private dollars in very successful project finance-driven public-private partnership infrastructure projects.

But there were speed bumps! Following the success of the Goethals Bridge PPP project, officials in Detroit broke ground on the Gordie Howe International Bridge project during the summer of 2018 summer to commence work on the long-awaited Detroit-Windsor crossing.

Importantly, Canada understood the infrastructure investment opportunity for financing the project, along with a $250-million customs plaza on the US side. Michigan would repay its share of the cost via toll fees collected on the Detroit end of the bridge after the Michigan legislature naively voted not to pay for the bridge, missing a terrific infrastructure investment financing opportunity. Canada's pension funds will probably earn a very attractive rate of return on their investment while Michigan will earn nothing.

The private owners of the nearby Ambassador Bridge had continued trying to prevent construction and turned to President Donald Trump in an appeal to halt the project through a TV commercial that aired on the Fox & Friends channel.

I was slated to give my Stanford Spring lecture in April 2018 and was hopeful for some congressional direction. I told the student audience that the Trump Plan, when it was finally unveiled, fell flat. We really lost a tremendous opportunity to do some educating in Congress as there was a certain amount of interest in some new ideas.

The private sector is now energized. There's a lot of money in numerous infrastructure funds as the long-term yield focus of the asset class is very appealing to investors. However, state and local governments need to open up their procurements in order to be paired with new public-private partnerships amidst competitive bidding. The ever-increasing federal, state, and local debt levels demand that these innovative project finance funding strategies be adopted.

And the governors, as I have told some, are to hire some young MBAs to staff an infrastructure project office and issue an executive order requiring a comparison of the best financing strategy for a given major project.

Leadership is needed in the public policy infrastructure sector at all levels of government to ensure public partnerships are able to stimulate new infrastructure finance models. While there were Biden expectations in this regard, their political finance/grant approach was discouraging.

Even the universities were having challenges as tuition had skyrocketed over the last twenty years and $1.3 trillion in student debt has accumulated. The University of California's new campus at Merced finally issued public-private partnership procurement for campus buildout after we urged such action over a decade earlier. This is the future as universities partner with long-term infrastructure investors to more efficiently oversee the totality of their infrastructure requirements, particularly in the recovery from the damage of the 2020 coronavirus pandemic.

In California, at the state level, retired Governor Jerry Brown learned his own infrastructure procurement lessons the hard way, ranging from his struggling high-speed rail project to his San Francisco-Oakland Bay Bridge rebuild (when he was Mayor of Oakland prior to being elected governor).

You must have the project finance infrastructure skills to finance and construct the infrastructure project. In the PPP process, the public sector does take the environmental/eminent domain risk and sometimes ridership risk, while the private sector takes on financing, design, and construction risk for water, transportation, and social. Energy and broadband have a different orientation, but the PPP is still an option.

Jerry Brown's successor was Governor Gavin Newsom, also from San Francisco, and earlier served as Lt. Governor. Newsom family members were old friends of our family, and this is the California Infrastructure Investment Strategy (2018) memorandum I prepared at his 2018 campaign staff's request:

1. Californians recognize that the state has not performed well on major infrastructure projects in recent years. Those days are over!
2. As your Governor, I will be establishing in my office an "Infrastructure Project Development Office"; and will quickly hire a two-to-three-person staff of project finance experts to provide guidance to major regional infrastructure projects throughout the state as to "best in class" strategies for both the funding and financing of these large-scale infrastructure projects.
3. I will also quickly issue an Executive Order to all state agencies, universities, and related infrastructure jurisdictions that they will be required to perform a "comparator" on all infrastructure projects estimated to cost more than $50 million so that all project development options can be compared in terms of the most cost-efficient, performance-based construction method to pursue.
4. This analysis will include the use of public-private partnerships; and important considerations will be risk transfer, time value of money, competitive bidding, project finance experience, and other parameters.
5. This Governor's "Infrastructure Project Development Office" will assist project sponsors in the development of competitively bid requests for proposals for these projects that will include transportation, telecom/information technology, water, energy, and the social sector, including medical centers, universities, state courthouses, and the like.
6. Public employee pension funds have discovered that the infrastructure investment asset class has consistently demonstrated quality returns on a long-term, stable basis and are very interested in projects here in California that will be of benefit to these pension funds and their retirees.

As the general election approached that November 2018, Gavin Newsom was way ahead in the polls, and our Stanford Global Projects Center invited his transition staff to a campus infrastructure off-site after their successful election. But they all disappeared into new jobs after the election in that funny California way.

Back in our nation's capital, I submitted a Washington Post Op-Ed in the spring of 2020 in hopes of influencing the congressional infrastructure process. It was entitled: Yes, We Need Infrastructure Investment; and Yes, We Need Infrastructure Legislation. I noted that the US International Development Finance Corporation (DFC) was created by the bipartisan (BUILD) Act of 2018 to provide financing for private development projects overseas with a $60 billion lending cap. This strongly supported the argument for a US National Infrastructure Investment Corporation for lending to our own US infrastructure projects, including the public health sector, per President Trump.

Earlier on April 10, the *Washington Post* printed seven principles for a post—coronavirus economy written by Henry "Hank" Paulson Jr., the former US Treasury Secretary in the George W. Bush administration. It is an excellent list, and I could not agree more with him that state-of-the-art infrastructure is essential to economic competitiveness and will require massive government and private investment.

This harmonized with Senator Daniel Patrick Moynihan asking me in 2000 to assist him in developing some new strategies to recruit new investment in American infrastructure, noting the coming limitations on government in the United States to exclusively serve that purpose in the future. As he succinctly put it, Dan, government can't do it all, help me with the infrastructure sector.

Senator Moynihan developed the "Infrastructure Investment Commission" approach incorporated in the 1991 transportation bill known as ISTEA, as I described in Chapter 5.

Around the millennium year 2000, infrastructure funds were launched in the United States and have invested billions in US infrastructure; the bulk of those dollars have come from pension funds. The results have been very positive for retirees, both active and prospective. In fact, virtually every US pension plan today has a significant infrastructure allocation, and there is capacity to invest billions more in US infrastructure projects.

In a way, we had moved infrastructure project finance into the mainstream of US infrastructure policy and prepared a House Ways and Means Committee memo entitled: Strengthen New and Existing Infrastructure Financing Tools. But the coronavirus was taking its toll and cities across the United States were hemorrhaging money as the pandemic shut down commerce, entertainment, and tourism activities that provide much of their revenue.

Nearly 90 percent of cities expected revenue shortfalls, according to a survey by two advocacy groups, the National League of Cities and the US Conference of Mayors, which polled 2,463 cities and towns that are home to 93 million people. Cities had long funded core services by capitalizing on their role as gathering places, charging to park in their downtowns, enter through their ports, and eat in their restaurants.

They now had to keep running their services without any sign of when those revenues would return to normal levels. For office buildings, metro services, restaurants, and the like it would be a challenge. In 2024, Washington, DC, alone lost seventy restaurants.

Congress had authorized $150 billion in aid to state and local governments to cover costs related to Covid-19, but that aid could not be used to replace lost government revenues. In June 2021, Congress was also exploring the need for infrastructure funding.

Federal lawmakers also laid out another option for large cities: Spending now and paying later. Congress gave $454 billion for the Treasury to use to backstop losses in Fed lending programs, and the Treasury had committed $35 billion of that money for a central bank effort to backstop debt with maturities of up to three years issued by states and large cities and counties.

Debt had long functioned as a fiscal band-aid for cities, because they are often limited in their taxing abilities by state law or the need for voter authorization. But now, that debt is interfering with expenditures like infrastructure.

I was surprised to read on December 18, 2020, that the US Department of Transportation would launch a new demonstration program to establish several Regional Infrastructure Accelerators that would expedite delivery of transportation infrastructure projects through innovative finance and delivery methods.

The Department's Build America Bureau (the Bureau) issued a Notice of Funding Opportunity to solicit applications to designate Accelerators that would serve defined geographic areas, act as a resource to qualified entities within the designated areas, and demonstrate the effectiveness of these Accelerators to expedite the delivery of eligible projects through Federal credit assistance programs, including the Transportation Infrastructure Finance and Innovation Act (TIFIA) and other innovative financing methods. A total of $5 million was available for the program.

The Accelerators would assist project sponsors in project planning, evaluating innovative financing options, accessing technical assistance and best practices, and developing a pipeline of projects ready for investment.

The Bureau would administer the Regional Infrastructure Accelerator program. The Bureau was established as a "one-stop shop" to streamline credit opportunities while also providing technical assistance and encouraging innovative best practices in project planning, financing, delivery, and operation. They had closed over $9.91 billion in TIFIA and Railroad Rehabilitation and Improvement Financing (RRIF) loans, supporting more than $33.16 billion in infrastructure investment across the country during the four years of the Trump administration.

With the Biden administration, we all know that billions have been spent on pandemic-related needs. It was important to grasp the role of private sector project finance knowledge and institutional investment in meeting the confluence of our environmental and infrastructure needs. But it did not happen as the giving away of grant money cancer spread in that peculiar political way. They used to call it street money, but it was not about asphalt. However, it was bipartisan.

The need for infrastructure investment and supply chain efficiency in the United States was clear to me, as I was well aware that

1. The US dedicates only 1.6 percent of gross domestic product (GDP) to infrastructure spending versus 2.9 percent for Europe, 3 percent for Japan, and a whopping 6.1 percent for China (Group of twenty).
2. According to the US DOT, in 2018, 25 percent of US bridges needed significant repair.

But the bipartisan infrastructure legislation had long passed the House and was signed by President Biden. However, it did not take long to realize this was not project finance but rather the old-fashioned political finance.

As noted several times in this chapter, our PIRC coalition had long urged governors to set up infrastructure project development offices with the necessary project finance expertise; unfortunately, that was not happening, as the January 4 *Washington Post* reported that Biden's infrastructure czar was urging governors to appoint their own infrastructure implementation coordinators.

As it happened, President Joe Biden's infrastructure czar, former New Orleans mayor Mitch Landrieu, sent letters to all the nation's governors in that new year urging them to appoint their own infrastructure implementation coordinators to smooth the rollout of the $1.2 trillion law.

Landrieu suggested governors could create their own infrastructure task forces modeled after the White House Infrastructure Implementation Task Force to help integrate all project aspects.

Landrieu also told governors in early 2022 that his team would be releasing formal guidance to agencies to "help set the policy parameters for much of the discretionary and remaining formula funding in 2022 and beyond." They were also preparing a guidebook for state and local governments related to programs coming this year.

There was nothing about project finance, infrastructure funds, and public-private partnerships. It was just the same old political mantra and was very disappointing. I could just see the spending fiasco coming.

The rhetoric in 2021-2 seemed to be centered on how much federal money goes out the door versus how many successful projects there are. But the pandemic had left its infrastructure scar tissue. Mass transit was hemorrhaging millions of dollars as passenger usage had plummeted, remote work seemed to have become a permanent fixture, and large-scale metro downtowns throughout the country had lost their economic rhythm.

The State of Maryland, in its post-pandemic 2024 legislative session, discovered that they had an enormous budget deficit and, at the same time, its infrastructure projects were in total disarray, with local budgets were similarly impacted.

And while we now have many major infrastructure funds and very interesting projects, there was still a tension in 2022 within the political and congressional sector as to the role of private capital infrastructure investment and their preference for doling out grant dollars, their so-called real money. They ignore the discipline of project finance, preferring what I call political finance.

But there was a very positive story as well: The new public-private US infrastructure timetable truly began with our 1993 Infrastructure Investment Commission Report, with its emphasis on the need for the United States to develop a project finance discipline that intersected with my work in passing the 1992 Energy Policy Act creating the US independent power industry (project finance).

There was a TIFIA passage in 1998, with Macquarie entering the US market around 2000, followed by other Canadian, European, and Australian infrastructure firms, prompting Goldman Sachs to launch their platform. The WIFIA passage in 2014, and around the same time, in July 2014, the Department of Transportation Build America Bureau was established via President Obama's Memorandum Expanding Public Private Collaboration on Infrastructure.

There were the House hearings on public-private partnerships (we hosted the Canadians for dinner), and I assisted ULLICO's launch of their infrastructure fund during that period, real progress, there was good news: Over the last twenty years, numerous large infrastructure funds have received millions of dollars in commitments from US pension funds for investment in investment-grade projects. Their projects have proven to be successful.

Here is some commentary on the linkage of ERISA, the Fiduciary Standard, Pension Funds, and the Real Estate and Infrastructure Asset Classes, which would be timely. In late 1973, I was working in New York for the Martin E. Segal Company, a large pension/health fund actuarial consulting firm at 730 Fifth Avenue, then owned by the Wertheim Investment Banking firm, and commuting from Scotch Plains, New Jersey. It was a training program for six months before returning to its San Francisco office.

During that time, the Employee Retirement Income Security Act of 1974 (ERISA) was the subject of congressional hearings and legislation that, as a federal law, set minimum standards for most voluntarily established retirement and health plans in private industry to provide protection for individuals in these plans. One of the most important provisions was the establishment of fiduciary standards for the overseers of pension funds. I did meet with congressional staff at the time.

At the Segal Company, I was intensely interested in the role that pension funds could play in the US economy while earning healthy investment returns. I would often go to multi-employer trustee meetings with the firm's Executive VP, Vincent O'Hara, in Washington, DC, (national funds) and to local New York metro area pension and health and welfare funds. It was a very interesting perspective, and I saw a lot.

Several times at such meetings in the New York area, trustees would openly discuss real estate investment deals with the developers of projects. This was unseemly, and ERISA's fiduciary requirements ultimately ended the practice. Professional investment managers, as third parties, were selected to oversee the various investments for the fund.

Returning to the Segal San Francisco office in late 1974, I adopted Democratic Party politics as my outside activity while continuing to consult with pension and health plans on the West Coast. During this time, I became acquainted with Walter Shorenstein, a wealthy Democratic Party contributor, and his real estate investment company based in San Francisco. I suggested that pension funds had the potential to be major investors in his projects, but it was too early. Today, some forty years later, that firm owns interests in 23 million square feet of office space throughout the United States. The company has sponsored twelve closed-end real estate funds, with total equity commitments of $8.8 billion, primarily from pension funds.

The infrastructure asset class was to follow in the millennium year 2000, and I was proud of the role our team played in its launch in the United States.

Yes, this infrastructure journey has taken years, but it reminded me of my Navy days on the bridge of the USS Coral Sea aircraft carrier when it was time, as the Officer of the Deck, to give the order to turn the ship into the wind to launch and recover aircraft. The turn took close to half an hour, but then we went to full speed ahead at over thirty knots. And that is happening out in the new infrastructure marketplace, underway now in the United States for some twenty years.

9

Thoroughbred Racing Reform Effort, 2007 and 2022/3

My wife, Fonny, and I were invited to the charming city of Lexington, Kentucky, home of the University of Kentucky, to enjoy the Keeneland Stakes in 2007 by the Clay family, owners of Runnymede Farm, an American horse breeding farm located outside Paris, Kentucky, and named after the site in England for the signing of the Magna Carta some seven hundred years beforehand. David Blee had been a colleague at a Washington firm, and he and his wife, Biz (Clay) Blee, were our hosts.

The 365-acre thoroughbred breeding farm had been established in 1867 by American Civil War Colonels Ezekiel Field Clay and Catesby Woodford. Colonel Ezekiel Clay (1840–1920) was a cousin of Henry Clay. The farm has had a long history of breeding success. US Racing Hall of Fame inductees Miss Woodford, Hanover, Ben Brush, and Roamer were bred at Runnymede Farm.

During our visit, we attended several pre-Keeneland Stakes receptions in Lexington, the capitol of the bluegrass Kentucky thoroughbred racing industry. On one occasion, at Mrs. Josephine Abercrombie's beautiful estate, I was asked about my Washington, DC, professional background by Robert Clay, owner of the famous Three Stables Horse Farm. He brought Gary Biszantz over to join us. Gary was the owner of Cobra Farm at the time (made his fortune in Cobra Golf Clubs) and had a place in Del Mar near San Diego, and we were up the road in Carlsbad.

When I noted my "deregulation" history in response to the question, a coterie of quests surrounded and queried me as to what their racing industry needed. I responded that the major tracks needed regulatory reform; that is, they needed to have their own national thoroughbred racetracks league with uniform federal regulatory standards within a self-regulated mode, like football and baseball, combined with the pre-emption of antiquated state regulation. There was enthusiastic agreement (maybe it was the wine and the Peter Duchin piano), and they asked for my help.

The strategy of a national thoroughbred racetracks league would entail federal regulatory reform in order to preempt the antiquated state regulatory model for thoroughbred racing. We would be advancing uniform federal regulatory standards within a self-regulated mode like the football and baseball leagues in the United States as the trade-off for the state regulation preemption.

Those league standards would include federal requirements for medication use, track conditions, and other safety standards to protect the horses, as well as uniform baseline standards for horseracing.

This could be popular as a consumer-driven platform for needed change, but it would require a well-thought-out public relations effort.

There could be other reforms included, such as restoration of intellectual property, broadcast rights, and conformity to traditional corporate tax policy. They need rescue from the suffocating state regulatory environments for thoroughbred racing!

We worked hard at it over a two-year (2007–9) period, but the industry was just too fragmented.

Finally, the Horseracing Integrity and Safety Authority (HISA) was created by Congress in 2020 to oversee thoroughbred racing safety and horse trainer drug practices. This happened as the multiple deaths of thoroughbreds at tracks convinced Senate Majority Leader Mitch McConnell from Kentucky that the time had come for the safety and drug topics to be regulated nationally.

It still seemed desirable to add the issues of a league, national standards, and restoration of intellectual property to the mix. We tried, and here is that story:

Runnymede Farm's Chairman is Catesby Woodford Clay, a grandson of the founder, Ezekiel Clay, and father-in-law of David Blee, a former member of my firm and a close friend. David and his wife, Biz, would spend their summers in Kentucky assisting Biz's brother, Brutus, a Georgetown grad, who oversaw the Runnymede operation for the Clay family. We would stay at their ancestral home several times during this project.

In early 2020, we were all shocked to read that David had passed away in Kentucky during the Christmas break that year. After Catholic Church funeral services in Lexington (David had been a convert), my wife Fonny and I attended the mass of celebration of his life at their parish church, Holy Trinity, in the Georgetown neighborhood of Washington, DC. (We had been parishioners there ourselves years earlier.) The church was packed, including many students from Georgetown Prep, where their son, Cooper, was a sophomore.

The Clay family members were very committed Catholics and, sharing the same faith, we enjoyed being not only their house guests but also church fellows as well in Lexington and even singing in their church choir. Knowing that their famous ancestor, Henry Clay, had been a Baptist, in response to the obvious question, it was explained by the family that Catesby Clay's great-grandfather married a McAvoy from Baltimore. They were a dedicated Catholic family whose business was supplying vestments to Catholic priests throughout the East Coast. At that point, the Clay family became devout Catholics, and the tradition continues to this day.

With the running of the Kentucky Derby (some 150 including 2025), there is not another major sport in the United States that can compete historically. And that is the paradox; as virtually every other major sport in the United States has a completely different and more modern approach to regulation.

I was asked to research this further back in 2007 by the National Thoroughbred Racing Association and make recommendations, which we did while also working as well with the faculty at the University of Louisville, incidentally the alma mater of Senator McConnell.

You have to remember that most of the major racetracks in the United States have a birthright going back to the 1920–1930s which invited a focus on state regulatory oversight at the time.

The Interstate Horse Racing Act of 1978 (in the midst of other regulatory reform measures at the time) maintained this principle, reaffirming that states would have the primary responsibility as to what forms of gambling might take place within their borders. This allowed the state regulators to "give away the signal," the track's intellectual property, to off-track betting parlors (OTB), thinking that this would spur new revenue.

The Congress did confirm its own role, in the 1978 Act, as to regulating interstate commerce with respect to wagering on horse racing, to further the horse racing and legal off-track betting industries in the United States. I was working on railroad deregulation during this same time period, and one of our goals, which we accomplished, was to preempt onerous state regulation.

In 2006, Congress passed the Internet Gambling Prohibition Act, and the horse racing industry found itself in disagreement with the Department of Justice over whether its interstate simulcasts were legal under the federal law. During House Judiciary hearings, the Department testified that existing criminal statutes prohibit the interstate transmission of bets or wagers, including wagers on horse races. While the racing industry was exempted from the Act, virtual chaos reigns in the simulcast racing market itself even today.

In May 2018, the Supreme Court ruled that states could allow betting on sports, which set off a pandemonium of sports leagues wanting to be paid for their content, their intellectual property. Churchill Downs Corporation, the owner of the racetrack and the Kentucky Derby, was one of those! In August 2024, articles appeared about the tremendous earnings of their gambling subsidiary, with more than two dozen casino and gambling locations.

In 2008, Congress held hearings, prompted by the so-called Mitchell (former Senate majority leader) Report, on the use of steroids and other drugs in US sports. The NTRA testified in those hearings and agreed with the congressional suggestion that states either adopt the industry-sponsored model rule for thoroughbred drug testing by year-end or lose their right to oversee simulcast racing and revenue.

This, to me, was an important step for thoroughbred racing in recognizing the issues of national drug standards, integrity in the sport, and the intellectual property of that sport. I thought there was a chance. I became a regular commuter to Lexington, Kentucky, attending meetings of owners, track presidents, and public officials but avoided trainers; in my view they were the problem.

In years past, certain horses had captured the imagination of the American public. Whether it was Secretariat, Seattle Slew, or Smarty Jones, their fame was imprinted on the public's mind. But never have we had the phenomenon of Barbaro.

Even American Pharoah, the best of them all with both his 2015 Triple Crown and Breeder's Cup wins, while very popular, did not rival Barbaro, nor did the 2018 Triple Crown winner, Justify. They were great thoroughbreds, but Barbaro had the story!

Barbaro was an American thoroughbred racehorse who decisively won the 2006 Kentucky Derby but shattered his leg two weeks later in the 2006 Preakness Stakes at the ancient Pimlico Racetrack in Maryland, ending his racing career and eventually leading to his death. In fact, every network was reporting on a minute-by-minute basis regarding Barbaro's surgery at the University of Pennsylvania, and Dr. Dean Richardson was now among the most famous medical practitioners in America.

Gretchen Jackson, owner of Barbaro, emerged in the public eye as a loving, caring person illustrative of the deep affection that Americans have for horses and their intrinsic beauty. The letters and phone calls of support for Barbaro poured in, and I remember reading that Mrs. Jackson had suggested that people were making a deep connection with the struggling horse's story. I thought the political stage was set!

At the same time, newspapers throughout the country in 2006 carried John Clay's excellent article, Breakdowns, Part of the Game? (Lexington Herald-Leader). In the article, John Clay pointed out the attributes of a polytrack racing surface, as better for the horses than dirt, in a very effective manner.

The Pimlico Race Course, where Barbaro was injured, is a traditional dirt track that opened in 1870. Its name is derived from the 1660s when English settlers in Baltimore named the area in honor of Old Ben Pimlico's Tavern in London.

In his memorable article regarding the need for action, I read John Clay's recommendation that racing should fund more research to obtain needed information and even appoint a commission for investigation as the sport was in dire need of leadership. My research was reaching a similar conclusion!

And we responded by organizing an industry leadership roundtable at the University of Kentucky Alumni House. The turnout was excellent, with many prominent owners in attendance, along with leaders in various aspects of the industry, including the National Thoroughbred Racing Association (NTRA). Arthur Hancock was an attendee and an excellent contributor to the discussion.

Congressman Ed Whitfield from western Kentucky flew in and attended as he was both an old friend from railroad days and a senior member of the Energy and Commerce Committee, which had jurisdiction over horse racing.

This was the genesis for the report we later did for the National Thoroughbred Racing Association (NTRA). The timing was good as the thoroughbred racing industry now had America's attention with the focus on safety amidst a subtle love affair with the equine sport.

Sadly, most racetracks on a given day have a sparse crowd with a meager offering of competitive horse races and small purses discouraging investment. Many of these tracks have lost their attractiveness, and younger generations, including millennials, never visit—much less have seen a horse race other than the Triple Crown series on television.

Many racetracks have closed and are now shopping centers (Bay Meadows in San Mateo that I attended with my parents and Tanforan up the road by the San Francisco airport were two of many). Something was wrong. The era in which the American horse racing industry grew up was over.

Today we have ESPN, Fox Sports, the College Sports Network, the Tennis and Golf Channels, the NFL channel, and on it goes. This saturation, combined with huge player salaries (tax deductible as assets belonging to the wealthy team owner), agents, and the like, has its own sports content challenges, as noted in an earlier Chapter #2; but the continuing affection for horse racing has nostalgia worth capturing.

But back to wagering, we now have numerous Indian tribe casinos, legalized sports gambling, and a proliferation of gambling casino activity throughout the country, whether it is Mississippi's Gulf Coast, Atlantic City, or Las Vegas. So, the tracks may be empty of fans on a given day, but with 85 percent of pari-mutuel activity coming from simulcast to these venues.

In the 2006 House Judiciary Committee hearings that I attended, the transcript of the members' statements, as to the racing industry, suggested a lack of clarity as to what the regulatory regime for thoroughbred racing in the United States should be in today's modern economy.

Would not a national standard regulatory approach benefit the greater good? Other industries had been successfully deregulated in this fashion, including railroads, trucking, telecommunications, energy generation, and the list goes on. I have been centrally involved in all of them and, most importantly, the American consumer has been the winner!

Even today, industries lobby for federal preemption over state regulation. Even the wine industry, with Supreme Court victories, continues to seek federal internet sales standards.

Having been a veteran of those battles, I was pleased to use that experience for this good cause. With my deregulation/regulatory reform background, I thought we could be successful with thoroughbred racing reform and overcome its fixation with state regulation by introducing a federal regulatory strategy (top racetracks would have an approved league, own their restored intellectual property, and have a rational corporate tax system in exchange for national drug safety).

In analyzing the various component parts of the thoroughbred racing industry, whether they are related to taxation, the internet, safety, purses, or track conditions, it stands to reason that a new national standard be adopted to replace an array of inconsistent, worn-out state systems!

We reported our findings to the National Thoroughbred Racing Association in 2008.

First off, in the 2006 House Judiciary Committee hearings that I attended, the transcript of the members' statements, as to the racing industry, suggested a lack of clarity as to what the regulatory regime for thoroughbred racing in the United States should be in today's economy.

Other older industries had been successfully deregulated from their original regulatory regime, including railroads, trucking, telecommunications, and electric utility generation, where I had the good fortune to play a role. Most importantly, the American consumer has been the winner! Even today, industries lobby for federal preemption over state regulation.

Having been a veteran of those battles, I wanted to use that experience for this cause. With my deregulation/regulatory reform background, I thought we could be successful with thoroughbred racing reform. It was clearly in the public interest to move this US treasure—thoroughbred horseracing—to a new level of viability and economic integrity.

And we reported these findings to the National Thoroughbred Racing Association:

1. Deregulation of other US industries during the last thirty years—notably railroads, trucking, telecommunications, energy, and aviation—and their resultant prosperity, consumer benefit, and technology advancement present very attractive models for study and guidance to explore potential paths ahead for the NTRA and its membership.
2. Each of the above successful deregulation initiatives had a different economic formula that required thoughtful analysis to devise. But there were common threads of a vision that could be understood by public policymakers as leading to good purpose, progress, and revival.
3. In presenting the case for deregulation of railroads, trucking, telecommunications, energy, or aviation, proponents always stayed close to the themes of consumer benefit, competition, new technology, and the general public interest.
4. In all cases, it was vital to address the three tiers of the federal governmental process: Executive, judicial, and legislative. The administration had to be on board and initiate the policy recommendations, the underlying court cases had to be examined, and Congress, in the final analysis, had to act.
5. The unique ingredient with the thoroughbred racing industry is the intrinsic value of it being a national sport as well. One doesn't want to lose sight of that opportunity in making the case for not only deregulation but also for equity and fairness in having similar regulatory treatment relative to the other major sports in this country—wagering notwithstanding.
6. There are two different revenue platforms in thoroughbred racing that depend on the mutual success of each other. Track attendance with fan excitement and intellectual property revenue are a harmonic to dynamic purses and wagering volume. The regulatory interplay within this industry—in place for decades—is simply inefficient, inconsistent, intramural, and in dire need of reform.

Congressional legislation would deal with national standards for thoroughbred drug medication, simulcast revenues, wagering integrity and invite a "league" format and federal regulatory treatment like other sports. States would continue to regulate gambling, but Congress would look to a "league" for implementing these national standards for the sporting aspects of thoroughbred racing.

But some history here would be timely to appreciate the public policy challenge. The first US racing regulation was in 1906 with the creation of a state racing commission in Kentucky, one of a handful of states permitting gaming of any kind at the time. That commission process was soon repeated in other states, and as pari-mutuel racing was authorized more widely in the 1930s, primarily as a revenue source, each new state created its own racing commission similar to the railroad industry as well as telephone and electric utility service.

In part, this state-by-state approach reflected a variety of regional attitudes toward gaming and a general acceptance of the view that any issue with significant moral and social overtones should be dealt with locally. Congress, whatever the dispositions of its individual members toward gaming, had historically left gaming policy decisions to the states, which had made their own decisions on modes and forms.

Regulation of racing evolved similarly for the same reason. It was accomplished entirely at state levels, with the licensing and operation of pari-mutuel facilities being matters of local interest. Essentially, racetracks were looked upon—and saw themselves—as local firms whose customers and stakeholders were located mostly in their surrounding market areas. Additionally, racetracks enjoyed a monopoly on gaming, with all the attendant restraints and regulations that applied in local circumstances.

The model worked reasonably well until the age of television. With television, the growth in competitive entertainment options began to accelerate, and, over the last three—four decades, there has been a proliferation of state lotteries, the emergence of gaming on tribal property, and expansion of casino gaming. National policy was changing, but racing regulation was not.

As a result, racing's growth over this same period, if measured in money wagered, has been weak. In fact, the pari-mutuel share of the gambling market has declined from close to 100 percent in pre-Second World War days to less than six percent today.

Most of the major racetracks in the United States have a birthright going back to the 1920–1930s which invited a focus on state regulatory oversight at the time.

And the Interstate Horse Racing Act of 1978 maintained this principle reaffirming that states would have the primary responsibility as to what forms of gambling might take place within their borders. (The Act was amended in 2000 to permit interstate pari-mutuel wagering via the internet, telephone, etc. so long as such wagering was legal in both states.)

The Congress did confirm its own role, in the 1978 Act, as to regulating interstate commerce with respect to wagering on horse racing, in order to further the horse racing and legal off-track betting industries in the United States.

Congress passed the Internet Gambling Prohibition Act in 2007, and the racing industry, while in disagreement with the Department of Justice over whether interstate simulcasts were legal under the federal law, was exempted from the legislation.

In 2008, the thoroughbred racing industry joined other sports leagues in testifying about drug medication abuses in their respective sports and agreed to the suggestion of linking national enforcement of states adopting the industry-sponsored drug medication "model rule" by the end 2008 or lose their right to oversee TV simulcast revenues.

To seize the moment, a well-researched and documented economic and public policy report had to be prepared. Even the layman knows that the tracks were struggling and fans were disappearing; and yet it is a great sport! But gambling was just around the public policy corner.

In all the major public policy initiatives that we are familiar with, such an analytical report is essential for industry leadership to make the right public policy decisions, prioritize them accordingly, and assemble the appropriate legislative agenda.

The report was designed for the industry's leadership, but ultimately as a reference in making the case to both Congress and the Executive Branch, particularly the Department of Justice.

Absent this report's findings, it was somewhat difficult to chart the congressional course. Nonetheless, with Barbaro having been operated on at the University of Pennsylvania, and with Gretchen Jackson's residency there as well, it seemed at the time that Senator Arlen Specter, of Pennsylvania, who then chaired the Senate Judiciary Committee, could be a leading advocate for an omnibus measure. Even the great horse, Smarty Jones, had a Pennsylvania horse farm address!

The point is that both the Judiciary and Commerce committees would have congressional jurisdiction, and Kentucky's delegation, as the home of thoroughbred racing, would need allies from across the country.

There are a range of issues that will be explored within the report, including industry economics, taxation, competition, safety, medication, wagering, and the internet; the financial condition of the tracks, jockeys, and benefits. There is a mosaic of interests that need to be organized in a decision-making matrix that would allow the intersection of public policy purposes to take place. This compendium of compromise and economic opportunity is the goal of the report, which will include legislative recommendations.

As always, venturing into the public policy arena must be done with care. The goal must clearly be worth the effort. The Justice Department must be consulted.

All of this requires a coalition of interests. This coalition can include consumer groups, labor, and other organizations beyond the thoroughbred horse industry itself.

The excitement of the Triple Crown TV coverage must be conveyed in a political format.

Here, in summary, was our vision of what this sport would look like within a newly adopted national regulatory format:

1. As with the NFL, the NBA, or any of the other professional leagues—why not have a new National Thoroughbred Racing League (NTRL) made up of top US racetracks that agree to meet federal standards for safety, Poly-track, medication, and financial transparency regarding wagering.
2. In turn, the tracks would be committing, within their new league, to refurbish their facilities and upgrade their programs. Del Mar, Saratoga, and Keeneland are all destination resorts. All the member tracks in this new league would agree to a new, long-term track enhancement program, unlocking a new market value and, in effect, would be a concession within the new league.
3. National leadership will be provided by an NT/RL league selected commissioner, just as the NFL owners have commenced a search for their next commissioner.
4. Again, as with other professional sports that have adopted collective bargaining agreements, the horse owners and jockeys would adopt a similar negotiating platform and engage in collective bargaining with the new "National Thoroughbred Racing League" and its member tracks.
5. New national federal safety and medication regulations would be adopted, replacing individual state requirements as cumbersome, inefficient, and anti-consumer. (Interstate Commerce).
6. Intellectual property rights would be recognized and restored to the tracks as well as to TV/marketing rights.

7. Racetracks' financial integrity will be restored, allowing increased investments in facilities, purses, and attendance.
8. A new championship series could be offered by the league within the Breeder's Cup series and known as "The Nationals."

Thoroughbred horse racing is at one of those critical junctures in time where a great leap forward is in the offing.

The congressional legislation to address the above would deal with national standards for thoroughbred drug medication, simulcast revenues, wagering integrity and invite a "league" format like other sports. States would continue to regulate gambling, but Congress would look to a "league" for implementing these national standards for the sporting aspects of thoroughbred racing.

This preliminary report was completed and slated for review by the Board of Directors of the National Thoroughbred Racing Association (NTRA) at their 2008 annual meeting preceding their annual awards dinner, the Eclipse Awards, at the Beverly Hills Hotel in Los Angeles. Each year the NTRA rotates between Beverly Hills and Palm Beach, Florida, for this awards function.

At first, I did not understand the name for the awards other than the industry seemed to be facing an eclipse. So, I researched it and, lo and behold, modern racehorses are virtually all descended from a legendary British racer called Eclipse.

And recent studies confirm almost all English Thoroughbreds contain DNA from this famous stallion foaled during and named after the solar eclipse of April 1, 1764. He was undefeated, winning eighteen races, including eleven King's Plates.

My research continued and, as if it were today's Middle East wars, I read that some ninety miles west of Aleppo in 1700, a tight convoy of merchant ships set sail across the Mediterranean Sea. In the hold of one of the nine ships was a young desert stallion, a purebred Arabian born in 1700 and acquired along the caravan route from Basra. Once in England, over time this Arabian horse's real value became clear; and 95 percent of all thoroughbreds today trace back to this one Arabian stallion, the predecessor to Eclipse. Its speed became a valued commodity, ending the era of the plodders who raced multiple times in a single day.

And a racing milestone was the 1780 inauguration of the Epsom Derby, from which all other derbies, including the Kentucky Derby, take their name. The "Derby" moniker arrived in a coin toss won by the twelfth Earl of Derby. Talk about history!

As the 2008 NTRA board meeting started, I thought we were in good shape. I was seated next to the President of Keeneland, who had formerly worked for Senator Wendell Ford from Kentucky, and I had known the senator. We had a good chat!

Well, halfway through my presentation . . . the minute I mentioned federal legislation and federal regulation (state preemption) to the Board, that was it!

These Kentucky Colonels could not see through their political prejudice and would be damned if they were going to have federal regulation (even if it meant making money and getting rid of burdensome state regulation).

The NTRA staff had not done a very good job of setting the table even after I had flown to Lexington several times and had demonstrated over and over how well deregulated industries were doing. We even had the summit at the University of Kentucky Alumni House with Congressman Ed Whitfield flying in to be part of the discussion.

Eight years later, in March 2016, I noted an announcement by NASCAR regarding Charters for their racing teams. Instead of charters to teams, they were recommending charters, in effect, to the dozen or so top tracks to create a league akin to the NFL. While NASCAR probably paid McKinsey several hundred thousand dollars for designing this concept, we went even further in reclaiming the intellectual property rights (unlike NASCAR, which owns them) via a necessary federal preemption strategy.

I thought that maybe this NASCAR experience could assist in exploring a league approach once again as it would add great value! Obviously, the two sports are quite different in history and regulation. For example, NASCAR is relatively new and unencumbered with needless state regulatory burdens, and they control their signal and their intellectual property.

And then in May 2018, NASCAR itself and its owners, the Francis family, put their NASCAR business up for sale. Attendance had been decimated during the Great Recession and it never recovered. The millennials were not as interested as their parents.

During the 2020 pandemic, NASCAR resumed its racing programs at the various speedways for television but without any fans in the stands. It was the new normal!

Gambling per se will not be a panacea for the thoroughbred racing industry. We know well now the lessons Donald Trump learned in Atlantic City; that is, that gambling casinos themselves are overbuilt, with too much competition chasing that revenue stream and losing billions of dollars. However, wagering at the track, good restaurants, and attractive facilities all fit the destination market.

The Supreme Court's 2018 decision allowing states to sponsor sports betting will actually worsen the situation for thoroughbred racing unless they retrieve their intellectual property.

Ultimately, reform of the US thoroughbred racing industry is needed if it is to survive. With American Pharoah decisively winning the Triple Crown in 2015, the Breeders' Cup, and the multi-million Pegasus in early 2018, followed by a second Triple Crown winner in that same year, Justify, there should have been an introspective review and action taken.

Then in March 2019, over twenty thoroughbred horses were to die on the turf at the Santa Anita track in Southern California. This prompted Belinda Stronach, CEO of the Stronach Group, which owns numerous major racetracks, including Santa Anita, to announce a Lasix drug ban and increased restrictions on therapeutic drugs.

The 145th Kentucky Derby on May 4, 2019, would be horse racing's first national event since that dreadful winter at Santa Anita Park, the California track where twenty three horses died between December 26 and March 31, forcing it to shut down racing. In the Derby, twenty-one horses would be running. Ironically, this was the same number as the Democratic Party presidential primary contenders at the time. All—whether the horses or the candidates—were long shots!

Horse racing is among America's oldest sports; yet the multibillion-dollar industry was reeling as the Kentucky Derby approached. I'm concerned about the publicity we've been getting, said Bob Baffert, the Hall of Fame trainer who won the Triple Crown with American Pharoah in 2015. You can't defend a horse getting hurt.

Yet, you have to remember Churchill Downs' July 2024 decision to end the suspension of Baffert followed his contrition for Medina Spirit's positive test in the 2021 Kentucky Derby. I am responsible for any substance found in the horses that I train, and I have paid a very steep price with a three-year suspension and the disqualification of Medina Spirit's performance.

The 2019 Kentucky Derby was to be very different. After watching the interference, I wasn't surprised when the three race stewards, responding to lodged objections from two other jockeys, disqualified the first-place finisher, Maximum Security, and allowed the second horse, Country House, to win the Kentucky Derby.

They did what no officials had done in all the Kentucky Derbies since 1875: They took down the winner because of an infraction amidst a pouring rain. It was unreal! Some pundits called it a disaster for the sport, and I agreed.

And the Preakness would follow, in the Triple Crown series, at the dilapidated Pimlico track in Baltimore. Not an inspiring time! The fact is, the sport of kings needed a king! All of the weekend press coverage was extremely negative and suggested to me that there was a chance for a national governing body, as both Trainer Bill Mott and Congressmen Barr and Tonko suggested; but their legislation at the time only addressed the drug medication topics. Trainer Bill Mott went on to say that he felt terrible and had to apologize for winning, but the sport doesn't have a national governing body, leaving states to set their own rules.

So even an elite trainer such as Bill Mott, who has won over 4,900 races in his career, was confused. This crisis was an opportunity to create a new federal-state relationship with a top tracks league as the private sector partner. Thoroughbred horse racing was at one of those critical junctures in time where a great leap forward is needed.

And our congressional legislation would address not only national standards for thoroughbred drug medication but also simulcast revenues (intellectual property), wagering integrity, tax policy, and invite a league concession format like other sports. As I said earlier, states would continue to regulate on-track wagering (gambling), but Congress would look to a league for implementing these national standards for the sporting aspects of thoroughbred racing as well.

Years ago, for railroad deregulation (1980, the Staggers Act), we established national standards and essentially preempted the states, and it worked well. I really thought, based on my Washington experience, that it could be done here; but you need a critical mass of support from the industry sector. There was always opposition to our deregulation efforts (railroad, telecom, electricity), but we always had "the leadership" coalition and government support, and we won.

I sent this note to Alex Waldrop at the NTRA: "Alex, we all miss David Blee here in Washington, DC. He and I spoke often on this topic. His Washington, DC, funeral was absolutely packed. We keep in touch with his family here. Dan."

This 2019 crisis, not just at Santa Anita but also the Kentucky Derby fiasco, suggested once again an opportunity to create a new federal-state relationship with a top tracks league as the private sector partner. Even Bob Baffert, at the time, who had won five Kentucky Derbies, seven Preakness Stakes, three Belmont Stakes, fifteen Breeders' Cup races, and three Dubai World Cups, had this to say in a press release: "Horse racing is in crisis; and we need immediate, drastic federal action to fix it."

I was to recall the reaction of the Board of Directors of the National Thoroughbred Racing Association to our recommendations in 2007, as Baffert had always opposed federal intervention until now, in 2019.

As I said repeatedly, Congress would look to a league for implementing these national standards for the sporting aspects of thoroughbred racing. It was true reform that would have worked. But the Kentucky Colonels wanted nothing to do with the federal government; now Mr. Baffert did. However, it was not to be, and in June 2020, amidst the pandemic, the Triple Crown series was rearranged with the New York Belmont Stakes going first on June 20, a real blow to this sport that was already having its challenges and clearly unable to restructure its stifling regulatory structure. The Kentucky Derby was set for Labor Day weekend on September 5, 2020.

And then I was to read in the Sports section of the Washington Post on September 1 that Senate Majority Leader McConnell from Kentucky had announced a bill to help make horseracing safer, fairer, and more transparent. It would be entitled: The Horseracing Integrity and Safety Act, and a new independent authority will aim to help protect the sport and the over 24,000 Kentucky workers who support it.

It made me feel good—there had been speed bumps, all these years, but finally there was light at the end of the tunnel. I truly felt that a league approach (incentives for excellence) where the tracks in the league all subscribed to the requirements of this new Horseracing Integrity and Safety Authority Act would be a good addition for addressing other issues such as intellectual property, taxation, track conditions, and the like.

Everyone had saluted; now it was time to pass the legislation. It was September in a presidential election year. Majority Leader Senator McConnell was positioned to do so, and he represented Kentucky, so the thoroughbred racing industry would follow in lockstep.

Leading the advocacy charge in 2020 was Stuart Janney III, chairman of a Manhattan-based wealth management firm and son of a famed Maryland horseman. As chairman of the Jockey Club, the thoroughbred industry's inner circle, he had played a central role in the reform bill. Starting with fellow Jockey Club member Arthur B. Hancock III's poorly received "Drugs and Thugs" speech at a 1991 industry symposium, the exclusive 130-member Jockey Club had made itself an annoyance in racing by focusing on synthetic drug cheaters.

Arthur Hancock had attended our University of Kentucky roundtable years ago and supported our regulatory reform approach.

But some in this disjointed industry said the club had strayed from its role of registering thoroughbreds to maintain the purity of the breed. Members noted that when the Manhattan-based club was formed in the late nineteenth century, it was with a stated intent to ensure order instead of the growing chaos of racing.

The chaos they perceive these days is in the patchwork regulation of the sport, the purview of thirty-eight state agencies. Those bodies are their own fiefdoms, Hancock said in a 2021 interview, with racing commissions stocked by the horsemen who gave the most money to the governor.

Looking back at our effort, for years, the Jockey Club failed to get the rest of the industry and Congress, on board to overhaul horseracing's regulatory system. In 2013, a federal act that would have given USADA the authority over doping in thoroughbred racing died without being voted on.

As it would be for the rest of the decade, reform efforts had been opposed by Churchill Downs Inc., the company that owns the track where the Kentucky Derby is run each spring. The United States Anti-Doping Agency (USADA) is a nonprofit, nongovernmental organization and the national anti-doping organization for the United States.

In a Securities and Exchange Commission filing in 2015, the company said provisions in that year's incarnation of the bill, including allowing USADA to regulate a track's interstate wagering over doping concerns, could have a material adverse impact on our business. But that was to change.

And without Churchill Downs, the Jockey Club's Hancock said, they struggled to convince McConnell, the Kentucky senator who in 2015 became majority leader and was easily re-elected in the November 2020 election. To be clear he did introduce the bill before that election.

Coincidentally, the 147th Kentucky Derby was on that first weekend in May 2021. Maybe the Horseracing Integrity and Safety Act would be passed by this new Congress before that; and it was.

The Horseracing Integrity Act and Safety Act was signed into law on December 28, 2020, and focused on ensuring the integrity of thoroughbred horse racing and the safety of thoroughbred racehorses and jockeys by requiring national, uniform safety standards that include anti-doping and medication controls and racetrack safety programs to be enforced by the Horse Racing Integrity and Welfare Unit, a division of Drug Free Sport International.

Amen to that! But the economics of thoroughbred horse racing were still a muddle of regulatory confusion and inefficiency.

Interestingly, our son Clay now lives in the San Francisco Bay Area in the wonderful Sonoma town of Petaluma, where the main shopping street is Kentucky Street, but no one in town knows why. Again, the riddle continues!

During our weekend retreats at our Middleburg (Virginia) home in the late 1980s and 1990s, my wife Fonny and I became fans of the steeplechase races that took place in the fall and spring. In fact, the Gold Cup had the big name, but the Middleburg race was the best.

And Maryland had its Triple Crown series in April, with their Hunt Cup north of Baltimore in Glyndon being their main event. I attended a Hunt Cup in my final year at the Naval Academy, having just purchased my Alfa Romeo (used) sports car. It was a beautiful country like the Virginia countryside.

We became good friends with Maggie Bryant there from our Middleburg Tennis Club matches with her son and the Democratic Party receptions she would host. It was a sad day to read that she had died on June 28, 2021, at her 2,400-acre horse farm home in Middleburg, VA.

She was a member of one of Virginia's wealthiest families, but you would never know it. She had lived in Middleburg, regarded by many as the horse and hunt capital of the nation, for over fifty years. She built a stable of stake winners and was inducted into the Virginia Steeplechase Association Hall of Fame in 2014. Steeplechase was horse racing's amateur league, and it had the integrity and wholesomeness that its big brother lacked at their sad tracks around the country.

Maggie pursued entrepreneurial endeavors as well. In the early 1990s, she was the founder and leading investor of the $326 million, 15-mile Dulles Greenway toll road extension from Washington Dulles International Airport to Leesburg, VA, that I advised her on. It was fun!

Another neighborhood story here fits nicely. Paul Mellon's vast Upperville estate and stables were further up Rokeby Road from our 10-acre weekend retreat. We would hear his jet take off for the Kentucky Derby and lo and behold, he finally won the 1993 Kentucky Derby with Sea Hero. We drove down to his home expecting a big celebration after hearing his jet land. But it was very quiet! So, I mailed him a personal congratulatory note as a neighbor and received a very nice letter from him in return. Neighbor to neighbor, it was nice.

Surprisingly, Paul Mellon's son Tim, at age eighty-one, was the biggest donor to Donald Trump in 2024. A 1964 Yale graduate, he had contributed more than $75 million to a super PAC supporting the former president's bid to return to the White House. His net worth was estimated at $700 million in a 2014 deposition and, unlike his father, he was not engaged in the thoroughbred racing sport.

The run of tragedies again brings safety issues to the fore in racing, a sport in which a maze of state-by-state regulation, in the absence of an empowered national regulator, has made it difficult to impose reforms.

They should play Taps at the Derby instead of "My Old Kentucky Home," PETA senior vice president Kathy Guillermo said in a statement.

As noted, the Horseracing Integrity and Safety Authority, or HISA, had been finally launched to create a uniform set of rules for thoroughbred racing in the country. However, legal challenges had slowed the rollout of some initiatives meant to standardize safety enforcement across the industry. HISA was to be overseen by the Federal Trade Commission.

The HISA safety program, which took effect in July 2022, introduced regulations as opposed to different states testing at differing levels. The new rules were designed to replace the differing standards in the thirty-eight states that have horse racing.

HISA Chief Executive Lisa Lazarus had told the Associated Press that she was surprised at how efforts to create uniform rules for every racing jurisdiction had evolved into a political debate on states' rights versus federal rights, a new sign of the times, for example, blue states versus red states.

During that same 2023 period, a spate of horse fatalities occurred in Maryland at their Laurel track as the Preakness approached. The press reported that despite state subsidies of $91 million the prior year from the state lottery to the thoroughbred industry, the sport was in dire straits.

The Preakness Stakes that Saturday was to be the end of an era: The last Triple Crown event ever run before the launch of a new federal program meant to end thoroughbred racing's often chaotic state-by-state antidoping regime.

A national drug-testing program for the sport was finally set to roll out the antidoping program when major tracks such as Churchill Downs in Kentucky, Belmont Park in New York, and Santa Anita Park in California held races, and it would be the standard under which the Belmont Stakes were run later that 2023 Summer.

The new drug testing program was designed to bring more rigorous and consistent federal standards, yet the Horseracing Integrity and Safety Authority (HISA) faced a battery of legal and logistical challenges.

HISA is supposed to run the drug program and set and enforce uniform safety rules as well. It's being challenged in half a dozen different lawsuits around the country by opponents who variously say it's unconstitutional, tramples on state regulators who can do the job better, and its rules and procedures are too rigid and have been enacted without proper consultation with horsemen. It all sounded so familiar to 2007.

In keeping with their anti-federal bias, the Texas Racing Commission emerged as the most outspoken state opponent of the new body and joined the lawsuit filed against HISA in Texas. Texas tracks stopped exporting their simulcast signal across state lines—a maneuver that removed them from HISA's authority and continued the authority of the Texas Racing Commission instead (I was reminded of Texas electric energy regulation). The case challenging HISA was filed in Texas by the National Horsemen's Benevolent Protective Association, a trade group for thoroughbred owners, trainers, and backstretch personnel.

The splintering over the regulatory scheme was visible across the industry. Massive change in any industry is never easy, and we've seen pockets of resistance to HISA, said Tom Rooney, the new chief executive of the National Thoroughbred Racing Association, which is the trade association representing racetracks, owners, breeders, and trainers. But the fact of the matter is, we have to do better, and we are.

Around this time of the 2023 Kentucky Derby, the Horseracing Integrity and Safety Authority (HISA) called a public veterinary summit to examine the Churchill Downs situation, where twelve horses had died in the weeks before the derby itself.

HISA CEO Lisa Lazarus said at the time that she was hopeful some answers would emerge that would help explain the unfortunate situation. Some called for the elimination of dirt tracks, switching to synthetic surfaces such as I saw at Keeneland years earlier. Of the twelve horses, HISA indicated that seven died as a result of musculoskeletal issues while racing on the main track.

What I found perplexing was that Dennis Moore, a track consultant and the long-time track superintendent at Santa Anita, had also been brought in to look at the racing surfaces. Santa Anita had similar death events of horses on its track several years earlier.

It all raised the question of why Churchill should cease racing, as HISA does not have the authority to force the track to shut down. They can deprive the racetrack of being able to send out their simulcasting signal.

But Lazarus indicated her strong view that if HISA were to make a recommendation to Churchill Downs to shut down racing, they would accept that recommendation. Sure enough, the 148-year-old Churchill Downs (CDI) announced on June 2, 2023, that it was suspending racing following the twelve horse deaths, including the seven in the run-up to the Derby earlier in May.

The decision followed a recommendation by the Horseracing Integrity and Safety Authority (HISA), created by Congress in 2020 to oversee thoroughbred racing safety and horse trainer drug practices, that time was needed to investigate the spate of horse deaths that marred the Kentucky Derby and have persisted since.

HISA CEO Lisa Lazarus said that because the authority has been unable to recommend or require interventions that we felt would adequately ensure the safety of the horses running there, we made the decision to recommend to CDI that they temporarily suspend racing at Churchill Downs while additional reviews continue, and they complied.

I was now impressed with Churchill Downs' management. The new Horseracing Integrity and Safety Authority (HISA) was having a positive impact. In prior years, Baffert and other prominent trainers ran the show, so to speak. It was a good example that the narrow, selfish state's rights stance versus national standards had literally run its course.

When the Horseracing Integrity and Safety Act was signed into federal law, it charged the Horseracing Integrity and Safety Authority (HISA) with drafting and enforcing uniform safety and integrity rules in Thoroughbred racing in the United States. Overseen by the Federal Trade Commission (FTC), HISA is implementing, for the first time, a national, uniform set of rules applicable to every Thoroughbred racing participant and racetrack facility.

HISA is comprised of two programs: the Racetrack Safety Program, which went into effect on July 1, 2022, and the Anti-Doping and Medication Control (ADMC) Program, which went into effect on May 22, 2023. It was a new era!

Just maybe a national thoroughbred racing league, based on the major tracks, might blossom, mindful of my frustration years earlier at the Eclipse Awards meeting. The industry now had HISA for drug and safety issues but nothing regarding intellectual property restoration, rational taxation, national track standards, a successful league, and so forth. It was still a political orphan.

But I was glad to see that Tom Rooney, the new president and CEO of the National Thoroughbred Racing Association, in a statement noted that HISA was working to make the sport of thoroughbred racing safer and more transparent and has the NTRA's support. Bottom line: It took some fifteen years for the NTRA to finally adopt my original federal trade-off recommendations.

But the league approach was poached by something called the National Thoroughbred League with their 2024 announcement: After careful consideration and thorough evaluation, NTL has chosen Las Vegas as the new home, marking a pivotal moment in the league's history. The National Thoroughbred League (NTL) is a first-of-its-kind racing league reimagining America's oldest spectator sport by creating a team based professional sports league, consistently and safely running exceptional horses at various tracks and maximizing the wagering opportunity.

Part Three

Governmental Reforms

10

Technology Challenges within US Government Procurement

US government technology procurements present challenges and do not always have the best outcomes. Here are personal examples relating to the maglev (magnetic levitation) high-speed technology in which I was to be directly involved for several years.

In a 2013 report, the US Government Accountability Office (GAO) reported to Congress that the Navy faced technical, design, and construction challenges in completing the USS Gerald R. Ford (CVN 78) that had led to significant cost increases and reduced the likelihood that a fully functional ship would be delivered on time. Ultimately, this one aircraft carrier was to cost $13 billion and was years late.

The GAO reported that the Navy had achieved mixed progress developing CVN 78's critical technologies, such as a system intended to more effectively launch and recover aircraft. This was a reference to the maglev work that General Atomics in San Diego was doing for the Navy, and we will talk more about that in this chapter.

But first, here is some background from my experience representing Transrapid (Siemens/Thyssen) high-speed maglev in the United States. And yes, the US Navy was very interested in the maglev technology for its aircraft carriers; and here is that history.

United States Navy and Maglev on Aircraft Carriers

The US Navy planned to spend over $43 billion to produce three new Ford-class aircraft carriers. The first ship in the series, *Gerald R. Ford* (CVN 78), was scheduled for delivery in March 2015, and commissioning in Newport News, Virginia, did finally occur in 2017.

The carrier finally received its official Flight Deck Certification after two consecutive days of operations with a total of 123 launches and landings during the day and forty-two at night.

The carrier was then slated to be operational in 2020 from its San Diego homeport. In March 2020, the USS Gerald R. Ford completed its 1,000th flight using General Atomics electro-magnetic catapult and arresting technology. It would be, as a $13.3 billion aircraft carrier, the United States's most expensive warship in history.

The ship was to be the lead ship of the newest class of aircraft carriers since the Nimitz class was introduced over forty years ago. Advances in technology would allow the carrier to have a wider variety of planes and operate with several hundred fewer sailors. Flying missions would be increased by a third by utilizing a faster electromagnetic catapult system for launching aircraft.

But some of the advanced maglev technology used on the Ford ultimately led to significant delays. Problems included issues with the catapult system and the weapons elevators that bring munitions to the flight deck.

The Ford, at a length of 1,106 feet, is the largest aircraft carrier in the world and would carry 2,600 crew members when it officially deploys in 2020—a reduced number from the old carriers.

This was the first major redesign of a US Navy aircraft carrier in over four decades. It had its own nuclear plant inside (all US carriers were now nuclear), which generated enough energy that allowed the carrier to go at an impressive top speed of thirty knots (34.5 mph, 55.5 km/h). When I served on the conventionally powered USS *Coral Sea* (CVA 43) from 1965 to 1967 off the coast of North Vietnam after my Naval Academy graduation, we could attain similar speeds, as thirty knots was the minimum needed to launch aircraft when there was little or no wind.

Interestingly, the amount of nuclear energy produced by the USS Ford allows it to run without stopping to refuel for twenty to twenty-five years. There are two A1B reactor plants ("A" is for Aircraft Carrier, "1" is first-generation, and "B" is for Bechtel, the manufacturer) aboard the USS *Ford*, and they were specially developed by Bechtel for this new class of supercarriers.

Bechtel normally handled engineering and construction for nuclear plants in the USA and was a client of my firm for non-nuclear energy policy issues.

The second carrier, *John F. Kennedy* (CVN 79), was scheduled for delivery in 2020; and the Navy had awarded a $152 million planning contract to Huntington Ingalls Industries (HII) in Newport News, Virginia, for the construction of the third *Gerald R. Ford*-class nuclear-powered aircraft carrier, Enterprise (CVN 80). Construction on that vessel was scheduled to begin in 2018, and delivery was expected to take place in 2027. Additionally, a fourth carrier might be combined with the Enterprise procurement to achieve savings. However, this schedule was way behind, and US shipyards were unable to move the pace forward, jeopardizing national security.

And how to keep up with China's ever-expanding fleet of warships was a related challenge. Not only was China's navy already the world's largest, but its numerical lead over the United States was getting wider, with the head of the US Navy warning that American shipyards simply can't keep up. Some experts estimate China can build three warships in the time it takes the US to build one. On the other hand, US allies in South Korea and Japan were building some of the highest technology naval hardware on the oceans at affordable prices. Buying ships from these countries, or even building US-designed vessels in their shipyards, could be a cost-effective way of closing the gap with China, it seemed. The longstanding problem was that US law currently prevents its Navy from buying foreign-built ships—even from allies—or from building its own ships in foreign countries due to both security concerns and a desire to protect

America's shipbuilding industry. Some foreign shipbuilders have opened US-based subsidiaries to overcome this hurdle, but it is not that simple.

Based on my US Navy—Transrapid (Siemens/Thyssen) maglev experience, it may be time to rethink that law to give the United States an edge in the battle for the seas. And from a related shipyard maintenance perspective, Rahm Emanuel, US ambassador to Japan and former White House Chief of Staff, suggested in a June 2024 Op Ed that Japan was ready and able to maintain US naval vessels; and it is time for our two countries not only to train together but also to maintain maritime readiness together. Japan is key to our regional deterrence strategy, and we need to begin maintaining ships with our allies in theater. It had been many years, but I remember my USS *Coral Sea* Vietnam War tours and always going to Yokosuka, Japan, for routine maintenance. I was always impressed with their work ethic and maritime ship maintenance skills. Plus, I would add that US Navy ships, their crews, and families had been homeported in Japan now for years, primarily at Yokosuka. To have to rotate all of this back to the United States just for major maintenance is nonsensical.

Sure, there are some 18,000 skilled shipyard employees, primarily in the Norfolk, Virginia area, working on these new aircraft carrier projects, and they have a huge impact on the regional Tidewater economy. But we need more US Navy surface warfare ships beyond what US shipyards seem able to produce; so having certain US ships built overseas in allies' facilities makes sense.

Now all four aircraft carriers are to be equipped with electromagnetic (maglev) systems for the launch and recovery of aircraft; and that is a different story. First off, General Atomics in San Diego was providing its newly designed and untested technology, not the German consortium's that many of us felt had the superior technology. Here is that story!

My Naval Academy roommate for three years was Paul Reason (Washington, DC, native), who was to serve as Commander in Chief, United States Atlantic Fleet from 1996 to 1999. Earlier in his career, as a commander, he was the naval aide to the president of the United States, Jimmy Carter, from December 1976 to June 1979. In 1996, Paul became the first African American officer in the United States Navy to become a four-star admiral, and there is a special commemorative display at the impressive Naval Academy Museum in his honor.

By coincidence, my firm was representing the German Transrapid maglev consortium (Siemens/Thyssen) primarily on entry into the high-speed surface transportation market in the United States. As such, I had traveled to Germany several times with guests to ride on the 270-mph maglev test track in the small municipality of Lathen located in Northwest Germany by the Dutch border. We often socialized with the Reasons, and I had mentioned this very impressive technology.

When Admiral Reason, as CINCLANTFLT, visited Germany in 1998, at his request I had arranged with Transrapid for him to visit this maglev testing facility at Lathen. He rode the maglev at 270 mph and must have been very impressed.

Upon his return to Norfolk, Virginia, where he was headquartered, he called and asked if Transrapid representatives could come to Norfolk to meet with Navy aircraft carrier staff, go out on an aircraft carrier for two days, and report to him on the viability of electric motors (maglev technology) to replace the Second World War vintage steam catapult aircraft launch and recovery systems.

I called the President of Thyssen Marine Systems in Kiel, Germany, Dr. Eckhard Rokamm, who was also a captain in the German Naval Reserve. Dr. Rokamm was very excited about this opportunity to go out on an aircraft carrier and be of assistance to the US Navy.

A schedule was set, and a month later Dr. Rokamm arrived in Washington, DC, and we flew together to Norfolk, Virginia. The night before we headed out to the USS Abraham Lincoln (CVN 73), we had dinner with Admiral Reason and the Air Systems Command reps on his Admiral's barge in very good weather. It was very informative and pleasant!

The Admiral explained that all eleven of the US aircraft carriers were now nuclear with surplus electricity, and the steam technology for the aircraft launch and recovery systems was outdated and wasteful. Could the system for the next planned aircraft carrier design be designed for electric motors/maglev technology?

The Navy had been experimenting with the design and production of a carrier launch/recovery system that used linear induction motors and electromagnets instead of steam-powered turbines because engineers realized that they could improve three things: Eliminate the need for housing a separate steam boiler, increase the level of control during jet or drone takeoffs, and reduce the amount of maintenance in two ways—using solid-state components and reducing wear and tear on the supercarrier from repeated launches.

The reason electromagnetic catapults cause less stress is due to the increased control over acceleration, thereby allowing launches and recoveries to be at accelerated speeds, but more gradual and steadier than steam pumping through a turbine from a traditional steam catapult system. Steam had replaced the hydraulic systems used during the Second World War.

I had witnessed hundreds of such abrupt, steam catapult launches and recoveries from the bridge on the Coral Sea in 1965-6 for raids over Hanoi and Haiphong harbor, and many of those pilots were good friends.

The next day, bright and early, we departed from the Naval Air Station by transport plane (the cod for Carrier Onboard Delivery) to the carrier and remained onboard for three nights, one extra due to weather, as it turned out. Dr. Rokamm enjoyed the shipboard life, and we explored every aspect of the ship's steam generation-based launch and recovery system and its suitability for an electromagnetic launch and recovery system.

After completing our very positive research findings, and before flying back to Norfolk to brief the Admiral, I made the point (both of us sitting up on the Admiral's Bridge watching flight operations) that the US Navy might be interested in having Transrapid as a technology provider for this new system. Transrapid would be working with Newport News Shipbuilding, owned then by Northrop Grumman, which was the exclusive provider of aircraft carriers. It is now owned by Huntington Ingalls.

Dr. Rokamm did not think it was realistic that the US Navy would allow a foreign contractor into this US defense industry procurement. I countered by pointing out that there was much US-European NATO commercial interaction now; and with my Washington experience, I thought we could do it. But he demurred; however, I encouraged a partnership with a US firm as a backup.

Since then, I have read advertisements sponsored by Germany Trade & Invest that referred to the US-Germany special relationship; but it was not to be this time. Despite my urging, Dr. Rokamm's caution hindered this opportunity; and it was unfortunate as the German technology was not only the best, it was also unique.

Upon our return from the carrier at the Norfolk Naval Air Station, Dr. Rokamm reported to Admiral Reason, in an office by the airfield, that the aircraft carrier's transition to electric motors (maglev) for aircraft launch and recovery was very realistic and should proceed.

General Atomics, in San Diego, was the only US firm that had been doing maglev research (they did not have any operational product, just a design); and at first, they were very anxious to play the intermediary role between Transrapid and the Navy.

After several months of dialogue (no confidentiality agreements), General Atomics informed us that the US Navy did not want a foreign contractor involved. In fact, I was disappointed that General Atomics and the Patuxent River Naval Air staffs did not invite Transrapid to partner, as they were very willing not only to partner but also to be generous in technology transfer.

I do think we could have had a very successful Transrapid/General Atomics US Navy partnership.

Now, some twenty years later, in 2020, the USS *Gerald Ford, CVN 78* was progressing, finally in its San Diego sea trials. I was told that the launch and recovery systems were working, but that they were not the optimal technology that could have been available from Germany. There were system problems, cost overruns, and delays; and that was where procurement reform was in order.

What is wrong with outstanding foreign technology being available to the US military from an ally? Open the procurement up to joint ventures! The work would have been done in the United States, and that technology transfer would have been invaluable.

And this Foreign Ownership, Control or Influence (FOCI) section 2104 under the National Industrial Security Program suggests it can be done and provides criteria for determining whether US companies are under FOCI; prescribes responsibilities in FOCI matters; and outlines security measures that DSS may consider to mitigate or negate the effects of FOCI to an acceptable level.

To illustrate how a foreign shipyard can participate, in February 2018, some twenty years after our 1998 USS Abraham Lincoln tour, the US Navy announced it had shortlisted five shipbuilders for its new frigate FFG(X) program: Lockheed Martin, General Dynamics, Huntington Ingalls, Austal, and Fincantieri.

The five were awarded research-and-development contracts, and the Navy indicated that they would pick a single company to oversee the program in 2020.

Fincantieri is an Italian shipyard, but they had a shipbuilding facility in Wisconsin. Similarly, Austal is Australian, with a facility in Alabama. That was the catch!

On Jun 10, 2015, Newport News Shipbuilding sponsored a demonstration on the Gerald R. Ford (CVN 78), seventy-three years after the first super carrier (non-nuclear) the USS Forrestal CVA 59 began service. The press release that same day explained that the electromagnetic aircraft launch system (EMALS) to be integrated on the aircraft carrier Gerald R. Ford (CVN 78) would be demonstrated to give the media an up-close view of the catapult system in action. The EMALS design was to replace the existing steam catapults being used by the US Navy.

Well, the testing process took an additional two years as it turned out at great cost, because the USS Gerald Ford was initially having problems with the electronic systems. It was clear to me that the Navy and General Atomics could have benefited from the German technology and expertise. But Dr. Rokamm was truly a gentleman and not familiar with the US government procurement system. They were not Beltway Bandits!

But I was right years earlier to suggest to Dr. Rokamm that they could have a US partner and should have strongly recommended that ThyssenKrupp open an electromagnetic/maglev facility in the United States. It probably would have worked as they had the technology.

But the procurement reality was that General Atomics, now the lead for the Gerald Ford project, was selected for the launch and recovery systems for future John F. Kennedy class aircraft carriers; and in August 2014, the US Naval Air Systems Command (NAVAIR) awarded General Atomics (GA) an initial sole-source contract for the Electromagnetic Aircraft Launch System (EMALS) and Advanced Arresting Gear (AAG) for the CVN 79 aircraft carrier to be named John F. Kennedy.

This contract was for the initial procurement of the long-lead-time materials in support of a full production contract for the installation of EMALS and AAG into CVN 79, the second of the Gerald R. Ford-class aircraft carriers. CVN 79 was scheduled to be delivered to the US Navy in 2023. But the trouble had begun years earlier! General Atomics was winging it as they were just testing out their new concepts and somehow had the Navy out on a limb with them.

And, as it was, the USS *Gerald Ford*, the newest and costliest US aircraft carrier at $13 billion, was finally delivered to the Navy in May 2017; but it took another three years of sea trials to get it all working.

First of the problems was that the electronic maglev launches and recovery system (EMALS) had ballooned in cost, tripling to $961 million from $301 million, according to news reports. While the Navy said the landing system had been fixed, the *Gerald Ford* built by Huntington Ingalls Industries Inc. still had not been cleared until 2020 to launch F/A-18 jets carrying a full complement of fuel tanks under their wings.

These two issues underscored the technical and cost challenges for the planned three-ship, $42 billion Ford class of carriers to increase the carrier fleet from eleven authorized by law to twelve. The increase in costs for the development phase of the advanced arresting gear—built by General Atomics to catch planes landing—was borne by the Navy under the terms of that contract. Ultimately, the program acquisition costs of the three systems built more than doubled to $532 million each from $226 million.

Years earlier, it was learned that the carrier was delivered without working elevators needed to lift bombs from below deck magazines for loading onto fighter jets. The problems with the eleven elevators for the ship added to the technical problems with the two other core electromagnetic systems—the system to launch planes and the arresting gear to catch them when they land. In early 2019, I was told that finally the maglev system seemed to be working, although the elevators were still a problem. Then

Huntington Ingalls said all the elevators were installed, noting they were the most advanced technologies being incorporated into the carrier and that its completion had been delayed due to a number of first-in-class issues.

Again, all they had to do was call ThyssenKrupp in Germany as they had designed and were constructing commercial maglev elevator systems in Berlin buildings that were working. But this Navy "buddy system" cost the taxpayer billions in waste. It is unfortunate that the Patuxent River Navy EMALS team would not return my calls twenty years earlier when I was offering the German technology assistance.

Coincidentally, at Stanford, one of the impressive graduate students—in our Global Projects Center—working on his PhD in Civil Engineering, Robert Wilhelm Siegfried Ruhlandt, was from Germany and intrigued to learn from me that maglev technology would be launching and recovering aircraft on our new US aircraft carriers.

Surprisingly, in June 2018, rumors were that ThyssenKrupp was examining a full or partial exit from its naval vessels business as its consortium was excluded from a German military procurement for Germany's new MKS-180 warship project, one of the German military's largest armament initiatives designed to combat targets in the air, above and below water, and to conduct land operations.

That might have been different if ThyssenKrupp were a US partner for the EMALS activity, as Huntington Ingalls Industries Inc., the sole US builder of aircraft carriers, continued to fall short of the Navy's demand to cut labor expenses to stay within an $11.39 billion cost cap mandated by Congress on the second in this new class of warships.

Meeting the labor goal would help demonstrate that the Navy could be trusted to keep costs in line and earn public support to increase its fleet to 355 vessels from the 282 that could be deployed at that time, and ThyssenKrupp's maglev technology was a given.

While President Trump had said at the May 2018 Naval Academy graduation that he wanted to build back this 355-ship Navy, the Congressional Research Service and the Congressional Budget Office found that the Navy's long-term shipbuilding plan to build a 355-ship Navy would not be attained until at least 2050 under their current budgets. In September 1985, the US Navy had 571 ships. The sad fact was that the Navy acknowledged it had only 283 full warships in 2018, of which over 40 percent of surface ships were underway and roughly 35 percent were on overseas deployment.

The US Navy indicated it wanted to start buying new frigates in 2020, one or two per year, at an estimated cost of $800 million to $900 million each as we were now in a Cold War-type environment again. I was to say to another Naval Academy classmate and retired admiral that the US Navy is starting to look like the proverbial big hat with no cattle.

Relatedly, one of the most crucial Biden decisions involved handing over Bagram Air Base to the Afghans in 2021 as the last step of the overall withdrawal. Bagram had been the hub of the American military effort there for the past twenty years, and generals had stated that leaving 2,500 troops would be sufficient to maintain stability; but instead, all troops were removed.

Worriedly, of our eleven US aircraft carriers, in the fall of 2018 only two were at sea and the remainder were in port or the shipyard for long overdue maintenance. That is why Bagram was an important US asset.

A few years later, and no longer representing Transrapid, General Atomics retained us for several years in the 2004–2008-time frame to assist them in finding private sector applications for the electromagnetic talent base they had built up for the Navy effort. I positioned them in the renewable energy business as the new wind farms being built around the country, in rural areas, would require new long distance DC transmission lines to connect with the electrical grid.

We designed a top-notch medium voltage inverter for Clipper Wind to convert the AC current from the turbine to DC current and send it directly along the long distance wire. Clipper has since been bought and sold by United Technologies to a private equity firm.

It was rather ironic for me to watch on television the new Commander in Chief at the time, President Trump, visit the USS Gerald Ford on March 3, 2017, in Norfolk, Virginia, on his way to his weekend retreat at Mar-a-Lago in Florida.

Going to his properties incurs additional security expenses, unlike a trip to Camp David, which is protected year-round as a military installation. In that same cost context, here is a new ship that has been delayed for two years and is over budget. He was very brash in speaking to the crew and shipyard workers about how he was going to spend even more dollars—$54 billion or a ten percent defense increase.

Yet months later he criticized the new aircraft carrier technology. In an interview with Time Magazine in May 2017, Trump called on the Navy to abandon the new technology. "You're going to goddamned steam; the digital costs hundreds of millions of dollars more, and it's no good," he told the Navy in the interview. He repeated the criticism in a speech to Navy personnel later that month.

I wondered how President Trump got onto this. It is a shame the Transrapid technology was not used. I worked very hard at it; but General Atomics and the Navy bureaucrats seemed to have an understanding (no foreign technology). I suspected some of the Navy civilian personnel at their Patuxent River Naval Air Station facility were interested in General Atomics employment.

Back on May 19, 2020, I read that General Atomics' electromagnetic systems business had announced a new contract from the US Navy to engineer and sustain electromagnetic aircraft launch systems. This presumably signaled that the program was now moving from the design and development phase into concurrent production and sustainment phase, providing sustaining engineering, material, and maintenance support for all Ford-class aircraft carriers.

Scott Forney was the president of General Atomics' electromagnetic systems business. I knew him well and wondered how, despite their disappointing performance, the Navy was precluded from using the German technology as it was foreign. Clearly, procurement reform in this technology sector would be a real benefit to our military/naval force.

In a February 2019 report titled, Navy Ford (CVN-78) Class Aircraft Carrier Program: Background and Issues for Congress, the Congressional Research Service noted that estimated procurement costs of CVN-78, CVN-79, and CVN-80 had grown by 24.7 percent, 23.2 percent, and 15.1 percent, respectively, since the fiscal year 2008 budget request was submitted.

It noted that the main sources of risk included the electromagnetic launch system, the advanced arresting gear, and the dual-band radar. To lower costs, the Navy opted to double down and award Newport News Shipbuilding a two-carrier contract. The decision was expected to save the service about $4 billion, according to reports. Yet General Atomics was slated to deliver the dual EMAL and AAG systems for the future USS *Enterprise* and USS *John F. Kennedy* vessels as they did with the USS *Gerald Ford* amidst record cost overruns and delays in delivery.

Since CVN-78 (The Ford) was commissioned in 2017, it has completed over 1,000 aircraft launches and recoveries by mid-2020. But the ship was ordered in 2008 by the Navy; and it took over a decade to complete various tests, including flight deck certification and shipboard launch and recovery.

In June 2022, China launched its third, largest, and most cutting-edge aircraft carrier. It was the first domestically designed and built vessel of its kind. In a ribbon-cutting ceremony held at the Jiangnan Shipyard in Shanghai, officials unveiled their Type 003 warship, the *Fujian*, which, according to officials cited in state media, would not be battle-ready for five years. But it was an important milestone in Beijing's ambitions to develop a blue-water navy, capable of projecting power far beyond its shores.

Interestingly, according to press reports, it was equipped with an electromagnetic catapult for launching aircraft and a similar electromagnetic landing system on its upward sloping deck. You had to wonder where the technology came from. For sure, it was not the US General Atomics version, so maybe it was Germany, as their maglev technology had been utilized for the Shanghai airport connector.

The two antiquated laws behind this are the 1933 Buy American Act, which requires the Pentagon to purchase domestically produced products for purchases over a $3,500 threshold, and the more restrictive 1941 Berry Amendment, which applies mainly to clothing and food products purchased by the military. Together, these laws require that the US military's entire supply chain be sourced from inside the country.

And finally, US Navy shipbuilding was expanded to US-based shipbuilding—which could have been the solution but that was to wait for the frigate procurement.

In practice, various free trade agreements had allowed American defense manufacturers to rely heavily on foreign materials. But now free trade agreements were being terminated. The lesson learned is that second-rate technology could be advantaged in what would be a Buy America cartel.

Now let's take a look at the defense supply chain market. In fiscal year 2013, for example, approximately $19.7 billion, or only about 6.4 percent of all US military spending, went to foreign entities (May 2014 report from the Defense Department), while US arms sales jumped thirty-five percent, or nearly $10 billion, to $36.2 billion in 2014, according to a Congressional Research Service report.

The top weapons buyer of US goods in 2014 was South Korea, a key American ally, and Iraq was the second biggest weapons buyer, as the country sought to build up its military capacity following the withdrawal of the bulk of American ground troops there. In 2020, President Trump was threatening to reduce the US military presence in South Korea as he had with Germany. He wanted them to pay more for these troops as if they were mercenaries.

The facts are that those bases in South Korea and Germany were of great value to the United States, and President Biden restored that position upon taking office and succeeding President Trump in 2021. Many thought he should have done the same in 2021 with the strategic Bagram Air Base in Afghanistan.

For perspective, on March 9, 2023, the Biden-Harris administration submitted to Congress a proposed Fiscal Year (FY) 2024 Budget request of $842 billion for the Department of Defense (DoD), an increase of $26 billion over FY 2023 levels and $100 billion more than FY 2022. At the same time, the long-term US deficit projections were alarmingly high. It seemed logical that this procurement system's cost was unsustainable and that reforms were urgent.

For comps, as they say, in the 2019 period, China was #2 in defense spending at almost $100 billion, with the United States far ahead at over $700 billion for the Fiscal Year 2019 budget. The United Kingdom spends roughly $69 billion, as does France, followed by Russia at $61 billion, according to the Stockholm International Peace Research Institute.

But the UK displayed its superiority in pomp and circumstance at Queen Elizabeth's death in October 2022, with the immense years-long planning effort paying off with a week-long festival of military parades, marching bands, and the like.

Today ThyssenKrupp is downsizing the steel business to focus on capital goods manufacturing, including elevators for skyscrapers that will use electromagnetic technology instead of cables to whisk passengers not only up and down in these very tall buildings but also sideways on certain floors of newly designed large high-rises. The first such building began construction in Berlin in 2017, but they were no longer in the maglev technology business.

Lesson learned: Technology is key wherever the superior product is found. It is clear that the United States defense establishments need a new procurement discipline that is flexible and disciplined for the best project result, not how much funding goes out through the archaic Federal Acquisition Regulations.

And just before Memorial Day 2021, the US Navy announced that the USS Ronald Reagan aircraft carrier would exit its longtime Japan home port and transfer to the Indo-Pacific region to relieve the aging USS Dwight Eisenhower. The Navy needed more ships to meet its mission. The Chief of Naval Operations had said he hoped the nuclear negotiations with Iran would go well so they could be relieved of covering that region. By 2024, with the Israeli-Gaza warfare, the Red Sea was a significant American Navy operation.

And our US ambassador to Japan made the case in 2024 that China now had the world's largest navy and the world's largest shipbuilding industry and had harassed and bullied its Indo-Pacific neighbors, from the Philippines to Japan to Taiwan. Over the same period, chronic maintenance and repair delays, cost overruns, extended sea tours, and construction backlogs had led to a reduced American fleet and a broken naval industrial base. While we try to modernize a handful of government-owned US naval shipyards (we have exactly four) in the United States, Japanese, and South Korean facilities—which together produce 47 percent of the world's ships each year—need to turn to our allies in the Pacific to be full partners in repairing and maintaining our fleet.

Ambassador Emanuel had been President Obama's chief of staff, and during the second Obama term, on a Sunday morning after Catholic Mass at the Naval Academy, my wife and I stopped by the Academy Museum to see the new Forrestal CVA 59 model that had been recently donated. Fonny had been born at the Naval Academy when her father was a Navy surgeon there. We learned the donated model was elsewhere in the yard (the campus). It was 12 feet long and weighed some 3,600 pounds, and there was not enough room available at the Museum. We finally found it on the second floor of Alumni Hall. An acceptance letter from Navy Secretary Ray Mabus said the model was appraised at $2.6 million. It sounded so simple!

Maglev for US Surface Transportation

As to the surface maglev transportation topic, Transrapid—as noted—was a joint venture of Thyssen Krupp and Siemens, and my firm was retained by them in the mid-1990s to advance the cause of high-speed maglev surface transportation in the United States.

Zoltan Merszei was the former Chairman of Dow Chemical, a large Thyssen shareholder, and a mutual friend of Admiral Bud Zumwalt. Bud had heard me talking about New York Senator Daniel Patrick Moynihan's interest in the maglev technology stemming from work he had observed at the Brookhaven National Lab on Long Island.

Zoltan, who fled Hungary in his twenties, led Dow Chemical Co.'s hugely profitable expansion in Europe in the 1960s and early 1970s. His reward was to be named chief executive, but his volatile personality and management style offended many US-based executives, including me. He always wanted to meet the senators and was then was rude.

I get my best ideas from the shouting at my staff meetings; he told Fortune magazine. Zoltan died on July 26, 2019, at the age of ninety-six. He wanted to run the Transrapid operation in the United States but was totally unequipped for the public policy application and created much confusion.

I was to go to Bremen, Germany often escorting various US groups to the Lathen test facility (by the Dutch border) that were interested in bringing the technology to their communities including Los Angeles, Pittsburgh, Baltimore/Washington, and Florida (too many, as it turned out!).

After working hard to develop a plan for maglev deployment with the Federal Railroad Administration, $50 million was authorized and appropriated by Congress in 1998 in the highway bill that year per Senator Moynihan's direction.

In the 1998 legislation, we had wanted the Department of Transportation/Federal Railroad Administration to select one project in a competition, and the $50 million would have been designated accordingly. This is what I had told Senator John Chafee when we rode the maglev in Lathen, Germany again at 270 miles per hour in response to his question: What does Pat Moynihan want to do with this?

I responded to build one US maglev transportation project as a demonstration model to assist other metro regions in designing their systems.

The US maglev legislation was unfortunately focused on the US subsidizing project competition, and for five years, the emphasis was on multiple payments from the $50 million to different regional sponsors and their consulting firms doing the planning for these various projects. At the end of the consulting period, there was little to show for those dollars.

Transrapid had opened a small office in Washington, DC, as well as their main office in Berlin, focusing then on the ill-fated Hamburg-Berlin line. They had an excellent project finance plan there with the government building the guideway, and a privatized Deutsche Bahn railroad making long-term lease payments to amortize the infrastructure cost.

The German technology for both the aircraft carrier and surface transportation applications had the maglev electromagnetic infrastructure embedded in the guideway itself and not the train sets. The Japanese maglev technology, I am told, is the reverse and not as practical.

In Germany, the Christian Democratic Party had strongly supported the 270 mph Hamburg—Berlin maglev line as a giant step forward in facilitating the economics of the 1990 reunification of Germany. I attended many briefings around 1995 and 1996 at the Deutsche Bahn headquarters in Frankfurt and was very impressed with the infrastructure/project finance strategy for that project.

Essentially, the government was to:

1. Create a government-sponsored "guideway corporation" that would be responsible for the financing, design, and construction of the maglev guideway above ground level.
2. Deutsche Bahn was being privatized and would sign a long forty-year lease concession for the exclusive use and operation of the guideway and the high-speed train sets.
3. The forty-year lease payments were designed to repay the Guideway Corporation for the cost of the construction.
4. Being a private carrier, Deutsche Bahn would lease the train set from Transrapid (Thyssen/Siemens), which would depreciate its investment on its corporate tax return.
5. A similar model was designed for the new stations with the value-added strategy of owning the land by the stations in Hamburg and Berlin, and selling or leasing parcels to building developers.

I have often thought this would have been a good model for the California High Speed Rail Authority project from Los Angeles to San Francisco, as it broke down a very expensive project into manageable project financing platforms. I had testified before the earlier California High-Speed Rail Commission (as Chairman of the US Infrastructure Commission), but my reception was very insulting at the time.

But, as a native Californian, I continued my efforts and explained that this procurement/business model would allow for the advantages of a true public-private partnership with risk transfer, transparency, accountability, and other attributes, particularly in clearly identifying how the private sector could efficiently contribute to the project's success. However, the California High Speed Rail Authority maintained its traditional procurement practices, resulting in billions wasted while traveling the world's metro centers.

But back to Germany, the Christian Democratic Party lost the elections in 1998 as the Social Democrats took over; and surprisingly their coalition partner, the Green Party opposed maglev. Their opposition was not on environmental grounds, but because it went too fast and was contrary to the bucolic (bicycling) nature of the German countryside as they saw it.

So that was the end of German government support for the Hamburg-Berlin line. The Germans also failed to build a maglev line (airport connector) in Munich as well. This failure in Germany did hurt our US efforts accordingly.

I went to Berlin many times, but it was all for naught. A shame, as it was an impressive technology: safe, efficient, quiet, with no emissions and energy efficient.

There was an accident at the test track in Lathen years later, but that was the only accident in all that time.

Finally, the Chinese built a Shanghai Airport maglev line in a competition with high-speed rail. Zhu Rongji was the Mayor of Shanghai from 1989 to 1991 and was an engineer very interested in maglev for surface transportation. He was a member of the Politburo Standing Committee from 1997 to 2002, serving as Premier from 1998 to 2003, and was responsible for the Shanghai project. My Transrapid colleagues often talked about Zhu Rongji from their meetings with him, thinking that his interest in maglev would be the breakthrough.

He had told the Germans that China's plan was to build out a new high-speed network for its 1.3 billion citizens, and the technology was the only remaining question. The Shanghai Airport project was to be the test, and in that process, the Chinese found maglev to be more expensive, which vectored them accordingly. (Coincidentally, my nephew got to know Zhu Rongji while working for a Washington firm that represented Shanghai.)

I can remember the German Transrapid team showing us the construction photos from the Shanghai Airport to the city itself. But Siemens was always double-breasted on surface transportation, and politically that hurt. While the Chinese opted for rail versus maglev, claiming the latter was more expensive, the real challenge I felt was that Siemens could sell their existing high-speed trains off the shelf, while maglev was a first of its kind.

The first of its kind is always more expensive at the beginning, plus Siemens had its order book out to the Chinese for their ICE model, and this huge market represents a first mover opportunity!

In 2019, Siemens (the ICE train) and Alstom (the French TGV model) attempted to merge in order to compete more effectively with China's huge CRRC, which had become the world's largest carrier in just those sixteen to seventeen years—very impressive.

High-speed rail (HSR) in China, at speeds of 155–190 mph, is the world's longest high-speed railway network. It is hard to believe that this vast network was built over the last fifteen years to connect thirty of the country's thirty-three provinces with over 16,000 miles of track, accounting for about two-thirds of the world's high-speed rail tracks in commercial service. As impressive as this infrastructure statistic is, it has plans to continue building out this high-speed rail system.

Compare this impressive record with the US effort over the same time period, with billions spent and little to show for it. California is struggling just to complete some two hundred miles in the San Joaquin Valley after spending billions! The governor, Gavin Newsom, has walked away from this project and seems to avoid the needed infrastructure agenda for California as he does not understand project finance, thinking more about political finance for infrastructure purposes.

And in the 2021 Biden infrastructure proposal, billions more would be wasted on high-speed rail as there were no lessons learned from the California debacle. In fact, they called the President Amtrak Joe.

Sure enough, Alstom and Siemens had both opened plants in the United States. Alstom had won the Amtrak Acela contract for providing new Acela trains capable of speeds of 160 mph before there was the so-called 2022 bipartisan infrastructure funding. But even with the hundreds of millions of dollars provided to Amtrak, the Northeast Corridor in 2023 was capable of only 90 mph as the track infrastructure was old and there was congestion with local and freight trains.

As the saying goes, what a way to run a railroad!

And I had read in August 2020 that China was planning to double its high-speed train network by 2035. China Railway Group (CRRC) would increase the country's high-speed rail network from 36,000 km to 70,000 km, as part of the development of regional hubs.

The railway expansion would increase the total length of track from its present 141,400 km to over 200,000 km. After the new tracks are laid, every Chinese city with a population of over 200,000 will be served by a high-speed rail line. Every city with over half a million people will have a service that travels at over 250 km/h.

The new high-speed train network was being constructed with the aim of facilitating the creation of new regional hubs in inland China. Making smaller cities more accessible to migrant rural workers would go some way to preventing further overpopulation of the country's coastal megacities.

Rail transport is a priority for the Chinese government: Over $1 trillion has been spent on the nation's rail network since 2009, including almost $50 billion so far in 2020. But China Railways is struggling to recoup its investments and currently has a debt of around $770 billion, similar to real property excesses, so infrastructure investment, as the last pillar, cannot fail. The construction work on the additional rail lines is expected to be completed in 2035, the year that President Xi Jinping has set for China to become a modern socialist country, albeit his Communist Party's dominance of China's economy is baffling. So, exports are key!

Almost all HSR trains, track, and service are owned and operated by the China Railway Corporation under the brand China Railway High-speed (CRH) with substantial funding from the Chinese government, especially the economic stimulus program during the Great Recession.

The United States started a similar program at that same time, with billions put to work on several projects; but no lines have been completed, a sad commentary on our political infrastructure incompetence. In the United States, we have project infrastructure finance confused with political infrastructure finance.

China's early high-speed trains were imported or built under technology transfer agreements with foreign train-makers, beginning with Siemens but including Alstom, Bombardier, and Kawasaki. Since this initial technological support, as expected, Chinese engineers have redesigned internal train components and built their own trains. This seems to drive these same GOP senators into tirades. The fact is China does a great job on infrastructure, and we don't!

The advent of high-speed rail in China has greatly reduced travel time and has transformed Chinese society and the economy. The Beijing–Guangzhou High-Speed Railway (1,428 miles) is the world's longest HSR line in operation, and the Beijing–Shanghai high-speed railway is the world's fastest train.

The Shanghai Metro—Pudong Airport Maglev is the world's only high-speed commercial magnetic levitation line, running on a 27-mile guideway, reaching a top speed of around 270 mph with seating for 574 passengers, and they arrive in just over seven minutes. It is quite a story!

But there was no comparative US story!

Lockheed Martin (Maryland) retained me when I was at USC on the public policy faculty for project/infrastructure finance in the early 2000s as they became interested in maglev; and ultimately a joint venture was organized with Transrapid. Back I went to both Dusseldorf and Berlin, this time at Lockheed's offices on Unter der Linden, which now apparently is the K Street of Berlin where all the corporate governmental affairs and lobbying firms are located.

Unter den Linden is a boulevard in the Mitte district of Berlin, the capital of Germany. It is named after its linden trees that line the grassy pedestrian mall between two carriageways. Berlin is a very impressive city! I became very familiar with its neighborhoods, shopping districts, cultural halls, and the like. Hard to believe there was a Second World War.

On one occasion, I invited former McLean neighbor and then US ambassador to Germany Dan Coats (2001–5), to attend the Lockheed—Transrapid team at a private club in Berlin for cocktails. Dan accepted and gave a terrific talk.

In keeping with a term-limits pledge he made to the Hoosiers community, Dan had stepped down from his Indiana Senate seat in 1999. After leaving the Senate, he joined a quality Washington, DC, law firm and in 2001, was named Ambassador to the Federal Republic of Germany, arriving in that country only three days before the tragic events of September 11, 2001.

As Ambassador, Dan played a critical role in establishing robust relations with German Chancellor Angela Merkel and in the construction of the new United States Embassy in the heart of Berlin, looking out on the Pariser Platz just across from the historic Brandenburg Gate.

I was in Berlin often for Transrapid meetings the following year with Lockheed Martin, and would contact Dan at the US Embassy. It was great. Dan, his wife Marcia, and I went out to dinner together, picking me up in their ambassadorial BMW car with the German security detail driving and following. Dan asked me to compare a BMW with a Mercedes for US purposes, but his driver interjected, stating the BMW was the superior automobile.

But there are reports from 2018 that BMW has retreated from its leadership in innovation, a good example being the electric vehicle.

After Germany, Dan had returned to the US Senate for Indiana, and it was like old times. I visited him in 2012 in his Senate office, having been in a Brookings Institution session with him earlier. We talked about our children, and it was nice to learn that his son had purchased a house in Potomac Hills, the same McLean, Virginia, area where we had all enjoyed living some thirty years earlier.

As I wrote this chapter, Dan retired at the end of his term in 2016. He was often described as a GOP conservative. The truth is, Dan was a moderate who was very popular in our neighborhood. My son, Clay, would string his tennis rackets.

And President Trump was to appoint Dan as his Director of National Intelligence. We were very pleased as he is a true Millennium person, with a conscience that allows us to sleep well at night. Dan served a total of sixteen years in the Senate during two separate stretches.

His selection was critical and came at a time when the Trump administration's views on the quality and value of US intelligence-gathering were unclear at best. We were fortunate to have Dan Coats in that job and gravely disappointed when he resigned under Trump's pressure in the late summer of 2019.

The reunification of Germany occurred in October 1990, so these trips to Germany (a dozen or so) took place in that ten-year aftermath. The impact on Berlin was amazing. One hotel I stayed at on Unter der Linden (the former East German side) had been the hostelry for the East German Communist leadership and was quite ornate in a funny way.

On one Berlin trip, I was staying in a hotel by the Transrapid offices off the Elbe River. It was a weekend as the meetings were to start on Monday. As it happened, the Women's World Basketball Championships were being played in Berlin at the Max-Schmeling-Halle, a multi-purpose arena named after the famous German boxer Max Schmeling. The US and Russian teams were staying at the same hotel, and the US parents noticed me in the lobby as a tall American and invited me to join them for the game that evening.

It was a real treat, driving over in a van with the parents and sitting with them. The US won, which was terrific! But the next morning, I was startled to see several of the Russian players in the lobby. They looked drunk, as if they had been drinking all night as they awaited transportation to the airport. I knew that Russia had a drinking problem, and this confirmed it!

Returning to Washington, I arranged a Lockheed Martin/Transrapid dinner at the Georgetown Club that impressed all (I had been on that club's Board). We were just short of signing the joint venture papers. But backroom dealings continued, and the joint venture was never consummated. The Transrapid CEO was from Siemens, and she was hesitant to sign. Finally, we all gave up!

That was the end for surface maglev transportation in the United States, but there was still a tribe of consultants feeding off of earlier congressional earmarks. Lessons learned: The unveiling of new technology such as maglev is very difficult in a US government funding/procurement scenario.

The German maglev launch/recovery technology was superior to the US General Atomics version, but under the guise of national security, it was not invited to participate. Another unfortunate phrase is Buy American, which can have a similar negative impact—the focus should be on the best technology. This was some twenty years ago, and since then global supply chains have become a standard business practice for large-scale government contractors.

In late 2018, with Donald Trump in the White House, the so-called US-China Economic and Security Review Commission, which includes appointees by Senate and House leaders of both parties, found that Chinese dominance of networking equipment manufacturing threatens the security of US fifth-generation, or 5G, wireless infrastructure.

In addition, China's position as the world's largest manufacturer of internet-connected household devices creates "numerous points of vulnerability for intelligence collection, cyberattacks, industrial control, or censorship."

I was skeptical as no US firms had complained. But in March 2024, the Biden administration announced an $8 billion dollar grant to Intel Corporation toward building a semiconductor manufacturing enterprise.

This grant followed from the 2018 National Defense Strategy Commission comprised of twelve former top Republican and Democratic officials selected by Congress. In its list of thirty-two recommendations, the commission urged the Pentagon to explain more clearly how it intends to defeat major-power rivals in competition and war.

And here is the procurement reality. This National Defense Strategy Commission described current Pentagon acquisition programs as too risk-averse and urged the Defense Department and Congress to create a new category of pilot programs aimed at leap-ahead technologies that could serve as breakthroughs to help retain American military dominance.

And in June 2021, the Senate endorsed $52 billion in subsidies for computer-chip manufacturing. The measure was supported by President Biden, who stated, "We are in a competition to win the twenty-first century, and the starting gun has gone off," after the Senate endorsed the bill.

It earmarked (1) $10 billion for the Commerce Department to establish regional tech hubs that would help create new companies and boost manufacturing and workforce training; (2) an extra $81 billion for the National Science Foundation over five years, partly to fund a new directorate of technology and innovation to accelerate the commercialization of technology in fields such as artificial intelligence, robotics, and advanced computing. And (3) it provided $16.9 billion to the Energy Department over four years for research and development and energy-related supply chain activities, which could involve supporting battery production.

Of the $52 billion set aside for semiconductors, three quarters would go directly to chipmakers, like Intel, that were expanding existing factories or building new ones. Another $10.5 billion would fund a new National Semiconductor Technology Center.

I had my doubts about all these dollars going out the door to the existing procurement matrix. In 2024, there were a number of articles and reports about the surge of venture-capital funding for defense technology.

One 2024 report released by the Silicon Valley Defense Group indicated that the top 100 venture capital-backed national-security startups raised a combined $53 billion in private funding since their inception, $11 billion of which came in the 2023-2024-time frame.

The report indicated those same startups collectively earned $22 billion in revenue from federal awards, $6 billion of which came from the Defense Department. The average age of the startups noted in the report was seven years; however, their analytical challenge is that government award data suffers from absolute opaqueness fostered, in my view by the national security creed.

That same year, 2024, Donald Trump was elected a second time to return to the White House—it was a stay tuned moment!

11

Government Information Technology (IT) Reform

In this chapter, we will discuss the Navy Marine Corps Intranet strategy that occurred in the year 2000. Essentially, the Navy Marine Corps Intranet was a service contract strategy that I recommended to Naval Sea Systems Command to meet the immense challenge of replacing the twenty-eight legacy carriers and installing the new system to provide that intranet service so the different services could communicate with each other. It was common knowledge in the Navy community that they could not. As a Naval Academy graduate, I was very active in that community and was a founder of the US Navy Memorial complex on Pennsylvania Avenue in Washington, DC.

EDS won the competition, and EDS took the risk, not the taxpayer! They did not get paid until the agreed service was delivered. I carried the idea from my work in the 1992 Energy Policy Act and the passage of PUHCA Reform Title VII (Electricity), which created the independent power industry and changed electric utility power procurement. From then on, most new utility generation was secured through competitive bidding in the new wholesale power market.

The independent power producer (IPP) that won the competition took the risk, based on a power purchase agreement, to build the new generation facility and deliver the power (natural gas, wind, solar). The IPP did not get paid until the contracted power was delivered. It worked very well.

As successful as that procurement was, it is still unique, a one of a kind. Unfortunately, until Amazon's Cloud Services won the CIA IT competition in 2013, the same year as the Obama health care rollout with the failed IT component.

This $600 million computing cloud developed by Amazon Web Services for the Central Intelligence Agency over the following year began servicing all seventeen agencies that make up the intelligence community.

The Department of Defense was to follow in 2018; however, delays and lawsuits focused on President Trump's personal intervention and animosity toward Amazon's founder Jeff Bezos (being the owner of the *Washington Post*) stalled the award.

The Beltway Bandit club did not like the Navy Marine Corps approach and managed to keep the old procurement system in place elsewhere, with the government taking the vendor's systems integration risk, coupled with numerous system buildout failures in many federal agencies. Later, during the pandemic, we were to learn of the state and local government's antiquated IT systems.

There is a critical need for similar federal government procurement reform, particularly in the IT sector, and this includes the Federal Acquisition Regulations, otherwise known as the FAR.

You have to salute President Obama, after the 2013 Affordable Care Act IT announcement failure, for accurately explaining that the way the federal government does procurement and particularly IT is generally not very efficient. In fact, he emphasized that there's probably no bigger gap between the private sector and the public sector than IT; and what we probably needed to do on the front end was to blow up how we procure for IT and start anew.

How and when President Obama learned of this IT procurement is unclear; but his staff should have known the only government IT success to that date was the Navy Marine Corps intranet procurement in 2000, for which I take much pride, and coincidentally we did it in that millennium year.

IT, or Information Technology, is infrastructure, and it has a severe government procurement problem. In a March 2017 edition of the *Wall Street Journal*, there was a special section on IT procurement. The main theme was the rapid advances being made in the private sector and featured executives from Google, Microsoft, and others.

No one from the government was featured as they would be embarrassed. Bottom line: virtually all government IT procurements have failed as the winning bidders insist on building out new, unique systems while taking zero risk for this approach, leaving government and the taxpayers holding the bag.

As President Obama accurately described this unfortunate government Information Technology (IT) history on Friday, November 15, 2013, in his Affordable Care Act postmortem and again before a 2013 CEO Council (Wall Street Journal), there had been a long history of Federal Government IT failure. So, in my own words, it was time to follow up Obamacare with Obama Tech, a surgical approach if you will. And that is what they did; and we will talk about that later in this chapter.

But the next president, Donald Trump, unfortunately told CEOs at the White House in mid-April of his first year in office that he would throw money at it, inferring, amidst laughter, that our US computer system, being forty years old, was going to have a massive program to modernize our equipment—ideally buy brand-new equipment.

Interestingly, the President's former counsel, Michael Cohen, was to testify in public before a House Committee. In response to a question, Cohen stated the President doesn't use the computer, emails, or texts! Dan Scavino, Trump's assistant, does.

This governmental IT systems failure syndrome exists at all levels of government, unfortunately: federal, state, and local. For example, I was driving up to San Francisco years ago from my spring lecture at Stanford's Global Project Center and had the local NPR station on my car radio when a national news report came on the air, stating, per my notes, the only place in San Francisco still pricing real estate like it's the 1980s is the city assessor's office. Its property tax system dates back decades.

The situation speaks for itself! More than 3,400 state, local, tribal, and territorial governments in the United States suffered ransomware attacks between 2017 and 2021, according to data from the Multi-State Information Sharing and Analysis Center, a threat intelligence group for municipalities. Local governments are ripe targets because of the financial and personal information they hold, and they are often easier to attack than major companies, plus their technology is archaic.

After the 2013 Obama healthcare IT speech, the Washington Post was filled with very informative federal government information technology (IT) articles relating to the healthcare website failure. Those articles were late to the game, but still important to be unveiled.

In total, there had been some two-dozen major federal agency IT failures over that earlier 2000–2010 decade while the private sector (Google, Amazon, etc.) seemed to always get it right. Their data centers were completed on time and on budget; but look at the colossal failure of the Utah NSA Data Center complex and the Washington state Veterans Administration pilot electronic records failure.

And in 2020, the census count would capture a country that had changed significantly since 2010. But Census Bureau officials worried that disinformation spread over social media could taint the count. Most importantly, the Government Accountability Office had been worried about Federal IT and was concerned that the new technology underpinning the online count was not ready, pointing out that the bureau switched to a backup system to manage households' online responses that wasn't tested extensively by the contractor.

From what I have personally observed, the traditional defense firms hide behind the existing procurement process, avoid risk, and fail to innovate, and then there are these failures. Their three-word glossary is composed of RFP (Request for Proposal), the FAR (Federal Acquisition Regulations), and finally Systems Integration, which means many companies in a procurement pyramid with no one taking risks. It was noteworthy that the General Accounting Office had identified government IT procurement as one of its needed reforms.

I could not have agreed more. The Federal Acquisition Regulations (FAR), all 1,897 pages, need to be reformed—a total overhaul. When these IT projects fail, only the government (the taxpayer) loses money, not the vendor, with one exception: the Navy Marine Corps Intranet, and here is that history.

Navy Marine Corps Intranet 2000

Admiral J. Paul Reason USN, as noted earlier, in his tenure as CINCLANTFLT (1997–9) called me at my Washington, DC, office and told me that, after listening to me for several years about our 1992 success in opening up electricity generation to independent power producers (IPPs) who would supply the utility under a power purchase agreement (PPA), he decided to explore a risk transfer/leasing services approach to his Navy IT procurement. He had finally found a procurement officer at the Navy's Philadelphia contracting office who appreciated the concept and issued a leasing/services/risk transfer-based Request for Proposal (RFP) that prescribed the desired services over a ten-year period.

He explained to me that no equipment was being purchased; rather, the required equipment services were being leased over a period of years. If the services (and the leased equipment) were not delivered, there was no payment. And because of this leasing/services procurement approach, the CINCLANTFLT staff in Norfolk, Virginia, had completed a very successful transition to this new IT services platform.

Admiral Reason told me that he now had all new equipment for his 600-person staff and that they were very happy with this service lease, and would have new equipment rotated in every three years. He was going to call CINCPAC and suggest they do this fleet-wide, which he did.

Naval Sea Systems Command was to oversee the initial procurement process, and I was then asked by them to attend several meetings at their headquarters as an informal advisor and assist them in the design of the groundbreaking Request for Proposal (RFP). This was the beginning of the innovative Navy Marine Corps Intranet (NMCI) procurement.

As I said, I had developed the idea based on my experience leading the effort to open the electric utility wholesale power market in 1992, where utilities now pay for electricity generation services delivered by independent power producers. Customers no longer paid for utility-owned power plant (including nuclear energy) construction cost overruns that were conveniently moved into what was known as the rate base.

On October 6, 2000, the NMCI contract was awarded to Electronic Data Systems (EDS), now part of Hewlett-Packard. Secretary of the Navy Gordon England summed up the Navy's IT environment prior to the commencement of NMCI, indicating that the Navy basically had twenty-eight separate commands budgeting, developing, licensing, and operating IT autonomously, which was inefficient and produced results that were far from optimal. Admiral Reason used to tell me the same thing: that the Navy could not talk to each other!

The NMCI consolidated roughly 6,000 networks—some of which could not email, let alone collaborate with each other—into a single integrated and secure IT environment. EDS updated more than 100,000 desktop and laptop PCs. The program also consolidated an ad hoc network of more than 8,000 applications to 500 in four years and 15,003 logistics and readiness systems to 2,759 over a two-year period.

It was common knowledge in the Navy and the Marine Corps that their existing legacy systems could not talk to each other, and 9/11 illustrated how government departments themselves could not talk to each other!

EDS's subcontractors included: Apple Inc., Cisco, Dell, McAfee, Microsoft, Oracle Corporation, Sun Microsystems, Symantec, Harris, and Verizon.

NMCI quickly suffered some widely publicized setbacks, including rollout delays that caused EDS financial losses (importantly—not the government's) due primarily to intransigence by the incumbent legacy providers. This risk transfer/services approach is the key element! The vendor had equity in the game and was taking the risk, not the taxpayer.

While losing money at the beginning, it was a very successful long-term business opportunity for EDS and a win for the Navy and Marine Corps. They now had a brand-new operating system that worked well and had avoided any risks or costs of failure under the NMCI contract. Today, NMCI is considered the core enterprise network for Navy and Marine Corps forces in the United States and Japan, providing secure access to integrated voice, video, and data communications.

NMCI has been a hugely successful program for the Navy. It has been a cost-effective way to deliver unprecedented level of service. I was pleased and very proud to make my contribution to the United States Navy. I anticipated it would be successful eventually and adopted throughout the federal government IT world.

As pointed out, during the buildup period, EDS lost significant dollars as they were on the hook to succeed, not the government or the taxpayer. But over time, EDS turned the corner and the NMCI was very profitable. They were respected in the IT market and garnered other contracts.

Still, the Navy had complete control and authority over how it operated the network. That allowed it to maintain extremely high degree of security, which was its number one issue, and always is, often to the detriment of the procurement itself.

What I never understood is how this Navy Intranet success story was ignored by the other federal agencies as they continued to issue procurements for building out their systems, which seemed to never work, resulting in billions of taxpayer dollars being wasted. It was that way until President Obama's 2013 Affordable Care Act IT announcement failure; then, there was some change.

On a Saturday in early February 2016, I attended the Army-Navy gymnastics event at the Naval Academy in Annapolis, Maryland. It was fantastic; the crowds were into it, along with the athletes from both service academies, urging their teammates on to a record performance. Sitting next to me were three Naval Academy female plebes (freshmen) in their weekend khaki trousers and blue jackets and personal shoes.

I asked what their major course of study was, and they told me, "Probably IT!" I then explained the above history of the Navy Marine Corps Intranet procurement so they would understand how important that process is, with the vendor taking the risk for delivering the service. They were very attentive, and I hoped they would remember that lesson when they graduated and became officers.

The Navy had awarded EDS, since purchased by Hewlett Packard (HP), this $6 billion contract in 2000 to manage its network from soup to nuts for 700,000 sailors and Marines in 3,000 locations around the world. This management services contract, which included all hardware and software, grew to more than $8 billion and would end up being worth almost $12 billion by the time the Navy fully implemented the succeeding NGEN (Next Generation) phase.

It worked, and the Navy and Marine Corps were very pleased with the services rendered, equipment received, and technology used. I had volunteered my advice and was very pleased.

By way of background, ten years later, on September 30, 2010, the NMCI contract ended, and a new Continuity of Services Contract (COSC) began. The COSC presumably gave the Navy and Marine Corps the best of the current NMCI IT environment.

Under the COSC, the Navy retained the same scope of NMCI services with HP (EDS); but the network became a government-owned, contractor-supported, managed services environment. This new approach was called Next Generation (NGEN). It was a paradigm shift, in my opinion, because under the original NMCI contract, the government managed the network but did not own any IT assets used in the program.

Rather, they were owned by the prime contractor, and services were provided to the government on a service's per capita basis. Most importantly, it worked! In a way, this was a precursor to the service contracts to be awarded to Amazon's cloud technology services years later by the CIA and the Pentagon, much to the chagrin of the traditional Pentagon suppliers.

The Navy awarded HP this NMCI continuity of services contract to serve as the transition between NMCI and NGEN. The deal was for forty-three months and worth $3.4 billion. It was now 2020, and I did hope the transition had been successful. Frankly, I was concerned as this new procurement process had the potential to revert back to the traditional command and control model. But I was pleased to read that a Navy spokesman, at the time, was reassuring, saying that NMCI had been a hugely successful program for the Navy. It has been a cost-effective way to deliver unprecedented level of service. We learned a lot about how to do it and how not to do it.

Yes, NMCI was a very good IT procurement model for other federal government agencies to emulate, and that is what this chapter is about.

I spoke on this at a House Public Private Partnership Caucus panel in 2013, and one of the Pentagon participants told me he was unhappy with the Navy Marine Corps Intranet because he could not take his laptop home at night! Yet, months earlier there was a Washington Post article about a government employee who had left his laptop in his parked car, and it was stolen in a car burglary.

NMCI was the first and only successful large-scale federal government IT centralization and outsourcing services project. By contrast, the IT procurement failures list at the IRS, Customs Service, DHS, Veterans Administration, and other federal agencies was practically endless. They all had problems! And billions of dollars have been or will be wasted!

The NMCI success should have informed these other government agency efforts on how to consolidate and outsource IT services. The new Department of Homeland Security, created after the IT inter-agency failures in the aftermath of 9/11, surely should have paid attention. The General Services Administration (GSA) is the fallback IT agency, and there has been some progress, but still the Federal Acquisition Regulations prevail.

In Congress, Matt Lira, senior adviser for then House Majority Leader Kevin McCarthy, said the gap between the government's information technology and the private sector had grown larger than ever. The Government Accountability Office in 2015 reported that about 25 percent of the federal government's 738 major IT investments—projected to cost a total of $42 billion—were in danger of significant delays or cost overruns. It seems the Veterans Administration IT transition begun in the 2018 time frame was hopelessly in shambles and its congressional sponsors were at a loss as to what to do.

One reason for such overruns is the government's reliance on big, monolithic projects based on proposal documents that can run to hundreds of pages as required by the Federal Acquisition Regulations (the FAR) and are preferred by the vendors (no risk of failure). This approach to software development was at least twenty years out of date (reminder: The Navy Marine Corps intranet RFP was in 2000).

Modern software development, I am told, focuses on small chunks of code accomplished in sprints and delivered to customers quickly so that problems can be identified and corrected.

You must give the Obama administration credit for developing a novel way to address these issues after the Affordable Care Act IT rollout disaster by quickly assembling an expert team of coders and project managers from the likes of Google, Amazon, and Microsoft. They were immediately assigned to large government projects to help existing IT staff revamp their approach to be more in sync with the private sector.

In fact, you often read often about the critical role that Chief Technology Officers (CTOs) play in today's corporate management structure; finally, every governmental agency is starting to have a CTO, including the Defense Department. The Obama White House, in 2014, after the health care announcement fiasco, had one named Megan Smith, a Google executive with decades of experience in Silicon Valley. The Obama administration named as her deputy US CTO, Alexander McGillivray, a former Twitter lawyer known as a staunch defender of the free flow of information online. They were both steeped in the workings of some of Silicon Valley's biggest and highest-profile companies, one an engineer with a record of executing ambitious, even innovative ideas, the other a lawyer who had navigated some of the internet's trickiest policy questions.

And shortly thereafter, two new government coding organizations, known as 18F and the US Digital Service, were established in 2014 and quickly built up to 500 staffers (a government geek squad, if you will, and long overdue).

The United States Digital Service is a part of the Executive Office of the President of the United States. It provides consultation services on retainer to federal agencies on information technology and was launched on August 11, 2014.

18F is a digital services agency within the General Services Administration. Their purpose is to deliver digital services as well as technology products, and technology products; and were established about the same time. I read that Aaron Snow, now executive director of 18F, explained to the press that we transform government services by transforming the practices that create those services. The way to do that is to change the culture that creates those services.

In March 2014, I knew that a group of Presidential Innovation Fellows had started 18F to extend their efforts to improve and modernize government IT. Its name refers to its office location in northwest Washington, DC, on 18th and F Streets. 18F is within Technology Transformation Services, part of the Federal Acquisition Service. In addition to its Washington, DC, office, the agency has offices in New York, San Francisco, and Chicago.

In 2021, the US Senate confirmed Robin Carnahan as administrator of the General Services Administration (GSA). A nationally recognized government technology leader, she received broad support across party lines and indicated after her confirmation that she was grateful for the support of the Senate, was honored to serve as the next administrator of GSA, and was committed to doing all she could to support that important mission.

Prior to her appointment, Carnahan impressively founded and led the State and Local Government Practice at 18F, the tech consultancy inside the GSA. In this role, she helped federal, state, and local government agencies improve customer-facing digital services and cut costs.

Before her time at GSA, Carnahan served as Missouri's Secretary of State, where she served as the state's Chief Election Official and State Securities Regulator and oversaw an organization that delivered in-person and online services to hundreds of thousands of customers.

Her father was the Governor of Missouri from 1993 until his death in a plane crash in 2000. A Democrat, he was elected posthumously to the US Senate; his widow, Jean, served in his stead for two years until a special election.

As it turned out, Ed Smith, the president of ULLICO and my infrastructure fund client, knew the Carnahan family well, and he told me about a breakfast meeting he had with Robin earlier that same day. I complimented her experience and explained to Ed how important this was.

As to the history of the Obama administration's health care IT crash, HealthCare.gov had been launched months earlier in October 2013; and when users tried to sign up for health insurance plans, despite $600 million in private contracts to construct the website, it crashed as so many government IT programs had done so earlier. This included the Center for Medicare and Medicaid Services, which managed the Affordable Care Act (Obamacare), and hired private companies in the conventional way to build Healthcare.gov to be the federal marketplace for health care plans through which millions would enroll in health insurance coverage.

Problems began well before the website's disastrous debut on October 1, 2013, when the employees charged with handling those private contracts failed to oversee and manage the companies, the investigative report from the Office of the Inspector General showed. President Obama understood the vulnerability of the conventional IT procurement approach and made it known.

I suspect he would have been fascinated by the Navy Marine Corps Intranet approach; but just a few months later, in response to this embarrassing IT failure, 18F began to host the Presidential Innovation Fellows program that had started in May 2012, before 18F's own inception, in the Digital Government Strategy office.

The existence of the 18F agency in general, and such projects, has always led to resistance from established government IT firms (the so-called Beltway Bandits) who most importantly spawned dozens of major federal government IT failures.

In 2016, 18F became part of the Technology Transformation Services (TTS), which also included the Presidential Innovation Fellows program, the Office of Acquisitions, the Office of Products and Programs, and the IT Modernization Centers of Excellence. In 2017, TTS became part of GSA's existing Federal Acquisition Service (under Robin Carnahan in 2021).

The Affordable Care Act IT problem was a blessing in disguise—a wake-up call! Finally, we saw the inept procurement practices! And it was time for dramatic federal government procurement reform as at least $10 billion in federal technology contracts were currently at risk of failing, according to a review by the Government Accountability Office. Chief information officers across federal agencies had reported that 183 of 759 major IT investments were at medium to high risk of failing before completion.

The GAO's IT management director, David A. Powner, at the time in 2017 pointed out that information technology should enable the government to better serve the

American people; yet despite spending hundreds of billions on IT since 2000, the federal government had experienced failed IT projects and had achieved little of the productivity improvements that private industry had realized from IT. Despite the success of the Navy Marine Corps Intranet risk transfer strategy during that same 2000–2015 period, it had been ignored.

But now the politicians and political appointees had discovered they can be held liable as well politically—so there would be change. The government's handling of federal IT programs is closely watched in the Washington area because so many contractors are based there close to the procurement platforms themselves.

While the 2017 GAO report did not identify specific programs or contracts at risk, federal agencies were required to publicly update the progress of their technology programs to correct what the GAO described as a troubling trend toward decreased transparency in federal IT reporting. Still, the GAO indicated sites such as the IT Dashboard make the federal government more transparent than in the past, building a culture in which agencies share information. And in 2017, both 18F and the US Digital Service were to be up and running.

In a non-federal example, 18F staffers joined a massive effort to create technology for California's child-welfare system, which must work with the federal Department of Health and Human Services. The system serves 20,000 social workers who track half a million reports of child abuse and neglect each year.

It began as a typical big government project, with a design specification of more than 100 pages. Taking an approach typical of private enterprise, 18F broke it into eight smaller projects, each of which could be tackled with more modern agile techniques, they said. The first two projects are operating and came in under budget, they announced.

But the inside-the-beltway system integrators did not like it. Nor did the appropriations-oriented lobbying firms representing their clients go after the estimated $406 billion in federal contracts set to expire in 2017, according to the publication, Trump's Swamp: The Reprogramming Potential for Agencies and Contractors.

But here is a good example of progress. In 2020, the General Services Administration planned to contract with privately run e-marketplace platforms, making them available to other federal agencies as an alternative to existing government-run purchasing websites.

Walmart Inc. and eBay Inc. had joined Amazon in showing interest, and bids fulfilling the government's requirements were due in November. But guess what? Government contractors were up in arms. "We're going to lose our shirts," said Steve Armstrong, general counsel at MSC Industrial Supply Co., a Melville, New York, distributor of safety goggles, ladders, and other items. This seems to point to the supply chain collapse during the coronavirus pandemic.

Mr. Armstrong said his biggest customer was the GSA, the federal organization that facilitates purchasing by other agencies. He worried that he would now have to list his wares on Amazon to reach the same buyers—and pay a fee to Amazon on sales that already have thin profit margins. Government officials are hoping e-commerce saves time (Amazon Prime) and creates more competition for the government's business. We will stay tuned!

And Now the Cloud

After years of IT failures, the Department of Defense deserved credit for facing up to its deplorable IT infrastructure situation and taking a very innovative path to solution.

A key reason, no doubt was the Pentagon's arrival earlier in 2018 of Dana Deasy as the new Department of Defense Chief Information Officer. His earlier assignment was doing the same for JP Morgan Chase, with thousands of employees under his leadership. I was hoping to brief him, as well as his staff, on the Navy Marine Corps Intranet procurement.

And at the same time, Ellen Lord, the Pentagon's undersecretary for technology and logistics, pointed out that if we keep doing business the same old way, our software will be outdated; it will cost far more than it needs to. We won't be able to attract the best software talent, and we'll lose our technological edge.

The Pentagon had long led the way in developing advanced technology that found its way into civilian applications, such as GPS and the internet. That balance had shifted, according to tech leaders and others. They contended that the private sector had more talent and greater research budgets than the government—and more advanced capabilities in artificial intelligence and cloud computing—all while the military was more reliant on technology. Robert Work, a former US Deputy Secretary of Defense, suggested that everyone is saying we are in a competition with China, but we are not organized to win the competition, and if we do not correct that, we are doomed to lose. Work was the vice chairman of the National Security Commission on Artificial Intelligence, a panel created by Congress in 2018 and chaired by former Google Chief Executive Eric Schmidt. Other members included Andy Jassy, chief executive of Amazon.com Inc.; Oracle Corp. CEO Safra Catz; and top scientists from Microsoft Corp. and Alphabet Inc.'s Google.

In a report released in 2021, the commission laid out a road map for the Pentagon to buy commercially designed software and hardware to maintain a strategic edge, as China and other nations stepped up their tech investments. Google stepped back from a software project with the Pentagon when employees in 2018 found out about it and revolted.

They probably could have handled the Silicon Valley-type procurement process and optics differently; but be that as it may, the beltway vendors did not like the new procurement cloud services approach that emanated from this development.

But I was glad to see that this did not deter Mr. Deasy or Ms. Lord as they maintained the Defense Department's cloud services procurement. In early April, they announced that Amazon and Microsoft would be the finalists, eliminating Oracle and IBM.

The cloud is conceptually thought of as a digital exchange of bits, but it's actually all about physical infrastructure—data centers and transoceanic cables carrying petabytes of information. Amazon, Microsoft, and the other big cloud players enable other companies to outsource vast computing requirements to these costly infrastructures that can process billions of online transactions without having to undertake major construction projects themselves, which is the beltway bandits' preference.

The "cloud" IT services approach was not available in 2000 for the Navy Marine Corps Intranet procurement; however, it was the services concept that was critical, and now the Pentagon was on it.

President Trump in his first term said on the campaign trail that he was going to drain the swamp in Washington and remove the influence of lobbyists and special interests. However, the earlier Pentagon cloud services article excerpt suggested otherwise. It clearly makes the case for federal procurement reform, with the contractors taking risks for providing services and bidding accordingly.

The Pentagon contract, along with Trump's criticism of Amazon, drove the procurement into the appeal process, which served as just a detour away from a solution. And I am sure the traditional vendors will run to Congress; however, I have found real interest in my perspective with several committees and their staff. My suggestion was to duplicate the Navy Marine Corps intranet!

About this same time, artificial intelligence (AI) made its research debut in computer science, which develops and studies methods and software that enable machines to take actions that maximize their chances of achieving defined goals. However, huge data centers were needed and built as they consumed enormous amounts of electricity from the grid. All of a sudden, Microsoft was signing a power purchase agreement to restart the undamaged Three Mile Island nuclear unit.

On January 21, 2025, one day after his second inaugural, Donald Trump announced the $500 billion Stargate joint venture between OpenAI, Softbank, MGX, and Oracle to build new data centers to power the next wave of artificial intelligence (AI). CEOs such as Larry Ellison from Oracle were in the Oval Office for President Trump's announcement. And while no US government funds were supposedly involved, the private sector funding would support the construction of large US data centers containing thousands of advanced computer chips required to train new AI systems. You had to wonder what was going on!

This is my March 2019 note to senior professor Dr. Ray Levitt, Dean Emeritus of the Stanford Graduate School of Civil Engineering and founder of their Global Projects Center, where I served on their Board of Advisors:

> Ray, I am still in the Bay Area; but an article in today's Washington Post regarding Palantir winning the competition to build the Army's intelligence system reminded me of a chapter excerpt from my book, "Real Regulatory Reform". The Chapter deals with government's (at all levels) failed approach to information technology (IT) infrastructure procurement.
>
> I sometimes think this IT infrastructure topic should be a Global Projects Center initiative—it is all about procuring services from a successful infrastructure platform and not taking risks to build out customized systems that repeatedly fail. Dan

Inside the Beltway–Government IT Stories

It happened that I worked with former White House Chief of Staff Governor John Sununu while advising energy colleagues in 1999–2000, developing the first independent transmission company in the United States known as Trans Elect. Their offices were in adjoining leased space in the old, yet famous, Clark Clifford law firm offices on Connecticut Avenue, looking directly at the White House, with the network TV cameras permanently ensconced below on the US Chamber of Commerce roof in a white tent. It was quite a view! That building has been totally rebuilt since then—but it looks like the cameras are still there.

I was on the USC faculty at the time, living in the San Diego area, and commuting to Washington, DC, on a regular basis. In fact, I invited our Vice Dean, Dr. Detlof von Vinterfelt, to meet with John Sununu as Detlof was serving on the Nuclear Waste Advisory Panel, and John Sununu was an MIT PhD and a strong advocate of nuclear power.

As the three of us chatted in Clark Clifford's old office, Detlof mentioned several studies that they had completed over the last several years. Sununu became exasperated as to why, when he was White House Chief of Staff, he had never seen these reports, which would have been helpful to him in national energy matters. We were all surprised at this lack of communication!

Then came 9/11 in 2001! We would be hammered as a nation by that terrible 9/11 attack. On that dreadful day, I was at the Radisson Hotel across from USC, working out in the hotel fitness center while watching the TV morning news. All of a sudden, they began showing videos of the planes hitting the World Trade Center. I had been in those World Trade Center buildings several times, including the restaurant on the top floor, Windows on the World, a complex on the top floors (106th and 107th) of the North Tower of the World Trade North Tower. The restaurant operated from April 19, 1976, until 2001, when they were destroyed in the September 11 attacks and was not to be rebuilt in the new World Trade Center.

Hurrying over for my meeting with David Seltzer and our USC Public Policy School counterparts, we both realized that David was stranded. He explained that his brother-in-law, Brian Roberts, CEO of Comcast, had flown out to LA on a corporate mission to discuss a transaction with Walt Disney Inc. With him was Steve Burke (then NBC president), who coincidentally had purchased our cousin's beachfront home in Mantoloking, New Jersey, where we had spent many family holidays. It had been rebuilt by new owners after being virtually destroyed in Hurricane Sandy.

David had hitched a ride with them on the Comcast jet from Philadelphia, and now they were stuck at Burbank Airport. I took David out there, but they were unable to fly out after their meeting for two days.

When I flew back to Washington, DC, the following week, the airports and planes were packed. We had a bevy of Red Cross volunteers heading to Washington to support the Pentagon relief mission.

The testimony that ensued from the 9/11 episode revealed that the government's IT practices were totally unacceptable. The FBI could not "talk" to the CIA, and so it went! The notion of a new Department of Homeland Security was spearheaded by Connecticut Senator Joe Lieberman. I went to his chief legislative staffer Bill Bonvillian, an old friend (who went on to run MIT's Washington office), and suggested some new IT procurement thinking like the recent Navy Marine Corps Intranet. They were all for it!

When I went by to see John Sununu at his office in Washington, DC (he was always in New Hampshire on the weekends), he noted that the Bush White House had not wanted to support a Department of Homeland Security. But Congress was moving forward as the 9/11 fervor was quite high, and it was difficult to oppose the idea. He told me he had spoken to Tom Ridge, the first DHS secretary (former Pennsylvania governor), who had reservations as well but agreed to serve.

And sure enough, under the Trump administration and their strident anti-immigration policies, I regretted the creation of this new cabinet-level agency as its behavior had changed. Instead of being protective, it became invasive! Working with Trump's immigration czar, Stephen Miller, in the White House was an impossible task! And then Kevin Cuccinelli arrived as acting DHS Deputy Director. Kevin had gone to Gonzaga Prep High School close to Capitol Hill with our sons; but unfortunately, he had forgotten his Jesuit training. He was to lead some of the worst DHS operations!

But let me continue with the IT and public building procurement topic and the Department of Homeland Security (DHS) Headquarters Buildings and Information Technology project.

I explained to John Sununu what I had in mind, that is, a first-class IT technology/construction consortium would prepare an unsolicited proposal to construct a best-in-class headquarters and IT system for the new Department of Homeland Security based on the "provision of services" approach of the Navy Marine Corps Intranet procurement that I had assisted with two years earlier.

John said sure he would set up a meeting with White House Chief of Staff Andy Card, who had worked for him under President Bush in the early 1990s, if I could put the public private partnership consortium together—a Catch twenty-two, as it turned out.

Lockheed Martin was a client, and I asked them if they would be interested in forming this consortium to make an unsolicited proposal to build a new, first-rate headquarters facility with a best-in-class IT infrastructure in an NMCI format. They wanted to go after the assignment but not take that risk.

I called on contacts at Oracle and Nortel to see if they would come on board. No, they would wait for the RFP and would work the process accordingly in their preferred role as a system integrator, which means they are at the top of the commercial pyramid. In the "Beltway Bandit" community, the US government was often referred to as the "customer." A better title might be the "victim." The system integrator's title is code for running their procurement pyramids in a quasi-low-profile manner while avoiding project risk responsibility.

Fifteen years after 9/11, Lockheed Martin Corp in January 2016 announced a $5 billion tax-free deal to combine its information systems and government services business with Leidos Holdings Inc. Leidos had been spun off from Science Applications International Corp (SAIC) in 2013.

The combined company would have annual revenues of $10 billion, making it the largest US government services provider. For government IT work, they deserved each other! SAIC was a long-time San Diego founded and headquartered company but moved to the Washington, DC, area some ten years ago to be closer to the customer.

And in February 2018, General Dynamics announced that it was acquiring CSRA, another government IT firm, formed just three years earlier in a wave of consolidation. General Dynamics would now have almost $10 billion in IT revenue, second only to Leidos. The other government IT vendors in sequential order were Booz Allen Hamilton, CACI, and SAIC. And at the end of the day, many of their IT government agency procurements would fail.

But they were betting on more procurement activity now that Congress had boosted military spending. In March, CACI made a counteroffer to purchase CSRA for $7.2 billion, a higher offer than General Dynamics. Government IT procurement contracts were quite lucrative, it seemed albeit few, if any, were actually successful.

And then we watched the IT procurement process play out. On March 22, 2018, the Senate Intelligence Committee held a hearing with then DHS Secretary Kirsten Nielsen testifying along with her predecessor, Jeff Johnson, on the topic of Russian hacking (cybersecurity) during the US elections.

The Secretary was asked an IT question about needed software for one of her agencies, and she casually responded that they would obtain that software from the General Services Administration (GSA). This was actually not a bad answer, as that agency had beefed up its IT in the previous Obama administration, as noted earlier in this chapter.

Secretary Nielsen was a Georgetown Foreign Service graduate with a University of Virginia law degree. While cyber was her specialty, she did not seem versed in government IT procurement.

The Department of Homeland Security was officially established in 2002 and was originally slated to move into its new DHS headquarters in 2018. However, it was located for many years in a set of buildings known as the Nebraska Avenue Complex, whose address is 3801 Nebraska Avenue, just off Massachusetts Avenue. Originally, the site was known as the Mt. Vernon Girls Seminary, and during the Second World War it became the Navy's Washington, DC, Communications Facility until the DHS took it over.

The new Department of Homeland Security Headquarters was to be permanently located at the old St. Elizabeth's Mental Hospital site in Northeast Washington, DC, on the hills above the Anacostia River. From the beginning of this project, the General Services Administration had been spending an enormous amount of money and was increasingly behind in both budget and timetable, another typical GSA federal building procurement failure. It is very difficult to do federal public-private partnerships for a variety of reasons (OMB scoring on long-term leases to eventually own); this is one of our infrastructure reform proposals discussed in Chapter 5. In 2014, reports indicated that the entire headquarters program would be scrapped after spending over $1.5 billion and completing only the new Coast Guard headquarters building. In late 2015, funding was provided in House Speaker Boehner's omnibus appropriations Christmas "present" that would keep the DHS headquarters site project alive. From my infrastructure finance experience discussed in earlier chapters, my public-private partnership approach would have worked, but no, the same old outdated procurement models continued.

The initial phase of the DHS headquarters project, unfolding on the 176-acre site of the former campus of St. Elizabeth's, had been the design and construction of this new headquarters for the US Coast Guard, a unit of DHS. A design-build contract on that portion of the overall project had been awarded by the US General Services

Administration (GSA) to Clark Construction, of Bethesda, MD, and the impressive building itself was completed.

A total of eleven agencies, out of the twenty-two in the DHS, were expected to be headquartered on this St. Elizabeth's site by the time the entire program was completed. Finally, in April 2019, the new $5 billion headquarters of the Department of Homeland Security, with its commanding view of the nation's capital, opened. Thousands of DHS employees would relocate to the new campus that month.

Meanwhile, President Trump had been purging the department's leadership and, in effect, changing this agency focused primarily on counterterrorism to one defined by its immigration enforcement efforts—and buried in some of the White House's immigration controversies.

Unfortunately, several of the senior DHS leaders who had gathered to cut the ribbon the previous week at the new campus—the largest federal construction project in Washington since the Pentagon—would not be staying long enough to work there.

In a span of six days, Trump fired Homeland Security Secretary Kirstjen Nielson; her deputy, Claire M. Grady; the head of Immigration and Customs Enforcement, Ronald Vitiello; and the director of the Secret Service, Randolph D. "Tex" Alles. He also left the Transportation Security Administration and US Customs and Border Protection—the country's largest law enforcement agency—with leaders in acting roles.

The firings prompted senior GOP leaders to publicly ask the president not to fire anyone else, while DHS officials noted humorously that their new offices were on the grounds of the government's first mental institution.

Indeed, John Sununu and I looked back on this experience with great disappointment. Now in 2023, I agree that creating the Department of Homeland Security was a mistake, and the George Bush administration had been correct when you look at its bureaucratic structure and implementation. By 2024, US immigration policy was a third rail for the entire DHS family.

The US Citizenship and Immigration Services assumed responsibility for the immigration service functions of the federal government in 2003 after the Homeland Security Act of 2002 reorganized the former Immigration and Naturalization Service and separated the former agency into three components within the Department of Homeland Security.

Federal immigration and naturalization agencies date back to 1891 when the Office of the Superintendent of Immigration was created and placed in the Treasury Department.

In early 2018, the US Citizenship and Immigration Services director announced the agency's new website mission statement to staff members.

The old mission statement read that the USCIS secures America's promise as a nation of immigrants by providing accurate and useful information to our customers, granting immigration and citizenship benefits, promoting awareness and understanding of citizenship, and ensuring the integrity of our immigration system.

The new statement, in the first Trump administration, now reads that the US Citizenship and Immigration Services administers the nation's lawful immigration system, safeguarding its integrity and promise by efficiently and fairly adjudicating requests for immigration benefits while protecting Americans, securing the homeland, and honoring our values.

Actually, other agencies like the US Agency for International Development, the Housing and Urban Development, and the Consumer Financial Protection Bureau made similar "mission statement" modifications to their websites in the early days of the Trump administration.

These federal building fiascos happen because of so-called OMB scoring, wherein long-term operating leases have to accrue their long-term costs in that initial year. Consequently, federal agencies are effectively precluded from engaging in public-private partnerships, although Congress has been reviewing that infrastructure issue once again.

Years ago in 1992, Senator Moynihan was asked by the Chief Justice to assist the Supreme Court in expediting the construction of a much-needed administrative center. The Senator was then Chairman of the Senate Environment and Public Works Committee with jurisdiction over federal buildings and the Capitol Architect.

Quickly, under the leadership of his Legislative Director, Bob Peck (later Public Buildings Commissioner), the Capitol Architect established a trust fund. That fund issued the design-build competitive RFP, and Boston Properties was the winning bidder. The Supreme Court, as the third co-equal branch of the government, did not have to go through the OMB scoring nonsense.

Earlier, I noted working closely with Senator Daniel Patrick Moynihan, and amongst the many activities was the public-private partnership concept that was put in place by the Senator, as Chairman of the Senate Environment and Public Works Committee, for this project. Today, the resultant Marshall Building houses agencies that support the work of federal courts, including the Administrative Office, Judicial Center, and Sentencing Commission. It was completed in 1992 and two years later named for Thurgood Marshall (1908–93), the first African American to sit on the US Supreme Court.

And the project was very successful, on time and under budget! This approach is what I had in mind for the new Department of Homeland Security Headquarters.

I did talk about the low audit rates, staffing shortages, and revenue collection challenges at the Internal Revenue Service earlier in the third chapter on tax reform. Now we will review their IT situation, particularly in light of the 2017 tax cut legislation, which seems to be more complicated than its predecessor regulations. The law made the farthest-reaching changes to the US tax system since 1986, lowering tax rates, limiting tax breaks, and restructuring the way the US taxes multinational companies.

But like so many other agencies, IRS information technology efforts have struggled for years, most recently during the 2017 individual tax filing deadline when an IT failure prevented the agency from processing returns and forced a one-day extension in April 2018.

The IRS was also bracing for a 17 percent increase in phone calls due to the new tax law, planning to revise forms and publications and provide staff training. So, the agency, in a rather conventional way considering their IT track record, announced at the very end of May 2018 that they would spend $291 million updating 140 computer systems.

The CBO estimated that hiking the agency's budget by $20 billion over the coming decade would boost federal revenue by $61 billion. A $40 billion raise would result in $103 billion in revenue. Increased IRS enforcement would likely promote higher levels of voluntary compliance, but this budgeting trend coupled with an already weak IT platform suggested trouble ahead.

And then the pandemic laws of 2020–1 required an already strained department to rise to the challenge of moving billions of dollars into American bank accounts. Somehow the IRS scraped through administering the various coronavirus programs, calling back employees, and reopening their large regional centers.

The Biden administration aimed to alter this situation in the September 12, 2022, Inflation Reduction Act, which included about $79 billion in additional funding over ten years for the IRS, much to go to IT. The issue was what IT strategy would be pursued: the "beltway bandits," or alternatively what the US Digital Service and 18F would recommend.

A new IT issue had cropped up because of the Edward Snowden disclosures regarding US government National Security Agency (NSA) metadata retrieval and analysis. Congress passed reform legislation in 2015; however, private sector metadata gatherers such as Google and Facebook insisted that government activities be even further restricted under the guise of privacy, while they gather personal data on every American for their own commercial benefit.

Google and Facebook know more about American citizens than the NSA ever will; and with their enormous Washington, DC, lobbying operations have so far carried the day. It is noteworthy that a slight majority of Americans (51 percent to 49 percent), per Pew Research, supported the FBI request to Apple in 2016 to "open" the encrypted iPhone of the San Bernardino terrorist assassin.

Apple, Amazon, Facebook, Google, and Microsoft spent a combined $64 million to shape US regulations and stave off government scrutiny in 2018, according to their disclosure reports filed in January 2019, an uptick in lobbying that reflects the industry's policy battles.

The tech sector's biggest spender was Google: it shelled out more than $21 million in 2018 to lobby Congress, the White House, and key federal agencies on issues including online privacy. That marked a new record for Google, the second time in two years that it has outspent companies across all industries to influence policy in the nation's capital.

In the spring of 2018, a sweeping set of new European Economic Union data privacy regulations impacted US internet companies, requiring them to modify their data practices to avoid steep penalties. Companies sent notices to their users about updates to privacy policies and user agreements aimed at making their data collection practices more transparent.

The moves were an effort to prepare for the General Data Protection Regulation (GDPR), which went into effect that Friday, May 25, and required companies to give full disclosure about what they do with the digital data they collect and offer their users more control over their information. The EU was way ahead of the US in this important IT regulatory approach.

A key perspective on government spending is the federal contracts in the twelve major consulting areas, which totaled $43 billion in fiscal 2010, with companies such as Lockheed Martin, Deloitte, and Booz Allen among the biggest recipients of awards. As pointed out earlier, many of these contracts are in the IT communications sector, and chances are that they have or will fail.

And here is another perspective: Vicki Hildebrand, Transportation Department CIO, pointed out during an April 2018 panel hosted by Foreign Affairs and the Advanced Technology Academic Research Center that she knew it was not a very common thing that you hear from people in government; that is, we have a lot of spending out there; we need to spend more wisely.

Hildebrand also pointed to the government procurement process (as opposed to insourcing), which she suggested lends itself to higher prices than private sector acquisitions. Prior to joining Transportation, Hildebrand spent thirty years at Hewlett-Packard Enterprise, ultimately serving as vice president for customer and partner advocacy, and indicated she was rather surprised when she arrived from the private sector that the government is charged more than the private sector. And sometimes for services that aren't quite as good.

A few years back, there was a July 2015 announcement about the winner of the huge Department of Defense's Healthcare Management Systems Modernization, or DHMSM, project. Contrary to expectations, DOD awarded the contract to the team of Cerner, Leidos (SAIC/Lockheed), and Accenture at a "discounted" price of $4.3 billion.

The project—which aimed to update the Defense Department's IT health records system and, most importantly, establish seamless medical data-sharing between the DOD, Veterans Affairs, and the private sector—would be watched closely over the next couple of years. Its success was not only important for the DOD but would also have a significant impact on the national health IT landscape and the challenges it currently faces.

There was a good chance it would fail, and there was serious slippage noted in a Senate Veterans Affairs hearing in the fall of 2018. It seems to never end, as I told the Committee staff afterwards, briefing them on the services' approach via the year 2000 Navy Marine Corps intranet.

Unfortunately, individual departments have traditionally taken the lead on their IT procurements.

The General Services Administration now plays the pivotal role; this is a summary I prepared of the GSA Government IT Initiatives from their website:

1. *Cybersecurity: Improving federal cybersecurity is a key initiative of the Administration and an integral part of the mission for all federal agencies. GSA plays a strong leadership role in providing innovative cybersecurity products, services, and programs to our customers.*
2. *Data Center Optimization Initiative (DCOI): We help federal agencies optimize and modernize data centers and IT infrastructure, and encourage shared services marketplace participation as part of DCOI in compliance with the Federal Information Technology Acquisition Reform Act (FITARA).*

3. *Digital Strategy:* We are building a twenty-first-century government that procures and manages devices, applications, and data in smart, secure, and affordable ways, enabling the American people to access high-quality digital government information and services anywhere, anytime, on any device.
4. *Emerging Citizen Technology:* The demand for more automated, self-service access to public services grows each day. Join our efforts to find practical use cases for modern technologies like artificial intelligence, blockchain, virtual and augmented reality, and social technologies.
5. *FedRAMP:* We lead efforts to launch, maintain, and manage the Federal Risk and Authorization Management Program by providing technical expertise, coordinating efforts across government, and staffing the FedRAMP program management office.
6. *Identity, Credential, and Access Management (ICAM):* We help contractors and federal employees navigate the security clearance and credentialing process.
7. *Mobile Government:* Mobile technology is changing the way people find and use information and services. Find out how the government uses these tools to serve citizens in this anytime, anywhere world.

It sounds good; it is progress; but reform is missing. I noted earlier that in 2015, the Code of Federal Regulations totaled 178,277 pages in 237 volumes, according to studies. At the end of the year, there were 3,297 new rules in the pipeline; 218 were economically significant, meaning that they were projected to have an annual impact of $100 million or more.

And again, the Federal Acquisition Regulations, under the General Services Administration, are a part of this Code of Federal Regulations.

I am proud to say: The Navy Marine Corps Intranet Procurement in 2000 was—and is—a very good information technology (IT) "services" model for government. It was competitively bid so all concerns had a chance; but risk transfer dissuaded some firms from participating.

What is surprising is the use of the "national security" buzzword to buttress their beltway bandit arguments, ignoring the lessons learned from the breakup of the AT&T monopoly in the early 1980s, as I talk about in Chapter 2. The Pentagon back then supported the AT&T monopoly at the time, not realizing the new technologies that would evolve to the benefit of the armed services of our country, as noted in Chapter 2.

In 2024, the Justice Department antitrust suit against Apple brought back the memory of how AT&T owned everything; Apple wanted to sell you everything.

As the pandemic mushroomed in size, underfunded and understaffed state unemployment offices nationwide were struggling to do their jobs. In Florida, according to press reports, the state's phone lines were jammed, and its website repeatedly crashed, creating delays for stimulus checks and other coronavirus relief hindered by dated IT technology, government rollout, and significant corruption in filing false claims.

It seems that Florida's problems started about a decade earlier under the leadership of then-Gov. Rick Scott (R), who slashed unemployment benefits in the name of austerity. He was, on the other hand, a technology business executive and should have known better. But when local officials put in place a $77 million computer system to process applications, auditors reported on repeated deficiencies, including errors that denied people benefits.

And at the Centers for Disease Control and Prevention (CDC) early on in the pandemic, hospital data acquisition was crucial. According to the press reports, the United States had tried—and failed—over the past fifteen years to build a system to share such information in a crisis. When the pandemic started, nothing existed except the National Healthcare Safety Network.

Nearly 70 percent of corporate boards cited the impact of Covid-19 for an increase in spending on IT and digital capabilities, and the coronavirus pandemic had put corporate information technology in the spotlight, as companies turned to digital tools to keep running amid lockdowns and travel restrictions. The shift to remote work during the coronavirus pandemic also enshrined cloud-native cybersecurity companies.

CIOs and other corporate technology leaders over the 2020–1 time frame found themselves in greater positions of leadership, taking a critical role in facilitating the shift to remote work, reconfiguring supply chains, speeding up the automation of factories, and moving stores and restaurants online, executives and industry analysts say.

CIOs also had a hand in strengthening the security and resilience of their companies, which were tested as never before as the shift to remote work and collaboration tools opened new vulnerabilities for hackers.

Chief information officers with above-average skills and experience are expected to draw average annual salaries of $260,250 in 2022, up 2.7 percent from 2021, after rising 0.5 percent this year from 2020, according to data provided by recruiting firm Robert Half International Inc.

Interestingly, in terms of IT personnel, I read elsewhere that only 6 percent of federal employees are under age thirty, and nearly five times more federal IT employees are older than sixty than under thirty. No wonder federal IT infrastructure has been a challenge over the years. Many belonged to the so-called Potomac Officers Club, which is a membership organization within the government contracting community. It is one of four publications belonging to Executive Mosaic and hosts several series of annual events that discuss trends and opportunities in the defense, artificial intelligence, intelligence, cybersecurity, and homeland security industries. It also regularly reports news on the government contracting industry and the many types of companies involved.

A 2018 report from the National Center for Education Statistics found United States, workers ranked last among eighteen industrial countries when it came to problem solving in technology-rich environments or using digital technology to evaluate information and perform practical tasks. This was one of the reasons educators, leaders, parents, and students wanted schools to reopen in the fall of 2020.

And in early 2024 I was impressed to read that almost twenty universities, including the Massachusetts Institute of Technology, the University of California at Berkeley, and Indiana University, offered clinics as part of a Consortium of Cybersecurity Clinics. The US Cybersecurity and Infrastructure Security Agency was supporting these university-based clinics as well. The National Security Agency recently awarded grants to three universities to create cybersecurity clinics, and a $20 million grant program from Google was funding expansions of these clinics.

The Naval Academy (my alma mater) had some very smart young midshipmen; hence, construction was completed in the summer of 2020 after four years for a new and very large cybersecurity academic building called Hopper Hall on the campus (the "Yard"). In 2005, the Navy merged IT and cryptology and created career paths for these specialists, and this new cybersecurity academic building will be needed.

Having graduated from the Naval Academy in 1965, we never envisioned this technology in our curriculum. Computers had just started in the 1950s, and coding with FORTRAN was it. Originally developed by IBM in the 1950s for scientific and engineering applications, FORTRAN came to dominate programming early on, and to my surprise, has been in continuous use.

I made this point at a Naval Academy discussion, noting that the new Hopper Hall could be a fine venue for IT-related symposiums. And I added that as an American computer scientist, mathematician, and United States Navy rear admiral, Grace Hopper was increasingly being recognized as a pioneer of computer programming amidst this semiconductor deluge.

Admiral Hopper earned a PhD in both mathematics and mathematical physics from Yale University, and the annual Hopper IT conference would, in my experience, be very successful for alumni association outreach and Naval Institute publications. Coincidentally, the Naval also re-introduced a mandatory celestial navigation course due to concerns about satellite navigation reliance and being hacked. It was a back-to-the-future moment.

12

The Need for Regular Order, Congress, and the Executive Branch

In mid-2018, based on years of experience with the congressional process, I drafted an article on the concept of what was called Regular Order in the Congress, which is critical for real regulatory reform entitled: "Congress Can Work; It Has the History to Prove It, Returning to Regular Order."

Reading fellow Naval Academy graduate, Senator John McCain's best-seller "The Restless Wave," he talks at length about the congressional legislative process and, in fact, devotes his Chapter to the title, Regular Order. The late Senator described regular order as the key to restoring the bipartisan legislative process that has been in absentia for many years. I totally agree!

As I was involved in many congressional initiatives—particularly the successful 1975–95 deregulation efforts outlined earlier—let me describe what congressional regular order entails.

The US Senate divides its tasks among twenty committees, sixty-eight subcommittees, and four joint committees; and is generally symmetrical with that of the House of Representatives, with a few unfortunate misses.

The United States House of Representatives similarly has twenty-one congressional committees: twenty standing committees and one select committee. All but three committees—the Budget Committee, the Ethics Committee, and the House Administration Committee—are subdivided into subcommittees, of which there are a total of ninety-five, each with its own leadership.

Staff, on both sides of the Capitol, are numerous and play a major role in leveling out the legislative product under a regular order scenario. Regular order is the term applied to the traditional congressional legislative work process, which includes committee hearings, bill markups, and committee and conference reports. Bills must be reported from their committee before being taken up on the floor of the House or Senate.

In recent years, congressional committees have stagnated amidst leadership legislative struggles, gridlock, and continuing resolutions to maintain funding for the next fiscal year beginning October 1. In fact, due to the lack of regular order in the Congress, that is, committees reporting the bills before they go to the floor, members of Congress, in their frustration, have continually introduced their own legislative proposals in historic record amounts, severely taxing the Office of Legal Counsel and sparking record turnover there.

There is a consensus that this Speaker leadership trend began under Newt Gingrich, who was Speaker of the House between 1995 and 1999, and has continued since under Hastert, Boehner, Ryan, Pelosi, and McCarthy/Johnson.

The so-called Speaker Hastert Rule, requiring the majority of the majority GOP approach to voting, was a major part of this House gridlock.

Not only has this led to top-down legislative initiatives, denying committees their pivotal role in regular order; but in recent years there has been a constant river of partisan votes in both chambers, particularly on the House floor.

There is a policy trinity of the Executive, Legislative, and Judicial branches. The President, for the Executive Branch, starts the process normally by giving the annual State of the Union address in early January and then sending a budget request to Congress by the first week in February at the beginning of each legislative year.

This early February budget deadline for Congress synchronizes with the regular order congressional rhythm of the Budget Committees in February and early March, then the Authorizing Committees from late March into June, and the Appropriations Committees follow through July. During the August recess, the House and Senate staffs complete the funding legislation for members to vote first in their respective chambers, then a House-Senate conference and, finally, the final conference report is voted on by both Houses and sent to the president for signature by the end of September as the federal fiscal year begins on October 1.

For the authorizing committees, there are hearings in subcommittees and full committees, followed by markups overseen by the respective Committee Chairman. Then, House Senate conferees are appointed to meet in conference and produce the compromise policy legislation and conference report.

Prior to 1999, major State of the Union presidential recommendations would often be submitted to Congress later as a legislative proposal that could be introduced by request. To simply say, we want to work with Congress is not enough. Congressional members on both sides of the aisle want specific Executive Branch proposals.

In her 2018 book entitled "Leadership," Dorothy Kearns Goodwin draws upon the four presidents she has studied most closely—Abraham Lincoln, Theodore Roosevelt, Franklin D. Roosevelt, and Lyndon B. Johnson. In reading the book, I was struck by Johnson's 1964–5 legislative leadership approach and achievements in the passage of the Civil Rights Act and his Great Society initiatives, including Medicare, Medicaid, the Older Americans Act, and federal education funding, which continue to the present day.

I was just graduating from the Naval Academy in 1965; and it was some twelve years later, in 1977, that my own Washington governmental affairs career began. Somehow, it was the same legislative embroidery: the President had to make specific recommendations to Congress and then create the outside coalitions to effectively demonstrate support so that Congress would be both enabled and able to pass effective bipartisan, consensus legislation, not executive orders, and the excessive ping pong of regulatory rulemakings under the Administrative Procedures Act.

There was a legislative rhythm in Congress, and it started with the target date for the annual budget resolution's to be completed by April 15; but that has seldom happened since the millennium year 2000. In 2018, I watched a House Budget Committee markup in June! This tardiness leads to separate House/Senate budget target complications.

During the traditional August break, House and Senate staff members would optimally work out proposed "conference" compromises and reports so that when the members returned after Labor Day, they could expeditiously pass all appropriations bills by the September 30 fiscal year deadline. This timetable can be expedited.

In summary, Congress should reassert that all bills must be marked up and reported by the relevant committees before going to the House or Senate floor rather than emerging from congressional leadership office suites. The House Democrats adopted this reform when they became the majority in 2017 but seemed to ignore it in practice. Additionally, terminating the GOP Hastert majority of the majority rule in the House would be very helpful in encouraging bipartisan cooperation.

Lastly, the differences between House and Senate bills should be reconciled by actual conference committees rather than in informal talks at the leadership level. Before the late 1990s, a House-Senate Conference would typically have a side-by-side analysis of the various legislative provisions under four columns, that is, House, Senate, and the Executive Branch versions plus a recommended compromise.

This is what regular order is all about. The committee process is what builds the fraternal bonds of civility and friendships! I witnessed some fantastic committee legislative markups in that historic 1975 to 1995 period, which was the key to quality legislation. The members were articulate in their advocacy, polite to their fellow committee members, and respectful of seniority in terms of expertise.

From my own career of thirty years of legislative advocacy from 1975 to 2005, it is critical to restore congressional regular order, which is simply the congressional process through which all legislation must be reported from a related committee to be considered on the floor of the House or Senate. That committee process itself encourages legislative expertise, bipartisan behavior, and cohesive, on-time policy results. The Committee Chairs are well recognized as the leaders of this legislative process, working with the Ranking Member of the other party. The Speaker of the House is essentially the conductor of this orchestra.

In tandem, the Congressional Budget and Impoundment Control Act of 1974 established a new congressional budget process and timetable, a budget committee in each house, and a Congressional Budget Office.

And the traditional State of the Union address was in January as the president outlined his budget proposal and priorities and sent that message to Congress in early February so that the congressional budget process began on time and was completed (authorizing and appropriation) before the end of the federal government's fiscal year on September 30.

Yet today, the lack of substantive legislation and the use (abuse) of continuing resolutions have become common any time that Congress and the president do not reach agreement on spending levels and fail to enact regular appropriations by the start of the federal fiscal year on October 1.

Between fiscal years 2010 and 2022, forty-seven continuing resolutions passed, allowing Congress to delay its duties for as long as 176 days at a time. On three occasions, not even a continuing resolution was approved, resulting in a government shutdown. This astonishing record of legislative failure is a direct result of not adhering to the important committee role, the fundamental precept of regular order.

I would add that if Congress is going to function in the way intended by our founders, it will need to know that the Supreme Court, in the recent removal of the Chevron Doctrine priority for regulators, has tasked lawmakers to return to the writing of much more detailed legislation that courts can readily administer. This will require a return to regular order and the expertise of committees and their staffs amidst timely oversight policy hearings with sequential open markups of their legislative products.

There was a time, decades ago, when the *Washington Post* published on a daily basis the Congressional hearing schedule for that day and reported on those hearings, establishing the Post as the national newspaper for congressional coverage. But that is no longer the case for some reason. The Post has lost much of its talent for coverage in this legislative/administrative scenario. And, as a result, it has been losing subscribers and millions of dollars.

Real regulatory reform was possible then as Congress and the Executive Branch were in tandem regarding the public policy process, and substantive legislation reported from authorization committees was the norm.

Since around the millennium year 2000, regular order in Congress has collapsed, leaving in its place the partisan regulatory rule-making jungle that law firms might enjoy but ignore the public interest. I have labeled this regulatory ping pong, and we will never be able to legislate the types of bipartisan policy initiatives I talk about in this book until we return to regular order.

Perhaps the June 2024 Supreme Court demise of the Chevron Doctrine, which strongly supported the role of federal agencies' rulemaking authority and the resultant ping pong, will hasten that return.

It was January 6, 2025, and I thought about a return to regular order as we approached the second Donald Trump inauguration on January 20, noting the invasion of the US Capitol four years earlier on January 6 and the Democratic National Committee chairmanship election to be held on February 1, 2025.

Yes, it might be time to reflect once again on last year's November 5, 2024, election and the resounding Democratic Party defeat. What did it mean? Numerous articles have tried to analyze what happened.

It was actually quite simple; Democratic voters didn't turn out—and those who did moved toward Donald Trump. (And CNN reported a drop from 1.8 million prime-time viewers in 2020 to only 394,000 in 2024, a 45 percent drop.) Why did this happen? Nationwide voter turnout for both parties was down slightly from 2020. But among counties that President Biden won in 2020, declines were sharpest among Democrats. While Vice President Kamala Harris's efforts moved some Democratic voters to the polls in battleground states, Trump won them all.

Trump won just under half the popular vote, only 1.6 percent more than Vice President Kamala Harris received. With a public disapproval rating of 50 percent, he is the least popular presidential winner in modern times. Yet he has won twice against Democratic opponents Hillary Clinton in 2016 and Joe Biden (nee Kamala Harris) in 2024. Joe Biden received some 81 million votes in 2020, but his unfortunate surrogate, Kamala Harris, received only 68 million votes in 2024 as of the following morning after the Trump victory had been announced. As the West Coast voting results came in, Harris was to add to her tally, but it was meaningless.

One of the political realities today is that a new generation of leadership is essential; candidates in the thirty-to-fifty-year bracket are needed, no more folks in the sixty-five to eighty age spectrum. Let them join the AARP. And with that new leadership must come a return to congressional and White House "regular order," wherein legislation must be reported from committees, State of the Union presidential addresses are in early January, and federal budgets are delivered to Congress by early February. Hakeem Jeffries, the Democratic Minority Leader, has indicated support for this return to regular order.

The public policy chaos of the last twenty-some years, with unending continuing resolutions, has to be replaced with stability, statesmanlike behavior, and results including reducing the federal deficit. The Fed reduced its interest rates, but mortgage rates are stubbornly high, with their reliance on the US Treasury's ability to market its borrowings, the historically large federal deficit clouding that market.

It now seems clear that Democratic voters were very disappointed when Joe Biden (being advised by his White House team) announced on April 25, 2024, that he would run for a second term despite polls at the time showing a majority of Democrats did not want him to seek a second term. In doing so, Amtrak Joe launched one of the greatest political train wrecks in US history.

Beginning with the inaugural, those early years 2021–2 in that first term were, for the most part, stellar. Whether it was Covid, the economy, family, or whatever—it was good and his team was good. Why they went for that second term will be for the historians, as it invited the secrecy to make Joe look good; he had to be responsible for everything good.

Yet the American public became suspicious as no other political leaders were on the team, there seemed to be no collegiality, very few White House cabinet meetings were held, and most consequentially, there were no primaries no excitement, and no new candidates. And when Biden finally handed the baton to the little-known Harris, the Democrats were too far behind to make up the distance amidst the low Democratic turnout.

Harris, or another Democrat, nominated at a convention following exciting primaries, could easily have won the White House and Congress. But eighty-two-year-old Joe and his White House silenced the Democratic Party, and the price now seems to have been a very steep four years in the penalty box.

Support sagged despite efforts by Harris's campaign to shore up Black and Hispanic votes with targeted rallies and policy proposals. But who knew that the then DNC Chairman was a Black Yale/Georgetown lawyer named Jamie Harrison? We have since read that the Democratic National Committee laid off staff shortly after the election due to financial problems, only to read that the Democrats had not spent millions they had raised.

Yes, the 2025 Democratic National Committee chairmanship election is to be held on February 1, 2025, at the party's winter meeting in National Harbor, Maryland, to determine the next chairperson of the Democratic National Committee. They better get it right! IDs should be checked at the door; no one above sixty-five is allowed.

In 1983, I was a Founder with Chairman Chuck Manatt of the Democratic National Committee Headquarters Building on South Capitol Street and now I am eighty-three years old in 2025. I will emphasize real regulatory reform will always be essential for political leadership, and it will require regular order in our Congress and the White House to achieve.

Following President Donald Trump's Inaugural on January 20, 2025, he signed twenty-six executive orders that same day including, in his first executive action, the rescission of seventy-eight executive actions implemented by the prior Biden administration. In his first inaugural day in 2017, he signed only one executive order but then set the record of 220 executive orders in his four-year term. These had been prepared quietly in the weeks beforehand by various interest groups.

Real Regulatory Reform and the Need for Regular Order were never more apparent.

Conclusion

In writing this book, it developed from a broader undertaking to write a non-fiction memoir leading up to the Millennium year and beyond, and how we failed to take that opportunity here in the United States to reflect on where we have been, so to speak, and where we are going as a nation. Unfortunately, we fell to the vicissitudes of a narrow security argument called Y2K in the millennium year 2000.

While that Millennium memoir project is still underway, it seemed timely to concentrate on a separate work regarding my own professional journey, participating in the very successful economic deregulation efforts that began just as I was arriving in Washington, DC, in the mid-1970s. I have always been very proud of these public policy endeavors and their public benefit.

In this book's various chapters, I addressed Railroad Deregulation, Telecom Reform/AT&T Breakup, Tax Reform, Electric Energy Deregulation, Infrastructure Investment Commission and Subsequent Public-Private Partnership renaissance, Health Care Reform including the 2020 coronavirus pandemic, NAFTA/Mexican Energy Reform, Transportation Infrastructure Investment Reform (TIFIA), Foreign Technology Challenges in Government Procurement, (Maglev), Federal Information Technology (IT) Reform, Navy Marine Corps Intranet, and Thoroughbred Racing Reform.

I had the good fortune to personally play a leading role in all of these major economic reform endeavors.

From the 1970s to the 1990s, there was always a triad of the Executive, Legislative, and Judicial Branches of government involved. Congress passed railroad and electricity deregulation with White House support.

Regular Order in the congressional legislative process was the critical bipartisan pathway. Since that time, rulemakings under the Administrative Procedures Act had become the go-to partisan option, resulting in a sort of regulatory ping pong that the Supreme Court addressed in June 2024 by removing the dominance of the Chevron Doctrine in a Securities Exchange Commission case.

Indeed, even the MCI-Sprint inspired breakup of AT&T gained its early momentum in congressional hearings but eventually culminated in a momentous court decision based on a consent decree.

Two decades ago, the US government tried to break up Microsoft Corp. It accused the company of leveraging its operating-system monopoly to squash the rival Netscape browser. An epic yearlong trial ended in the summer of the millennium year 2000 when a federal judge found Microsoft guilty of antitrust violations and ordered it split in two. But the breakup order was reversed on appeal, and the Microsoft case was settled.

Microsoft was not the same business monopoly model as AT&T. Additionally, it was new technology, as was Google, Apple, Facebook, and the rest. However, they are all now under the microscope, particularly Google and Facebook, regarding the privacy topic.

It is a different time when one notes that since 2000 there have been

1. Six airline mergers, reducing the number of major carriers from ten to four.
2. At least forty-two pharmaceutical mergers.
3. Four companies that control 76 percent of the nation's soybean market and
4. Only four major national consumer banks are left: JPMorgan Chase, Bank of America, Citigroup, and Wells Fargo.

What we did in that 1970s–1990s time bracket were all very challenging bipartisan public policy endeavors, and I was proud of this track record. But after the year 2000, it seemed different, and I now thought it important to write this book as what we did was real regulatory reform, not political rhetoric (get rid of red tape) or regulatory rulemaking ping pong, as I termed it.

The various industry restructurings that I described in this book were essentially completed before the Millennium year, with the exception of the public-private partnership infrastructure investment sector in the United States, which went into high gear shortly after 2000 following twenty-five years of missionary work, congressional testimony, and policy leadership.

That started with Senator Daniel Patrick Moynihan's request to me in 1990 to help him open the infrastructure sector as government could not do it all, which led to my chairing the 1992 Infrastructure Investment Commission and the publishing of our report, Financing the Future, the following year recommending a federal focus on credit enhancement, lending, and project finance.

I was fortunate to participate in a number of the earlier 1975—95 regulatory reform efforts as an advocate here in Washington, DC. Typically, there was a coalition formed and an analysis was performed regarding the problem(s), often by top economists. Then, the appropriate public policy solution was done.

Much of the regulation stemmed from the 1930s or earlier (railroads!) and was simply outdated. For Republican members of Congress, I would emphasize the phrase, let the market work, and for Democrats, it was simply, let competition thrive, for the very same recommendation.

These massive undertakings have, for the most part, worked out very well. Railroad CEOs, even today, talk about the Staggers Act as their renaissance moment. Telecom and electric energy have had similar successes. As the reader will have noticed, I told each industry's story, chapter by chapter, illustrating my own personal role.

As to the Need for Regular Order, in writing this book both at the start and finish, it was increasingly clear that real regulatory reform requires a period of stable, bipartisan, good government-type congressional hearings and policy discussions. That is what we had in the 1970s through the 1990s. Sure, there were speed bumps, but regular order prevailed; committee markups were impressive, and quality legislation, such as I have described from my own personal involvement, advanced.

I recall back in June 2023 when then Speaker McCarthy promised to pass all twelve appropriations bills that make up the annual budget and send them to the Senate, and called on the Senate to do the same, and then conference. He was right, and my *Wall Street Journal* agreed that this is the process Congress is supposed to use, entitled Regular Order, but it hasn't been done since the 1990s. Instead, lawmakers often end up merging the bills or negotiating them outside of a formal conference process. I knew all of that, but it was confirmational to read the same.

Because without regular order, you do not have the congressional committee process in place to develop bipartisan legislation, particularly in the budget and regulatory sector. Speaker McCarthy failed in passing the appropriations bills; chaos prevailed and he was gone shortly thereafter. His successor, Mike Johnson, in 2024 was running the same gauntlet.

Earlier, in the 2019 budget year, the government ran up a deficit of $984 billion, the most in seven years. The Congressional Budget Office was forecasting that the deficit for 2020 would hit $1 trillion and stay above $1 trillion for the next decade. The country last ran annual $1 trillion annual deficits from 2009 through 2012 during and after the Great Recession financial crisis. Think tanks kept reminding their audience of this bipartisan spending and partisan tax cutting to no avail. And continuing resolutions became the annual soup du jour of congressional budgets.

Issues like regulatory reform were now left to the agencies and partisan regulatory rulemakings or as, I termed it, Regulatory Ping Pong, which I talked about in the prologue and introduction; but now curtailed by the June 2024 Supreme Court Chevron Doctrine ruling limiting that practice.

In 2000, there was talk of the urgency for much-needed bipartisan immigration reform legislation, an excellent example of how regular order can be so effective. I remember in 2018 when then White House Chief of Staff Mick Mulvaney told a crowd at a private gathering in England that the Trump administration needed more immigrants for the US economy to continue growing. In this world of problems, regular order, wherein committee members trust their colleagues, tough issues can be solved. But if not, the issues get even tougher.

Now let's look at our GDP situation in the context of economic normalcy and the evasive political path to needed regulatory reforms. Over the course of President Obama's first year in office, GDP dropped 2.5 percent amidst the Great Recession. But in 2010, GDP growth recovered, surging 2.5 percent. And growth was already positive when President Trump first took office, jumping from 1.6 percent in 2016 to 2.2 percent in 2017. The economy was estimated to have gained 4.2 percent in the second quarter of 2018, but that still paled in comparison to the 5.1 percent and 4.9 percent growth in the second and third quarters of 2014 in the Obama administration. However, Larry Kudlow, Director of the National Economic Council, in political remarks to the Economic Club of New York in September 2018, said he expected US budget deficits of about 4 percent to 5 percent of the country's economic output for the next one to two years.

A year later, in 2019, Kudlow was to follow our infrastructure investment panel at a Washington D.C. infrastructure conference. Citing our panel in his remarks, he told the audience that infrastructure investors would provide the financing and his White House would streamline permitting.

And despite his opinions, the facts were that the federal government was now—at the end of 2018—projected to borrow a total of $1.3 trillion, more than double the amount borrowed the previous year and the largest annual borrowing figure since the 2010 Great Recession, according to estimates released at the time by the Trump Treasury Department.

None of us were aware at that time of the lurking coronavirus which spawned massive spending by both the Trump and Biden administrations, thus unleashing an added deluge of deficit spending. I really did not see a clear path to the regulatory reforms needed if this fiscal misbehavior continued.

As the coronavirus entered the picture and was taking its human toll in 2020, the deficit was exploding! Some 80 percent of the federal government workforce is located outside of the Washington, DC, metropolitan area; but now all federal employees were in the remote, virtual Zoom world.

At the time, unemployment mushroomed from state by state. I had read a few articles on the European subsidized employment model. It had limits; but certainly, its advantages in terms of a focus on corporate employment stability in a crisis made sense.

We did the opposite, focusing on the individual, and now the equivalent US subsidies had to work through new congressional programs, and everyone suffered while antiquated state IT programs were severely challenged. I had the thought that the US labor community might study this European approach and take a strong stand. Keep the workforce on the job!

The United States's political bickering since the millennium year 2000 has impacted our ability to make quality bipartisan decisions. Now we need to turn to the European Union for regulatory answers.

Margrethe Vestager was a Danish social liberal politician and served as Executive Vice President of the European Commission for a Europe Fit for the Digital Age. In that role, as European Union competition chief since 2014, Vestager targeted Alphabet's Google, Amazon.com, Apple, and Facebook for allegedly abusing their market positions or dodging taxes. Her heavy fines and penalties earned the EU antitrust watchdog a reputation around the world as one of the only regulators unafraid to stand up to US tech giants.

Interestingly, her plan to use regulation to restore trust in technology—starting with artificial intelligence (AI)—was something even Google and Facebook Inc. were conceding was necessary for the sake of their businesses. It reminded me of our zone of freedom in the railroad deregulation context.

When Vestager unveiled her proposal in February 2020 to regulate artificial intelligence (AI), she said the EU wants to embrace the benefits the technology brings while also tackling its risks. Her approach now is to focus regulation on the applications that affect people's lives or legal status.

And I was encouraged after their 2018 midterm elections victory when House Democrats began detailing plans to wield their newfound oversight power in the next Congress. They signaled that House Democrats, while wary of the risks of alienating voters who backed the president, are fully embracing their midterm victory as a mandate to dig deep into the actions of the executive branch. But the reality was that little happened without congressional regular order and corresponding executive branch legislative proposals.

About the same time, the US Treasury under the Trump administration announced it had collected a record $7 billion in import tariffs in September, as new duties kicked in on apparel, tools, electronics, and other consumer goods from China.

Two years later, the incoming Biden US Trade Representative mysteriously maintained the Trump status quo for leverage, she would say. Talk of trade reform disappeared. There were no regular order trade oversight hearings in Congress, and the policy process of the United States continued to meander.

As mentioned in the prior chapters, I served on the Board of Stanford's Global Projects Center (Infrastructure Finance), a well-regarded university platform, as it was very timely and needed for the public policy path. Real regulatory reform needs this type of intellectual discussion and research. It is about modernizing the regulatory process to make it more efficient and effective, not playing retail politics for partisan advantage.

In a back-to-the-future moment, noting the book's Chapter 2 covering the AT&T breakup, I was fascinated to read that the Department of Justice Antitrust Division had determined that rules limiting film studios' influence over theaters had outlived their usefulness in a movie business that had changed considerably since the curbs were first imposed.

The rules were laid out in decades-old legal settlements known as the Paramount consent decrees. The decrees followed the Supreme Court's blockbuster 1948 ruling in *U.S. v. Paramount Pictures* that covered the nation's eight major motion-picture distributors. Amazingly, we never brought this case up in the 1982 AT&T breakup, which today surprises me.

This 1948 ruling largely prohibited the studios from owning the theaters where their movies played, as well as from requiring theaters to play either several of their movies or none at all, or when and how films could be shown in specific metro areas. The decrees were no longer needed, according to the Justice Department, because the conspiracy among movie-industry giants from the 1940s no longer existed.

And that reality hit when, in July 2023, the national board of the Screen Actors Guild-American Federation of Television and Radio Artists, or SAG-AFTRA, voted unanimously to go on strike. It was the first time film and television performers had staged a work stoppage since 1980, when former SAG president Ronald Reagan was campaigning for the White House. Hollywood's writers were already striking over these artificial intelligence issues more than two months earlier after the Writers Guild of America, a union that represents film and television writers, started striking for similar reasons. But again, there were no regular order oversight hearings.

Interestingly, in 1996 under regular order, the Communications Decency Act (Section 230) was passed by Congress. While allowing the Googles, Facebooks and Twitters to not be held accountable for what their users post on their sites, it does prohibit certain kinds of content, including violence and hate speech, without the threat of liability if they remove a user's post—or expel them entirely. This was new economic territory, and creditably these three digital technology companies, under public pressure, had invested heavily in new rules, creating powerful artificial intelligence tools and hiring thousands of employees to monitor what happens on their sites.

In fact, UC Berkeley's fastest growing class was data science 101 to study the science of mining the tidal wave of digital information that floods our lives. More than 300 universities offer data majors, as companies like Google can't hire enough specialists.

In June 2020, Alphabet Inc.'s Google said it had reached agreements with selected publishers around the world to license (and compensate) news content, a significant development in the years-long tug of war between the tech giant and media companies. So, now in the digital economy, we have arrived at the intersection of public policy and privacy. But again, no regular oversight hearings.

The European Union (EU), as a large consumer of Silicon Valley digital commerce, had already moved by addressing new regulations known as the General Data Protection Regulation (GDPR) in EU law on data protection and privacy for all individuals within the EU and the European Economic Area (EEA). However, the United States was in the midst of an intensifying debate over monopoly power and privacy, with Democrats calling for much tougher antitrust enforcement and Republicans joining them in accusing big tech companies of abusing their market dominance. Yet again, no bipartisan legislation; and it turns out that US cellphone plans are more expensive than those in Europe due to this concentration and lack of competition.

While the second chapter in the book deals with the 1982 telecom breakup of AT&T, the eleventh chapter focuses on government information technology (IT) procurement reform, noting our groundbreaking 2000 Navy Marine Corps Intranet procurement.

In the absence of regular order and real regulatory reform, presidential executive orders were common and, as an example, the Biden administration's unfortunate July 9, 2021, White House competition executive order was over fifty pages of unfounded regulatory nonsense. Even our very successful Staggers Act railroad deregulation was singled out for criticism.

So, it is fair to say that there is an important role for reform where there is consensus as to not only the need, that is, the problem, but also a well-grounded economic solution.

But with the lack of regular order, Presidential Executive Orders were popular. In 2014, I remember well when there was the GOP spat over Obama's issuance of Executive Orders, and in November 2014 I pointed out to Jeff Zients at the White House (Jeff, in 2024, had been the Chief of Staff for President Biden) that by any measure, President Obama had been very judicious in using that privilege and Josh Earnest in your press office ought to make that point continuously. As for strategy, early next year the President gives a first-class State of the Union focused on the economy, makes clear his budget will be sent up on time shortly thereafter for Congressional Regular Order review, and informs that major recommendations for Congressional action, including infrastructure, tax reform, immigration reform, and trade, will be sent up as well in legislative form to make this the most effective Congress in years.

President Obama issued a total of 276 executive orders, per the American Presidency Project at the University of California-Santa Barbara. That's fewer than the total of 381 issued by Ronald Reagan and the 291 used by George W. Bush during their eight years. Among Democratic presidents, both Bill Clinton (364 executive orders in eight years) and Jimmy Carter (320 in four years) turned to executive orders more than Obama.

As I have noted, Joe Biden's staff seem wedded to them as well, setting records with the number of Executive Orders, Memorandums, and Actions taken in the first two months of his presidency, with 117 as of July 2023. Donald Trump issued 219 executive orders during his four years between 2017 and 2021.

1. Harry S. Truman 907
2. Dwight D. Eisenhower 484
3. John F. Kennedy 214
4. Lyndon B. Johnson 325
5. Richard Nixon 346
6. Gerald R. Ford 169
7. Jimmy Carter 320
8. Ronald Reagan 381
9. George H. W. Bush 166
10. William J. Clinton 364
11. George W. Bush 291
12. Barack Obama 276
13. Donald Trump 219
14. Joe Biden 162

Biden issued an average of forty-one executive orders per year in office, the third lowest average among the seven presidents who held office since 1981. Donald Trump's (R) average was highest, at fifty-five executive orders, and Barack Obama's (D) average was lowest, at thirty-five.

On another front, regulatory rulemaking, in his first seven years the Obama Administration agencies and departments issued 392 major regulations (economic impact greater than $100 million) with another forty-seven for 2016. This number marginally surpassed George W. Bush at 358 and Bill Clinton at 361. Many of these regulations are required by congressional mandates and are "monitored" in the congressional hearing oversight process, as they should be.

And in the regulatory ping pong race, a 2020 Washington Post analysis from October 30 analysis that I read found that as Trump's first term wound down to a close, his team had rolled back more than 125 rules and policies aimed at protecting the nation's air, water, and land, with forty more rollbacks underway.

Amidst all these government agencies in the Executive or Legislative Branch of our Federal Government, the Judiciary also has its own organizational structure led by the Supreme Court and its Chief Justice John Roberts, who has been a very effective leader of the court in my view despite the partisan challenges posed by a very partisan nominating/confirmation process that has been in place since the millennium year 2000 breakdown of congressional regular order.

In a speech in 2020 at the University of Minnesota Law School that I read, he emphasized the importance of judicial independence from the political branches and civility among his colleagues noting that, for a century, justices had shaken each other's hands before taking the bench to hear arguments. He went on to point out that it's a small thing, perhaps, but it is a repeated reminder that, as our newest colleague put it, we do not sit on opposite sides of an aisle, we do not caucus in separate rooms, we do not serve one party or one interest; we serve one nation. And I want to assure all of you that we will continue to do that. It was their version of regular order.

Relatedly, in June 2024, the Supreme Court had overturned the so-called Chevron Doctrine that had given agencies a priority standing. I actually applauded as Congress would now have to recognize regular order and pass well-written legislation.

A good example would be legislation commonly referred to as immigration reform that has been stalled in Congress primarily due to the lack of regular order and the bipartisan benefit it brings. Whether it was to be the August 2021 Afghan refugee crisis or the thousands of Haitians under a Del Rio, Texas bridge, or just the US need for immigrants, no legislation had moved due to a lack of regular order, oversight, and real regulatory reform. Amidst the unfortunate political rhetoric about the border, the US Immigration and Customs Enforcement (ICE) released its annual report on December 19, 2024, stating that it had deported 271,484 immigrants to nearly 200 countries, the highest tally in a decade, from fiscal year October 1, 2023, to September 30, 2024. In that same annual report, US Customs and Border Protection reported 46,610 encounters with migrants along the US-Mexico border in November, the lowest one-month total since President Biden took office. But you would never learn these facts in the absence of a regular order oversight hearing.

The Biden administration sent Congress a bill in 2021 that would have allowed most of the 11 million undocumented immigrants in the country to get on paths to citizenship. However, due to the lack of hearings and public education, no legislative reforms were enacted, and surging border crossings resulted in ICE expanding rather than reducing detention and deportations.

So, the Biden administration in September 2021 moved to a rulemaking process to make permanent protections for those brought to the US undocumented as children under President Obama. However, earlier in July 2021, a ruling from a federal judge in Texas appointed by President Trump argued that the Obama program violated the Administrative Procedures Act, which governs lengthy rulemakings.

It was unfortunate to see how important policies such as immigration often needed to be subject to a rulemaking process that could be quite partisan, bouncing from one judge to the next as legal briefs were filed, and regulatory ping pong ensued while political rhetoric escalated.

In fact, there were bipartisan immigration legislative proposals, but in a way, they were ad hoc and not in a formal legislative regular order process.

I can resolutely state there are real regulatory obstacles to progress in the governmental sector, particularly in the procurement process. Government IT procurement is the most glaring, as illustrated by the rollout website failure with the initial unveiling of President Obama's 2010 Affordable Care Act. During the 2020 coronavirus pandemic, the IT systems for federal/state unemployment processing were found to be antiques, unable to perform with weeks of delays.

Amidst the pandemic, in September 2020, more than 860,000 women had dropped out of the US labor force to take care of their children as school opening policies were very confusing, even though studies showed that school children were at very low risk for the virus. Additionally, the two national teachers' unions wanted hazardous duty pay.

By year-end, predictions were 200,000 and we were at 250,000 deaths just before the November 2020 election. CDC's Dr. Fauci predicted a surge, and that happened; but the vaccine was slowly gaining traction, with deaths slowing so that only 112 were to die on Memorial Day 2021, bringing the total to almost 600,000 deaths nationwide. The CDC had announced that masks would not be required outdoors for vaccinated individuals. There was a very cautious relief, but still killings and crime were up and some airline passengers were unruly, refusing to wear required masks.

There would be hearings in the aftermath, and clearly our public health care infrastructure would require major changes in regulation, procurement, management, research, and investment including public-private partnerships. However, I had been alarmed to read a May 2020 Wall Street Journal op-ed entitled "Deregulate for the Coronavirus Recovery," which suggested that the suggestion that this first Trump administration should also look for opportunities to use regulatory relief to amplify the eventual recovery effort. The op-ed's author did give credit to President Obama's 2011 and 2012 executive orders directing agencies to think more creatively in identifying and reducing regulatory burdens and improving their regulations by conducting retrospective analyses of old regulations. Mr. Obama even issued an order asking traditionally independent regulatory commissions to rethink their regulations. But as you read this book, I hope to have made the case for real regulatory reform, that is, well-written congressional laws versus regulatory rulemaking ping pong, and maybe the Chevron decision will help make this happen.

Chapters 10 and 11 focus on government procurement reform (IT and Tech) as that marketplace is huge, and the Government Accountability Office (GAO) released a May 2020 report noting that agencies spent more on procurement in fiscal 2019 than in any of the previous ten years.

The GAO report noted that agencies spent $584 billion on procurement in 2019, which marked an increase of approximately $20 billion since 2018 and more than $120 billion since 2015, reaching a six-year low of $442 billion that year.

The Department of Defense (DOD) had accounted for $381 billion of that total, while civilian agencies spent $205 billion. GAO said agencies procured 83.5 percent of all contracts competitively, which is significantly increased from 64.4 percent in 2015.

GAO stated that agencies continued to spend more on services than on products across the government. Given the increase in overall spending, multiple award contracts also reached their peak in 2019.The top markets for this spending in 2019 were IT at $38 billion and professional services at $35 billion. As a reminder, the Federal Acquisition Regulation (FAR) is the principal set of rules in the Federal Acquisition Regulations System.

The FAR System governs the acquisition process by which executive agencies of the United States federal government acquire (i.e., purchase or lease) goods and services by contract with appropriated funds. The FAR System is codified at Title Forty-Eight, Chapter 1 of the Code of Federal Regulations. While nearly all federal government executive agencies are required to comply with the FAR, some executive agencies are exempt, for example, the Federal Aviation Administration and the US Mint.

In May 2020, I watched a C-Span interview with Brad Smith, the president of Microsoft headquartered in Seattle. He joined that company in 1993, pointing out that they had 4,000 employees then and some 150,000 in 2020.

He had just finished co-authoring a book entitled Tools and Weapons, which generated most of the questions from the interview host. Mr. Smith pointed out that Microsoft founder Bill Gates had always opposed a Washington office, as he was averse to regulation in the early days of the internet. But today, Microsoft has offices all over the world in fifty-six capitals, including a major operation in Washington, DC.

He indicated a strong preference now for the need for regulation (not getting rid of red tape), particularly in the area of privacy. I talked about this in the second chapter on telecom. In the future, Mr. Smith also indicated that regulation would be needed in areas surrounding artificial intelligence and the cloud. Certainly, the Need for Regular Order was quite obvious.

Microsoft had won the Department of Defense JEDI contract, albeit still under appeal from Seattle neighbor Amazon. And I review federal technology procurement and the JEDI procurement in depth in Chapter 11.

This was the cloud approach versus agencies building out their own intranet systems, which government procurement had compiled at a miserable rate of major project failures.

The cloud technology relied on huge data centers, now the largest consumers of electricity globally, and to my surprise, I noted that Ireland, with its clean weather, was the leading center of data center concentration, serving thirty-five percent of the European market. I review our US deregulation of electricity generation in Chapter 4, which created the independent power industry that became a global powerhouse as well. Now in 2024, the AI data center revolution is prompting an electricity renaissance, and even old nuclear plants are being recruited.

Again, Brad Smith talked about the cloud and privacy regulation. He advocated for investigatory purposes that governmental agencies had to go to the customer to get whatever information they were seeking, not attack the cloud, which was merely a high technology enabler but essentially an information pass-through service with no proprietary rights.

Yes, it is complex and regulation is very important. To be effective, real regulatory reform needs to be bipartisan and ultimately written into the law. The rulemaking process is necessary but has become a very partisan. It was a pleasure to look back at all of my public policy regulatory experiences and incorporate those into this book entitled Real Regulatory Reform and the Need for Regular Order.

In the early chapters, I described how we opened up important sectors of our economy to new competitors, technology, and economic market success. In the last three chapters, I turned my attention to where the next era of Real Regulatory Reform should focus, and that is government procurement. This effort will require congressional regular order!

And hence, that last Chapter 12 focuses on the nuts and bolts of regular order.

The year 2020 had been a difficult post-millennium year with the pandemic, the recession, the lockdown, and the election. Twenty difficult years had passed since 2000. But the Biden presidential victory seemed like the beginning of the end in Churchillian terms, with good things expected to follow. Seeing those millennials manning the 2020 election centers was part of that good news.

President-elect Joe Biden had secured more than 80 million votes as absentee ballots continued to be counted, making them the first presidential ticket in US history to achieve this milestone.

I had known Joe Biden and his family for many years. He was the youngest senator in history and would be the oldest president as well. He went right to work delivering remarks the Monday after the elections on combating the coronavirus, announcing members of a thirteen-person advisory board to help shape his response to the pandemic after receiving their briefing.

Finally, on November 23, the head of the General Services Administration received the related signal to begin the official transition process.

Trump stated on Thanksgiving that he would leave the White House if the Electoral College voted for Joe Biden. The GOP lawyers, believe it or not, were trying hard to prevent the Electoral College from performing their duty of representing the vote count in their respective states. States must certify their votes before the Electoral College met on December 14—many already had—and resolved all challenges to the outcome by December 8. An ominous January 6, 2021, Capitol invasion to prevent the Electoral College Vice Presidential certification would occur. I was reading about the Lincoln election before the Civil War, and this certification process was an issue then.

Joe Biden, upon taking office, pledged to reverse a number of Trump's executive orders, having the power to issue new orders to the agencies requiring their regulations to be amended. The same applied to unfinished rulemakings. Again, even this rebalancing illustrated this game of political ping pong. It was not good governance by any measure, and it takes valuable time.

But the need was there, as here are examples of the record number of rulemakings the outgoing Trump administration was jamming through in its last weeks:

1. In early December, the Environmental Protection Agency issued an interim decision allowing farmers to use a pesticide linked to brain damage in children.
2. A few days later, the EPA finalized a rule rejecting tougher standards on soot, which is emitted by industrial operations, vehicle exhaust, smokestacks, and other sources. This deadly air pollutant is linked with asthma, heart attacks, and other illnesses, including Covid-19. EPA scientists have noted that these fine particle emissions disproportionately harm low-income and minority communities.
3. On December 9, the EPA finalized a rule designed to make it harder to issue new clean air safeguards in the future. It achieves this by rigging the accounting in the cost-benefit analyses required to justify new rules—specifically, by forbidding the agency from counting huge categories of benefits while still counting all the costs.

This is all about transparency and conducting our work in a transparent fashion, EPA Administrator Andrew Wheeler said as he announced the rule during a webinar at the Heritage Foundation, the Trump think tank. Our goal with this rule is to help the public better understand the why of rulemaking, in addition to the what. He argued that the agency's past approach has meant inconsistent rules and a disoriented private sector.

In all, Trump's EPA had rolled back more than 125 environmental policies. Nearly fifty more were on the way. Other Trump agencies, meanwhile, were rushing to finish up their own eleventh-hour poison-pill regulations. It illustrated the theme implicit in this book: We needed to return to Regular Order and Real Regulatory Reform.

All the bipartisan regulatory progress of the 1970–2000 period provided evidence that this was the solution. The political paralysis since 2000 has been detrimental in many ways. This Regulatory Ping Pong was not the answer. President Biden, in announcing his bid for re-election, experienced a real downward turning point in his polling, which ultimately led to the re-election of Donald Trump. However, Biden and his team were rolling out last-minute executive orders that were quickly rescinded by the newly inaugurated Donald Trump shortly after his 2025 swearing-in ceremony indoors at the US Capitol.

It was clear to me that the successful regulatory initiatives outlined in this book required a political atmosphere with all three branches working as they should. Returning to that balance was a national priority, particularly regular order in the Congress.

And I would add emphasis to these fundamental traditions in that regard:

1. When I first arrived in Washington, DC, in the mid-1970s to begin my legislative (regulatory reform) journey, the Washington Post published the daily Congressional hearings schedule for both the House and Senate when they were in session. This legislative information greatly enhanced the regular order process. For some reason, the Washington Post discontinued this practice about the same time the regular order tradition itself was enfeebled. It would seem timely for the Post to resume this reporting practice and, as a long-time subscriber, I hope that they will. In 2023, they lost some $77 million, and maybe this lack of unique congressional information was a reason.
2. Executive Branch and Timely Budget Submissions are essential. Recent administrations have strayed from the disciplines of sending the fiscal year budget proposal to the Congress on time in early February, per the law, following the annual (early January) State of the Union address. This discipline enforced the sequential legislative review process of the Budget Committee, then the respective Administrative Committee (Policy), and then the Appropriations Committee (Funding), with the next fiscal year budget authorization passed no later than September 30 in time for the October 1 federal fiscal year. We have seen a series of continuing resolutions (funding) passed instead as a result of this Executive Branch timing failure. Even President Biden, with his years in the Senate, has lapsed every year, not meeting the law mandate early February deadline for submission.
3. For years, legislation (bills) to be taken up on the House floor had to be reported from the jurisdictional committee (per the Parliamentarian), then on to the Rules Committee regarding the floor agreement (amendments, etc.). This

encouraged the policy roles of the committee; it produced better legislation that was often bipartisan, written in final form by the Office of Legislative Counsel. However, the committee staffs have been weakened along with their chairman's influence. As a consequence, record numbers of bills have been introduced by members since 2000; yet burnout turnover at the Office of Legislative Counsel has also been at record levels as the bills went nowhere. There were debates and votes in committee markups, and respect and friendships were formed, with decorum observed. As I noted earlier, Senator John McCain endorsed the need for regular order in his Restless Wave biography, with Chapter Ten, entitled *Regular Order*.

I can forthrightly say that without this political stability, the important budgetary and regulatory reform laws that we were able to promote and support, and are discussed in this book, would have been impossible to reach final congressional passage and presidential signature.

As I noted and worth repeating, Congress since the millennium period has enacted a total of 127 continuing resolutions (CRs) into law during the period FY1998–FY2023, ranging from zero to twenty-one in any single fiscal year. The most glaring was the recent last-minute December 2024 struggle to complete funding (a continuing resolution was expiring) as incoming and returning President Trump, and his informal advisor, Elon Musk, announced opposition to the bipartisan funding bill. Yes, we had returned to the Trump way, and with his second inaugural just a month away in 2025, one wondered how.

Well, it now seemed clear that Democratic voters were very disappointed when Joe Biden (being advised by his White House team) announced on April 25, 2024, that he would run for a second term despite polls at the time showing a majority of Democrats did not want him to seek a second term. In doing so, Amtrak Joe launched one of the greatest political train wrecks in US history as the GOP won the White House and the Congress. Biden's early years (2021–2) in that first term were remarkable. Whether it was Covid, the economy, family, pro-union issues—whatever it was, it was good and his team was the best. Why they went for that second term will be a question for the historians as it invited the secrecy that made Joe look good; he was responsible for everything good. Yet the American public became suspicious as no other political leaders were on the team, no collegiality it seemed, few White House cabinet meetings, and most consequentially, no primaries nor excitement.

And it was now clear from the budgetary confusion in the Congress just before Christmas in 2024 that the astonishing record of legislative failure year after year since 2000 was a direct result of not adhering to the important committee role, the fundamental precept of regular order, and the traditional budgetary process.

At the last minute on Friday evening, December 21, 2024, Congress narrowly avoided a government shutdown, approving a federal funding extension bill to March 14, 2025 (another continuing resolution) by over the required two-thirds vote. The Senate quickly followed suit to pass it early that Saturday. And Donald Trump re-entered his Oval Office a few weeks later.

It was clear that the stability of regular order was urgently needed, and hopefully that would happen just before St. Patrick's Day in 2025. But that would be sheer Irish luck.

I do hope the reader enjoyed this book. Its many observations are based on my long professional career engaged in congressional/legislative activity, testifying, chairing a commission, attendance at two presidential signing ceremonies, and the passage of significant regulatory reform legislation.

Afterword

An Image of the Author

The author, Dan Flanagan, a native of San Francisco, served as President of the Washington, DC, public policy advisory firm, The Flanagan Consulting Group Inc., from 1981 until 2009. The firm specialized in regulatory reform and industry restructuring initiatives both in the United States and overseas.

Dan Flanagan advised railroads, trucking, electric utilities, natural gas, and telecommunications companies in their successful and historic regulatory reform/industry structure initiatives. He also assisted governmental agencies in reviewing and upgrading their procurement practices.

For reference, early in the 1970s, the environmental regulatory role began with the establishment of the Environmental Protection Agency (EPA) on December 2, 1970. That same year, the Clean Air Act was passed (with major revisions in 1977 and 1990). The Clean Water Act followed in 1972.

But the period from 1975 through the Millennium year 2000 was unique in launching the dramatic economic regulatory reforms and related deregulation of industries that led to many economic breakthroughs for the American economy. The author, Dan Flanagan, was to play a leading role in many of these initiatives.

This transcendental economic regulatory reform period began with the Airline Deregulation Act, a United States federal law signed into law on October 24, 1978, by President Carter. The main purpose of the act was to eliminate the Civil Aeronautical Board's government control over fares, routes, and market entry (of new airlines) from commercial aviation. In 1977, President Carter appointed Alfred E. Kahn, a professor of economics at Cornell University, to be chair of the Civil Aeronautics Board; and he was truly the catalyst in launching this transformation.

Amidst this regulatory transformation, Dan Flanagan began his Washington, DC public policy career that same year of 1977 at the age of thirty-six, overseeing Southern Pacific's Washington, DC office. In that capacity, he devoted significant professional time to transportation deregulation (rail and truck both in 1980) and their Sprint subsidiary's efforts leading to the 1982 AT&T divestiture. He met with Dr. Kahn on several occasions to discuss deregulation strategy.

He was present, on two occasions, to witness the President of the United States sign major deregulation policy initiatives: President Carter signing the Staggers Act of 1980 (Railroads), and President Bush signing the Energy Policy Act of 1992 (Electricity).

He also was the guest of the Speaker of the US House of Representatives for the historic 1993 passage of NAFTA, having served as an adviser to the Mexican government on its infrastructure and energy reform initiatives.

He served as Chairman of the Alliance for Philanthropy in 1986 (tax reform), as well as Chairman of the 1993 US Investment Infrastructure Investment Commission, assisting in both cases, Senator Daniel Patrick Moynihan, then Chairman of the Senate Environment and Public Works Committee.

He also an informal advisor to Senator Moynihan, later Chairman of the Senate Finance Committee, serving as a facilitator with the Clinton White House in their 1993 health care reform effort with Ira Magaziner, Special Assistant to President Clinton.

As the Chairman of the US Infrastructure Investment Commission (1992–3), he testified before Congress on lending, credit enhancement, innovative finance, and the public-private partnership concept, emphasizing the potential for "private capital investment" in our nation's infrastructure.

In 1998, he was pleased to witness Congress pass the resultant Transportation Infrastructure Finance and Innovation Act (TIFIA) to initiate federal lending to major infrastructure projects, a commission recommendation that would encourage private capital investment.

Also in 1998, Dan's firm was retained by the German Transrapid alliance (Siemens and Thyssen) to introduce the maglev technology to both the US transportation and US Navy sectors.

The following year, in 1999, Dan was asked by the US Navy to assist them in what became the uniquely successful Navy Marine Corps Intranet Information Technology (IT) Procurement. In October 2000, EDS was named by the US Navy as the winner of its five- to eight-year computer services delivery contract worth up to $9 billion. At the time, this was the largest computer outsourcing IT services contract ever awarded, and it worked.

Today, Dan Flanagan advises infrastructure funds from his Washington, DC, area office on investment strategies in these same sectors and led a national infrastructure policy coalition during the Obama administration. He is well-known as the father of the US infrastructure fund sector, giving speeches and advice over the last thirty-five years, as well as the public-private partnership concept itself.

Dan Flanagan is a 1965 graduate of the United States Naval Academy, B. S. Engineering, with five years of naval service, including two Vietnam assignments (Bronze Star recipient). He served as a Founding Board member of the US Navy Memorial Foundation and served on the Board of Advisors of the Global Projects Center at Stanford University. Dan and his wife, Fonny, live in Annapolis, Maryland, and often commute to California to visit their families and friends there.

When asked what he accomplished in his Washington career, Dan first noted the deregulation reforms from 1970 to 2020 that are chronicled and discussed in this book.

But there were others, and here are those stories from Dan.

ERISA, Fiduciary Standards, Pension Funds, and the Real Estate and Infrastructure Investment Asset Classes.

In late 1973, I was working in New York for the Martin E. Segal Company, a large pension fund actuarial consulting firm at 730 Fifth Avenue, owned then by the

Wertheim Investment Banking firm, and commuting from Scotch Plains, New Jersey. It was a training program for six months before returning to its San Francisco office.

During that time, the Employee Retirement Income Security Act of 1974 was the subject of congressional hearings and legislation that, as a federal law, set minimum standards for most voluntarily established retirement and health plans in private industry to provide protection for individuals in these plans.

One of the most important provisions was the establishment of fiduciary standards for the overseers of pension funds. I did meet with the congressional staff.

At the Segal Company, I was intensely interested in the role that pension funds could play in the US economy while earning healthy investment returns. I would often go to multi-employer trustee meetings with the firm's Executive VP, Vincent O'Hara, in Washington, DC (national funds) and to local New York metro area pension and health and welfare funds. It was a very interesting perspective, and I saw a lot.

Several times at such meetings in the New York area, trustees would openly discuss real estate investment deals with the developers of projects. This was unseemly, and ERISA's fiduciary requirements ultimately ended the practice. Professional investment managers, as third parties, were selected to oversee the various investments for the fund.

Returning to the Segal San Francisco office in late 1974, I adopted Democratic Party politics as my outside activity while continuing to consult with pension and health plans on the West Coast. During this time, I became acquainted with Walter Shorenstein, a wealthy Democratic Party contributor, and his real estate investment company based in San Francisco. Eventually, I joined his firm, which was focused on large urban office buildings, primarily partnering with large insurance companies such as Mutual Benefit Life.

I suggested that pension funds had the potential to be major investors in his projects, but it was too early. Today, some forty years later, that firm owns interests in office space throughout the United States, and the company has sponsored twelve closed-end real estate funds, with total equity commitments of $8.8 billion, primarily from pension funds in the now mature real estate asset class, including $723.5 million from the company as general partner.

The infrastructure asset class was to follow in the millennium year 2000, and having chaired the US Infrastructure Investment Commission in 1992–3 for Senator Daniel Patrick Moynihan, I played a key role (the pied piper) in its launch in the United States. It had five investment areas, including water, transportation, telecommunications, energy, and social, which was public sector real estate. I was pleased to assist ULLICO to launch its own infrastructure fund in 2010.

The urban center, trophy properties continued to be the prime real estate asset investment sector, and large-scale firms were very successful. Trustees under ERISA fiduciary standards continued to utilize these outside managers. Then the pandemic of 2019–22 was to turn downtowns across the country into virtual commercial deserts as work from home with Zoom sessions replaced going to the office. These same pension funds and their advisors had been very successful, but the pandemic was set to drastically change that paradigm.

Home Health Care and Medicare 1978–9

My brother-in-law Neal McNamara, as a San Francisco law firm leader and Hospice Board member, called me in Washington, DC, around 1978 to meet their Director Hadley Hall. We had a very good meeting here at my Washington office as I found Hadley's cost-effective argument for Medicare coverage of home health and hospice care to be persuasive.

Fortunately, at that time, a good friend, Senator Frank Church (D. Idaho), was then Chairman of the Senate Committee on Aging. I called him, and he set up an appointment for Neal, Hadley, and myself to meet with the Staff Director, Val Halamandaris.

I am convinced our 1978–9 visit had a big impact on his commitment to include home health care in Medicare. It was around that time frame when the Health Care Financing Administration (HCFA, later termed CMS in 2011) was established to regulate the federal portion of Medicaid and funding to healthcare agencies. Meanwhile, states were looking for next-step solutions to expand care beyond the skilled nursing setting, reaching patients in the comfort of their own homes.

Orphans Airlift 1975

After returning from my 1969 Vietnam tour and retiring from the Navy at Treasure Island near my hometown San Francisco, I had two initial careers: consulting and campaigns.

Fast forward, in early April 1975, just before the fall of Saigon, Vietnam; I spent three weeks at the San Francisco Presidio managing the Orphans Airlift operation there, delivering over 1,500 infants, arriving on a dozen flights primarily at Travis Air Force Base from Ton Son Nhut Airport in Saigon to their adopting parents throughout the United States. This was done by heroic Braniff airline stewardesses.

With the evacuation of Kabul in 2021, it stirred my 1975 memories; faith was front and center. After the last infant was transported and our base closed up in May 1975, I did go to our nearby church and prayed for them all.

Council of Viet Nam Veterans 1977

When my wife Fonny and I and our two boys moved to Washington, DC, in 1977, I was very concerned about the economic plight of the Vietnam veteran. They were not receiving the benefits in education, employment, housing, and health care that veterans of the Second World War and Korea were awarded for their service.

Senator Alan Cranston, from California, was a good friend and Chairman of the US Senate Veterans Affairs Committee. I requested an appointment and explained my concerns to the Senator. He was very agreeable and told me to call Stuart Feldman, which I did. That began my membership, that year, in the Executive Committee of the Council of Vietnam Veterans. We were quite an organization, incorporated and headquartered on Connecticut Avenue, hell-bent to "right the wrong"; and we did it!

Hearings were held, and Robbie Muller, our Executive Director and paraplegic Vietnam veteran Marine Captain, was our witness. I personally would wheel Robbie, in his wheelchair, through the halls of Congress to those House and Senate hearings. What amazed me was the opposition of the incumbent American Legion and Veterans of Foreign Wars representatives. They saw the Vietnam veteran taking from their members' benefit structure. Talk about hypocrites! It was the old vets versus the new vets, a trend that continued with the Kuwait, Iraq, and Afghanistan wars.

On the Council, we had made an oath not to be such hypocrites; but to achieve our goal of righting a wrong and then moving on! We were very effective and did achieve victory (an ironic twist on the war itself!) in the Executive Branch.

Much to my surprise, Robbie Muller called me and wanted to stop by my office in 1979 to go national and to start a membership organization. I responded that we had agreed to get the equity policies in place for the Vietnam veteran and then declare victory.

Robbie wheeled around, went off and founded the Vietnam Veterans of America, chartered before Congress, and essentially became another American Legion.

Democratic National Committee Capitol Hill Headquarters Building, 1983

After the 1980 election, the Democrats faced $2 million in debt. The party's headquarters was a rented space on Massachusetts Avenue in the Airline Pilots Association Building, and twelve of the fifteen electric typewriters in their offices were broken.

Shortly after Chuck Manatt from California became Chairman, I called him and made the case that the Democratic National Committee should have its own headquarters building financing it and taking advantage of the law. Paying rent all these years (campaign or "hard money") for a suite at the Mayflower, the Watergate complex, or the Airline Pilots Association Building was a waste of campaign resources.

The DNC stayed on at the Watergate, and in June 1972, the famous burglary took place there, destroying the Nixon presidency. However, the Democrats moved out of the Watergate shortly after the burglary and into a building owned by the Airline Pilots Association on Massachusetts Avenue, where the rent (political funds) reportedly now was nearly $500,000 a year.

Under the law, in those days, both parties were entitled to finance a headquarters building with corporate or union treasury ("soft money" campaign exempt) contributions.

The GOP had done this long ago with their Eisenhower office complex on the House side of Capitol Hill. Chuck agreed, and we went to work!

Chuck and I, along with Maryland developer Nate Landow, made an offer to the National Democratic Club Board to purchase their complex, including an adjacent gas station located at the intersection of South Capitol and Ivy Streets on the House of Representatives side of the US Capitol for $2 million.

We would be doubling their recent investment of $1 million in buying what was then the Rotunda Restaurant (a murder had occurred there, allowing the bargain price) and moving from their long-time basement facilities in the old congressional Ford Building, which is now a parking lot.

With the help of Senator Pat Moynihan, we had the Capitol Architects' approval for a five-story building and offered the Club the top floor—what a view! The entrance was to be off New Jersey Avenue, covering up the train tunnel and canyon, and called Truman Plaza. As it was, we made sure the postal address was 430 South Capitol Street, and that identification has now been seen on television several times, particularly after the 2016 Russian hacker's invasion of the DNC computers.

After much procrastination, the National Democratic Club trustees turned us down, forcing Chuck to make an offer for an apartment building on the Senate side that now houses the Heritage Foundation. I told this story a few years later to Ed Feulner, our Old Town neighbor and Heritage Foundation founder. He couldn't believe it!

When Chuck told me about this, I argued that "there was no way the Democratic Party could be housed on the patrician Senate side; we needed to be on the plebeian House side." Chuck's political conscience agreed, and we returned and offered to buy the gas station for $1 million. And that is how it happened!

I helped Chuck raise the funds to build this permanent Capitol Hill Democratic headquarters complete with state-of-the-art computers, and ultimately with this political infrastructure in place, he cleared the party's debt. It was a pleasure to stand with him in April 1983, shovels in both our hands, for the groundbreaking!

The architects did the best they could, but we were not able to build out the Truman entryway plaza over the New Jersey Avenue rail tunnel. The new headquarters would be a four-story building next to the National Democratic Club and would cost some $6 million to build and outfit. It would house the DNC, plus the House and Senate campaign committees, and would contain about 42,000 square feet of office space, plus a major conference facility and an underground parking garage.

San Francisco Mission Bay UCSF—SP Railyards—1984

In 1984, I explained to then Mayor Dianne Feinstein that the derelict Southern Pacific railyards in San Francisco were now under the authority of the merged SPSF railroad in Chicago, and then following up with a new development team and an agreement with the city. Now fully developed as Mission Bay, it is the site of the prestigious University of California, San Francisco Hospital.

Navy Memorial and Admiral Zumwalt, 1980, 1985, 1987, 1991

In March 1977, Congress provided the first $29 million in funding and borrowing authority for the Pennsylvania Avenue Development Corporation, and shortly thereafter, Chief of Naval Operations Admiral Arleigh Burke proclaimed in 1977 that "we have talked long enough about a Navy Memorial and its time we did something about it."

Admiral Burke and several Navy colleagues got busy: They founded the United States Navy Memorial Foundation in 1980, under the leadership of Admiral Zumwalt. His team quarterback, Rear Admiral William Thompson USN (Ret.), was the president.

I was asked by Admiral Zumwalt to join the Board shortly thereafter, and the United States Navy Memorial sought and received the blessing of Congress to construct a Navy Memorial on public land in the District of Columbia. This was to be the initial contribution from my Naval Academy classmate, Spike Karalekas, who had worked for Admiral Thompson in the Navy Public Affairs Office.

Working with the Pennsylvania Avenue Development Corporation, the Foundation selected Market Square, across the street from the National Archives, as the Navy Memorial's site. Fortuitously, another Naval Academy classmate, Tom Regan, was now the Executive Director of the Pennsylvania Avenue Development Corporation (PADC) and helped with the site selection, acquisition, and design. PADC, having been created under President Kennedy, based on Senator Pat Moynihan's report, was a critical milestone.

Spike Karalekas was General Counsel for the Foundation during the same years when the legal framework with the Park Service/Department of the Interior and the PADC were being worked out. Tom and Spike were the two Naval Academy classmates from 1965 who set the foundation!

Although helping the effort as early as 1979, I officially joined the Board in 1980 at the request of Admiral Zumwalt, whom I had gotten to know in Vietnam; we had become close friends. He was the Chairman of the Board, and our first meetings were in donated office space in Arlington, Virginia, just across the Potomac River.

Our primary challenge now was raising the money for the Visitors Center as well as getting those office/residential buildings (#701 and #801) financed and built. Somehow or other, that was my assignment, and we got the job done via the popular annual Lone Sailor Dinners that we launched.

Construction began in December 1985, and the outdoor Memorial was dedicated two years later on October 13, 1987, the 212th birthday of the United States Navy. The surrounding buildings, #701 and #801 Pennsylvania Avenue, opened their doors for tenants, both commercial and residential, in 1991. The indoor facilities for the Navy Memorial Heritage Center opened that year as well in the lower floors of #701. The twenty-fifth anniversary of those facilities occurred in 2016.

Admiral Zumwalt, Agent Orange Law 1991 and the Marrow Foundation in 1992

Bud Zumwalt said to me that "he felt his son's cancer was mostly due to Agent Orange during the Viet Nam War." He had been the lead Admiral in Vietnam (COMNAVFORV) and had approved Agent Orange being sprayed in the Mekong Delta, so he felt very bad as his son Elmo had been a Swift Boat driver in the defoliated region of the Mekong Delta.

After Elmo became ill in the early 1980s, the experience of father-son visits to the many US cancer centers was a major factor in our founding of the National Marrow Donor Program (NMDP) in July 1986 and the Marrow Foundation in 1992.

Admiral Zumwalt, as noted, was the first chairman of the NMDP's Board of Directors, and I was privileged to be an advisor to that effort as well as the Marrow Foundation itself. That activism earned Bud the nation's highest civilian honor, the Presidential Medal of Freedom, awarded by Bill Clinton in 1998—and we celebrated afterward.

In the 1980s and 1990s, I was to support, coordinate, and attend many Agent Orange meetings chaired by Bud as we plotted the strategy to eventually have Agent Orange victims compensated; that law was passed in 1991 by Congress, as only a small percentage of claims had been honored prior to that date.

Presidio Trust 1996

Assisting San Francisco Congresswoman and good friend Nancy Pelosi in guiding the Presidio Trust legislation through the US Senate, with the good grace of Jim O'Toole, a fellow St. Ignatius High School graduate, being the key Senate Energy and Natural Resources staffer working for the Chairman, Senator Frank Murkowski. The legislation was passed by the United States Congress in 1996 to oversee the Presidio of San Francisco, transitioning from a large US Army base to an urban national park located at the base of the Golden Gate Bridge, comprising nearly 6 million square feet of buildings, including 469 historic structures that contribute to its status as a National Historic Landmark District.

After our initial meeting in his Senate office, Jim O'Toole and I were on the phone often as he organized the drafting of the legislation about the preservation of the Presidio.

During the Thanksgiving week of 2024, my wife Fonny and I were in the San Francisco Bay Area and suggested to good friends in the city that we have lunch at the Presidio Golf Club. It was agreed, and we had a wonderful time. Upon our departure from the clubhouse, we went our separate ways to parking. I was wearing a blue jacket from the Naval Academy with the initials USNA, and two young golfers walked by heading to the clubhouse. Spotting the jacket insignia, one said to me, "Are you Naval Academy?" And with my affirmative response, he indicated he was a plebe, or a freshman, at West Point, the military academy. He had attended Stuart Hall High School, which was connected to the Convent of the Sacred Heart, which Fonny had attended, a magnificent mansion on the hill looking out on San Francisco Bay and the Golden Gate Bridge.

I explained my St. Ignatius Presidio Trust story—we had a good time.

And a few weeks later, the Navy beat Army in a football classic, ending their season with nine wins and three losses versus the Army's ten wins and two losses.

Selected Bibliography

The bulk of discussion herein is based on the author's unique personal experience and the following references are provided for additional background:

1) **The economics of regulation: principles and institutions** by **Alfred E Kahn, 1970 New York, Wiley**
   Industrial policy, Trade regulation, Monopolies

2) **US Chamber of Commerce, April, 2023, Risk of Policy Options Report**
   Rapidly changing Regulatory Policies and Regulations Impede Corporate Activity

3) **Brookings Institute, Center of Regulation and Markets, Reg Tracker 2015—2025**
   Regulatory Ping Pong at numerous federal agencies (Administrative Procedures Act, Chevron)

4) **From Gutenberg to Google, Brooking Institution Press, 2019, by former FCC Chairman Tom Wheeler**
   Breakup of AT&T

5) **US Infrastructure Investment Commission Report 1993, Chairman Daniel V. Flanagan Jr.**
   Innovative Federal Project Finance, Lending, Credit Enhancement, Leverage

6) **Pension Funds: A Potential New Infrastructure Option**
   Presented by Daniel V. Flanagan Jr., University of Southern California, National Center for Innovations in Public Finance, National Research Council, Second National Conference on Transportation Finance, Scottsdale, Arizona, April 21, 2000

7) **Findings and Recommendations of the Special Panel on Public Private Partnerships**
   Committee on Transportation and Infrastructure, US House of Representatives January 16, 2014

8) **Reinventing Federal Infrastructure Policy: A 25-Year Personal Perspective, Public Works Financing**
   May 2017 National Infrastructure Week panel before a full audience in one of largest United States Senate hearing rooms, in the Dirksen Senate Office Building. Daniel V. Flanagan, Jr.,

9) **White House Build America Infrastructure Initiative, Summit at Treasury, 9/9/2014**
A recurring theme seemed to be the need for a national interagency infrastructure financing office (or a national infrastructure bank as the President called for since his 2008 campaign) with project finance expertise to be available to the federal credit/lending infrastructure programs, including TIFIA and newly established WIFIA programs to enhance project

10) **Bi-Partisan Infrastructure Investment and Legislative Recommendations November 2016**
After the 2016 presidential elections, our bi-partisan infrastructure working group, PIRC, had to refocus away from the Clinton/Kaine transition team to the Trump/Pence team; and we did so.

11) **Statement of Professor Paul L. Joskow, Before the Committee on Governmental Affairs, United States Senate, June 13, 2001.**
Paul Joskow and his MIT- NERA colleague, Richard Schmalensee, were a consulting team to our Utility Working Group (12 utilities) in devising the 1992 Energy Policy Act, Title 7 on the electricity sector. The latter was as a Member of the President's Council of Economic Advisers from 1989 through 1991 and we worked very closely with him.

12) **U.S. District Court Judge Harold H. Greene formally took control of the Justice Department's landmark divestiture agreement with American Telephone & Telegraph Co. on January 20, 1982**
That same day the Federal Communications Commission gave AT&T and 11 other large interstate telephone companies permission to greatly accelerate the depreciation of their equipment and facilities; and AT&T began taking steps to implement what it calls "the most significant change in the Bell System's long history" by announcing major organizational changes to help prepare the communications giant for the break-up.

Index

9/11/2001   262–4, 270–1
2017 GOP Tax Cut (Reconciliation)   77
2020 Presidential Campaign   296–8
2024 Election, New Generation   284

AARP   161
accelerators   220
Accenture   276
Adams, Brock   21, 37
Affordable Care Act (ACA)
   Constitutional   174
   Trump's attack on   169
Afghanistan   145
AFL-CIO   197
Akerson, Dan (MCI)   54–5
Alameda County 1975 Competition   153
American Association of Health Plans (AAHP)   157
Apple CEO Tim Cook   80, 87
Appreciated Property-Charitable Deduction   75–7
Association of American Railroads (AAR)   38
AT&T CEO Compensation   93
AT&T Consent Decree   43–4, 60, 287
Azar, Alex   163–4

Baffert, Bob   233–4
Barbaro, Preakness   225–6, 230
Bechtel IPPs   123
Bell, Bert   64
Beltway Bandit IT (Cartel)   259, 266, 275, 277
von Bertrab, Hermann (Mexican NAFTA Ambassador)   179, 184, 189–91
Biaggini, Ben   26, 34
Biden
   2019 campaign   172
   Bi-Partisan Infrastructure Bill (2021)   90, 128, 208
Blue Cross   149, 153, 157, 169

Bradley, Bill   68, 71, 75, 77, 79
Brookings   256
Bryson, John   104
Buckberg, Elaine   81
Build American Initiative, Bureau   81, 126–7, 139, 203–7
Burwell, Sylvia   151, 160
Bush, George H. W.   120–1
Business Roundtable   34, 117, 189
de Butts, John   46
Buy American Act   249

CACI wins IT Contract   272
Cailes, Tania Elias   190
California Infrastructure   129–30, 218
CBS   58, 63
CDC, Coronavirus Data   278
Cerf, Vinton   51–3
CFPB IT   274
Chamber of Commerce   147, 156, 216
Chao, Elaine   133, 144, 207
China
   2018 US China Economic and Security Review Commission   257
   High Speed Rail   254–5
   Shanghai Airport Maglev   253
   Siemens   253
   Zhu Rongji (Mayor and latter Premier 1999-2003)   253–4
CINCLANTFLT   261
Clinton White House   152
cloud IT services: DOD, GSA, US Digital Service   268
coal   33
Code of Federal Regulations   277
Congress
   Doctors in Congress   168
   Health Care Legislation   167
   Organization   281
Congressional Budget and Impoundment Act of 1974   283

Congressional Budget Office (CBO)
    Reports   84, 158, 289
continuing resolutions   283
coronavirus pandemic
    Hopkins Data   172
    Pandemic and Public Sector IT Fraud   277
    Trump and Fauci   172
    vaccine   295
Crandall, Bob   86
Cures Act   169
cybersecurity   276, 278

defense supply chain   249
Democratic National Committee Headquarters Building   285–6
Department of Defense (DoD)
    AT&T, support for   45
    Biden Administration   250
    IT update   268–76
    Microsoft   287, 296
    public utilities   107–8
    supply chain, lessons learned   250
DHS
    Established 2002, the Homeland Phrase   272
    The Homeland Phrase, 2015 Headquarters Procurement Failure   272
    Trump Administration   273
DOE   93–110, 121, 123
    Loan Program Office   139
DOJ   34, 45–7, 61, 63, 169, 225, 229–30, 277, 291
Dulles Greenway   130, 236

Einthoven, Alain (Stanford)   153
Energy Policy Act of 1992   98–9
    signing ceremony   121
energy transition   93, 96, 113–15, 122, 139
ENRON   96–8, 102–105, 184
EPA   298
executive branch proposals, introduced by request   282
executive orders   293
executive rulemakings   294

Facebook   25, 60–2, 120, 275
fake news, Twitter   291
Federal Acquisition Regulations (The FAR)   260–1, 295
Federal Energy Regulatory Commission   96, 99, 101, 105, 108, 115, 183
    Order 888 (1992)   99
    pipelines, transmission   106
Feinstein, Dianne   35, 163
fiscal misbehavior   290
Forbes, Steve   79
Franks, Marty   58

GAO—OMB/DHS   267
General Atomics   113, 243, 245–9, 257
General Electric   106, 117
generic drug pricing   163
Germany
    Maglev test track   243–4
    The Social Democrats Coalition with the Green Party   252
Ginsburg, Ruth Bader   156, 174
Glasgow UN summit 2021   147
Global IT/Data Regulation   275
global supply chain containers   32–3
Goodman, John   107
GOP
    ACA Repeal and Replace   160
    Welfare Reform   155–6
Gramm, Phil   102
Greene, Judge   43–7, 70
Gribbin, DJ   132, 141, 207

Hamburger, Ed   37
Hancock, Arthur   226
Health Care
    Costs   166
    Home Health Care   175
Health Savings Accounts (HSAs)   167
high speed rail   133–4
high tech   296
hospitals
    Costs and Mergers   166
Huntington Ingalls   242
Hutchinson, Kay Bailey   131

Ignagni, Karen   157
independent power producers/power purchase agreements (IPPs/PPAs)   101–2, 120
Infrastructure Financing Authority   129–31, 147, 214–15
Infrastructure Investment Commission Testimony   203
infrastructure investors   221
Intel   59, 257
Interstate Commerce Commission (ICC)   19–42
Interstate Horse Racing Act (1978)   225
IRS
  Funding   82–3
  IT   274–274

Japanese Maglev   252
Jeffries, Ian   38
Jockey Club   234–5
Johns Hopkins Pandemic Data   82
Johnson 1964-65 Legislative Leadership   282
Johnston, J. Bennet   98, 116

Kahn, Robert   51–4
Kaiser Family Foundation   150
Kansas City Southern   21, 27–8, 188
Kudlow, Larry   144
Kushner, Jerald   84

Laffer, Art   74, 84
Legislation and Committee Markups   282
Legislative Calendar and Process   282
Levitt, Ray   215
Lindsey, Larry   71, 76
Lockheed Martin   53, 255–6, 271, 276
  Berlin   255
  US Ambassador to Germany, Dan Coats   255–6

Magaziner, Ira   152, 155, 170, 174
Maglev Projects and Consultants   251–2
Maryland
  Health Care Commission (Costs)   159–60
McCain, John (*The Restless Wave*)   281
McConnell, Mitch   87, 146, 165, 224, 234–5
McGowan, Bill (MCI)   50–1

Medal for Energy Security   94–5
Medicare for All (2019)   170–2
Merszei, Zoltan   251
Mexico
  Crime, Cartels   184, 187
  energy reform   183
  Energy Regulatory Commission   183
  Modern Mexican Political History, the PRI   186
  New Mexican Embassy in Washington DC   193
  New President Lopez Obrador, 2018 Election, PRI Defeat   187
  Re-Regulation under Lopez Obrador   198–202
Microsoft   59, 268–9, 287, 296
Middleburg Virginia
  Maggie Bryant   235–6
  Steeplechases   235
Millennium Year 2000, Y2K   287–8
Mitchell Report   225
Moynihan, Daniel Patrick   288
  1993 Infrastructure Investment Report   12
  FRA's $50 million grant   251
  Navy Memorial   154
  Tax Reform Deal of 1986   71–2, 76
  Thurgood Marshall Building   274

NAFTA
  New NAFTA (Trump), Global Trade   188–90, 192–5
  Passage   181
  Success   190
National Academy of Public Administration (2015)   140
National Center for Innovations in Public Finance (at USC)   204
National Infrastructure Bank Legislation   130–40, 212
National Infrastructure Week   36, 87, 140, 142, 207, 216
National Security Commission on Artificial Intelligence   268
National Thoroughbred Racing Association (NTRA)   224
  2008 NTRA Report   229–31
  2019 Reform   234
  Waldrop, Alex   233–4

National Thoroughbred Racing
  League   223–4, 238
Natural Gas Industry   12, 33, 37, 101,
  106, 109, 113
Natural Gas Industry   106, 109–10,
  112–13, 184–5
Navy Marine Corps Intranet, a model for
  success   261–7
Navy Memorial   154
Neri, Rogelio Gasca   183
Newsom, Gavin   218
Nieto, Peña   185
nuclear energy   116–17
nursing homes   173

Obama White House
  11/15/2013 Affordable Care Act (ACA)
    Roll Out and IT Failure   260
  Blair House Health Care Summit   158
  transportation infrastructure   206
Office of Legal Counsel   281
Olea, Hector   183
Olympic Committee (USOC)   66
Orderly Transition of Executive Power,
  January 6 Insurrection   297
Otellini, Paul   59

Packwood, Bob   75–6, 79
Peck, Bob   274
Pelosi, Nancy   2, 98, 129–30, 144, 188,
  195, 282, 308
  infrastructure   129–30
Pentagon Cloud Computing
  Award   268–9
Performance Infrastructure Review
  Coalition (PIRC)   128, 133, 145,
  207, 216
PHARMA   162
pharmacy benefit managers
  (PBMs)   167–8
policy trinity, three branches   282
Prescription Drug Bill   162
Prescription Drug Reform   55
Price, Tom   165
privacy   275
Progressive Policy Institute   59, 83
public private partnerships (PPPs)   127, 204
Public Utility Holding Company Act
  Reform   96

Public Works Financing   128

Rail and Pipeline   31–3
Reagan Tax Cuts/Increases   71–2, 77
Real Regulatory Reform   285–6
Reason, Admiral Paul
  CINCLANTFLT, Transrapid, Germany
    Maglev test track   243–4
  Navy Marine Corps Intra-Net
    (NMCI)   261–4
Regulatory Agenda, Post-
  Pandemic   298–9
Regulatory Perspective, 1980-2020
  Period   32–3
Renewable Portfolio Standards   96, 98,
  101, 110, 112, 120, 121
Roberts, Chief Justice   150, 173, 293
Rokamm, Dr. Eckhard (Thyssen Marine
  CEO)   244–6
Rostenkowski, Dan   75–6
Rule Making Jungle, Regulatory Ping
  Pong   284
Runnymede Farm   223–4
rural hospitals   169

SAIC et al. Mergers
  &Consolidations   271–2
Salinas, Carlos (Mexican President)   180
Scavinio, Dan   260
Schlesinger, James   94
Schmalensee, Richard Lee
  "Dick"   96–7
Schmidt, Eric   268
Schultz, George   123
Section 230, Communications Decency
  Act   53, 62, 291
Seltzer, David   204
Senate 2021 Bi-Partisan Infrastructure
  Legislation   147
Skelly, Michael   100, 110, 119
Snow, John   26
Southern California Edison
  (SCE)   104
Southern Pacific   21, 26–50, 94, 153
Speakers of the House (7, 2000—2025)
  Leadership   282
Spectrum Auction   144
Sports
  betting   68–9

College Sports Financial
  Perspective 64–8
 as content 63–8
Sprint 43–61, 94
Staggers Act 19–51, 233
Stanford Global Projects Center 212, 215, 218, 291
Stanford Infrastructure Lecture 217
State of the Union 282
State Utility Regulation 101, 108, 111
Staubach, Roger 54
Successful Role of Private Institutional capital Matched with Federal Lending 209–12
Sununu, John 270
Supreme Court Rule Making 294
Surface Transportation Board 20, 28–30, 39–42

Tauzin, Billy 162
Tax Reform
 1986 71–2, 76
 2017 77–91
Texas ERCOT Freeze in 2021 98, 102
Thurgood Marshal Building (Court Administration) 1992 274
T-Mobile 48, 55, 61
Transportation Innovative Financing Act (TIFIA)
 enactment 203
 format 205
Transrapid 251
Trottenberg, Polly 208
Trump
 Executive Orders on Inaugural Day 286
 infrastructure 128
 Stargate Joint Venture 269
 Trade and China 291

ULLICO Infrastructure Fund 137–8, 221
unemployment policy 290, 294
University infrastructure 129, 136
University of Kentucky Alumni House Roundtable 231–2
University of West Virginia 108–10
US–China Economic and Security Review Commission 257
US Navy
 Cybersecurity Center 121
 Forrestal Model 108
 Ships, Procurement 242–7
 Trump 247–8
USS Forrestal CVA 59, 245
USS Gerald R. Ford, CVN 78, Maglev Launch and Recovery 241–2

Viacom–CBS 58, 62–3
Villarreal, Ildefonso (Office of Economic Affairs) 180

Wall Street's Public Finance 129
Warner, Mark 131
Washington Post 284
 2021 Infrastructure Op Ed 147
Wheeler, Tom 51, 59
White House Chief Technology Officer, 18 F and the US Digital Service 265–6
Wholesale Power Market 96, 100, 102–112, 117, 119, 262
WIFIA Format 205
Wiley, Dick 50
Wirth, Tim 46
World Bank 215

Yergin, Daniel 95

zone of freedom concept 24–9, 39, 62
Zumwalt, Bud 94

About the Author

Daniel V. Flanagan Jr. was present, on two occasions, to witness the President of the United States sign major deregulation policy initiatives: President Carter signing the Staggers Act of 1980 (Railroads) and President Bush signing the Energy Policy Act of 1992 (Electricity). He also was the guest of the Speaker of the US House of Representatives for the historic 1993 House passage of NAFTA, having served as an adviser to the Mexican government on its infrastructure and energy reform initiatives. He also served as Chairman of the Alliance for Philanthropy in 1986 (tax reform), as well as Chairman of the 1993 US Investment Infrastructure Investment Commission, assisting, in both cases, Senator Daniel Patrick Moynihan, initially as Chairman of the Senate Environment and Public Works Committee and later as Chairman of the Senate Finance Committee. In this latter case, he served as a facilitator with the Clinton White House in its 1993 health care reform effort, working with Ira Magaziner, Special Assistant to President Clinton. As the Chairman of the US Infrastructure Investment Commission (1992–3), Dan Flanagan testified often before Congress on lending, credit enhancement, innovative finance, and initiated the public-private partnership concept, emphasizing the potential for "private capital investment" in our nation's infrastructure.

www.ingramcontent.com/pod-product-compliance
Lightning Source LLC
Chambersburg PA
CBHW051804230426
43672CB00012B/2623